MW01077860

# Rays of Hope Devotions

## Carolyn R. Morris

Copyright © 2023 Carolyn Ruth Morris.

Published by ROH Publishing, Aurora, Colorado

Printed in the United States.

All rights reserved.

No portions of this book may be reproduced, stored in a retrieval system, or transmitted in any form or by any means—electronic, mechanical, photocopy, recording, scanning, or other—except for brief quotations in critical reviews or articles, without the prior written permission of the publisher.

Scripture notations are referenced after each scripture used. Holman Christian Standard Bible ® Copyright © 2003, 2002, 2000, 1999 by Holman Bible Publishers. Used by permission. All rights reserved. Used 939 verses (CSB); Scripture quoted by permission. Quotations designated (NIV) are from THE HOLY BIBLE: NEW INTERNATIONAL VERSION®. NIV®. Copyright © 1973, 1978, 1984, 2011 by Biblica. All rights reserved worldwide. Used 74 verses (NIV); Scripture taken from the New Century Version. Copyright © 1987, 1988, 1991 by Thomas Nelson, Inc. Used by permission. All rights reserved. Used 6 verses (NCV); Common English Bible, Copyright © 2011 Common English Bible used 5 verses (CEV). Other short quotes from authors noted on page where quote used by permission or in public domain.

Jean,
May your walk with
Jesus continue —
Carolyn Morris

## About the Author

Carolyn Ruth Traylor Morris is the daughter of Catherine and Charles Traylor (both deceased), wife of Rudy Morris (retired). They have three children, 13 grandchildren, and 2 great-grandchildren. They currently reside in Aurora, CO but have also lived in Arkansas, Texas, Tennessee, Illinois, New Jersey, Ohio, New Hampshire, on the road in a motorhome, Arizona and Colorado. Rudy's work transferred them to these states until retirement in New Hampshire. Carolyn was a stay-at-home Mom for 18 years and volunteered at their schools and churches. She and Rudy both met and graduated from Southern Methodist University in Dallas, Texas. Carolyn got a BS in Business, Personnel Management.

Finally, she went to work outside the home as a Director of Christian Education in Ohio and New Hampshire. Her work involved at lot of personnel management of volunteers, writing, leading bible studies and other stewardship activities. After retiring, she took up her interest in designing and making quilts, continued writing, and leading bible studies. Their love for the outdoors, camping, and being in nature hiking and photographing God's creations resulted from years in Scouting through high school. During the Pandemic, they learned how to provide Zoom meetings for their Chapel so members could attend. They are both still active in their retirement at Heather Gardens, a 55+ active community. You can find her work at her Etsy Shop, Rays of Hope Quilts, https://etsy.com/shop/raysofhopequilts/ or email her at raysofhopequilts@gmail.com.

# Acknowledgements

Praises and thanks first go to God, Jesus, and the Holy Spirit for their continued work in my life, for without them, there is no book. The grace and love shown to me undeservedly brought about the results in the 367 devotionals in this book.

Thanks also go to Dorinda Vaughn-Ponquis and Jean Baldwin for their patience and time in reading and initial editing the first round! The final editing done by Jan Wolfgram and Terri Scott, my quilting buddies, and Terri's husband Bob. My readers, during the years of writing each one, who encouraged me to continue writing were helpful in letting me know they were appreciated. Pastors who read and gave good feedback provided support.

Over the years before these were written, many mentors enabled me to grow, learn, and absorb scripture. Ladies in my different bible studies enjoyed hearing them when we covered a scripture that I had used in a devotional. Thanks also to my husband, Rudy, for helping with photos and a listening ear!

Thanks to Joe and Jan McDaniel at Bookcrafters for their skill in getting my pages into book form. Without them, again, the book might still be on my computer. She spoke at a Women's Christian Network in Aurora about self-publishing, I bought her book and four years later, met with them, leaving very encouraged with a deadline!

This work is about seeing God at work in my life and how you can see Him in your life. It is a work about seeing more of Him not me. I am merely a tool in His tool box, but He is the master, creator, Lord over all.

*To all my family whom God gave to me, my parents for giving me life.*

*To Rudy's parents who prayed me into the kingdom, Mary and Rudolph.*

*To my husband, friend and father of our children, Rudy, for a great life together.*

*To my adult children, Scott, Chris, and Cindy, who are such blessings.*

*To their spouses, Erika, Tracy, and Bob who are answered prayers for this mother.*

*To my grandchildren, all 13 of them who I love dearly.*

*To my 2 great-grandchildren.*

*To all the saints who touched my life in such positive ways,*

*teaching, encouraging, and challenging me.*

*Thank You, Lord Jesus!*

# Table of Contents

# Introduction

How do you recognize the work of the Holy Spirit in your life? The easiest way is in retrospect as you evaluate a series of events and realize the Holy Spirit was leading you in your decisions. Occasionally, you have very definite events happen that instantly make you aware of the Holy Spirit's presence. These can be pivotal points in your life. In Acts 16:6-10 Paul has such an experience. He wanted to take the message of Jesus to Asia and as he traveled, he could never get headed in that direction. ***"When they came to Mysia, they tried to go into Bithynia, but the Spirit of Jesus did not allow them." -- Acts 16:7 (CSB)*** The passage goes on to tell of the vision Paul had to preach the gospel in Macedonia (in Europe not Asia) so that became his destination.

In late 1998, Rudy and I tried to find a way for him to get transferred to Denver with his job. They were hiring there, and it appeared to be a good time to try. For the next few months, he made calls, sent emails, got names from friends, but got NO response! Nothing, not even a "sorry, we have no openings." He thought he was not ready to retire at age 55 and, as preparation for the next year, we started doing some research about full timing in a motorhome. The week that we got serious about financing a motorhome, doors suddenly opened. EVERYTHING we did suddenly happened immediately. Of course, we were praying for God's direction, and it was becoming very clear, God wanted us to retire, sell the house (in 1999, it sold in one day for just over the asking price which we thought was overpriced). At the time, we wondered what God must have in store for us as He was facilitating this decision whereas our attempts to get transferred failed.

We Praise God that the Holy Spirit blocked our path to Denver and opened our path to retirement. After he retired, his company did not do well and that saddened us for our friends that were still there. It humbled us to

know that the Holy Spirit chose that time to clearly send us direction. The fullness of God's work for us was being unveiled to us gradually and we praised Him for closing one door and opening another.

After nearly a year of living in our motorhome my comfort zone changed. Most of my married life I have either volunteered quite a bit of time for or been employed by the United Methodist Church in the field of Christian Education. The first year of retirement was a very new and different lifestyle as Rudy and I moved into our motorhome, sold our house, and freed ourselves from a lot of stuff (some missed and most not missed). One aspect of my life that I found missing was the connectedness to a strong prayer and study life. I struggled with getting that aspect of my life into some kind of routine in a very un-routine lifestyle. During my working years, I wrote a thought for the week for all the teachers and volunteers. I needed the discipline that it took to write them. With the help of email, I planned to write a thought for the week for myself and share it with friends while we traveled.

How is God calling you beyond your comfort zone? What might be out there waiting for you to follow the lead of our Savior Jesus? I praised Him for the changes Rudy and I were able to make and the challenges He helps us through. Each of us has a comfort zone where life feels safe. For an infant that zone is usually wrapped in the arms of a parent. As we grow older often our comfort zone changes and expands. Then at some point most of us reach a zone that becomes a daily habit.

When we lived in New Hampshire, my zone was between the house, the job, and the church for the most part. Sometimes my job stretched my comfort zone once I started traveling to other churches to work with different groups or individuals. But because it was job related, the stretch wasn't too bad.

Then we moved into the motorhome. That really stretched the comfort zone and forced us to create a new zone. What enabled us to make that radical change? Several things. One, a desire to be nearer our grown children and our grandchildren. Two, a sense that God was calling us to a new place. Three, the faith to trust that God would lead us.

I had not compared our journey to a specific scripture until I heard a great sermon. Matthew 14:22-32 tells the story of the disciples on the boat in a storm and Jesus walks on the water toward them. " *'Lord, if it's you,' Peter answered him, 'command me to come to you on the water.' " -- Matthew 14:28 (CSB)* Rudy and I prayed wondering if we should retire, financially could we do it at age 55?

*"He said, 'Come.' " -- Matthew 14:29 (CSB)* We made the commitment to retire and put money down on a motorhome, sold the house and the stuff.

*"And climbing out of the boat, Peter started walking on the water and came toward Jesus. But when he saw the strength of the wind, he was afraid, and beginning to sink he cried out, 'Lord, save me!' " -- Matthew 14:29-30 (CSB)* About a year after being on the road, I began to miss the activity of ministry in a local church. I prayed for God to fill that void because I felt the loss of those connections to my faith.

*"Immediately Jesus reached out his hand, caught hold of him, and said to him, 'You of little faith, why did you doubt?' " -- Matthew 14:31 (CSB)* Jesus filled my mind with my desire to begin writing a weekly "Thought for the Week." From 2000-2010, friends and others took this journey with me. I never dreamed anyone would even want to read my thoughts much less to continue to do so for that long. The secret, though, is that the thoughts come from God and not from me. I am merely a vessel. Because of my commitment to you in His name, I found myself looking for His presence in my life. During that time, many asked if I had them in a book for which the answer was always, NO. That would be a lot of work and I wasn't sure I could do that. Where to even begin? That was my answer for about 13 years after I stopped writing them. God wasn't finished with me yet! People would ask periodically, and then a speaker at a Women's' Christian Network brunch was a self-publisher and knew about getting a book published. It took me only four years to contact her! As you can see, I dragged my feet on this one! Matthew once again brought me to accountability! *"You are the light of the world. A city situated on a hill cannot be hidden. No one lights a lamp and puts it under a basket, but rather on a lampstand, and it gives light for all who are in the house. In the same way, let your light shine before others, so that they may see your good works and give glory to your Father in heaven." -- Matthew 5:14-16 (CSB)* I determined to be accountable to Jesus and get it published. He will oversee how it does. If only one person comes to know Him because of this work, then my efforts have been successful.

During the years we traveled, we worked with a mission organization called NOMADS. Do a search and learn more about them! They are volunteers who travel in RVs and do mission projects around the US. Since it is under the umbrella of The United Methodist Church, the agencies NOMADS support have some affiliation with UMC. Projects are determined and authorized, listed on the members web site and members, like we were, would choose which projects they wanted to work on. Projects usually were three weeks long, working Monday-Thursday six hours a day. The agency provided places for us to park our RVs for the duration of the project. The work always varied, sometimes it was construction, office work, sorting of goods, sewing, remodeling of homes for elderly or poor, food pantry work, or many other things. God always seemed to provide the right help for each project. Once a year the members gather in a different location around the US for an annual reunion to help raise funds for those agencies that needed help with supplies as well as labor. We were all volunteers giving of our time and our funds. With that background, here is the new project God gave to me. I wanted to make a special quilt for the Reunion auction to help raise funds for the organization's work. But I wanted something very special for this group, not just any quilt. For two months, I prayed for a design. On Easter Sunday morning of 2011 at 4:30 am, I awoke with a vision of a quilt. For the next two hours that morning, I constructed it in my head. It went with me to Forest City, IA, in September.

Three of the people who took that journey to Forest City, Iowa found their lives intersected in a God inspired way. Ed and Cora's journey began some time earlier with NOMADS, and, at that time, their local church in West Ohio was diminishing in members. Their church finally decided to merge with another church. Ed and Cora's church had supported NOMADS over the years of their involvement. When the church finalized their funds, they were able to give a sizeable check to Ed and Cora to bring to the NOMADS Annual Meeting and donate or use as needed for the organization.

When I took the quilt to the auction committee, Cora was there to check it in. As soon as she saw it, she told me she planned to get it to take back to her church. They had given her some money, but she did not mention how much she had. In an auction you never know! Once the live auction began, the auctioneer's wife told the story to about 300 people of how I got the design and what each part meant to me. It was a gift to me from God! I named the quilt "Thank You God." The bidding began.

Enter Alan. His journey began with his recent retirement where his co-workers described him as a "humanitarian, adventurer, entrepreneur, visionary, philanthropist." His business card reads "Serving the Lord by helping others." He joined NOMADS and had only done a few projects, one being in Ruston, Louisiana, at a children's home. While there, he attended a small country church which welcomed him graciously and befriended him as he traveled alone. Alan had no idea why he began bidding on the quilt, but he did. So much so that he helped run the price up to $4,800 where he stopped, and Cora bid $5,000 which was the exact amount of money she had to give from their old church. By this time, I was shaking, tears rolling down my face in awe of what was transpiring in the room. Cora told her story, and everyone was in awe! I stood and told the auctioneer that if the second bidder wanted, I would make another quilt for him for his last bid. He not only accepted but matched Cora's winning bid! The quilt was certainly not worth that, but they were willing to give that amount to NOMADS. My part was all donation!

At this point everyone in the room knew that the Holy Spirit was running this auction! The two quilts brought significant funds to the organization. But it wasn't because of the material value of the quilts; it was because God brought three people together on a journey for different reasons. Alan gave his quilt to the Ruston church. Cora gave her quilt to her new church in honor of the church that closed. We all obeyed God by responding to the opportunities given us.

*" 'For I know the plans I have for you' — this is the Lord's declaration — 'plans for your well-being, not for disaster, to give you a future and a hope.' " -- Jeremiah 29:11 (CSB)* But that isn't the end of the story. While making three more of the quilts in Arizona, Alan and two friends, my quilting buddies wanted to make the quilt for their churches, pastors, etc. They asked me to put it into a pattern! I had never created a written pattern, but I did have graphic, photography, and writing skills. After several days of praying about this new request, once again this scripture, Matthew 5:14-16 convinced me to proceed by not hiding the light of the gift of the quilt that God gave me in the depths of my mind but to let it shine for others to see.

If God gave me this gift, I must let it be a light for Him. Four months later, the pattern was ready to distribute. Six months later, I tried a new stained-glass version using 14 colors in the rays. It became the favorite version of quilters, and I tweaked the pattern drawing. After working with a team of ladies to make the new version, we decided the text of the pattern needed to be on video showing ladies how to make it. My grandson, Sam, over a course of six weeks filmed me making one and

prepared the videos that are now on YouTube in a series of five sections. The story of the quilt is also on YouTube. I set up an Etsy shop to sell the pattern in 2012. Since then, the patterns have gone global to Australia, New Zealand, Germany, United Kingdom, Holland, India, Canada, and all over the USA including Guam.

God had far exceeded my plans to make one special quilt. In the first year, the quilt acquired a new name. The name, *"Rays of Hope Quilts,"* came about as a family member, who had just finished chemo treatments for cancer, saw it, and with tears streaming down her face, said, "That reminds me of rays of hope." My response was, "You just named the quilt."

I always have and continue to give God all the praise and glory for this journey. I asked and God gave. He opened the door that I obediently walked through. Was I afraid, yes, and no, but how could I not follow! This book is also a journey of faith that has taken me a lot longer to be obedient about. Once again, I give all the praise and glory to God for this venture. He knows the plans He has for it; I just need to be obedient.

During the years of my writing my Mom suffered from Alzheimer's Disease, thus the section called "Mom." It was a difficult time in my life yet eventually, very rewarding. I included it all together in one section simply to provide some help to those who may be facing a similar situation. That section ran over a ten-year period beginning in 2003 and ending with her death in 2013 after I quit writing.

As you read your way through the 367 devotionals, remember that it took ten years for me to write them all. Many of them did not make the cut for the book! They are not in sequential order as I tried to put them in themes. So, geographical locations are not important to sequence! If you find one you like, remember the title and mark it in the index in the back so that you can find it later. I pray that God will give you eyes to see and ears to hear from Him. May the words I wrote be simply tools to see more of Him not me. Faith is about a personal relationship with Jesus that you seek. He is always there waiting for you! Jesus is the Son of God and He died so that we would be seen by God, just as God sees His Son, Jesus, a precious, forgiven and loved person.

God Bless!

—Carolyn Ruth Traylor Morris or simply Carolyn

# My Journey With Mom's Alzheimer's

## *Eye Laser Surgery*

My mother was terrified of doctors and medical problems due to a couple of bad experiences. Much of this stems from her early life and lack of education at that time. (She graduated from high school when I finished my junior year in college.) Once fear took over, she wanted to close everything out and do things her way, regardless of the consequences. I had a difficult time with telephone calls as she was miles away. At 79 and very independent, she had cataract surgery on her left eye and could not see out of it very well. Returning to the surgeon, a film had grown over the lens and while laser surgery would fix it, she refused the procedure out of fear.

Now five years later, I accompanied her to see an ophthalmologist who had seen her a few months earlier. This ophthalmologist recommended cataract surgery on her other eye! Mom was petrified that she would go blind in the only good eye she had. As I was on the way to the doctor's office with her, she cried just trying to fill me in on her history. On the way, I learned for the first time that she never told this doctor in her earlier visit about her previous cataract experience. When he said surgery, she just froze and left. I filled the student doctor in on much of what had happened while Mom added the things I did not know!!! During the eye exam it was obvious even to me that her vision in the left eye where the cataract had been removed was not as good as the eye with the cataract still. During the exam, I could hear her choking up again and getting tense. Suddenly she started crying again and we had to stop. Finally, this doctor told us a film had grown back over the left eye and it was something that often happens. That was when Mom said her previous doctor told her that five years ago, but she couldn't handle it. When Dr. Kaufman, the lead doctor, saw her he agreed to fix the film on the corrected eye before we even thought about the other eye. I was able to ask the questions that Mom wanted to ask. Suddenly she agreed to have the laser process done and they could do it while we were there.

Another student doctor had to dilate her eyes and turned the lights down. Mom had been very nervous up to this point and closed her eyes. I began speaking to her very softly telling her to relax, keep her eyes closed and imagine herself being wrapped in warm caring love. I spoke so softly I wasn't sure how much she heard. Then I began praying silently asking God to bring a peace to her that only comes from Him. *"May the Lord of peace Himself give you peace always in every way. The Lord be with all of you." -- 2 Thessalonians 3:16 (CSB)* I prayed for soothing warm water of Christ to pour over her starting at her head allowing it to flow over and through her bringing peace to her soul and comfort for the procedure. As I prayed for the next 20 minutes, I watched a transformation take place in her. She never opened her eyes, her shoulders relaxed, her breathing became easier and clearer, her facial lines relaxed. I was seeing the peace of God descend upon her as we sat there. My prayer was being answered as I prayed it! She was calm, the procedure was all done. On the way home, she'd only heard me say a few words about relaxing, but she was aware of the change happening in her body. Never in all the years of knowing my mother have I seen her relax so quickly and completely. She even said if she had to go back for more of the laser work, she could do it!!! She said the light was brighter in that eye. Yes, Jesus answered prayers in a time of stressful fear.

### Wasting Away?

God is good. My Mother sounded on the phone as though she needed help, but would not ask because she knew our kids needed us. Rudy and I left to go to New Orleans to check on her. God brought us exactly where we needed to be. As I reviewed some scriptures this is what I found, *"Therefore we do not give up. Even though our outer person is being destroyed, our inner person is being renewed day by day. For our momentary light affliction is producing for us an absolutely incomparable eternal weight of glory. So we do not focus on what is seen, but on what is unseen. For what is seen is temporary, but what is unseen is eternal." -- 2 Corinthians 4:16-18 (CSB)*

My mother was 80 years old and her body was allowing arthritis to attack her knee and hip. She was fiercely independent, which in many respects was wonderful. She simply did not want to accept that her body couldn't do what it once did. All of us get to watch our bodies change and fail to perform as perhaps they once did. How easily we can focus on such temporal things. How readily we fight to maintain what we once had, and certainly we should, up to a point of some balance. How easily we take our eyes off Jesus, when we encounter a daily struggle just to walk across the room. How easily I found myself absorbed in Mother's daily struggles and forgot to take the time to have my own prayers. I smiled when I read the scripture above – do not lose heart. No, I won't! The very realization became a renewal issue for me,

### Facing Difficult Times

As Rudy and I travel to be with my Mom, my thoughts centered on the Psalms and the wonderful words of encouragement offered by David. King Saul chased David for 17 years trying to kill him yet David never tried to retalitate. At 82 my Mom faced a biopsy of a growth in her throat behind her tonsil. Who was her enemy? We did not know. Suspicions abounded! How could I help her as we await the procedure?

*"Give thanks to the Lord, for he is good; his faithful love endures forever... Let those who fear the Lord say ,'His faithful love endures forever.' I called to the Lord in distress; the Lord answered me and put me in a spacious place. The Lord is for me; I will not be afraid. What can a mere mortal do to me? The Lord is my helper; therefore, I will look in triumph on those who hate me." -- Psalms 118:1, 4-7 (CSB)* Of course, many other Psalms offer hope and encouragement. They also offer a focus on what is valuable in our life, our relationship with our Lord. I could not make Mom promises, fix what was wrong, or take away what already was. Hopefully, prayerfully, I could offer her a peace that comes only from our Lord.

Many of us face difficult times with loved ones, and if not now, we will in the future. What is it that we can offer during those times? God uses us as His instruments of care and grace. Sometimes just our presence is all that is required. Perhaps our ability to think clearly provides reassurance when the world is fuzzy. Additionally, our relationship with our Lord allows us to share our source of peace and comfort in stressful times. It is my prayer for you and for me that in those times of need with our loved ones that God will hear our prayers for one another and stand firmly beside us, guiding us minute by minute to uphold one another in His name. Let us all lead those in need to You, O Lord! *"I love the Lord because he has heard my appeal for mercy. Because he has turned his ear to me, I will call out to him as long as I live. The Lord is gracious and righteous; our God is compassionate. The Lord guards the inexperienced; I was helpless, and he saved me." -- Psalms 116:1-2, 5-6 (CSB)* These words are part of a song, and they echo in my heart, mind and soul. May they be a blessing for you.

### Reassurance Needed

During the week, activities, events, and discussions seem to lead us toward or perhaps away from thoughts of our Lord. Occasionally events thrust me into a situation that truly God led me into. It sometimes is easy to walk away from those situations, thereby missing an opportunity to allow God to work through us.

As Rudy and I left my Mom's house to return to the motorhome for the night, she asked me to write down my phone number in case she needed me during the night. The anxiety in her voice confused me since she had been fine all evening. The more I tried to figure out what was wrong, the more anxiety she expressed. I offered to spend the night at her house, which she immediately did not want me to do as that meant Rudy would be by himself! I came close to leaving, but something held me back. Finally, I looked at Rudy and we made the decision I must stay!

After he left, I found her sitting on her front porch. Since it was after 11 p.m., I was surprised to see her out that late. I joined her and for a while we just sat together. The next hour led to a time of sharing how Jesus provides comfort during times of stress. Her anxiety about the unknown concerning her health had simply overwhelmed her. Her fear of the future, her concern at not being good enough for heaven was paramount in her thoughts.

Our blessed Savior had me where I was to be that night. Prayers for us enabled me to assure her through stories, through scriptures, and through our prayers together. In the midst of our troubles, we all need reassurance. John the Baptist even needed that reassurance when he was in prison. ***"Now when John heard in prison what the Christ was doing, he sent a message through his disciples and asked him, 'Are you the one who is to come, or should we expect someone else?" -- Matthew 11:2-3 (CSB)*** Jesus responded with positive affirmation. He did not belittle John for his lack of faith. Jesus wanted to encourage and uphold John in time of trouble.

### Do Not Be Anxious

What does tomorrow bring for you, for our loved ones or for me? Boy, how I wish I knew the answer to that question! I know some of you are facing anxious times ahead. Some are in the process of waiting for physical healing to progress to the next level, some awaiting surgery for various reasons, some enduring chemotherapy or radiation, some expecting new life to cry out announcing a new birth, some awaiting results of tests – medical or educational, some saying goodbye to a loved one no longer with us on this earth. Perhaps the waiting might be for a job or an event to happen that we hope will bring us lots of joy.

A friend recently reminded me of my favorite scripture found in Philippians ***"Don't worry about anything, but in everything, through prayer and petition***

**with thanksgiving, present your requests to God. And the peace of God, which surpasses all understanding, will guard your hearts and minds in Christ Jesus." -- Philippians 4:6-7 (CSB)** As I face biopsy surgery with my Mom, I know that God is in control and my anxiety about her future is not helpful to her or to me. Many of you share your prayer requests with me and I want us to remind one another as we pray for each other about Paul's message in Philippians. It is timeless, always important and brings profound comfort.

As I picture you, I see the arms of Jesus surround you. As I participate in your prayers for health and wholeness, I feel your prayers helping to ease my anxiety. How I praise God for the kingdom family as we stand in place for one another.

As you think about tomorrow and the unknowns in your life, take with you the words Paul gave to us in Philippians. They are strong words available to carry us through each day.

### Answered Prayers

God heard our pleas as we prayed for healing, for peace amid the unknown and for wisdom in searching for health answers. Upon seeing the size of the tumor in Mom's throat on the MRI results, the neurologist emphasized its size as very large. Psalms 143:1 *"Lord, hear my prayer. In your faithfulness listen to my plea, and in your righteousness answer me." -- Psalms 143:1 (CSB)*

We invited the priest from Mom's Episcopal church to visit. He brought her communion and anointing oil. We laid our hands on one of my prayer cloths, prayed for her and read scriptures together. God opened so many doors for us to really share the value of our faith with one another. During these times of sharing, you could see the anxiety in Mom disappear. Her coping skill was to pace around the room. I encouraged her to pray rather than pace.

We were off to the hospital for the biopsy on that tumor. Mom wanted her prayer cloth with her, and the nurse gave us tape to hold it next to her tummy. Mom was absorbed in our prayers for her. I held her hand as the final preparations took place to send her off. The doctor came in, talked with her and then with me in the hall. He fully expected the tumor to be malignant and talked about radiation and chemotherapy it since was too big to remove. Then off she went while Rudy and I waited.

Her doctor sang a different tune when he returned to give us the great news. It was benign! Turned out to be a salivary gland tumor that was deep, large, and doing no harm. Pathology analyzed a frozen section and found nothing and assured the doctor it was easy to diagnose. The doctor only wanted to put her to sleep once at her age and he wanted to be absolutely sure! The comprehensive report confirmed it was benign.

When Mom came back, I could not hold back my tears of joy at seeing her, knowing the peace that lay before her. We praised God together with joy and prayers. ***"Hallelujah! My soul, praise the Lord. I will praise the Lord all my life; I will sing to my God as long as I live." -- Psalms 146:1-2 (CSB)*** Prayer is the only way to take such a journey!

## God's Truth and Love

I praised God for my Mom's answers to prayers over the tumor in her throat. We are back in New Orleans after she spent two days in the hospital with more testing. The testing ruled out any abnormalities in her brain leaving only one probable explanation for her memory loss – dementia, probably Alzheimer's disease.

We now know what was causing her problems. Was it the answer we wanted? Hardly! Didn't God hear my prayers? Doesn't God know we have other plans? Doesn't God know how independent Mom was? Yes, yes, yes, but God still said, *"NO, I have other plans for you."*

What were those plans? What was the next step? What do we pray for now? His love carried us daily from one moment to the next as we found our way on a path we'd never taken. Am I angry? Of course, but at the situation, not at Mom and certainly not at God.

***"The Lord is my strength and my shield; my heart trusts in him, and I am helped. Therefore my heart celebrates, and I give thanks to him with my song." -- Psalms 28:7 (CSB)*** God was my hope, my peace, and my source of strength for taking us through whatever may come. My prayer was for God to bring those people to us that can share their help, their experiences, their support, their advice, their faith, their strength, and their encouragement. I continue to pray for healing according to God's plan. What form that healing takes was for us to discover as our journey proceeded.

### Comforting Mom

I remember as a child sitting in a pew and, on many occasions, laying my head in my Mom's lap. As a parent, I remember my children having their turn resting their heads in my lap. It is a peaceful feeling. No matter what happened that morning on the way to church or earlier in the week, the sense of peace that comes from being held in your mother's or father's arms is merely a sampling of being in the arms of God.

As Rudy and I sat in the chairs in the sanctuary, and my Mom sat next to me. The air conditioning was circulating more air than was needed and many were cold. After having spent much time with Mom in the last few months, I recognized her discomfort and she confirmed she was cold. Having no jacket to offer her, I asked her if she wanted to sit outside. She wanted to stay but indicated if it got too bad, she would go into the hallway.

The choir was doing their Christmas cantata when suddenly it occurred to me to put my arm around her to help keep her warm. Once I did, she scooted closer to me and snuggled right into the warmth I offered. The cantata took the place of most of the service, so I knew I was in for a long haul with my arm around her. As I prayed for the circulation to continue for the rest of the service, the music began to provide peace.

My thoughts drifted back to times years ago when she held me. Though much has happened in our relationship over the years keeping us emotionally apart, I sensed God bringing us together in a new way. By the time the last song began, I found a part of me thanking God for this moment. The words from the later verses of "*O Holy Night*" came through loud and clear helping me to see why we were here with her that Christmas rather than with our kids and grandkids. That was where God wanted us to be.

*"Truly He taught us to love one another; His law is love and His Gospel is peace. Chains shall He break for the slave is our brother and in His Name all oppression shall cease. Sweet hymns of joy in grateful chorus raise we, Let all within us praise His holy Name!" ***

*"O Holy Night*," Lyrics by Placide Cappeau, 1847, Public Domain

### Mary's Example

Some of you do not look forward to family gatherings at Christmas. Previous events and personalities often interfere with the happy thoughts most associate with what should compose a family gathering. Illness, deaths, disputes, tactless statements, angry feelings all hinder looking forward to these gatherings.

I remember a wonderful story that hit Mom and me right in the face! Luke 1:26-38 tells the story of the angel speaking to Mary. I have often marveled at Mary's response to the angel telling her about her impending pregnancy. Of course, being a virgin, meant a pregnancy would cause family problems, community problems, possibly death, and most certainly rejection from Joseph – her intended marital partner. I knew her faith was immensely powerful to allow her to accept the angel's proclamation despite the possible consequences. Mary accepted what came her way. *" 'See, I am the Lord's servant,' said Mary. 'May it happen to me as you have said." Then the angel left her." -- Luke 1:38 (CSB)*

As we actively sought moving Mom to a retirement community with assisted living features, she was feeling a total loss of control over her life. The future was difficult to envision, especially in some other place than her home.

Many of us have times when we feel out of control over the circumstances surrounding us. The issues vary greatly. But God accepts us right where we are and takes us to places we never thought possible. We can do whatever we set our minds to do. How many times have you heard that? Yet, how many times do we fail to think positively about situations that seem impossible? God does walk with us as He leads us to spots where He wants us to go. Let us trust His judgment and give up control this Christmas. May all of us allow the Mary Miracle to happen in our lives this season and all year long.

### Difficult Transition

During stressful activity, I cling to the words, *"I love you, Lord, my strength. The Lord is my rock, my fortress, and my deliverer, my God, my rock where I seek refuge, my shield and the horn of my salvation, my stronghold. I called to the Lord, who is worthy of praise, and I was saved from my enemies." -- Psalms 18:1-3 (CSB)* Rudy, my brother, Charles, and I helped Mom sort through and pack her belongings to take to her new home in a retirement community apartment. When the big move day arrived, Charles took Mom on errands and visits with her sisters for the day while Rudy and I loaded the truck for the physical move in pouring down rain! With the help of our cousins, we finally arrived at the new location.

All afternoon, after the cousins left, Rudy and I arranged the room, set up the bed, arranged the furniture, unpacked all the boxes, set out her knick knacks, carried out the trash, and got it organized. We kept Charles advised as to when to bring Mother to her new home.

Finally, she arrived. Of course, she had some tears! But as she walked into her new home, her eyes brightened as she allowed her eyes to go from one spot to another. *"How pretty,"* she kept saying. She exclaimed, *"It is nicer than my own home!"* We brought her back to the house once more after supper to pick up some personal items so she and Charles could spend the night at her new home. We couldn't keep her there long, as it was too frustrating with all the mess from moving still left over.

I felt the power of our mighty God who helps us through such ordeals. We prayed for her adjustment as she acclimated to her new home. I continue to rely on the strength that God gave me to now manage her old home, her new home and my home for the next month or so. My prayer for all was that the New Year brought new ideas, new reliance on our faithful God, new meaning for our lives, and a renewed faith that would carry us through whatever came our way during the year. May peace find its way into many areas of the world. May we help to bring that peace about one person at a time.

### *New Journey*

Rudy and I relocated my Mom from her home to her new home in a retirement community. It continued going very well, for which I praised God. I sought His guidance at the beginning for I was lost about what and where to go. He provided abundantly by sending me to the people who could help, by preparing Mom for the inevitable, by enabling me to remember the scriptures to share with her to calm her during stressful moments, and by giving me the courage to follow through with needed actions when I worked through mixed emotions. My praise was to my Lord who is my rock, my strength.

Many of you have a wide variety of situations that existed one year and carried over to the next year. All of us have situations yet to come of which we have no knowledge or maybe an inkling looming ahead. How do we prepare for things to come? From a sermon I once heard, "Are you willing to let God lead you through the day-to-day events of your life?"

We asked God for help with the day-to-day events and also for His help in the overwhelming events that will occur. As the magi came looking for the Christ child, they sought guidance, found the child, and received additional guidance to protect the child by not returning to Herod. (See story in Matthew 2:1-12.)

A very familiar scripture to me, *"Ask, and it will be given to you. Seek, and you will find. Knock, and the door will be opened to you. For everyone who asks receives, and the one who seeks finds, and to the one who knocks, the door will be opened." -- Matthew 7:7-8 (CSB)* My addition to this verse would be to offer praise to God for His giving, His guidance and His open door receiving us. God loves our praise and I know He is responsible for the smooth transition we experienced with Mom. All my praise is for my worthy Lord!

What can you present to God for guidance? How open are you to God's leading? Are you willing to go wherever God leads?

### Letter to Mom

Mom lives in the misery, mystery, and agony of Alzheimer's. She was giving up all she has known of her life since Dad died nine years earlier. To her this new life with early-stage Alzheimer's was not her choice and, even though it was filled with nice people, she wants the past back again. Though she may not be able to remember the ideas in the letter, perhaps in her good moments it will bring her comfort.

Dear Mom,

On those occasions when you feel as though you are lost, or perhaps are facing a future that scares you, I want you to open your Bible and read the following excerpts: *"Do not fear, for I have redeemed you; I have called you by your name; you are mine. When you pass through the waters, I will be with you, and the rivers will not overwhelm you. When you walk through the fire, you will not be scorched, and the flame will not burn you. For I am the Lord your God, the Holy One of Israel, and your Savior... Because you are precious in my sight and honored, and I love you,... Do not fear, for I am with you" -- Isaiah 43:1-4, 5 (CSB)*

God is saying that you, Mom, are special in His sight. Just as the Israelites fled from Pharaoh only to face the Red Sea, God opened the waters to allow them safe passage. He also allowed them to make it across the Jordan River, despite the peril of deep water. As in the story found in Daniel about Shadrach, Meshach and Abednego surviving the fiery furnace, God, who stood with them, stands with you in your trials. Why? Because He created you and He loves you!

When fear takes over your thoughts, turn to God, seek His comfort, and let your thoughts turn to His goodness. *"God's solid foundation stands firm, bearing this inscription: The Lord knows those who are his." -- 2 Timothy 2:19 (CSB)* Hebrews repeats and continues with instructions: "Be satisfied with what you have, for he himself has said, I will never leave you or abandon you. Therefore, we may boldly say, The Lord is my helper; I will not be afraid." -- Hebrews 13:5-6 (CSB)... Mom, God is with you even when the disease controls your life. When your life feels like it is out of your control, know that God is your foundation, and He is there for you always. He made you. He loves you. You are His. No matter what happens. And I too love you no matter what.

Love, Carolyn

Do you know anyone that needs such a letter today? Write your own or use mine, just make the necessary changes. Do you need this letter for yourself today? God made you; He loves you and you are His.

### *Simply Cannot Pray*

Have you ever had one of those days when you simply did not know how to pray or what to pray for? The gloom of a situation or a moment loom so heavily over you that hope seems impossible. These moments occur frequently with Mom when she is able to think as herself without the interruption of memory loss. She wants to see hope, but the ravages of dementia offer no hope. Her despair reduces her to tears when she considers her future.

Once again, I am reading scripture searching for those verses to bring her hope. *"In the same way the Spirit also helps us in our weakness, because we do not know what to pray for as we should, but the Spirit himself intercedes for us with inexpressible groanings. And he who searches our hearts knows the mind of the Spirit, because he intercedes for the saints according to the will of God." -- Romans 8:26-27 (CSB)*

These words apply to many situations as varied as the many personalities who read them. Life is far from perfect. No matter how hard we try on our own, we simply cannot do everything right all the time. But through Christ, we are forgiven and seen as right in God's sight. By allowing the Holy Spirit to intercede for us when we simply do not know how to pray or what to pray for, we place ourselves in the hands of God. His love and comfort become available immediately to calm our heavy hearts.

Of course, as soon as we begin to feel better, guess who takes control again? Right! The cycle begins once again. When we finally reach the point of hopelessness, we seek God. Some of us reach the point of seeking God's help sooner than others. The more we do so, the more we reap the wonderful benefits of allowing the Holy Spirit to dwell in us regularly rather than occasionally.

Praying for one another is an important part of our faith. As we intercede for one another, the Holy Spirit also intercedes for us. God is for us as described in the rest of Romans 8:27-39! It is another favorite passage of mine.

### Love is Difficult

Finding the ability to love someone that loves you one minute and threatens you the next is a challenge. As a novice dealing with Alzheimer's disease, I had so much to learn the hard way! Over the past months, I had experienced a level of stress that made me want to walk away and never look back. Rudy and I helped my Mom move to another living arrangement, empty her house, sell it, sell her car, reassign all her personal financial matters to me at my address, care for her medical condition of dementia and while dealing with her demands for attention and take care of our own living needs.

All of that was fine, except for her many outbursts of demands, accusations, and threats to her life if I did not bring her the car or return her to her house. The struggle involved many days where she gave permission for all the above to happen and the next day or moment she would explode with screaming and issuing of threats to revoke the power of attorney, and of killing herself. When the phone rang, I began to not want to answer it since I did not know what mood she was in.

Our time to leave approached and we gave careful thought as to how to do it to prepare her for our departure. All the time spent getting the house and car sold ended up falling through in the last week! We finally got a contract for the house right before we left. We got Mom to sign it the next morning, as well as a Power Of

Attorney for my brother to sell the car in Texas. The next morning, we had breakfast with her, said our goodbyes and she was fine. We left to get the motorhome and pick up her car. For the next three hours she called and demanded we return the car with threats to call the police, screaming and accusing me of all sorts of uncaring acts. How little I knew at that time. My brother and I made the decision to leave Mom's car but gave a neighbor the keys. I was not in any shape to drive a long drive! Mom called us all day as we drove. We simply had to turn off the cell phone. The next morning, I called her. She calmed down some as we talked. She returned to the cooperative person she had been earlier in the week.

We arrived in Denton for our grandson's dedication at his church. As our God is so good, He had a message for me *"This is my command: Love one another as I have loved you. No one has greater love than this: to lay down his life for his friends. You are my friends if you do what I command you. I do not call you servants anymore, because a servant doesn't know what his master is doing. I have called you friends, because I have made known to you everything I have heard from my Father. You did not choose me, but I chose you. I appointed you to go and produce fruit and that your fruit should remain, so that whatever you ask the Father in my name, he will give you. 'This is what I command you: Love one another.'" -- John 15:12-17 (CSB)*

Yes, Lord, I can make this work but only with YOU! I am way too weak to continue on my own. Please abide with me daily and enable me to care for and love Mom during these difficult days. Enable her to deal with her losses and enjoy the joys she still has in her life. Help me to define limits and continue to honor them. I praise You for Your message.

### *Gift From Mother*

As a daughter, I greet Mother's Day with mixed emotions. I sent my mother flowers with a Mylar balloon coming out the top. She needs little in the way of stuff, but she needs something to visually remind her of someone who loves her.

As the ravages of Alzheimer's continue to attack her mind, she no longer remembers talking to me the day before. Much less does she remember being nearly hysterical because she could not reach me by telephone (why is still unknown to me as I had my phone on and with me all day). The office of the facility where she lives called me and let her talk to me quickly. She at least still knows who I am and for that I am grateful.

When I found this scripture about mothers, I had to smile. ***"Listen to your father who gave you life, and don't despise your mother when she is old… Let your father and mother have joy, and let her who gave birth to you rejoice."* -- *Proverbs 23:22, 25 (CSB)*** All of us can remember good times with our mothers and yes, we also remember some bad times. Hopefully more good times emerge than bad. But regardless of which memories linger on, our mothers gave us a great gift – life!

But what have we given our mothers? I know for one, I gave her lots of grief simply because I was the quiet silent child who appeared to behave but who tried things I was told not to do! Fortunately, that was only one period in my life. But God is good and continued to mold and shape me into one who now chooses to honor and love my mother. That does not mean that I agree with everything about her. I choose to love her as my mother and honor her for the role she played in my life. Now in her late years, as her memory wanes and as fear seizes her, I know that God is with her and with me while we try to make the best of the time we have. I pray that God will allow me to continue to give her reasons to be glad that she is my mother. I pray even more for her to remember the good moments of each day.

### With You Always

Several of the prayer cloths that I made have the scripture ***"And remember, I am with you always, to the end of the age."* -- *Matthew 28:20 (CSB)*** Rudy and I were en route to New Orleans to begin moving Mom to Dallas. It has been two years since we moved her into a retirement community environment. She has survived two evacuations for hurricanes. When she finally returned from the latest evacuation to New Orleans in late January, she simply did not remember the building where she lived. She did not know New Orleans, nor does she remember where Dallas is. It is time for my brother and me to get her to a place nearer to one of us. My brother lived in Dallas and found a place for her. Rudy and I also spent a couple of months a year in that area to visit our son. We were ready to begin the move.

I entered this activity with many reservations while knowing what we were doing was best for her and for all of us. Will she be agreeable? On the phone she was agreeable. How will she respond to her new place? What attacks will come our way because of her illness? After talking with my aunt and a couple of cousins, we learned more about the astonishing level of devastation in New Orleans. Some places appear more normal, but, at the same time normal was a long way off. In so many ways, I wish we had more time to remain in the area, but this must be a very quick trip. Right now, we are paying for two rooms at a very large price, one in Dallas and one in New Orleans. The U-Haul truck was reserved for four days to return it in Dallas! My aunts were all getting together to visit while Rudy and I packed. Then we began driving to Dallas.

Would my stress level be high? You bet! That was why I must remember, *"I am with you always."* Jesus is my constant companion even during trials and tribulation. I pray for any happy surprises for us during the week. I pray for peace for my Mom. I pray for safety for all of us as we travel. I pray for the many people still trying to sort out their lives in New Orleans and the surrounding areas after all the hurricane destruction. I pray for the NOMADS who were attending drop in and long-term projects in the area. I pray for the bitter and angry people who felt abandoned by insurance companies, by families, by local, state, and national governments. As each of you face whatever life has before you, remember Jesus' words that bring hope and comfort, *"I am with you always."*

### Relocating Mom

We arrived in New Orleans and were able to get Mom packed and ready to move without any meltdowns or outbursts. The reason for that docile mood was the extreme loss of memory since the last move over two years ago. Yes, she still knows who we are but our children, her grandchildren, are fading from her memory.

My good memories of this week center around her visits with her sisters perhaps for the last time. She spent two days visiting one sister's home where the five sisters came together to tell stories, laugh and just be together. All the way back to her place, Mom kept remarking about how much fun she had. She didn't remember anything they had done, but she remembered the good feeling she had about the day. They all knew that Mom
was leaving and that would be the last time they ever saw one another again. No one mentioned that possibility, but they all were aware of it (except for perhaps my Mom).

Her illness has progressed a lot over the last year. She was very dependent on me and fearful of me being out of her sight for very long. God has taught me so much over the past two years about dealing with Mom's memory loss, and I know there is more to learn. My brother and his wife met with the home health care nurse about managing her daily medications. The nurse told them, after talking to them and to Mom, that we may have to move her in a few months to an Alzheimer's unit, so she can get the special care that will be needed. That was hard. Yes, I knew that would happen, but when you hear those words, it is hard. I pray for her to feel safe in her new place and to find a special friend to aid her in getting to and from her room for meals and other activities. She seems to like her new room, but it confuses her not knowing where her room is in the building.

I praised God for the good days we had together during the move. I thanked Him for the many people who helped her during the hurricane evacuations. He was my source of strength when I got tired and grumpy. He found answers for us when problems arose. Now as I begin a search for her next home, I am secure in knowing once again that God leads us. *"I am able to do all things through him who strengthens me." -- Philippians 4:13 (CSB)* Know that Christ gives you strength to do all kinds of things you are putting off. Just ask Him for that strength! Yes, ask right now!

### Medication Starts

After only two weeks in the first place we moved her to in Dallas, she needed Assisted Living! So, another move, this time to Denton near our son. Being a caregiver for a parent requires making some hard decisions for them. Mom is continuing to have outbursts of emotions. The director of the residence and I discussed giving her a mild antidepressant. The problem is getting Mom to take the medicine!!!! She is against taking pills for nearly all reasons and has been most of her life. It took us two months to get her to take her meds for her memory.

Knowing this, I spoke with the doctor about putting it in her food. The Physician's Assistant decided to speak to Mom about adding medicine. Of course, she exploded, which really blindsided the PA. Fortunately, Mom's dementia does not allow her to remember the incident. However, everyone else around remembers it in vivid detail. We all decided that she needed a stronger medicine and that we needed to put it in her food. I discussed this with my brother and our spouses. We agreed that we needed to try it and not telling her was the best method. On the one hand that is hard to do! On the other, very easy, as it is in her best interest. Why do I still have this nagging feeling that we are deceiving her?

I found help as I read through Proverbs and found, *"A fool's way is right in his own eyes, but whoever listens to counsel is wise." -- Proverbs 12:15 (CSB)* I had to listen to the advice of professionals to make this decision. Mom's way is foolish. If there is medicine that will help her with mood swings and allow her to have a better quality of life, then we need to try it. Since her judgment is impaired now, we must make the best decision for her. I picked her up to take her to our son's house to spend the evening with us and she questioned why I had her in this new place. It is not where she needs to be according to her perceptions. How could her daughter ever do this to her, she wondered out loud. As she cried and continued to speak out against our decision to have her at this new place, I tried to reassure her and to distract her all to no avail. She did at least quiet down when we arrived at the house. Soon afterwards the baby's antics began to get through to her causing her to forget all the anguish. By the time we took her home, she raved about what a good time she had!

Sometimes we must make decisions, as parents or bosses, that might not be the most popular but when we listen to wise advice, we know that God is providing us with support. What decisions are you facing that perhaps requires listening to wise advice? Help us to recognize the difference in wise advice versus our own way.

### Therapeutic Listening

I sat with my Mom, on Mother's Day, at a tea for Mothers at her new home. It was a joy! We had two other ladies sitting with us who gave me some food for thought. One lady talked on and on about how she has walked all over the country and climbed every mountain. The other lady walks constantly around the building and can often be observed talking to herself out loud. Now picture this, as one lady is talking about climbing all the mountains in

the country, the other lady is telling me off to the side, that *the daughter* of the lady who is climbing mountains *tells her that all of that is not true!* But she is smiling, and you can tell she also enjoys the stories. Both ladies seem to be enjoying the conversation and the laughter emitted from all of us. My Mom is smiling and laughing with us.

As I left the table with Mom, I couldn't help but think what a fun time we had at the table. Now who cares if the stories were true! What fun they were having either making up stories or telling their own version of their lives! What freedom they have. I guess, as dementia invades, you can get away with life like that because what they see in the moment is their reality. Learning to deal with it is our responsibility. We become too tied to the truth. Recently, someone sent me a phrase they used for helping a parent or loved one who is suffering from memory loss, "therapeutic fibbing," that makes perfect sense to me. Listening to someone, like the ladies I encountered, can be "therapeutic listening." That concept, "therapeutic listening," makes me wonder if perhaps we need to do more of that with some people. To me that term means to just listen without evaluating the content, without trying to fix or understand the content, and without arriving at judgments based on content.

Immediately a caution comes to mind… Jeremiah 29 is a letter to the Exiles from the Lord presented by the prophet. ***"You will call to me and come and pray to me, and I will listen to you." -- Jeremiah 29:12 (CSB)*** But for years the Israelites ***" 'have not listened to my words' — this is the Lord's declaration — 'the words that I sent to them with my servants the prophets time and time again. And you too have not listened.' This is the Lord's declaration." -- Jeremiah 29:19 (CSB)*** Sometimes our listening needs to be much more intense by paying attention to the words, the instructions, the intent, etc. Lord, give us the wisdom to know the times for intense listening and for therapeutic listening

### Mom's New Home

An update on my Mom! God led us to the right place and the right people! She is doing so much better than ever before! No tears, no anger spells, no "why doesn't God take me" crying sessions. She is interacting at her new home with the staff and other residents. The doctor comes to see her and adjusts her medicine as needed. We have noticed the difference over the last three weeks. For now, it seems my prayers are answered. How I praise God for leading us to this place.

***"I proclaim righteousness in the great assembly; see, I do not keep my mouth closed — as you know, Lord. I did not hide your righteousness in my heart; I***

*spoke about your faithfulness and salvation; I did not conceal your constant love and truth from the great assembly." -- Psalms 40:9-10 (CSB)*

After lamenting over the years about the struggles of caring for Mom, I know that prayers are answered. Does that mean we are free entirely for the future? Goodness no! When situations or personnel change, we may be back in the seeking wisdom stage again. But for now, we embrace the joy of her happiness with her new home.

Isn't that the way many other situations go? We pray, get answers, and after a while find our need for new answers. Does that mean our first prayers were not enough? No, our life's journey takes twists and turns all along the way. It becomes time to re-examine God's plan for our journey. Time to ask, "Who is leading, God or us?" Perhaps it is time to reach out once again to those supporters who enabled us earlier in our journey.

Life has cycles. We need to plan God into our cycles by allowing Him to guide and direct us through the valleys and over the mountain tops. I praise God for answered prayers!

### A Blest Mother's Day

The past four years have certainly not been easy (nor fun) in many respects. I am happy to relate the tale of the blest Mother's Day weekend.

Mom lived in Texas in an assisted living residence. She had Alzheimer's Disease and was 86 years old. Our son and his family also lived nearby. They visited Mom and took her over to their house about once a week. We were also in Denton for Mother's Day. For our youngest twin's birthday, we took them to the Fort Worth Zoo. Since the Zoo also has wheelchairs, we took Mom along. She loved it. I pushed her all over the place while she saw the animals, watched the antics of the great-grandchildren, and enjoyed being outside with all of us. She kept asking me to sit down so she could push me! But of course, I graciously declined. The smile on her face and the joy in her eyes as she experienced the world around her as a child meant a lot to me.

Mother's Day morning her residence had a brunch for mothers and their children. My brother, his wife, Rudy and I joined Mom in her home for a time of sharing. She was so surprised that both of her children were there. Her disease has robbed her of the joy of anticipation of an event. She simply lives in the moment. After the event was over, we kept her with us for the rest of the day. Even though our afternoon consisted of quiet time in the motorhome, she loved being with us. As she slept for her afternoon nap on our recliner, I enjoyed watching her and remembering how we arrived at this point.

Scripture was not always easy to follow. ***"Honor your father and mother, which is the first commandment with a promise, so that it may go well with you and that you may have a long life in the land." -- Ephesians 6:2-3 (CSB)*** Mom was so unpredictable, but that was the disease. She needed medication to control what her brain would not allow her to control. Now with that medication given to her, she is calmer and more trusting.

Many of us face issues with our mothers and/or fathers. Some of us don't have good memories of our parents. But honoring our parents is not about whether we like them or agree with them. It is about respect that they gave us physical life. Without that gift we would not be here to experience anything, even God. Sometimes, we must learn how to follow their example and other times we must learn to follow a new path so as not to be like them. That is why each of us is an individual. God's examples come to us in many ways and through many different people. We still need to honor our parents by offering them care as they age. God forgives us for many digressions when we seek that forgiveness. We need to offer forgiveness to our parents even before they ask for it. Forgiving has nothing to do with approving their actions or agreeing with their decisions. It is about loving the child of God within the individual.

### Dressed and Ready

What does tomorrow hold for us? If we only knew! Yes, we know about the plans we make but what about God's plans for us? Aha, that we cannot know until it happens. Jesus' words for us are, ***"Be ready for service and have your lamps lit. You are to be like people waiting for their master to return from the wedding banquet so that when he comes and knocks, they can open the door for him at once." -- Luke 12:35-36 (CSB)***

My morning began very unexpectedly. The 4:45 am call from Mom's residence of her need to go to the emergency room got me out of bed. I was not near her so I had to manage it all by phone. My mind was groggy, and I captured as much information as I could. Fortunately, her complaint was a repeat of other occasions, but it still needed checking. After getting done all I could at that point, I crawled back into bed but was unable to sleep. After enough time passed for her to arrive at ER and get checked, I called the ER and spoke with the nursing station to confirm my suspicion of her situation. They did pick up a low oxygen saturation level that required hospitalization to learn why. Again, sleep was fitful as I thought about her anxiety of not knowing what was happening or why she was there.

My next call found her moved to her room and I got her nurse on the phone. We had a great talk that helped the nurse understand Mom's anxiety. She was very reassuring, helpful, and considerate of Mom's Alzheimer's disease and her being alone so early in the morning. As the day wore on, our son spent some time with her. The nurse suggested a way that I could talk with Mom since Mom can't operate a phone.

The events of my day went on, but it was filled with prayers for her, filled with prayers for guidance for those helping Mom, and for me in making decisions. As I considered this the scripture above in light of my early morning call, I know that life as we want it to be can change in a heartbeat. Jesus can come for us any time. Are we dressed and ready for service? Are we waiting for Him passively without thinking about how we wait? Or, are we waiting by being involved in service to others in His name?

I praise God for those people available to help us! I praise God for reminders to always be ready. I praise God for the many friends that cross our paths along our journey. I praise God for Mom and ask for her to feel His presence.

### Caring for Parents

I have much to praise God for concerning my Mom. Over the last five years, many of you have walked this journey with me, my Mom and her dementia (which is probably Alzheimer 's disease). We moved her to Texas where my son and his family live so I get to visit there much more often than in Louisiana. Since then, she appears to be much more content most of the time. The medications help with her anxiety, the staff makes her feel really cared for, and medical care is readily available for her even if I am not in town.

Yes, she has lost some more memories, but she is content most of the time now. When I visit, she is delighted to see me. Each time I show up is like the first time in a long time! Once she asked me to make her a quilt and I was dubious for a long time figuring she would either lose it or someone would take it from her. I am confident about where she lives and the people there, so I made her a lap quilt. I embroidered her name and mine on it, with the date, so that she knew it was hers from me. The delight on her face when she got it, and the joy on her face as she showed it off to all her facility residents, let me know that, regardless of what happens to it, I made her day for that moment.

Our relationship has been a rocky one over the years, especially the first couple of years after her diagnosis. Now I can enjoy her company even with the repeated questions. Even those questions are diminishing. My prayers for peace for her are being answered. I love taking her out for ice cream. She loves it and is like a little child holding and eating her cone with this wonderful smile on her face. She still occasionally has a bad day or blue mood, but the staff is patient with her.

Scripture is clear about aiding our family. *"Support widows who are genuinely in need. But if any widow has children or grandchildren, let them learn to practice godliness toward their own family first and to repay their parents, for this pleases God. -- But if anyone does not provide for his own family, especially for his own household, he has denied the faith and is worse than an unbeliever."* *-- 1 Timothy 5:3-4, 8 (CSB)* Though at times this is tough, it is worth the effort and agony to provide. I praise God for guiding me over the years, for bringing special people to me at the right moment, for helping us find the right place for her care, for finding the medical care suited for her and for the family that I have that supports me in all of this.

To other caregivers, yes, the job is hard. You need to take time to care for yourself in the process. Take time to include God in all that you do and look for ways to improve the situation rather than give in to the status quo. I pray that as you find yourself in a care giving situation, you will include God as your most important partner. Seek others as prayer warriors on your loved one's behalf as well as your own. For those of you who know someone who is a caregiver, offer something valuable to them - time out, a home cooked meal by you, a listening ear, or whatever you know they need.

### *Music, Dance, Joy*

This week the residence where Mom lives had a Family Night activity with supper and a Dixieland Jazz Band providing entertainment. Rudy and I attended and Mom was so surprised that we were there. Each day for her is a surprise!

The residence is fully occupied with 36 men and women. With the staff and family members present, about 70 people remained to hear the band. The band members were also seniors and sure enjoyed performing. As the music filled the room, one of the residents began to dance around the front of the room. She was oblivious to the people in the room watching her. The smile on her face, and the smooth rhythmic movements in time to the music indicated that this was a lifelong skill she possessed. Occasionally she would make eye contact with someone in the band or at one of the front tables and her smile increased.

I could not help but wonder how many times she and her husband (who apparently has passed on) went through those same steps together over the years of their lives. The staff kept a close eye on her as she got flush from many minutes of activity that she is not accustomed to daily. She was not to be deterred! Though they tried occasionally to get her to rest and drink some water, she simply would not quit. As long as the music played, she danced.

*"You turned my lament into dancing; you removed my sackcloth and clothed me with gladness, so that I can sing to you and not be silent. Lord my God, I will praise you forever." -- Psalms 30:11-12 (CSB)*

Many of these residents have some form of dementia which takes away much of their memory. Something as basic as dancing remains in the genes of their lives and is brought to the surface with the sounds of music. As I immensely enjoyed her expression of joy in the moments of her dancing, I prayed that God would protect her and allow her this pleasure. I know that many of us who witnessed this amazing display of joy felt blessed to share it with her.

God created us with a sense of life's rhythm. Some find that rhythm and use it while others search for it, but can't allow it to be released out of fear or embarrassment. What form of expression is a part of your genetic makeup? How can you use that gift to help bring joy to others? She certainly shared her joy with many that night. I shall never forget that evening.

## Caregiving

My Mom was in the hospital with pneumonia and a fever. I also happened to be in Denton, Texas! I was with her all day and night. How grateful I was, if this had to happen, it happened while I was already there to be with her. Her Alzheimer's disease leaves her clueless as to where she is or why. So, we spent many hours together.

I did have lots of hours of quiet time too. I brought her to the ER one afternoon and she was there until she quit running a fever. I read the book by Lee Woodruff, *"Perfectly Imperfect: A Life in Progress"*\* and found some very wise words for caregivers. Lee is the wife of Bob Woodruff, the ABC News Anchor who suffered a severe brain injury in Iraq several years ago. As I read this book, I thought of so many of our friends who have or are going through crisis in their lives. The last chapter of her book was worth the price of the book as she listed 10 lessons, and each has many words to clarify and explain their importance.

*"Who can separate us from the love of Christ? Can affliction or distress or persecution or famine or nakedness or danger or sword? ... No, in all these things we are more than conquerors through him who loved us." -- Romans 8:35, 37 (CSB)*

God was in control of my Mom and her situation. As I looked at her face so filled with childlike trust in my care for her, I felt blessed that God had allowed me to persevere for many years when we first learned of her illness. Those times were tough, heartbreaking, and stressful. Her disease has progressed to total dependency on others to care for her. She wasn't fighting us anymore, thanks to some good wise professionals who know so much more than I do about medicines that help with her anxieties. Yet, I saw her fear of not knowing what was happening. God has granted me this time to show her the love that she deserves from me. Many questions still hang in the balance about her future, but I knew that God was my guide and would walk with us throughout not only that illness, but whatever was ahead of us.

May God be with her and with each of your situations in life. I prayed that God would watch over Mom every day that she has left on this earth. None of us knows when or how our time to leave this earth in our bodily forms will occur, but let us always be ready. Mom was ready, but she still had something to offer, at least to me.

*\*"Perfectly Imperfect: A Life in Progress,"* by Lee Woodruff, 2010, Randon House Trade Paperback Edition

### Mom's Next Move

Mom was still in the hospital. Yes, she had pneumonia, but she also had COPD and emphysema from years of smoking (teenager to nearly 50). This was a frustrating, special, and tiring week. Because she also has Alzheimer's disease, I stayed with her 24/7 with relief from Rudy during the day to run errands, get showers, etc. She was getting better but we had a major change to make this week when she gets discharged from the hospital. She was going to skilled nursing care rather than assisted living. It would involve a new facility and a whole different environment. I did not know what her response would be. Would she be combative? Would she be frightened? Could she possibly be compliant? Would she need me there constantly to feel safe? How much did I need to be there for her as opposed to letting the new staff get to know her? For the most part, she was not as combative as she once was, for which I am eternally grateful! God still had new experiences for us that's for sure!

That week was a gift for me. On several occasions, I looked over at Mom and she had this slight smile and look in her eyes as she gazed at me that reminded me of how I looked upon my babies many years ago. I knew she was seeing me as her baby. She even asked me once where her little girl was. I responded by telling her I was her daughter and that her little girl had grown up. She even told me she was my baby, and I was the parent. What a moment of reality that she had! She didn't seem to mind as she smiled with pleasure that I was here for her. As she slept, she talked as though she was reliving conversations she had over her lifetime. Rudy and I listened and sometimes we heard nearly a full sentence but usually, it was just a series of words. Many times, she told me how glad she was that she had a daughter.

*"Listen to your father who gave you life, and don't despise your mother when she is old. -- Let your father and mother have joy, and let her who gave birth to you rejoice." -- Proverbs 23:22, 25 (CSB)* Though for years we did not have a close relationship, I was so very grateful for the time that we had then. I would not abandon her as she was the person who gave me life. The love I have for her transcended past difficulties. God's grace allowed us to be together in ways that were never possible in the past. Our summer held other plans for us, but those plans could wait while I cared for her first.

Many of us have had difficult relationships with family members over the years. As those journeys come closer to an end, perhaps we need to reflect on what God wants us to do about restoration. My journey with my mother was not unique just to us. Others have similar situations. What was God leading you to do or say? How was God guiding you to respond to your loved one? I know for me God was helping me to see Mom in a new and more beautiful light and I praise Him for that vision.

### Decisions for Mom

Some days are good and other days not so good. After her long hospital stay with pneumonia, Mom needed to go to full skilled care. Once again, every day was a surprise. This day was a very bad one that took me back to the early days of her disease. She was terrified of her surroundings. She thought all of us were in danger and that I had to get her out of this evil place. After nearly 20 minutes of talking with her, I was too stressed to handle any more. I told her how much I love her, kissed her, walked away, and left her with the nurses who were with her. My head told me what I was doing was in her best interest. My heart wanted to scoop her up and take her away from her fear. My head told me no matter what I did, nothing would take her fear away. When I got out of her sight, I lost it, and Rudy was there with the support I needed.

When I called later, she was fine. When she was anxious, I was able to calm her down by telling her I would come see her later. I also learned on Monday that her swallow test showed that thin liquids (milk, water, etc.) were seeping into her windpipe. When she swallows, the muscles in her throat are not keeping the windpipe closed off. That is probably what caused her pneumonia. Now, they must thicken her fluids, which she does not like. The speech therapist was working with her to find what liquids she likes. Eating was not as natural an activity as it once was.

We decided that she needs to see less of me to give her time to adjust and the staff agrees. We went to Denver to see our daughter whom we had planned to be helping anyway. We hoped that by the time we got back Mom would be better. I called every day.

Psalms 4:1 is David saying, ***"Answer me when I call, God, who vindicates me. You freed me from affliction; be gracious to me and hear my prayer." -- Psalms 4:1 (CSB)*** Mom's constant request was for God to take her. She doesn't want anything done to prolong her life, yet where do you draw the line? Allowing her to have the thin liquids ensured she would get pneumonia again. Was that what God wants me to do for her? That was a preventable outcome for the most part, but did it grant her wish? Allowing her to drink something that I know will hurt her was not something I wanted to do. We tried to find thicker liquids that she likes and would drink enough of to keep her from dehydrating.

I prayed for guidance and strength to do what I must to care for Mom. For Mom, I prayed for peace, for her safety, and for freedom from the fear that grips her. Many of you have walked this journey before me and many will walk this journey after me. For those of you on this journey as well, keep your eyes upon Jesus, allow your friends and family to be there to bolster you in your weak moments. Share your struggles with others. You never know when those stories can help you

### How's the Weather?

God is good and very present in our lives. Life with Alzheimer's disease continues with surprises, but the distance from Mom was needed. I checked with her by telephone nearly every day and things seem to be going well. Yesterday, I had a funny call from her. The aide called and said Mom wanted to talk to me. When she got on the phone, her voice was pleasant. She informed me that she was leaving to go back to Louisiana and wanted me to know. When I asked how she was going to get there, she said she was taking either a bus or the train. I asked her if she would wait a couple of days until I got back from Denver so that I could tell her goodbye. She said she could wait but she would have to see if they had a room for her where she was. They did, so she agreed to wait. She put the aide back on the phone and I explained what I told her. She very wisely repeated the instructions for Mom to wait until I arrived. The aide understood what I was doing and went along with the story. Mom was doing better, or at least it seemed that way.

This scripture passage described our time. *"So they left the crowd and took him along since he was in the boat. And other boats were with him. A great windstorm arose, and the waves were breaking over the boat, so that the boat was already being swamped. He was in the stern, sleeping on the cushion. So they woke him up and said to him, 'Teacher! Don't you care that we're going to die?' He got up, rebuked the wind, and said to the sea, 'Silence! Be still!' The wind ceased, and there was a great calm. Then he said to them, 'Why are you afraid? Do you still have no faith?' And they were terrified and asked one another, 'Who then is this? Even the wind and the sea obey him!' " -- Mark 4:36-41 (CSB)*

A pastor once asked the question, "How is the weather in your life?" Rudy and I just grinned at each other! Yes, the storm surrounded us and threatened to take us under. *"Be still, and know that I am God." -- Psalms 46:10 (NIV)* God prepared the way for me as we came to Denver and as we made our way to church. The rest of our day found us in Rocky Mountain National Park, hiking around Bear Lake and basking in the wonder of this world.

Thank you, Lord Jesus, for your guidance and for the peace you are bringing Mom. I know it won't last for every day, but things are progressing in a positive direction. Prepare the way for her to come be with You, which would grant her wish to be in Your presence rather than here on earth.

### Agitation Escalates

News came to me about my Mom's escalating agitation at the skilled care center. With safety concern for her and the other residents, Mom had to be transferred to a geriatric psychiatric ward about 30 miles away. She was living in another era in her mind. One that included the school children she used to help, one that existed before my Dad passed away, and one that cannot be explained. As I read through the stages of Alzheimer's disease, she was now mostly in stage 6 or 7.

On our return to Texas, I went to see Mom in the psychiatric ward at their one hour visiting time. She spotted me and cried out my name and held me in a tight embrace exclaiming how glad she was I came to get her. She wanted me to meet the "teachers," who had helped while she was there. For the next 45 minutes she talked, and I tried to follow her conversations. Yes, she was rambling. I could only imagine the random thoughts that emerged in her mind from the damaged pathways caused by her disease. As she talked on, I noticed the calm in her as she sat next to me. I thanked God for that moment of peace. When it was time for me to leave, she planned to go with me, which was a problem. It was a less than desired departure. The staff came over to her and held her hand and immediately began trying to redirect her as I left the area. Her desire to go with me was powerful. She broke away, came to the locked door with windows in it, pounded on the door, screaming to go with me. I waited (it seemed forever) for the elevator doors to open so I could get out of her sight. God provided five witnesses who had just left the same area and they rode down the elevator with me. Their comfort was needed and appreciated! I was a mess of tears!

For the next visitation, I called and learned that she was calm. All the way over I prayed for her peace. What a different response I had on this visit. She was given medicine shortly before I called to help calm her as she was getting agitated again. Her conversation was the same, random with unconnected thoughts, but her demeanor was much calmer. I chose to leave a few minutes before everyone else. I made up a story about having to leave and that I would be back to see her soon. I told her I knew the way out so she could just enjoy her sitting time. She agreed! I quickly and quietly made my exit. By the elevators, one of the people who brought me comfort previously noticed the difference.

I walk this journey battling a demon of disease. To do so, I must wear the armor of God as described in *"Finally, be strengthened by the Lord and by his vast strength. Put on the full armor of God so that you can stand against the schemes of the devil." -- Ephesians 6:10-11 (CSB)* We find ourselves in many different and difficult situations where we need to wear the armor of God. Caring for loved ones who are no longer able to care for themselves requires wearing God's armor to do what needs to be done.

### *God Provided*

During emotional work, God provides respite! A trip to the park with our grandkids in Texas was such a respite. As we watched them play on the playground equipment, heard their laughter, and their words "Hey, Gramma come here!" brought joy to my heart. We then took a walk down the pathway under the umbrella of the trees. As one of the boys remarked about a unique noise, I spotted a dead but intact cicada on the path. Boys do like bugs! They gathered around to see up close the source of that "noise" and, naturally, one of the boys wanted to hold it and take it with us. I soon found another dead one that was a better specimen, so we kept that one too. Rudy and I love nature and the boys all know it. When they spot a bird, they tell us. One of the boys literally caught a leaf as it fell from the tree and had to show me. Rock naturally attracts kids, and we give them the right amount of ohs and ahs. Thank you, God, for the joy of that morning. Mom continued at the psychiatric hospital. She did not sleep at all for two days, but she took her medicines. She would be transferred out once they got her sleep schedule settled. Rudy and I visited her new skilled care home and were pleased with the accommodation.

A dear friend reminded me that armor protects our front leaving our flanks and rear open. Other people's prayers and supportive words, as God's warriors, added the additional protection that I appreciate. The professional staff from all three facilities that I worked with have also added much comfort, support, and wisdom to help deal with things with which I had little experience. Because I knew Mom, that knowledge helped them help her. All these people, friends, prayers, and wisdom come together through the coordination of God's work to form that protection and guidance that I needed. His armor from Ephesians 6:10-20 led me. The rest of God's army brought up the sides and the rear to provide all that I need.

Mom attended Episcopal churches for many years and helped start one when I was a very young girl. One of the Psalms that they used frequently was ***"Shout for joy to the LORD, all the earth. Worship the LORD with gladness; come before him with joyful songs. Know that the LORD is God. It is he who made us, and we are his ; we are his people, the sheep of his pasture. Enter his gates with thanksgiving and his courts with praise; give thanks to him and praise his name. For the LORD is good and his love endures forever; his faithfulness continues through all generations." -- Psalms 100:1-5 (NIV)***

Yes, I praise God for all the blessings He has provided for us, even for my Mom in her current state. May God's peace descend upon her and fill her. When your mind plays hide and seek with you, peace is hard to find. I know that God is near and providing care for Mom. I pray too for the cure or prevention of Alzheimer's disease and other dementias that affect so many people.

### *Friends, Final Home*

Sometimes God presents us with gifts when we least expect them. Our decision to return to Texas to attend to Mom caused many changes of plans. We weren't sure when we would feel comfortable leaving, so we parked back in Texas for as long as we were needed there. I suddenly remembered that our daughter and her family were coming through our location sometime in August on their way to Florida. Three days later, they arrived! We got to spend one night and all day with two of our three kids' families (nine grandchildren too!) If not for Mom, we would have been in Iowa, unable to be here for their visit. What a joy as all six adults got to go out to dinner without the children, very rare for us! Our laughter probably annoyed those around us. Refreshing, restoring!

We went out to see Mom, but she slept through nearly all our visit. Since my daughter and family were coming back here the next weekend, we hoped to find her awake next time! Mom was apparently adjusting much better to her environment. Our time there appeared to be ending in the next couple of weeks.

Our prolonged stay allowed me to help honor the lady who inspired me to make quilted prayer cloths (more about these in the Prayer section). Her 88th birthday was Saturday and I got to attend her birthday party. She recently had to quit making them herself and other ladies in the Sunday school class were now making them for the class. Refreshing, restoring.

The lady who sold us a recliner chair for my Mom called us so that we could visit again. She originally bought the chair for her mother to use in a nursing home, but right after they purchased it, her mother fell, broke her hip, and never recovered. As we drove up to their house, we saw a big fifth wheel camper parked next to their home. We had a brief, but wonderful visit since we wanted to get the chair to my Mom as quickly as we could. When she called me later, she and her husband wanted to talk to us about full-time living in their RV. So, we had lunch with them. New friends! Refreshing, restoring.

*"Let the whole earth shout to the Lord; be jubilant, shout for joy, and sing. Sing to the Lord with the lyre, with the lyre and melodious song. With trumpets and the blast of the ram's horn shout triumphantly in the presence of the Lord,*

*our King." -- Psalms 98:4-6 (CSB)* I look for the blessing of each day and there are many! One of the blessings was the people at her skilled care home who were caring for my Mom. They were really making her feel at home and dealing with her disease in a caring and helpful manner. The medication also helped a bunch! Feeling refreshed and restored!

### Anger Over Care

After running some errands, I got to the nursing home, but Mom was not there! I learned she was sent to the hospital several days earlier for mental disorientation. They had called my brother not me! He wasn't sure she went to the hospital, and he didn't bother to call them back or to call me. I went into my "righteous indignation" anger mode! I found out where she was, picked up Rudy and headed to the hospital. After talking to the nurse, I learned they found a large mass in her throat! In 2003, she had a biopsy of that mass in Mom's throat and learned it was an enlarged salivary gland not a cancerous growth. That information didn't get sent to the hospital with her medical records from the nursing home. Of course, my brother didn't remember, and no one called me! So, I waited for the doctor, and he was very helpful filling in all the blanks. It was time to discharge her.

We got her back to the nursing home, and I planned a visit to the Director of Nursing to see how we can prevent this from recurring. I also talked to my brother, and he agreed to call me if he gets any medical calls about Mom.

Many emotions flooded through my body and mind. With Mom's inability to relate what is happening or any personal history, I feel the burden of being that memory bank for her. It made me think of how she was my memory bank when I was a baby, toddler, and young child. She took care of me, and provided the needed information to doctors for my physical care. It is the very least I can do now for her.

*"Refrain from anger and give up your rage; do not be agitated — it can only bring harm. For evildoers will be destroyed, but those who put their hope in the Lord will inherit the land." -- Psalms 37:8-9 (CSB)*

*"A fool gives full vent to his anger, but a wise person holds it in check." -- Proverbs 29:11 (CSB)* The anger I first felt could have continued in rants, raving, accusing, and destruction. But I knew that was not going to be helpful to me, to Mom, to caregivers, or to my brother. God enabled me to rest and do some processing. My purpose was not to blame others for what went wrong, but to see how we can

make the next time better. I worked it out with my brother and the nursing home to contact me about any health issues.

Many things in life make us angry. Anger in and of itself is not bad. What we do with that anger is either helpful or destructive. How has anger affected you? Let us pray that God's words can come to us before we say or do things that cause long term harm.

### *Words of Kindness*

We arrived in Texas a couple of days before Mother's Day, and I immediately went out to see Mom. She looked great for her age and mental condition. She recognized both of us, but she did not remember Rudy's name. She was as delighted to see us as I was to see her.

Sunday afternoon, we drove out to see her with a Mother's Day mylar balloon, some chocolates, and a rose corsage. Chris, our son, and his family all came too. We arrived first and brought Mom out to the lobby so all the kids could visit with her. She was so excited and loved every minute of our time together. The smile on her face, when the kids brought her the drawings they made for her, brought warmth to our hearts.

I showed her the two-generational quilt that I made from the shirts she made back in the 1980's as they traveled. I wondered if she would remember the stars she made as I put them into

the quilt. She did not, but she loved the quilt anyway. I looked for and found the photo in her room with both Mom and Dad wearing their shirts that are now in a quilt. That photo is going into a label for that quilt. At first, she wanted to keep the quilt, but soon agreed that I should keep it. I had hoped that she would remember her detailed embroidery work on the shirts but alas, Alzheimer's disease has taken that from her.

Mother and father figure types could change the course or strengthen the course of a young person's life by the words that they speak. *"A word spoken at the right time is like gold apples in silver settings." -- Proverbs 25:11 (CSB)* That young person can be one of our own children but can also be a student, a friend, an acquaintance, a co-worker, a stranger, or another relative. People I don't even know, but have heard via TV, speeches, Internet, etc., have influenced my life. Books or mere quotes I've read are powerful too.

This scripture is a reminder that our words go far beyond merely saying them. We need to be conscious of what we say and how we speak. Let us offer to those around us the best we have to offer as often as we can. Slow down our tongues and engage our prayers to ask God for the right words, especially in difficult situations, so that we can be uplifting rather than destructive. Those who work with children, or any young people, need to be aware of the influence they have on their charges. On Mother's Day, I honor all those women who influence children regardless of whether the role is biological or a role model mother.

### *Journey to Heaven*

Rudy and I were at our son's house in northwest Washington State when the calls began about Mom's decline. We got hospice started and they advised she did not have long to live. It would be a four-day drive from where we were to Texas or one day if we flew. Decisions are so difficult. Flying meant we would have to come back to get our car and stuff to then drive to Arizona. We finally decided to drive and we prayed that she would still be with us when we arrived. God answered that prayer!

We went straight to her place when we drove into town. She had her eyes closed. I touched her shoulder and told her I was here. She opened her eyes, saw me, and her reaction confirmed to both me and Rudy that she recognized me. It was only a split second, and she closed her eyes again. For the next four days, I stayed with her 24/7 and she never saw me again during that time. The family came in to see her and say goodbye with no reaction from her. When my son and his family came the night before she passed, I told my grandchildren that we all owed her our lives.

She had me. Rudy and I then made our son, (their dad). He and his wife created all of them. So, without Granny, none of us would be here. We gathered around her bed and sang Jesus Loves Me (but changed the Me to You) for her. The next morning August 1, 2013, between 5:30 and 7:30 am she passed away at age 92. I was sleeping in a bed next to her and found her when I awoke. Thank you, Lord, for allowing me to be with her those last days.

*"In my Father's house are many rooms. If it were not so, would I have told you that I am going to prepare a place for you?" -- John 14:2 (CSB)*

We celebrated her life on August 10 with a graveside service. All her grandkids were there, though they were all adults with children of their own. We catered in New Orleans style food in her honor. We had a very good day telling Granny stories, enjoying one another, and rejoicing that her difficult life on earth was over. Her eternal life finds her reunited with my Dad and many of her family members.

# Nature Inspired

### The Light of God

***"Proclaim the praises of the one who called you out of darkness into his marvelous light." -- 1 Peter 2:9 (CSB)*** Whenever I am in the mountains, I look at them and think of the mighty work of creation, of bringing the world from a dark flat void to what we know of it today. How mighty is our God!

A flower bulb exists in darkness only to have light shine on it to bring forth beauty and fragrance. The blossoms follow the direction of the sun each day knowing their source of existence. How mighty is our God!

A newborn baby comes out of a dark womb into the bright lights of this world and into a whole new existence. Just imagine that journey. How mighty is our God!

We each can live our lives in the light of God's grace and love. His light can help us through the darkness that might exist throughout our lives. His light can help us focus on our blessings, take a course of action needed, have courage in troubled times, and bring comfort during periods of sorrow. But we need to invite the light of God to shine upon us, knowing that He is always waiting for us to seek His light. How mighty is our God!

How do you need the light of God to shine on you today? What darkness might be hovering over and around you? Is it a time of separation due to busy schedules? Is it a time of peace and calm that helps you take His presence for granted? Is it indifference to the people and events around you? Is it simply forgetting to take time to recognize His light in your life? Take time now to invite His light into your life. Praise Him for His presence! How mighty is our God!

### Hiking Trails

Walking through the forest and across the rocky mountain slopes reminded me once again of our mighty Creator. *"My soul, bless the Lord! Lord my God, you are very great; you are clothed with majesty and splendor." -- Psalms 104:1 (CSB)* Walking up near Hart's Pass in the Cascade Mountains, we crossed several slopes of

loose rock with a trail forged through the middle. The vistas were magnificent with the larch tree needles turning from lime green to yellow. The sharp-edged rocks, which had fallen from ledges above, showed us the movement that takes place especially during the winter under the weight of snow. Even without the snow, rocks tumbled. Trees grew. Picas scrambled gathering food and shouting alarms. A marmot sat sunning himself. The clouds rolled in bringing misty light fog at times. The beauty surrounded us, enveloping us with the wonder of God's creation.

Yet at a different Pass, we walked out to Rainy Lake through a forest of tall hemlocks, Douglas firs and silver firs. A Douglas squirrel made a quick meal from the meat of a cone from one of the trees. Woodpeckers' holes proved they lived there also. The forest takes a toll during the heavy winter snows as evidenced by the numbers of fallen mighty trees. A process called snow creep causes the trunks of trees to form a permanent bend at the base under the weight of the snow and yet turn upward again.

The trees again reminded me of God's work in us. Even the fallen trees are used for good – homes of animals, fertile ground for other plants and lichen to thrive - then eventually decaying and renewing the soil. God uses all that happens in our lives to enable us to grow into stronger, more persevering individuals, perhaps more compassionate and understanding as well. Let us be reminded of the purpose and comfort God brings to us.

## Barren Places

Driving across southern Arizona is quite an experience. It is like no other place we have been through. Barrenness appears to be all around you. Brown is the dominant color. Sand and dirt surround everything. Off in the distance is always a mountain of some size and shape looking equally barren. The desire is to just drive straight through to find some lush forest!

By searching our maps, asking questions, using our binocular and getting off the beaten path, we are learning to see the beauty in this apparent barren land. The strength of the saguaro cactus in enduring such hardships, while producing blossoms of beautiful white and yellow, amazed us. Birds sit on the cactus without the problems faced by other creatures that only come near the cactus. Changes in types of plants and animals occur from one mile to another as the terrain, the temperatures, the rainfall, and even the amount of direct sunlight affects each spot. We sometimes hear life before we see it.

Life with Christ is much like that. Words to encourage us, ***"Then the eyes of those who see will not be closed, and the ears of those who hear will listen." -- Isaiah 32:3 (CSB)*** As we search for life in the desert, suddenly those same barren areas take on new life. As Christians, we will encounter times in the desert. Just as the Israelites endured 40 years in the desert, we can also endure all things through Christ. How do you get through your "desert"? Can you see any beauty or hope in your desert times? Do you know someone experiencing a desert time? If so, how can you bring "water" to them?

## Lazy Eagles

Rudy was up at the lake in the mountains. A couple of eagles sat on a tree branch overlooking the lake. I had already heard about the antics of the "lazy" eagles, but Rudy got to witness their action.

A couple and a young child were fishing in one of the rowboats. The rule on the lake is that fish must be a certain size to keep them. Now, don't get ahead of me!

Of course, they caught a fish that was too small. In anticipation of their throwing the fish back, the eagles took off and soared above the boat! As soon as the family released the fish, the eagles instantly dove for the discarded fish. The first eagle missed the fish. The second was only 10 feet behind and tried to snag the same fish. Both missed on the first pass. They circled and repeated the dive once again, only to have the same disappointing results!

As I visualized this scene, the thought occurred to me that many of us are like those eagles in our relationship with God. We attend church and maybe an adult Sunday school class. We carry our bibles and we may even read them occasionally. We say grace at mealtimes when we remember. We imitate the actions of those we perceive as closer to God than we are. We try to "catch" our relationship with God the easy way from others by following the actions of others .

*"Idle hands make one poor, but diligent hands bring riches." -- Proverbs 10:4 (CSB)* Just as the eagle searched for an easy meal, do we search for an easy life with God without working hard to discover the biblical truths and promises available to us?

## Let Go, Let God

The cliché "*Let go and let God*" seems so simple! Somehow my humanity keeps getting in the way! The controlling instincts, the leadership characteristics, and the decision maker parts of me keep rationalizing the next step.

While on a Pacific beach, I saw big tree logs that were washed ashore during storms and was reminded of the power of the waters! In Matthew 14:22-33, when Jesus walked across the water to join the disciples in the boat during a storm, I remembered Peter's reaction was similar to the cliché above. Once he decided to let go and let God, he was able to walk out to Jesus. He could do it! How quickly he took his eyes off Jesus and took in the enormity of the waves and the wind. Dunkin' time for Peter! Fortunately for Peter and for us, Jesus rescued him and carried him to the boat.

How do we "*let go and let God*" in the economic times we endure today, with the uncertainty of jobs, questions about continued income, whether to retire or change jobs, and anger toward corporate executives,

Perhaps, the answer lies in finding how to continue to serve God in the midst of uncertainty. Doing what we can to promote changes in our laws, our accounting practices, our sense of honesty and our care for others, rather than greed and selfish gain. Perhaps, by trusting in Him to provide as we faithfully seek His will and seek His guidance.

*"Immediately Jesus spoke to them. 'Have courage! It is I. Don't be afraid.' " --*
*Matthew 14:27 (CSB)* This sums it up for me!

## God in Nature

Sometimes, God has gifts for us but we must look for them. We set out to see some birding spots in southeastern Arizona. While walking down the trails at San Pedro Riparian Area, we heard the leaves on the ground crackling all around us! The leaves were also jumping! Upon closer inspection, we discovered that the ground was covered with grasshoppers. We had startled them as we walked, causing them to jump and turn over the leaves. Praise God for the unusual entertainment as we wandered in the kingdom.

We drove up Carr Canyon Road starting at an elevation of about 4600' and ending high in the forest at about 7000' some six miles later. The road was washboard dirt and rock, narrow, steep and offered spectacular views. Despite the desert environment in town, we discovered large Ponderosa Pines up in the high country. Along the way we saw Western Bluebirds, Townsend Solitaire, Dark Eyed Juncos, a Vireo, Acorn Woodpeckers and, of course, gray squirrels!

We still had more of God's world to see as we came to Ramsey Canyon Preserve, owned and operated by The Nature Conservancy. The trail that we walked was only about a half mile long. The Sycamore trees were the most unusual ones we can remember. The trunks and limbs were contoured in many directions with such graceful lines while covered with white bark. The maple trees had very tiny leaves in red, orange and yellow. As the gentle breeze blew, the late afternoon sun sparkled in and out of the leaves dancing on the ground. During our walk we observed at least six different deer grazing along the trail. They watched us, but chose to stay nearby. As we sat drinking in the beauty, six wild turkeys ambled down the canyon within 50 feet of our location. We walked down the trail with them, and they finally decided to cross the trail. Several of them displayed their wings for us as they made the crossing. A hawk glided through the forest during this short walk. Another hawk soared overhead while the Acorn Woodpeckers stored acorns in the holes of trees.

Once home again, I thought of God as we had shared in the splendor of the kingdom. These words express my joy, *"Let the whole earth shout joyfully to*

*God! Sing about the glory of his name; make his praise glorious. Say to God, "How awe-inspiring are your works!" -- Psalms 66:1-3 (CSB)*

### Glorious Place

It was a gorgeous day in Washington State. At Jim Creek Wilderness Area where we are camp host, we assisted with a Triathlon. Individuals rode their bikes 10 miles up the mountain and down to the twin lakes where Rudy has worked for the last two months. Then they climbed into a kayak and paddled for two miles around the lake. After beaching the kayak, they began the last leg by running back down the mountain for 5 miles.

Many of the participants exclaimed about how they enjoyed the biking portion while they dropped their bikes and put on their life vest for the canoe portion. Several said it was the best bike ride ever! Some commented that the technical aspects were superb! Their adrenaline was pumping. After the event, several people remarked about coming back for more next year.

Move ahead to Sunday morning in church. While singing some praise songs that declared our joy for God being in our life, I suddenly remember the comments, the praise, and the joy from the previous day. What if we left church wanting to tell everyone about our experience in worship? What if we lived every day so enthusiastic for our Lord that we simply had to tell others about our joy?

- *"Sing to the Lord, bless his name; proclaim his salvation from day to day. Declare his glory among the nations, his wondrous works among all peoples." -- Psalms 96:2-3 (CSB)*

- *"Give thanks to the Lord, call on his name; proclaim his deeds among the peoples. Sing to him, sing praise to him; tell about all his wondrous works!" -- Psalms 105:1-2 (CSB)*

- *"Let the name of the Lord be blessed both now and forever. From the rising of the sun to its setting, let the name of the Lord be praised." -- Psalms 113:2-3 (CSB)*

Psalms are full of such scriptures. Our instructions are clear. Let us shout from the mountaintops about our love for our Lord! Who can you tell today?

### Seasons of Life

Fall is my favorite time of the year! I love the changing colors of the trees and other plants. Today we drove over an 11,669 'mountain pass. The aspens were beautiful as the sun bounced off the fluttering leaves. The rugged road was a challenge, but the traffic was bumper to bumper in both directions! Pull-offs were crowded and the trailhead parking at the pass was packed. It seems as though half of Denver came to see the same sights we were trying to see.

*"He has made everything appropriate in its time. He has also put eternity in their hearts, but no one can discover the work God has done from beginning to end." -- Ecclesiastes 3:11 (CSB)* This sums up for me today's experience.

As I think about the changing seasons and the many things related to that event, I marvel at God's creation. Animals seem to know how to prepare for winter and gather food. Plants lose the sap to endure the frozen temperatures. Many retired people head for warmer climates to live during cold months. Leaves change colors and fall to the ground.

We go through changes in our lives as well. Are we entering a time of challenge with "winter" coming? Are we entering a time of blossoming that happens when warm temps and rain bring flowers to bloom? At times do we question our own usefulness or purpose? Perhaps, we are in a stagnant time of standing still. Does a crossroad loom ahead? Do we stand wondering which way to go?

I cannot fathom what God does from beginning to end in my life, but I am so grateful that He is present in the changes. Just as He makes everything beautiful in its time, He does the same for me in His time. Look at the beauty God provides for you, and you can enjoy the journey even if the road is rugged.

### Charging Batteries

Does your battery ever run down? Yep! How do we recharge? Some people take naps, some take vacations, some soak in a tub, some read, some take walks, and on and on....

God gave us a clue when He created the world by resting on the seventh day. The Psalms are full of images of how to recharge. After a month of constant activity, stress filled days of dealing with Mom's illness, picking up our new motorhome and getting things repaired, getting to where we needed to be despite repairs, stress was running rampant in my life.

Our arrival high in the mountains was a mere 11 days later than we planned for volunteer jobs. Our first "duty" was to take a few days to get acclimated! Being at 8,500' of elevation requires some of that under normal circumstances. I needed it just to unwind! The first day was a leisurely day of rest, sightseeing, and eating. The next day was an even quieter day. The morning worship gave direction. Then we decided to attend the evening vespers and campfire.

Hearing this scripture allowed me to submit to the peace of this place which comes from God and became a means for recharging my batteries. *"You made him ruler over the works of your hands; you put everything under his feet: all the sheep and oxen, as well as the animals in the wild, the birds of the sky, and the fish of the sea that pass through the currents of the seas. Lord, our Lord, how magnificent is your name throughout the earth!" -- Psalms 8:6-9 (CSB)* As we sat listening to these words, the birds in the trees sang beautiful songs of nature. The crackle of burning wood in the campfire, the floating ash blown by the breeze, the warmth of human companionship, the words of scripture read, and the songs of praise soothed this weary soul.

During the busyness of this week, remember to find time for rest, for restoring and recharging your batteries. Find time for God to bring you peace.

### Working Hard

As Rudy and I hiked through the woods in the mountains, we heard baby birds chirping in their nest. Finally, we found a hole in an aspen tree in the direction of the sounds. Patiently we waited and watched. Mom and Dad were not far away. The red-napped sapsuckers came one right after another with insects to feed their young. While the parents were in the nest the babies were quiet, but as soon as they left, their chirping began in earnest trying to encourage them to stay. As the parents left the nest, we followed their flight from tree to tree as they swooped out into the air to catch flying insects for their babies. We watched for 30 minutes or so as they made constant trips back and forth. What effort goes into caring for their young!

Paul wrote to the Thessalonians in his first letter. *"Although we could have been a burden as Christ's apostles, instead we were gentle among you, as a nurse nurtures her own children. We cared so much for you that we were pleased to share with you not only the gospel of God but also our own lives, because you had become dear to us. For you remember our labor and hardship, brothers and sisters. Working night and day so that we would not burden any of you, we preached God's gospel to you." -- 1 Thessalonians 2:7-9 (CSB)* The Thessalonians despised manual labor, viewing it as fit only for slaves. Paul would do any sort of work necessary to keep from being a burden to others while preaching the gospel.

As I viewed the college youth and the seniors working at our location, I saw Paul in many of them. They did their work and in their free time they studied the scriptures. A young lady in the laundry shared Isaiah 53 with me while our clothes went around in the machines. Another young lady from Egypt glows with the faith of Christ while struggling with loneliness after being in the US only a week.

Can we share our faith as avidly as the sapsuckers found insects for their young? Can we work as diligently as Paul so as not to be a burden while finding ways to share the gospel? How does God call us to use the gifts and talents that we have in the places where we are? Pray for direction, seek out those around us, and listen for God's loving guidance.

### Satisfying Thirst

One of the first things we were told upon arriving in the mountains was to drink lots of water! At 8,500' of elevation the oxygen level is lower, so your body works harder to function, and water helps replenish fluids lost. Not drinking enough leads to dehydration or altitude sickness, which causes flu like symptoms. The best treatment once reaching that point is IV therapy to hydrate the body quickly.

I met with a small group of women who studied this verse. *"Come, everyone who is thirsty, come to the water" -- Isaiah 55:1 (CSB)* Water is an analogy used often in scripture because of its important role in our physical survival. Yet, when used in scripture, water becomes the source to meet our spiritual need. How thirsty for spiritual food are we? We use words that reflect spiritual awareness. Do our actions reflect our spiritual thirst? Do we live our lives in such a way that others see how we quench our thirst?

My thirst often comes and goes much like it does with my body's need for water. At times I seem to be satisfied and full and then suddenly altitude sickness sets in, and I crave the water that soothes me. How do we keep an even flow of water to the soul that satisfies the thirst?

Just as we were to carry water with us always everywhere, drinking eight bottles a day, we need to carry Christ with us allowing the Holy Spirit to minister to us. ***"Rejoice always, pray constantly, give thanks in everything; for this is God's will for you in Christ Jesus." -- 1 Thessalonians 5:16-18 (CSB)***

Keeping company with other Christians through worship, study, prayer, fellowship, and work allows us to encourage one another. The discipline of individual prayer and study centers our focus on God's will for us. The practice of these disciplines waters the spiritual thirst just as drinking eight bottles of water helps prevent altitude sickness. Are you satisfying your thirst for Christ?

## Waterfalls

Thank You, Lord, for special times with our adult children! Exploring the woods in the Cascade Mountains in Washington state is always spectacular. We've seen lots of waterfalls all with many twists and turns that reminded me of the awesome power of our Lord.

The mountains that helped create the waterfalls represented another form of God's majestic power. Standing at the top of Slater's Peak, the 360° view revealed two volcanoes, Mt. Baker and Glacier Mt. Also seen were: old gold mining scars, valleys filled with trees, fire destruction, sharp pointed needle like mountain tops, smoother more rounded mountains, and the colors of fall. The peaks reminded me of the many times God carried me to the mountaintops of life. The various other sights reminded me of the parts of life's journey.

Snowfields remained from the previous year's cold. Melted snow continued to run from them into low areas to join with other streams to form the waterfalls, which then eroded the rock. As you go down the mountains, life can erode your relationship with God by taking your eyes off him. The more we lose sight of God the harder it becomes to deal with the daily issues.

The constant freezing and thawing cracks the rock after many years, causing slides that change the landscape. Boulders as big as trucks and rocks as small as ones a child would throw into a stream all come to rest where gravity takes them. We cannot allow the daily trials and tribulations to erode our relationship with God and with our loved ones, causing changes to occur.

Scripture uses mountains and water to help us understand God. David, as he wrote the Psalms , was especially adept with his visualization. ***"At your rebuke the water fled; at the sound of your thunder they hurried away — mountains rose and valleys sank —to the place you established for them." -- Psalms 104:7-8 (CSB)***

*"You establish the mountains by your power; you are robed with strength."* -- *Psalms 65:6 (CSB)*

*"Deep calls to deep in the roar of your waterfalls; all your breakers and your billows have swept over me."* -- *Psalms 42:7 (CSB)*

Water gathers power as it falls, just as we gather power when we spend time concentrating on any issue. When I spend time having my own pity party, life gets more sour the longer I spend at that party. However, the reverse is also true. When I spend more time in prayer and reading scripture, the stronger I become as I recognize the power of the Holy Spirit living within me. How grateful I am for the reminders the waterfall and the mountains brought to me in how I seek to keep God a part of my life. He chose you, and me, and we need to acknowledge Him with our praise and presence.

## Invite All

Outside my window sits a mockingbird that never tires of singing! He wants to dominate the bird feeder even though he has trouble feeding from it himself. We watch him as he chases off other small birds that fit the size of the feeder better than he does. Sometimes he just sits on a nearby branch watching like a guard dog watching his home. He apparently has no interest in inviting others to dine with him. But he sings such beautiful melodies.

I know that mockingbird has a place in God's world even though some of his habits annoy me! *"According to the grace given to us, we have different gifts."* *-- Romans 12:6 (CSB)* There are people too in this world that annoy us, but God has them here in this world for a reason. Perhaps the annoyance that I/we feel is my/our problem. Perhaps I/we need to develop more understanding, patience, or tolerance.

It still annoys me that the mockingbird will not allow the other birds to join at the feeder! Mr. Mockingbird, I read to you: *"He also said to the one who had invited him, 'When you give a lunch or a dinner, don't invite your friends, your brothers or sisters, your relatives, or your rich neighbors, because they might invite you back, and you would be repaid. On the contrary, when you host a banquet, invite those who are poor, maimed, lame, or blind. And you will be blessed, because they cannot repay you; for you will be repaid at the resurrection of the righteous.' "* *-- Luke 14:12-14 (CSB)*

We put the feeder out for all and occasionally, when the mockingbird is not around, others do get to feed. We did not put a sign up for only certain birds. Besides, everyone knows that birds don't obey signs! Guess we need to be more tolerant of all! Lord, help us to see the worth in everyone and to be open to all of your people and creations.

### Unexpected Birds

We pulled into an RV park in a new location and learned that the owner's wife was an avid birder. She was currently off at a training session for becoming a master certified naturalist in the state of Texas. According to the owner, she would love to take us birding the next day.

We envisioned a walk across the highway to a birding center. God does have surprises for us when we least expect them! Since the next day was rainy, we decided to at least learn about some good birding spots for future trips. She packed us into her 4x4 and off we went, but not across the highway! She took us on a three-hour tour of the county. We saw a lot of birds in spite of the weather. She took us to the location on a mud road to a juvenile Whooping Crane who was hanging out with a flock of Sandhill Cranes. Now you don't find Whoopers in this area! This guy got separated from his parents somehow and joined the Sandhills. He is about 30% larger than the rest of the group and he is only a juvenile!

*"The birds of the sky live beside the springs; they make their voices heard among the foliage." -- Psalms 104:12 (CSB)* God wants us to enjoy His world and Psalms 104 clearly lets us know that. This scripture emphasizes the joy we find in locating and identifying God's creations.

*"And Abraham named that place The Lord Will Provide, so today it is said, 'It will be provided on the Lord's mountain.' " -- Genesis 22:14 (CSB)* God provides for us even to go birding by sending a special lady to take us to special places. How easy it would have been to skip going simply because of the rain and because we really didn't know this lady! After all, there was a birding center right across the highway where we could simply do our own tour. Look what God provided by simply accepting the invitation. Watch for invitations that may come your way this week, perhaps God provides even when we don't look for or expect His provisions.

## Waiting Patiently

In the quiet of the morning, I found myself admiring the beautiful green of the trees outside our motorhome. The green of early spring is so different than the green of summer. I wondered what scriptures I could find about spring and did a search. Most were about springs of water. A few in the Old Testament talked about spring as a time to go to war. When I found James 5:7. I found spring and water mixed to help develop patience.

*"Therefore, brothers and sisters, be patient until the Lord's coming. See how the farmer waits for the precious fruit of the earth and is patient with it until it receives the early and the late rains. You also must be patient. Strengthen your hearts, because the Lord's coming is near." -- James 5:7-8 (CSB)*

During the past month, we have waited and waited (but not patiently) for all our repairs to be finished so we could get on with our journey. During that time, though, we experienced the beauty of the area, met some local folks we would not have known, met some fellow travelers seeking repairs, and found a lovely church with a spirit filled message. I also had time to sew more prayer cloths and to share them with others in the area.

Perhaps God has a purpose for us to be here so long. Perhaps patience helps us to be more open for opportunities to share God's love for us. Perhaps the search for scriptures about spring enabled me to find a taste of living water in a way I hadn't expected. Then reading God's word always holds surprise and joy. What surprises does God have for you as you read His word?

## We Are Unique

This past week we were blessed with several evenings of gorgeous sunsets! Arizona is blessed with lots of open space and enough mountains to interrupt the horizon and add to the beauty of God's painting in the sky.

Naturally each one is unique, never to be repeated. God adds unique touches to each sunset. Each of us is like the sunset, unique and never to be repeated. Even our identical twin grandsons are unique and individual. Yes, they share many genes that make them very similar, but their personalities are uniquely their own! Sunsets share many of the same characteristics. The shapes and size of the sunset varies with each one. Even the same sunset as seen in two different spots is different. David claims, *"I will praise you because I have been remarkably*

**and wondrously made. Your works are wondrous, and I know this very well."**
**-- Psalms 139:14 (CSB)**

As we prepare for that celebration of Jesus coming into this world, let us remember that He is unique, a one of a kind. He is the *only* Son of God. His purpose on earth was to be the final sacrifice for us. Yet He lived His life with a brilliance that outshines even the beauty of the sunsets. Because of His life and love of you and me, I know that my life is better.

I stood and watched the sunsets develop and all I could do was praise God for His creations. His creations bring joy to me daily. I watch for the evidence of His presence all around me. This week let us look for the evidence that reminds us why Jesus came to earth as a baby so many years ago. Let us praise God for His uniqueness as well as all His splendid creations around us.

### *Look at Nature*

The immenseness of life and complexity of our earth is mind boggling. We drive around and see the amazing scenes all over the United States. The sights leave us with appreciation of our amazing earth. Yet there is so much we have never seen on our earth!

Television and DVDs have many programs about nature that help us to see some sights most of us could never begin to see in person. These programs took many years of gathering the pictures with patience and incredible endurance. One program had a mating dance of a species of Bird of Paradise that took eight weeks for the photographer to sit in a blind heavily camouflaged to get the dance he wanted. Another series took many years of shots in the same spots to get the progression of growth for plants over time. The details in nature, the spectacular colors, the behaviors of animal life, and the relationships between all life of plants and animals is fascinating.

Watching these programs simply reinforces the majesty of our God and creation. When Genesis tells us what God created each day, the words seem so simple, Then God said, *"Let the earth produce vegetation: seed-bearing plants and fruit trees on the earth bearing fruit with seed in it according to their kinds." – 'Let the water swarm with living creatures, and let birds fly above the earth across the expanse of the sky.' – 'Let the earth produce living creatures according to their kinds: livestock, creatures that crawl, and the wildlife of the earth according to their kinds.' "* -- *Genesis 1:11, 20, 24 (CSB)*

We can each look around us and see incredible creatures and plants. We must look! Is our life so full of activities that we simply don't see the world around us? God has richly blessed us with His creations. We need to not only take time to observe them but to take care of them. Scripture goes on to, *"Let us make man in our image, according to our likeness. They will rule the fish of the sea, the birds of the sky, the livestock, the whole earth, and the creatures that crawl on the earth."* *-- Genesis 1:26 (CSB)* God charges us with taking care of the plants and animals he created! Yes, they are also a food supply for us and for one another, but we still must take care of them to ensure a proper balance of each. How can you this week help to care for God's creations? Look around you at the beauty, the uniqueness of God's creations. Share it with someone and praise God for His magnificent work.

### The Elusive Bird

We found it! We found the elusive bird from Mexico we came to see! What a treat! Oh, the images that remain in my mind! Yes, in Sierra Vista, Arizona, we found the Elegant Trogon in its amazing splendor.

To a birder, this is exciting news! To most of you it probably holds no importance at all. To find this bird, we asked many people where to find him and got several answers. We learned about his unique call, and were told that once heard, it would be unmistakable. We visited several spots where he was said to be with no luck. Finally, we went to one of those locations that we had first visited years earlier looking for him again. Upon arriving to the suggested spot, we found another man also looking for him who said he heard the bird about 30 minutes earlier but still hadn't seen him. As we stood there talking to the man, Rudy looked up and there was the bird in a tree about 50 feet away in his entire splendor! He flitted from one branch to another and finally landed on a branch in the sun with all his colors sparkling for us to enjoy. All three of us got to see him in the spotting scope. After we all had a good look, Rudy put the camera up to the scope to get his picture only to have him fly away, but still in view. We followed him for at least another 30 minutes as he dodged from one limb to another keeping enough small limbs between him and us to prevent a good picture. Finally, he flew too deep into the forest for us to follow.

This search reminds me of how some people experience their relationship with God. Our relationship comes and goes (if you even find it to begin with). God is the one seeking us, and we are the ones dodging Him. God wants us to follow, and He shows us the way, but we are stubborn sometimes and refuse to let God get close.

*"Ask, and it will be given to you. Seek, and you will find. Knock, and the door will be opened to you. For everyone who asks receives, and the one who seeks finds, and to the one who knocks, the door will be opened." -- Matthew 7:7-8 (CSB)*

What are we asking for? God wants us to ask for a relationship with Him most of all and, of course, we receive! Asking does not always get us what we want because God may know that what we ask for is not what we need. Jesus even asked God if it be God's will to let the cup pass from Him. Jesus really didn't want to die but He knew it was best for all if He did and God gave Him the ability as a man to endure that death.

Yes, we found the elusive bird. We also find God (who is not elusive) and allow Him to guide and lead us as we ask, seek, and knock on door. God doesn't hide or flit away as the bird did for us, but He waits for us to ask Him into our lives. What in your life today are you seeking? Try asking God, search the possible answers, and knock on the right door to which God leads you. Amazing results are available. Expect answers. They may not be the ones you expected; they might be even better in the long run!

### Restoring Earth

Rudy and I are back at a church camp for a couple of months. Coming back again means coming back to folks we know and love. It means a time of offering our services to the camp to help with many tasks and to work with a wonderful staff. As I sit at my computer, the view includes the tall evergreen trees and the buildings of the center. Yet behind the buildings and trees is a mountain side ravaged by fire several years ago. The grasses are beginning to return as well as small shrubs. You still know where the fire was and how close to the buildings that it came.

I am reading a fictional book that weaves the biblical stories with fictional accounts not included in scripture about people's reactions to the biblical accounts. Again, and again God's people have wandered from him, been captured, and then rebuilt again. *"For this is what the Lord says: 'When seventy years for Babylon are complete, I will attend to you and will confirm my promise concerning you to restore you to this place. For I know the plans I have for you' — this is the Lord's declaration — 'plans for your well-being, not for disaster, to give you a future and a hope. You will call to me and come and pray to me, and I will listen to you.'" -- Jeremiah 29:10-12 (CSB)*

Yes, seventy years before coming back for Israel. And tree regrowth takes many years to come back to maturity! The trees and plants will come back. God has a plan for us and for all of nature. God is a masterful planner! God loves us enough to restore His people who are lost to a right relationship once again and to restore the earth from the disasters that occur.

God also gave us the responsibility to oversee the use and protection of this earth. Some disasters cannot be prevented, but others can. If we are to be good stewards of all the creatures of the earth as well as the waters and the land, we have much work to do. Find out how you can participate with your community and what you can help start doing in your community. We need to encourage one another to find alternatives to our lifestyle which do not destroy our environment.

God brings those who seek Him back to Him, but we must seek Him. God will help us restore the earth as we seek to restore a right relationship with our earth. Someday the trees behind the buildings at the church camp will cover the mountain side, but it will take time. How is your relationship with God? Are you in need of restoration? Take those needs to God in prayer, and find scriptures that help you to seek His grace and forgiveness.

### *Gardens Nourish*

I spent some time weeding this week and that gave me some time to ponder and think. You have a garden where you plant all kinds of pretty and/or healthy plants. We shop for good bulbs or seeds. We get cuttings from friends. Finding the right mulch and fertilizers to help get things started is high on our list as we shop. Planting the seeds/bulbs requires some precision as each requires different amounts of distance and depth from other types. Oh, don't forget sun or shade, what do the plants need? After hours of work, sore muscles, and lots of love, the garden is done for now!

Gardens come with many unwanted guests. Those guests come in the way of unwanted insects, animals who trample or eat plants/bulbs, or weeds. Maybe it rained too much and drowned the new plants. Maybe the weather changed and got too cool for the plants. Of course, a two-year-old wanted to pick his mother a flower and pull it out by the roots. Or the kids were playing ball and, as the ball headed toward the garden, an eager kid dove for the most fantastic catch of his life and landed, yep, you know where! Oh, the things a garden must endure to survive!

Gardens also come with wanted guests in the form of the right amount of rain and sunshine, food, helpful insects, and caretakers. We want our gardens to look orderly, with lots of color, texture, and shape. We know that gardens can be disorderly, overgrown, and a lot to care for.

Our relationship with God is often like our gardens in The Parable of the Sower, *"Then he told them many things in parables, saying, 'Consider the sower who went out to sow. As he sowed, some seed fell along the path, and the birds came and devoured them. Other seed fell on rocky ground where it didn't have much soil, and it grew up quickly since the soil wasn't deep. But when the sun came up, it was scorched, and since it had no root, it withered away. Other seed fell among thorns, and the thorns came up and choked it. Still other seed fell on good ground and produced fruit: some a hundred, some sixty, and some thirty times what was sown.' " -- Matthew 13:3-8 (CSB)*

We need the right amount of ingredients to nurture and grow our relationship with God. We need a caretaker to help us, and the Holy Spirit fills that role. Ponder the ways that your spiritual "garden" grows this week. What things hinder your spiritual "garden" and what things enhance your spiritual "garden"?

Yes, I pulled some weeds this week in the garden, now I need to pull some spiritual weeds out of my spiritual life.

### Praise Always

After the football games this weekend, and with not much on the TV we want to watch, we pulled out a DVD we received for Christmas. What amazing footage of our oceans and the life within them. There is so much life in the sand even after the tides roll out. As I watched I marveled at the scope of God's creations. Of course, seeing creatures from the oceans all over the world introduced us to creatures and aspects of their life we knew nothing about. Naturally, the extensiveness of creation under the seas is intriguing. It is also amazing to watch the behaviors of animals and creatures that we do recognize and the risks they take to feed and to reproduce. Yet somehow most manage to survive.

I thought of life in our cities and communities. We are so accustomed to the sights and sounds of humans. Our complexity doesn't seem so amazing at first glance. If we think about the details of function and design for humans, we realize how amazing our God is to have created such detail and diversity. Witnessing the birth of a baby, I am in awe of God's work.

David spent so much time as a shepherd in the fields admiring the heavens. Later in his life he was outdoors a lot. In the Psalms , he declares his praise to God for all creation and the beauty of life. Psalms 148 is literally a praise song, naming all the things included in creation. ***"Let them praise the name of the Lord, or he commanded, and they were created." -- Psalms 148:5 (CSB)***

What beauty do we see around us? Are we so focused on the details of living each moment that we forget to see God's creations and the splendor in everything? It rained in Arizona and was cold with unpleasant temperatures, but in Arizona the rain is beautiful! No complaints!

What about the people around us? What is there to praise about them? Find one feature or character trait to praise at least. If possible, make the list longer! Is that person someone you would call a friend? What about someone you might have difficulties with? Can you find something to praise in them? At your job or in your school or neighborhood is there some aspect worthy of praise? Where do you see God in your surroundings? Look for God all around you, as God is there!

### *Wonders of Beauty*

***"How magnificent are your works, Lord." -- Psalms 92:5 (CSB)*** This is the scripture on my March calendar. The picture is of wildflowers - Paintbrush and Colorado Blue Columbines from the Lower Ice Lake Basin in the San Juan National Forest, CO. The photo is so sharp you can even see the very fine hairs that exist on the petals of the paintbrushes.

I love wildflowers! This past week we went out to a local state park and the wildflowers were in bloom! The Mexican Gold Poppy lined the roads and other patches throughout the park. When we first arrived, they were closed as the clouds kept the sun away. As the clouds moved away, the sun warmed their petals causing them to open. The lupines were also in full splendor. Because we had a wet winter the wildflowers are particularly abundant this spring.

The many cacti plants that live in the desert are also preparing to bloom. A few have already blossomed but many more are preparing to open. I never cease to be amazed at the vivid color, the texture, the shapes, and the detail in each blossom.

I also experience the same kind of wonder when we go birding. The colors and the detail in the feathers, the songs they sing, the behaviors they exhibit that are different for each species and the migrations that they endure all come from our Creator. They are indeed wondrously made.

As I sorted through years of photos, the scripture again displayed wonder. The babies, the detail that goes into their lives, their personalities, and the journey from conception to birth are all spectacular miracles that our Creator gave to us.

Look around you and see what wonders our Creator gave you. Sometimes miracles are not the most beautiful or the most perfect items. Perhaps the wondrous work is a transformed person for Christ, a not so perfect person that chooses to live a God centered life despite the odds. Perhaps the great work is the saving of a life that beats the odds of survival, a God miracle. Let us praise God for every wonder.

### Handling Conflict

The ruby throated hummingbird is abundant at our current volunteer work location. The dining hall has two feeders on the windows where we watch them fight over the food constantly. We put our hummingbird feeder up outside the motorhome window. Within 30 minutes the first customer arrived! Within the first hour several began playing chase to keep one another away from the feeder. By the next morning the feeder was empty! As soon as I refilled it, they began the never-ending fights over the food. Though small, a hummingbird is very aggressive and will even try to chase off bigger birds. They fight constantly! I keep trying to tell them there is plenty for everyone and they can take turns, but they don't listen to me! They expend way too much energy chasing each other which then requires them to need even more food to survive.

All this activity made me very glad that Jesus teaches us ways to avoid conflict and be more loving toward one another. Conflict can be avoided through negotiation when we choose to follow that path. We need to listen to each side before jumping to conclusions. Perhaps an explanation can help us avoid actions we might later regret. Conflicts can be avoided by seeking a common goal. Let us look at the larger picture rather than just the moment before engaging in conflict. Is there something we can agree upon that will help settle differences or allow us to agree to disagree?

Conflicts can be avoided by remembering their source. Do we want more possessions, more money, more status, and more recognition? Is something within us driving our desire to enter a conflict? Is it something self-serving? Is it something good for others? What is driving our anger or the jealousy that leads to conflict? Instead, we need to submit ourselves to God's will and ask what God wants for us in this situation.

***"What is the source of wars and fights among you? Don't they come from your passions that wage war within you?" -- James 4:1 (CSB)***

Obviously, we can't ask the hummingbirds to resolve their conflicts. It is not part of their nature to do the things listed above. However, we can certainly learn from them about what doesn't work. Yes, they do all eventually get to eat but they could be so much more efficient with their time, their energy, and their food. Their conflicts do provide us with lots of entertainment when we remember they are birds and not our relatives or co-workers!

What conflicts might you need to resolve through negotiations or a common goal or by remembering the source? Seek to restore those relationships by allowing God to guide you. Pray for the Holy Spirit to direct your thoughts.

### *Hummingbirds*

The conflict among the hummingbirds at our feeder continues. After watching them and filling the feeder twice a day, I have observed some interesting behavior. Many times each day, two birds will feed from the same small hole at the same time. They achieve this feat by one sitting on the perch and the other hovering over the perched bird. Then they both stick their bills into the small hole. Now the only way this is possible is if the one on the perch allows it. Occasionally I have noticed that the one hovering will gently place her feet on the one sitting on the perch. Only the females do this.

We have probably 15-20 birds hovering around at times. We have the feeder hanging on suction cups to the window of the motorhome, and with the tinting of the window, they can't see us. One immature male was perched and another adult male was trying to chase him away by hovering over his back. The young male leaned back while still holding on the perch as if to say to the adult male, "I'm not done yet," but he leaned back too far and fell off the perch! The adult male promptly took his place.

Hummingbirds must eat 50 to 60 times a day due to the energy they burn just flying. Their heart beats around 1,200 beats per minute. When they migrate south, many of them fly 500 straight miles across the Gulf of Mexico. Before they make that journey, they must fatten up since they expend a lot of energy for the trip.

*"Consider the birds of the sky: They don't sow or reap or gather into barns, yet your heavenly Father feeds them. Aren't you worth more than they? Can any of you add one moment to his life span by worrying?" -- Matthew 6:26-27 (CSB)*

Yes, many of us are concerned about the cost of fuel, the weakened economy, job security, health care costs, and on and on. As I view the hummingbirds and read this scripture from Matthew, God does provide for us. If we were not feeding the hummingbirds, there would be plenty of flowering vines and plants in the area to feed them. Perhaps they would have to travel farther to find enough, but they would eat. Just as God provides for the birds, God provides for us as well. Let us thank Him daily for everything (even the hard moments that come) since God is in the hard moments also. Thank You, Lord, for the hummingbirds and the joy they fill me with each day (even when I must make their food).

### Forest Walk

Rudy and I took off to the woods south of Tucson on Valentine's Day to do some birding after hearing about an Elegant Trogon being spotted in Madera Canyon. As we drove toward the mountains surrounding the Canyon, we noticed snow on the south side of the ridge! This ridge is perhaps 20 miles from the Mexican Border at about 8,000' of elevation. Last weekend a front came through with rain at lower elevations and snow at higher elevations. Most of the snow had melted, but some small patches remained in shaded areas.

The area where we searched for the birds was between 4800' and 5400'. The creek that ran down the mountain had water in it from the melting snow. We saw many birds, including wild turkeys that really weren't very wild. They hung out at the bird feeders at one of the lodges and enjoyed being hand fed by visitors, as well as eating the bird seed that fell to the ground.

The highlight of the day was spotting a Painted Redstart and watching him flit and flutter from branch to branch, giving us great displays of his magnificent beauty. We watched him for nearly 10 minutes, but we never found the Elegant Trogon. We will in the future!

As I hiked along the side of the creek, taking in all the sights of the area, the sounds of the birds, and the pleasure of being there, I could only praise God for His creations. Our God considered many very intricate details putting our world together. The uniqueness of each species is amazing to behold and almost incomprehensible to understand. How I loved being in nature yesterday with Rudy. For us, it was a perfect way to spend Valentine's Day.

Psalms 104 is a praise to God who made the world. It speaks of trees, birds, animals, mountains, waters of the earth, winds that shape the trees, clouds in the sky, flames of fire, and so many other parts of creation. Yes, we saw and experienced these words. *"He causes the springs to gush into the valleys; they flow between the mountains. They supply water for every wild beast; the wild donkeys quench their thirst. The birds of the sky live beside the springs; they make their voices heard among the foliage. He waters the mountains from his palace; the earth is satisfied by the fruit of your labor." -- Psalms 104:10-13 (CSB)*

We came home refreshed. My prayer for each of you is that you take the time to renew your soul, replenish your batteries, and see God around you. *"I will sing to the Lord all my life; will sing praise to my God while I live. May my meditation be pleasing to him; I will rejoice in the Lord." -- Psalms 104:33-34 (CSB)*

### Grand Canyon

Rudy and I stood on the rim of the Grand Canyon in front of Bright Angel Lodge with our spotting scope, our binoculars, our coffee, and our warm jackets, gloves, and hats! Our son and his wife were in the process of walking out of the Canyon after two nights in the Canyon. Our goal was to spot a California Condor. A condor is the largest bird in North America. In 1982, only 22 birds existed in the entire world! A very elaborate captivity/breeding program was developed to save the bird from extinction. It worked and now there are over 300, with about half in captivity and the other half flying free. About 70 are in the Grand Canyon area. Our stake out took all morning and into the afternoon, but finally two flew into our area. Right after they flew in, Scott called to tell us they were about 30 minutes from the trailhead. We only got a short, but good, view of the condors as they flew by. As we walked toward the trailhead, we found the condors sitting on the top of a cliff in good view. For the next 35 minutes or so, they sat there showing off for us. They sure are ugly birds, but with a 9' wingspan they are large and worth watching!

The Grand Canyon is an amazing place. The size is simply awesome. The vertical climb down into and up out of the Canyon is over 5200' (more than a mile) each way straight up/down. To walk that vertical distance takes about 10 miles with lots of switchbacks to get down and another 10 miles to bet back up. Someone told me they heard a lady walk up to the edge of the Canyon and ask "Is this a man-made

Canyon or a God-made Canyon?" It is so big; man could not have made it! Yes, our God is a mighty God. The many wonders that exist in the Canyon, from the smallest lizard to the condors, to the majestic cliffs and rock formations, to the changing light as the sun moves across the Canyon, to the shrubs and plant life, all are evidence of God's hand in creating this work of art. Genesis 1 tells of God's creative work and Psalms 104 also goes into detail about the beauty of our world with a summary here, *"How countless are your works, Lord! In wisdom you have made them all; the earth is full of your creatures." -- Psalms 104:24 (CSB)*

Photo by Scott Morris

This trip was a Sabbath for me. It enabled me to take a break from daily duties and to enjoy nature as only God can provide. Look for God around you. Though you may not be in a place as grand as the Grand Canyon, God also created much of what is around you. Look for His work and praise Him for giving us such a wonderful home as this earth.

### Rooted in Jesus

The road called us back into the motorhome. Once again after six months in Casa Grande, Arizona, we are traveling. Our first stop was south of Tucson to visit one of our favorite birding spots, Madera Canyon. As we walked down a trail, I spotted an amazing tree. A sycamore with its roots still embedded in the ground, was bent over at the base, not broken, just bent at nearly a 90-degree angle. The leaves and branches still reached out to cross the creek that flowed next to the tree. This was amazing considering that the entire center of the trunk was missing! Yes, I said missing. The exterior of the trunk was only about 2/3rds of the way around the trunk. The top 1/3 of the trunk/bark was missing. Nothing there! I went over and literally stood in the empty tree trunk.

I looked at the miracle of this tree even being able to produce branches and leaves with so much of the tree missing. The roots were still in place! I thought of people who struggle with cancer, with missing limbs, and many other debilitating injuries. For those whose roots are deeply imbedded in God, they survive despite whatever parts of their bodies have failed. They not only survive, but they thrive no matter where God plants them.

*"The one who lives under the protection of the Most High dwells in the shadow of the Almighty. I will say concerning the Lord, who is my refuge and my fortress, my God in whom I trust." -- Psalms 91:1-2 (CSB)*

Just as that tree survives with much of its trunk missing, we can survive amazing difficulties when our roots are in Christ and when He is our refuge. We can still bear fruit for the Lord because of how He cares for us. Our lives can still have meaning. Regardless of what we think might be missing, we need to hold on to Jesus, our root system, our Savior, our Protector. How I praise God for showing me that tree this week. I love seeing God in the surroundings I find myself walking through. Where do you see God in your surroundings? Look for Him. He is there.

### Rest in the Lord

Rudy and I love going out to a nature preserve to enjoy being outdoors, watching birds, and seeing what spring flowers were blooming. We both have had a very busy winter at our park with activities, work and projects. This day of relaxation was very much needed. I packed light snacks for us since there are no easy places to get lunch. Rudy took his new camera to learn more about what it can do. At a leisurely pace we proceeded down the trails. Though we didn't see many birds, we did see many Phainopeplas, which are basically black cardinals. Looks like a cardinal in shape, but is all black with wonderful white spots on its wings visible only when it flies.

A creek runs through the park providing water for the animals that live there. A bench along this path allowed us to sit, eat our snacks, and enjoy the peacefulness of God's world. Even though there were more people along the path, we faced the creek and continued to soak in the sights of fresh green growth on the trees, the sounds of the rushing water, and the songs of the birds around us.

*"He will cover you with his feathers; you will take refuge under his wings. His faithfulness will be a protective shield." -- Psalms 91:4 (CSB)* The rest we sought was found in the pleasure of being in God's world of the outdoors. After lunch we wandered over to the demonstration gardens to see what was blooming. Some amazingly beautiful cactus blossoms had Rudy trying the macro features on his

camera, getting within a couple of inches of the blossoms. The detail that emerges at that distance is amazing! Toward the end of the gardens, we found two chairs in the shade of a tree overlooking bluffs of rock. For the next hour we just sat and soaked in peace. The scripture describes for me how safe I felt there. I even dozed off as best I could while sitting up in a chair! The peacefulness was a balm to my soul. We had a good day.

As we go through our week, where can we find the rest we need? What restores you? How can you clear your mind and allow God to fill your senses with His presence? Even during turmoil or other trying circumstances, allow God to be the feathers and wings that cover you with His protection and peace.

### *Nourishing Tree*

We had an opportunity to spend the weekend in Rocky Mountain National Park. We went with a group from our daughter's church. They all left at the end of the weekend, but being retired had its advantages! Rudy and I chose to stay another night to avoid traffic getting back to Denver and to enjoy more time in the park. Sunday afternoon found us cruising up Trail Ridge Road to an elevation of 12,000+ feet, photographing a couple of herds of elk along the way, enjoying the tiny flowers in the tundra and the majesty of the mountains.

Monday morning our check out wasn't until 11 a.m., so we took an hour and a half hike around Sprague Lake. One of the trees along the path caught my attention. It was on a slope, the lower limbs rested on the ground making a blanket like effect on the ground. As I stood studying the tree limbs, I thought of how God is my trunk, the center of my being just as the ground is a source of food that nourishes the tree,

As the limbs rest on the ground, new roots form to spread down into the ground to bring more nourishment to the tree. As I reach out to other Christians around me, study God's word, pray for others and for the issues in my own life, the roots of God's love continue to grow stronger and feed my soul.

The Cedar of Lebanon is described as a great tree. *"It was beautiful in its size, in the length of its limbs, for its roots extended to abundant water." -- Ezekiel 31:7 (CSB)* The passage goes on to say the tree is destined to death. We are also destined to death in this life. It is not the tree or us that lives on forever on this earth. It is God that lives on eternally and His chosen with Him. As I saw this tree embracing the ground in such an intimate fashion, I felt the arms of God embracing me and providing for me the grace and blessings to walk along my journey. As the tree gets it strength from its roots, I get my strength from God. Thank You, Lord, for the tree that again showed me the importance of God's nourishment as we reach out to the world and to one another.

## Spiritual Giants

Our son and his wife took us to one of their favorite trails in the mountainous woods of northwest Washington State. It was in a spot that day hikers don't normally frequent. It is an area where you find some of the largest and oldest fir trees and cedars along the path. The term "Standing among giants" describes the area appropriately. As I stood there looking at the enormous trees, I thought of a couple of things about our walk with Jesus.

On occasion, I find myself among a group of people that I feel are spiritual giants to me. People I want to emulate. People that I want to spend more time with to listen to their wisdom. Of course, the publicized spiritual giants that come to mind are Mother Theresa, Billy Graham, etc.

Then came the image of the three disciples with Jesus at the transfiguration. *"After six days Jesus took Peter, James, and his brother John and led them up on a high mountain by themselves. He was transfigured in front of them, and his face shone like the sun; his clothes became as white as the light. Suddenly, Moses and Elijah appeared to them, talking with him. Then Peter said to Jesus, 'Lord, it's good for us to be here. If you want, I will set up three shelters here: one for you, one for Moses, and one for Elijah.' While he was still speaking, suddenly a bright cloud covered them, and a voice from the cloud said, 'This is my beloved Son, with whom I am well-pleased. Listen to him!' When the disciples heard this, they fell facedown and were terrified. Jesus came up, touched them, and said, 'Get up; don't be afraid.' When they looked up they saw no one except Jesus alone." -- Matthew 17:1-8 (CSB)*

I can only imagine how Peter, James, and John felt during those events and even afterwards, as they remembered the event. Yet those three went on to become spiritual giants. Look at the events of their lives, the obstacles they had to deal with daily, and the faith they shared with thousands!

As I looked at those trees, I was in awe of the difficulties they endured over the years of their existence as well as the beauty and strength that they offered to passersby. God gave us so many images in this world He created to help us be reminded of His work.

Help me, Lord, to see the spiritual giants in my life and to pay attention to their wisdom. Thank you for the giant trees you also gave us to enjoy. May each of us recognize and appreciate the spiritual giants in our daily lives.

### Defending Nests

Rudy and I made a trip to southeast Arizona. We came to see hummingbirds that visit from Mexico during August. Over the three days, we identified seven new hummingbirds that we had never seen and a total of eleven different species of hummingbirds.

At the Nature Conservancy in Ramsey Canyon, we learned so much about these new birds. Ever wonder about the size of a hummingbird nest? Yep, we not only saw three different hummingbird's nests, but one even had a Mamma on the nest with eggs in it! Did you know that hummingbirds use spider webs in the construction of their nests? The strength of the web helps hold the nest to the twigs as it suspends in air. As the babies grow, the nest expands to make room for the growing babies. Our guide took us to a very small nest that sat on a small limb that hung over the creek. *"The birds of the sky live beside the springs; they make their voices heard among the foliage." -- Psalms 104:12 (CSB)* He also showed us several other nests, all made near the water. Here in Arizona that is an important location, and the birds know it. One of the species that we saw flies 4,000 miles from its winter location to its breeding spots. Their wings flap at a rapid rate of about 70 per second (70 x 60 = 4,200 wingbeats per minute)! What endurance for such a small bird!

Birds are very much like any other mother; they will defend their nests. *"Like hovering birds, so the Lord of Armies will protect Jerusalem; by protecting it,*

***he will rescue it; by passing over it, he will deliver it." -- Isaiah 31:5 (CSB)*** The fierce nature of the hummingbird reminds me of how our Lord will fight for us. It also reminds me of how we fight with each other trying to one-up the other. Like children, hummingbirds fight over who gets to sit on which perch.

We watched one poor young hummingbird sit on the feeder, unable to get to the hole for his turn to eat, while the older more experienced birds buzzed around pushing each other off the perches. The young bird just sat frozen, apparently afraid to move! He'll learn quickly to be just as aggressive as the others if he wants to eat. I look at our society today and see many of those behaviors as we push one another around to get ourselves into the prime position to be first. Reminds me of road rage!

When I remember the spectacular iridescent colors that seem to change in different angles of light, I thought of the many different faces we wear around certain people. To God, we are transparent, and He knows what is in our heart. How I praise God for knowing us so well and allowing us to see His beautiful birds.

## Daily Life

### Waiting for Answers

Have you ever wanted something that seemed to evade you time and time again? You even pray for God to grant you the desires of your heart. You hope for:

- an event to occur,

- a person you love to do something or act in a manner that you desire,

- a relationship to be mended

- a loved one restored to health

- a lost, confused friend to return to sensible behavior

- a million other things that you can add to this list.

You pray, you live a good life, and yet, your wish, longing, desire, whatever you call that missing piece, never comes to being. You find yourself like the psalmist anger, hurt, impatient, crying out *"Wake up, Lord! Why are you sleeping? Get up! Don't reject us forever? Why do you hide and forget our affliction and oppression?" -- Psalms 44:23-24 (CSB)* We love to question God and that process is acceptable to Him. The process is much like a child who questions a wise parent's decision. The child grudgingly and unhappily accepts the decision, and maybe years later finally understands the wisdom of the decision. Answers to our requests often take time, requiring patience on our part. Sometimes the answer is not what we want to hear or experience. A child sometimes doesn't get his way because the wise parent knows what is best at the moment. In my prayer life, I can look back over the years and see actual requests that took years to resolve and some that are still in request form! Do I sometimes get impatient and angry like the psalmist? You bet, and I use the words in scripture to help me acknowledge my emotions. Then I move on to looking for the good, the praiseworthy, the noble, and the blessings of today. I read in a "bad news" letter from an organization one day the phrase "making lemonade out of lemons." I have adopted that phrase and attitude for those bad, inconvenient, undesirable times in my life that I cannot control. When our prayers seem to go unanswered, let us not turn our backs on God and prayer. Let us wait for the answer and, in the meantime, make lemonade. In the process, we just might find that answer God has for us, not as we expected, but as His will intends for us.

### Sides of A Dispute

*"The first to state his case seems right until another comes and cross-examines him." -- Proverbs 18:17 (CSB)* I thought of disputes from the past that seemed to be one way until some time passed. Other events later shed more light on the issues, causing those who were on the opposite side of the dispute to now seem justified.

I thought of:

- the children and their arguments and how desperately each want the parents to believe their version of the story.

- family disputes that keep families from speaking to each other for years.

- Christians who disagree over interpretation of scripture and hold grudges ending friendships forever.

- church members divided over issues that lead to some leaving the church.

Taking sides in arguments is easy to do based on trust and love for a person. As a third party in a dispute, our role is not to judge or determine who is right. Based on what I read here, our role is to encourage the participants to look at all sides, to seek God's direction on the issue, and find resolution. Of course, to find resolution means each party needs to accept responsibility for their role in the dispute. Sometimes, that takes time to recognize what God is telling us. It is never too late to accept that realization and make whatever amends are necessary. Perhaps you say too much time has passed. Hurts get carried with us for a long, long time and hearing an apology always helps. True, we need to turn those hurts over to God too, but that becomes another discussion! Is there someone in your life that you owe an apology, perhaps just because you listened to one side of the dispute? Is it time to contact that person? I ask God to lead you and me into action this week. For the future, may we think carefully and ask God for His wisdom while continuing to encourage others toward resolution and peace. What additional scriptures might help? You can always do an online search to find some others.

### *Having a Bad Day*

Have you ever had a day when something you did made you feel really bad about who you are or what you had said or done? Guess most of us could answer, "YES" to that question. After having one of those days recently, I found this scripture the following day. David wrote it during his 17 years of flight from King Saul who sought to kill him. ***"Listen, Lord, and answer me, for I am poor and needy. Protect my life, for I am faithful. You are my God; save your servant who trusts in you. Be gracious to me, Lord, for I call to you all day long. Bring joy to your servant's life, because I appeal to you, Lord. For you, Lord, are kind and ready to forgive, abounding in faithful love to all who call on you. Lord, hear my prayer; listen to my cries for mercy. I call on you in the day of my distress, for you will answer me. – Teach me your way, Lord, and I will live by your truth. Give me an undivided mind to fear your name. I will praise you with all my heart, Lord my God, and will honor your name forever." -- Psalms 86:1-7, 11-12, (CSB)***

My enemies that day were my tongue and my emotions responding inappropriately with anger. When we have those days, we need to recognize our enemies and recognize our response to those enemies. Then we need to seek restoration not only with God, but also with ourselves and any other person(s) who might be involved. May this passage of scripture be meaningful to you.

### *Molding Iron*

How did I become the person I am? Not biologically how, but how was I molded and shaped personally? I read: ***"Iron sharpens iron, and one person sharpens another." -- Proverbs 27:17 (CSB)***

The first image that came to mind was that of a blacksmith. He takes a piece of iron in his tongs, heats it until it turns red, and uses an iron anvil and iron hammer to mold and shape the hot piece into beautiful and useful shapes. The blacksmith must love his craft to see the beauty in the finished task long before achieving that product. His patience and his thoughtfulness are evident. He shapes the hot piece, ponders the piece, plunges it into water to cool and examine it, and then may even heat it again to continue fine tuning the product.

God, Jesus, and the Holy Spirit are my "blacksmiths." They do not literally set me into a fire and beat me into shape. They do patiently and thoughtfully mold me, making me into the person they desire me to become. They use a variety of means to reach me. I think of so many other people who have contributed to my spiritual development. People who inspire me, who question me, who unconditionally love me, who lead me to certain scriptures, are some of the tools in the Trinity's tool pouch. Reading my bible, praying, watching videos of spiritual subjects, and listening to gospel music are also ways for shaping me.

I am so grateful for Jesus' willingness to die on the cross for my sins. What love He has for me and for you, unconditional love that we do not deserve. Understanding the events of Holy Week as best I can helped to shape me into a more thankful person, a more faithful person, a person better able to share the joys of discipleship with others. The process of learning for me has had times when I felt like a hot piece of iron, wishing I could find another way to reach the final product. The process is not yet finished for me as I am still being molded and shaped by the love of God through His son Jesus. Who have been the molders and "blacksmiths" of your life? Who are you helping to mold and shape? Send them a note, pay a visit or make a phone call to thank them for their work.

### Telling Others

The book of John ends with the following two verses, ***"This is the disciple who testifies to these things and who wrote them down. We know that his testimony is true. And there are also many other things that Jesus did, which, if every one of them were written down, I suppose not even the world itself could contain the books that would be written." -- John 21:24-25 (CSB)***

Witnessing is a very important goal for John. He wrote about his memories of life with Jesus and what he personally witnessed happening. He used the noun "testimony" or "witness" about 14 times and the verb "testify" about 33 times, which is many more times than the other three gospels. We have many books today seeking to do much the same about how Jesus has impacted the author's life. Just go to a Christian bookstore and browse awhile. In many of the stories, we can identify with the author and find similarities with our own stories. What about our own stories of our encounters with the living Christ? How do we preserve our stories? How do we use them? With whom do we share them? Why would we want to share our mere story? Are we afraid others will think us foolish? Did we misread the whole situation and chalk events off to coincidence?

I struggled with these questions and, when I finally trusted God enough to share the first time, I was truly amazed by the loving caring response I received. Over the years, the sharing has come much more frequently and with much more confidence. The responses vary. I still struggle with when is the right situation for sharing. Perhaps I need to be less cautious and follow the examples set by the disciples. This scripture encouraged me to do something I have not done too much of in the past – to write my stories for sharing. We need to identify times of Jesus working in our life, and use them as our stories, write them down, and be willing to share them verbally or in letters to others. The disciples shared their stories of Jesus that included their faults, their doubts, their strengths, their faith, and their courage, so that we might believe. Jesus died on the cross so that we might all be forgiven and come into the kingdom of God. How do I respond to His death and resurrection? For me, I need to record my stories of His action in my life for sharing as the Holy Spirit leads me. I invite you to share your stories with others. Remember, the sharing of our stories is often the opening that allows us to also share the story of the good news as related by the gospels.

### *Your Gifts*

Why do we do some of the things we do? Why do some activities almost feel like a compulsion, being driven by something inside us that we do not fully understand? We stop and wonder, "Why me? I am not trained for the task; I am not worthy or bold enough. Why me?"

My study of Paul this week led me here: ***"I was made a servant of this gospel by the gift of God's grace that was given to me by the working of his power. This grace was given to me — the least of all the saints — to proclaim to the Gentiles the incalculable riches of Christ." -- Ephesians 3:7-8 (CSB)*** Saul would be renamed Paul after his conversion. Saul was truly the least of the least to be selected to preach the gospel! He had persecuted Christians, standing boldly against them, imprisoned them, even (some believe) lead the execution by stoning Stephen (Acts 7:58). Yet, God chose Saul to preach to the Gentiles. To us it is a mystery, but God knew the passion of Saul and knew Saul would be dynamic once the Holy Spirit empowered him.

What about us? We may not have been selected to preach as Paul did, but we each have gifts for service. When I write, I often question what I may possibly have to say to you. As always though, the Holy Spirit enables me to know whom I serve. You too can listen to the Holy Spirit guide your service in whatever way He leads you. I urge you to discover your gifts if you have not already. If you know your gifts, use them boldly. Our world needs hearing God's good news of salvation and Christian living. Christians are needed to stand for what they believe scripture is saying. The needy are numerous among us. What gifts from the Holy Spirit will you recognize and exercise?

## Disagreements

We have all seen disagreements that destroy friendships, church communities, and self-respect. Paul wanted to return to the towns of their first missionary journey and Barnabas agreed but wanted to take John Mark with them. Paul did not want to do that since Mark had deserted them on an earlier trip. *"They had such a sharp disagreement that they parted company, and Barnabas took Mark with him and sailed off to Cyprus. But Paul chose Silas and departed, after being commended by the brothers and sisters to the grace of the Lord." -- Acts 15:39-40 (CSB)* Fortunately, we do not have to wait years to learn about the forgiveness and acceptance that Paul and Mark established later in their lives. Paul even learns to respect Mark so much that he requested him to come be with him during his final days.

Churches often run into difficulties over many issues like theology, interpretation of scripture, how sermons are preached, social issues, and innumerable aspects of people's personality and qualifications to minister. We experience hurt feelings, injured faith, anger at God, and a full range of negative emotions. Disagreements will always be with us as a part of our human condition. What do we do with those disagreements? We can dwell with them and allow the injuries to fester and stay infected. Or we can seek solutions, one of which might be to separate, follow a different path, but a path that still has us with our eyes fixed upon Christ and continue to be productive. Often, as happened with Paul, we can come to appreciate or accept that which once offended us. The ministry of Christ is where we need to keep our eyes focused. Sometimes, as in Paul's case, splitting became the better path because many more people were reached with the gospel message by the team splitting. Rather than continue to argue and one trying to win, they agreed to go in different directions. That does not mean that one is better than the other, they just chose different paths to take toward the same goal. What disagreements in our lives need new focus? Ask God to help in seeing new aspects of the issue that can bring about acceptance and forgiveness. Help us recognize when agreeing to disagree is the best course of action.

## A Handle on Life

I heard a comment from someone whose health had suddenly changed, but I was not sure it was meant in reference to her health or her life. I was not in a position to clarify the comment, I was left to merely ponder the many implications of the statement. *"I thought I had a handle on life and then it broke."* My first reaction was the sadness in the comment. I am sure that many of us at times could identify with such brokenness, such disillusionment, such hopelessness. My other reaction came very quickly if not simultaneously, *"Did her belief in Christ break also?"* Jesus' final instruction to the disciples before He ascended: *"And remember, I am with you always, to the end of the age." -- Matthew 28:20 (CSB)* What does "a handle on life" mean to you? My handle on life is my relationship with Christ. My study of the scriptures reveals that having a handle on life by holding on to Christ does not guarantee a smooth, trouble-free life. *"And the peace of God, which surpasses all understanding, will guard your hearts and minds in Christ Jesus." -- Philippians 4:7 (CSB)* Paul goes on in Philippians to tell how that peace has enabled him to be content in all kinds of living conditions. The disciples endured persecution and physical pain that many of us have not endured; yet they maintained their grip on Christ's message for them. My experiences include sometimes in my life when I have loosened my grip on the handle. How I praise God for the times my grip on the handle tightened when I recognized His work in my life and during times of unknowns, pain, and loneliness when He carried me.

What do we focus on in troubled or good times? By focusing on our relationship with Christ, our mind stays clear to possibilities, to avenues for resolution, to hope, to the love and needs of others. Then perhaps our comment can be, "I have a handle on life no matter what comes my way."

## Changing People

I attended my 40th high school reunion and one person especially captured my attention. I saw him 40 years ago as someone else in our class, someone with a talent, but not someone I cared to know. Now 40 years later, I would like to spend hours hearing his stories. I thought perhaps Paul could have been speaking to him many years ago with these words: *"I recall your sincere faith that first lived in your grandmother Lois and in your mother Eunice and now, I am convinced, is in you also. Therefore, I remind you to rekindle the gift of God that is in you through the laying on of my hands. For God has not given us a spirit of fear, but one of power, love, and sound judgment." -- 2 Timothy 1:5-7 (CSB)* I did not know much about my friend many years ago, but I assumed he lived a loose life with some unbridled habits. He had a gift and talent that others enjoyed. Somewhere along the line God came into his life (the story I wanted to hear but not enough time to do so) and fanned into flame the gift God had given to him. For more than 30 years he has been serving God with complete openness and joy. We did have time to do some sharing and I now see him as a radiant beam for the glory that God brings into our lives. He speaks openly of his faith with conviction and without judging others. I know, from the short time I was able to spend with him, that many lives have been changed because of his witness and love.

Again, I was reminded of how easily we characterize people, judging qualities as negative or positive according to our own standards. Fortunately, God has a different method and reaches out to include those whom perhaps the world is more likely to discard. God can fan our flames into action. We all have gifts to be used by and for God. Each step in faith we take leads us to take even more steps. What gifts might God be trying to encourage us to use for Him? How can we use the power of love and self-discipline to be effective witnesses for God?

### *Passing Down*

Praise is such a powerful motivator. All of us enjoy receiving praise, even if we deny it verbally. Our Lord also enjoys receiving our praise. Psalms 145 came to mind after the births of our twin grandsons. *"The Lord is great and is highly praised; his greatness is unsearchable. One generation will declare your works to the next and will proclaim your mighty acts." -- Psalms 145:3-4 (CSB)*

The impact of what one generation passes on to the next is often underestimated. I want my grandsons to know about the prayers that went into their development, the blessings that were sought on their behalf, and the joy their arrival brought to so many people. I want them to experience the love and grace our Lord gives to all of us who seek it. I want them to know about the wisdom and guidance their parents seek from God as they provide discipline, education, and all the other needs necessary for raising children. I want, most of all, for them to develop their own relationship with our Lord as they grow into adults.

These wants are something we all have for our children and our grandchildren. During their lives, we must continue to pray for them, to praise our Lord in their presence, to tell them of God's mighty works in our life, to praise their efforts at prayer, to encourage their times of meditation, to speak of the awesome works, and proclaim the great deeds of our Lord. Psalms 145 gives us our instructions and we need to read, reread, and respond to these instructions. Each generation carries that responsibility. I praise the Holy Spirit for filling you and me with the desire and the ability to fulfill those responsibilities.

## Finding Comfort

Hallmark and other card companies capitalized on a concept of God's work for us. Cards usually provide comfort. *"Blessed be the God and Father of our Lord Jesus Christ, the Father of mercies and the God of all comfort. He comforts us in all our affliction, so that we may be able to comfort those who are in any kind of affliction, through the comfort we ourselves receive from God." -- 2 Corinthians 1:3-4 (CSB)*

I have a habit of putting cards I receive in a basket. The messages usually touch a special need in my heart. When the basket gets full, I go through them again, allowing them to touch my heart again. Many then get saved in a storage box. When we closed our house down, I came across cards I received when I broke my leg, when I had my mastectomy, when we celebrated birthdays, anniversaries, and deaths of loved ones. I took the time to reread them all again, allowing them to once again touch my heart.

God is the God of comfort, and He enables us to pass comfort along to others in many ways. Cards are just one of the ways. So many acts of kindness exist that effectively pass along the feelings of comfort to one another. Praying for others is another means of passing comfort on to others. Technology is making the communication of prayer needs quick and enabling us to share comfort in a way we could not in the past. Sometimes listening to someone in trouble or in pain is the best comfort we can offer at that moment. Comfort also comes by enjoying the surroundings of this world in nature. The soothing sounds of water flowing, birds singing, and wind rustling through the trees bring comfort to our busy lives. Think of the ways that comfort comes to you and then consciously provide an act of comfort for someone today. Wouldn't life be wonderful if every day we each sought to bring comfort to others? God is the God of comfort and compassion. It is He who brings us comfort and He who uses each of us, as we are open to His leading to be the conveyors of His comfort.

### Calling You?

Many churches and other worthy organizations find themselves searching for volunteers, calling and asking, sometimes even pleading. How easy is it to say, "I am too busy," or "I don't know if I can do that?" Sometimes we do need to say "NO, not now," but how do we know.

The Lord called to Isaiah: ***"Then I heard the voice of the Lord asking: Who will I send? Who will go for us? I said: Here I am. Send me." -- Isaiah 6:8 (CSB)***

In considering a task, who is calling you? Yes, a friend may be on the phone, but is God also calling you through that person? You often need to respond with "Let me pray first for what God is calling me to do." When God calls you and you respond with, ***"Here I am. Send me."*** He will also equip you, lead you, support you, and help you with whatever task is at hand. Even though I had never taught Sunday school, gone on mission trips, led bible studies or prayer groups, worked with committees on stewardship, or preached sermons, He led me, not because I had experience, wisdom, or vast knowledge, but because I wanted to learn more about His world, His wisdom, and His teaching. Then He equipped me to do His work. He led me to the people I needed to help me. He guided me to the resources I needed to use. Many times, I asked myself what am I doing here? Many times, I could tell you about when He has enabled me to do that which I could not do on my own!!! When I take the advice from Isaiah with the words, ***"Here I am, send me,"*** God provides the guidance. How is God calling you? What does He want you to do in His world now? Is it as simple as deciding to follow Him? How can we be obedient to His calling today?

### Sharing Space

One of the most common questions we field for our lifestyle in our motorhome deals with space and the lack of it. Needless to say, a 36' x 8.5' floor plan is scaled down from our last home. We must share a lot of space, take turns, pick up after ourselves, talk with each other, and respect each other's needs. Actually, it is not any different than most other situations where people must coexist with others. In Hebrews, the author concludes with many encouraging words, especially: ***"Don't neglect to do what is good and to share, for God is pleased with such sacrifices." -- Hebrews 13:16 (CSB)***

Space is something of value in our society. Many of us are accustomed to having our own bedrooms, single-family homes, our own car, etc. At work, we have our own computer, our own desk, our own equipment, etc. Churches, some businesses, schools, and homes, however, often find it necessary to share space to make the best use of their resources. Sharing is difficult, as it requires talking to each other about needs, planning of activities that recognize the many users in the space, and cooperating with others who use the same space. Sunday school and preschools often share rooms, toys, bulletin boards, and furniture. Families often must share rooms. Jesus never had His own room, His own synagogue, His own car, or His own computer, yet His ministry thrived because of what He taught, the power of His message, and His encouragement of the people. What is the message we want to send to those with whom we share space? Is our energy spent in claiming and protecting space or nurturing one another? Is our time spent criticizing and complaining or spent in cooperating with and encouraging others? We try to teach our children to share and we, as adults, need to model the concept of sharing as well. What sharing is God calling you to do this week? Respect and communication about the shared space is required and most important to make the arrangement work. Pray for creative solutions.

## Uncertainties

Every time you turn on the TV or read a newspaper today, it seems there is more bad news about layoffs and ripple effects of various tragedies or other events in our world. There are also the stories of unity, acceptance, heroic deeds, amazing survival. Ahead is the uncertainty of tomorrow. Doesn't tomorrow always carry a great amount of uncertainty?

Ephesians helps put all this in perspective: *"Finally, be strengthened by the Lord and by his vast strength. Put on the full armor of God so that you can stand against the schemes of the devil. For our struggle is not against flesh and blood, but against the rulers, against the authorities, against the cosmic powers of this darkness, against evil, spiritual forces in the heavens. For this reason take up the full armor of God, so that you may be able to resist in the evil day, and having prepared everything, to take your stand." -- Ephesians 6:10-13 (CSB)*

These words seem especially true for national and world events occurring today. They also apply for us individually for the daily events that affect our lives. We still face illnesses, personal relationship struggles, the discipline needed for continued study of God's word, the expectations of job and family, and the list could go on and on. God's word comes to minister to us individually as well as collectively. During these days and months of uncertainty, may we listen to one another in ways we never have. May our conversations with one another contain more understanding. May we encourage one another with the strength found in scripture. May the armor of God enable us to conquer what lies ahead.

### Heart and Soul

For many years, I spent time seeking those who might be available for service in God's church. I spent much time in prayer asking God to bring those to me whom He wanted called. Sometimes it appeared my prayers were not heard. I often felt the temptation to just ask anyone just to get the slots filled.

A scripture that was of great comfort to me during those years was: ***"But the Lord said to Samuel, 'Do not look at his appearance or his stature because I have rejected him. Humans do not see what the Lord sees, for humans see what is visible, but the Lord sees the heart.' " -- 1 Samuel 16:7 (CSB)***

Do we know that much about a person from how they look? Definitely not! Jesus cares about the development of the heart and soul.

Our society spends a lot of time and money telling us how important it is for us to look good, to smell great, and to dress well. How much emphasis is placed on the quality of our heart? Disasters often bring about a renewed emphasis on the heart, prayers to God, interest in one another, and/or the values of living a Christian lifestyle.

May our conversations with one another seek to learn more about the condition of our hearts rather than a listing of accomplishments and job titles. May our thoughts revolve more around finding time for prayer than time for making our homes and ourselves appear in certain ways. Lord, fill our hearts with a love for You that overcomes our need for physical appearances.

### Running the Race

***"Let us run with endurance the race that lies before us, keeping our eyes on Jesus." -- Hebrews 12:1-2 (CSB)*** Our daughter recently ran her first marathon. Hearing her talk about the experience came to mind when I came across this scripture. She did a lot of preparation during the year getting ready for the big event. The preparations involved not only the physical running, but also the mental preparations. Since she was running for a purpose (American Diabetes Association), she learned a lot about the disease. To earn financial support in donations for her trip, she learned about friends and family who suffer from diabetes. As an athletic trainer caring for injured athletes and helping to prevent injuries, she studied the special needs of diabetic athletes.

During the event, the run was very demanding. The stress on her body and emotions was tremendous. Yet the preparations helped enable her to finish; the bystanders also provided encouragement to finish. The temptation to give up exists because of the pain, but with the preparations and the encouragement, she never gave up and she finished.

Christ brings us into His kingdom. We don't earn our way in by how we live. Living our life as Christians then becomes the race we run to the finish. He wants us to accomplish that similar to a runner preparing for a race, giving it our all and never giving up.

How do we prepare? What kind of a training program must we develop? What knowledge is necessary to help us live life with Christ? Are we merely a bystander watching others prepare or are we in the middle of a bunch of Christians? May we as Christians encourage one another to continue praying, studying, and practicing the life principles taught by Christ. May we endure the hardships and sacrifices necessary to spend time with Christ. Lastly, may we complete this journey, knowing we did our best to finish!

## Love Carries Us

Sometimes the circumstances of our life find us in places where we would rather not reside. I spent many hours with Mary, my mother-in-law, as she succumbed to the ravages of breast cancer. During that time, I found and clung to these verses: *"No, in all these things we are more than conquerors through him who loved us. For I am persuaded that neither death nor life, nor angels nor rulers, nor things present nor things to come, nor powers, nor height nor depth, nor any other created thing will be able to separate us from the love of God that is in Christ Jesus our Lord." -- Romans 8:37-39 (CSB)*

God's love is so vast! We can experience it in our most humble moments, our most desperate times;

- in the isolation of war,

- in the kidnapping of journalist and children,

- in the rubble of 9/11,

- in the aftermath of respiratory problems,

- in the life lived longer than desired,

- in the turmoil of muscles and agility that fails us as we age,

- in the body that remains whole, but the mind that can't remember,

- in the failures of systems we entrusted with our life savings,

- in the relationships that do not live up to expectations,

- in the churches and pastors whose humanness may cause us to flinch,

- in the numerous accidents that take loved ones away suddenly, and

- on and on...

God's love cannot be taken from us! It is always there, and we must believe and depend on His love to carry us through wherever circumstances surround us. Claim and count on His love for you today and always.

### Light the Fire

Light the fire within! The Olympics have dominated our viewing the past days. As I watch the closing ceremonies, I am touched by the events and their stories. The stories of determination to overcome adversity to compete. The stories of family hardships. The stories of years of trying and trying. The stories of parents' love and sacrifices. The stories of successes, failures, and sportsmanship. The stories of practice and hard work.

I am reminded of these words: ***"This is the message we have heard from him and declare to you: God is light, and there is absolutely no darkness in him. -- If we walk in the light as he himself is in the light, we have fellowship with one another, and the blood of Jesus his Son cleanses us from all sin." -- 1 John 1:5, 7 (CSB)***

And: ***"For you were once darkness, but now you are light in the Lord. Walk***

***as children of light — for the fruit of the light consists of all goodness, righteousness, and truth." -- Ephesians 5:8-9 (CSB)***

Our Olympic athletes carry a light within for their sport. It is a passion to participate at that level of competition. We, as Christians, have a light within that needs to shine for all to see and to recognize as easily as we recognize the dedication of our Olympic athletes. What would our world be like if we carried our light boldly, if we practiced and studied our faith as diligently as do our Olympic athletes? Let us begin or step-up conditioning for our Christian fire lighting!

## Solve or Escape

All of us find a reading or passage that we can go to and find immediate identity. The Psalms are that place for me! All of us have good days and bad days. There are days we would like to escape from life and rid ourselves of our responsibilities, our obligations, our problems, our thoughts, and other such things. Fortunately, for most of us those days are only occasional and short lived. My reading in Psalms shared this thought that brought a smile to my face! ***"I said, 'If only I had wings like a dove! I would fly away and find rest. How far away I would flee; I would stay in the wilderness.' " -- Psalms 55:6-7 (CSB)***

You may be asking how Rudy and I could possibly have that thought now that we can drive away in our motorhome from whatever bothers us! All of us take our problems, responsibilities, etc., with us! When you look at your life and wonder how to escape, just remember God is there to help us solve and correct.

In that same chapter is the offer of God's hope: ***"I complain and groan morning, noon, and night, and he hears my voice. Though many are against me, he will redeem me from my battle unharmed." -- Psalms 55:17-18 (CSB)***

Often, communication is a good place to begin when we feel like escaping. First communing with our Lord and searching out provisions, then communicating with those who are affected by our desire to escape. Facing our problems, our anger, and our responsibilities is the real solution that God leads us toward. It isn't always fun or easy, but certainly worth the eventual peace and comfort that it brings. God is always present for us no matter what! He cares for all of us!

### My Faith

*"Draw near to God, and he will draw near to you." -- James 4:8 (CSB)* These words from James reminded me of a time when God was a concept in my mind. Not having a personal relationship with Him prevented me from experiencing His comfort, grace, and forgiveness. Having grown up in a church as a child, and going through confirmation in an Episcopal church made Him a known concept. Events in my life led me to seek Him in a way I never had. Yet I could see no immediate change.

Many years later, I began to see how He answered my prayers in ways I never dreamed possible. As my knowledge of how God works through others and how He grants grace and forgives, I began to see how He worked in my life. My mother-in-law offered me unconditional love, no questions asked, and she became a witness of living a life with Christ as your guide. She showed me the meanings of concepts I had only heard about during my life. Other people crossed my path as I sought out more about life with God.

The bible was just a book on my shelf, covered in dust, unread, and beyond understanding. Once again, my mother-in-law supplied me with a paraphrased Living Bible that, at least when I read it, I could understand the words and sentences. Gradually, as I attended adult Sunday school classes, bible studies, and special events at church, my knowledge, understanding, and desire to learn grew.

My faith became my own - not that of my parents, or even my mother-in-law, but my own. As I consciously came nearer to God, He appeared nearer to me. Yet He was always there, and I was the distant one. No one could make that journey nearer to Him for me. We cannot make that journey for anyone else in our life either, but we can be a witness of living life with Christ for others. Let us never fail to be that witness who encourages a relationship with Jesus Christ, our Lord.

### Seeds That Bloom

Because of our travels, we enjoyed spring in three different states. Watching the trees bud out with blossoms and then with leaves enhances our enjoyment of God's world. Getting to see it happen three times in the same year is a blessing!

My daughter has a Christmas cactus blooming, and it reminded me that I could never make plants bloom that lived inside the house. I either gave them too much or too little water, or not enough sun, or not enough fertilizer. What we do to and with plants is obvious because results are evident fairly quickly. Sometimes I wish leading others to Christ were as simple (except I would be a complete failure if my luck with plants is any indicator).

*"So, then, neither the one who plants nor the one who waters is anything, but only God who gives the growth. Now he who plants and he who waters are one, and each will receive his own reward according to his own labor. For we are God's coworkers. You are God's field, God's building." -- 1 Corinthians 3:7-9 (CSB)*

That verse tells me to keep planting seeds by telling others about my life with God and what He does for me. It tells me that others are watering through additional education and witnessing. No matter how much any of us does, God is ultimately the one responsible for those who grow.

We may not ever see a particular person bloom, but we need to keep planting seeds and continue watering. Sunday school teachers, youth leaders, and pastors have many people come and go in their midst and often wonder what happened to someone. When we do see God at work, we must remember that He brought that person into full bloom, not us. How nice it is when we see blossoms like the ones on her Christmas cactus.

### *Keep Me Safe*

*"Protect me, God, for I take refuge in you." -- Psalms 16:1 (CSB)* A simple statement, but what an awesome statement of faith. It is one I see reflected in many young children as they unconditionally trust their parents. Often, those in immediate danger think and pray similar words. Upon hearing the verdict of a doctor concerning a series of tests, one might find this statement embedded in their hopes and prayers.

Situations happen that bring this scripture to our prayers. A forest fire is spreading. The TV constantly gives flash notices of several forest fires raging. Dry conditions due to lack of snow and rain for the last year contribute to the devastation taking place. Other areas of the country suffer from flooding and too wet conditions. Farmers cannot plant their crops due to wet fields. Homeowners and renters suffer when low areas hold high water. Those who fight fires or rescue people from floods, provide security and communications, or distribute meals and warm shelters, all need our intercessory prayers seeking to keep them safe.

Those facing illnesses, pain, and surgery need the security of this verse as well to know the peace of God waiting for them unconditionally. Violence in families, in our communities, and in our world emphasizes the need for the power of this verse to care for those in harm's way. Let us remember our request of God for ourselves as well as for those around us. ***"Protect me, God, for I take refuge in you." -- Psalms 16:1 (CSB)***

## Differences

Ever had one of those days when nothing seems to go well? No matter what you say or do, it seems that it was the wrong time, the wrong words, or the wrong action. Others misunderstand what you said, or perhaps they are having an equally bad day and that multiplied the miscommunication. Or is it our basic differences that often cause conflicts? Sometimes, our differences cause us to feel rejected as opposed to just being different, especially when the difference is with a loved one. As I spoke with a woman this week, I sensed her stress and her feelings of rejection just because she voiced some different opinions.

With humans we can often allow our differences to be barriers and separators from one another. God has a different plan. ***"He himself has said, I will never leave you or abandon you." -- Hebrews 13:5 (CSB)*** And I do believe He means it! How wonderful to have a God who accepts us even when He may disagree with us. He allows us to grow, to make our mistakes and yet always be there to accept us when we seek His forgiveness.

Sometimes it seems we keep making the same mistakes and I can't help but wonder how we get past the impassable. I do know that God is there with us no matter what, and He enables us to keep going, to keep pondering, to keep seeking answers, to keep searching for peace and to continue the journey towards wholeness with one another and with Him. May He allow us to carry His promise with us daily.

## Financial Stress

Financial stress can be physically and emotionally difficult. It can come after months of a steady market decline, or perhaps the loss of a job, or major health issues. For many of us that is scary, since many retired folks depend on some of those funds for income, and others hope to retire, send kids to college, buy a new house, etc.

Scripture offers a respite: " *'I am the bread of life,' Jesus told them. 'No one who comes to me will ever be hungry, and no one who believes in me will ever be thirsty again. But as I told you, you've seen me, and yet you do not believe. Everyone the Father gives me will come to me, and the one who comes to me I will never cast out. For I have come down from heaven, not to do my own will, but the will of him who sent me. This is the will of him who sent me: that I should lose none of those he has given me but should raise them up on the last day. For this is the will of my Father: that everyone who sees the Son and believes in him will have eternal life, and I will raise him up on the last day.' "* -- *John 6:35-40 (CSB)*

During the depression, so many suffered financial problems. Yet the very difficulties caused by lack of finances also helped develop strength, a need for resourcefulness, an ability to seek and find alternatives, a dependency on prayer, and a faithfulness that comes from need. Jesus tells us that He is all we need, and He will provide for our needs (not our wants). Yes, we want to keep all our financial funds intact and available to continue providing a way of life that we have become accustomed to enjoying. Is that financial security standing in the way of our total dependency on Jesus? The qualities in people who emerged from the depression and World War II have disappeared in several of the generations living today. We need to get beyond worrying about our financial situations, live in this world, and allow Jesus to be our bread of life.

### Trouble Sleeping

Have you ever awakened at night with an idea or a disturbed child? Or, during periods of dreaming, a thought comes to you that applies profoundly to a daytime situation? Encouraging words: *"I will bless the Lord who counsels me — even at night when my thoughts trouble me."* -- *Psalms 16:7 (CSB)* The night here could be literally nighttime or perhaps a dark time of our life. Many years ago, my seven-year old son suffered from night terrors and had for years. As a new Christian, I had little experience with urgent prayers. As I went to bed that night, I prayed for him to sleep as I was exhausted from caring for our one-year-old baby. His terror began about 2 am. I woke him up, but he could not quit shaking nor return to sleep. He slept on the top bunk with his brother below, so I had to stand beside his bed talking to him. Our ladies bible study was studying about the power of evil and how Jesus guards us when we ask. Finally, I laid my hands on him and began to pray that God's angels would surround him, that he was safely guarded by Jesus and after a couple of minutes of continuous prayer, he suddenly and instantly settled, rolled over and went to sleep! I, however, instantly came awake realizing that God answered my prayer. The confirmation came the next morning, when he ran into my room and said, *"Mom, God answered your prayer!"* For many years after that we prayed that prayer every night as I put him in bed, and he seldom had terrors.

Occasionally at night, my brain seems to get stuck on a thought, a problem to be solved, a design to create, or some other issue that needs attention. The only way I've found to unstick the brain is to get up! Once up, reading is the best way to distract the brain. Sometimes music helps. Then there are times resolutions come, creativity ensues, and God gets the praise! During the quiet moments of the day or night, I write down any message that God gives to me to bring me comfort, peace or strength for use at later times during the day or night. Listen as He speaks to us and jot down those messages!

### *Facing Fear*

Swooping up into the sky, leaving a trail of smoke behind, he rolled, he stalled, and he seemed to be suspended in air, defying gravity! As gravity won the battle, the descent began with all observers waiting for the sound of that engine coming back to life, thereby taking control once again to allow another maneuver equally as compelling to watch. As I watched this pilot perform repeatedly at the Air Show, I wondered what makes people do these apparently dangerous stunts. Was it his love for living on the edge and the adrenalin rush from doing the daring stunts, or was it his knowledge of the plane's abilities, his experience over years of practice, and his ability to face fear and go onward.

As I reflected on: ***"I always let the Lord guide me. Because he is at my right hand, I will not be shaken." -- Psalms 16:8 (CSB)*** I wondered about my own ability to face fear and go onward. Fear comes in so many shapes and sizes! The fear that immobilizes us is important for us to know, understand and to seek God's help in overcoming. The fear that keeps us from doing things that perhaps we do not need to do, is that healthy fear God embedded in us to protect us. For example, my fear of flying as well as my lack of knowledge about the plane is the healthy fear that keeps me from trying what that stunt pilot so gracefully completed.

Reading through my prayer list of the many health issues that cause struggle in lives, I see the evidence of those people setting the Lord always before them. Perhaps all that is needed is knowing He is at their right hand and going forward with a sense of peace and confidence. How easy it is to take our sights off Jesus, only to be shaken and filled with fear of the unknown. With the help of one another and the love and support of friends and family, our sights can once again rest upon our Lord giving us strength, courage, and peace. May our reading, our studies, our thoughts, and our prayers keep our Lord always before us so that we may walk, run and plow ahead knowing He is at our right hand so that we can remain unshaken in our task.

### Insidious Greed

Who among us does not want more? More money, more recognition, more possessions, more friends, more, more, and more of most anything! Out here in the Pacific northwest, more sunshine is always big on the list (at least for some of us!) We are greedy people in many respects.

It is easy to look at the news and see big companies charged with all kinds of fraud and other deceptions and declare them greedy. What about our neighbors who have more than we do and always seem to have the latest and greatest of whatever? Why is our vision always looking beyond what we have and comparing? What about those living in homes smaller than ours, or homes that one might call a shack or a shanty?

Then Jesus: *"told them, 'Watch out and be on guard against all greed, because one's life is not in the abundance of his possessions.' " -- Luke 12:15 (CSB)*

What generates our greed? Do we rationalize our greed away by comparing what we have with those who have more? Do those we label as greedy view themselves in a different light? Probably. Can't those who live in shacks also view us as greedy? Does living in an impoverished way guarantee living without greed? They probably struggle with envy! Is there a difference between a desire for more possessions and a desire for more peace? To me, the difference is whom the desire benefits. Is peace something wanted for selfish purposes or for purposes beyond self? Are possessions something collected for self or for helping in serving others?

Lord, my request is to help me see myself for who I am and who you want me to be. Help me not to be tied so tightly to my possessions, my money, my (you fill in the blank). Show me how to use what I have for your work, for your glory, and help me to do so out of my love for You! Help me also to let go of whatever needs to go.

### *Communication*

Defiance starts very early in life! I witnessed our 17-month-old grandson cry for his Mom to pick him up because he did not want to stay in his bed where his Dad had deposited him. She gently told him no and did not reach out to pick him up. She did, however, ask him for a kiss, which he usually gives. He chose to ignore her for a moment. When she asked again, he simply shook his head from side to side saying a silent no. He obviously was mad at her for not picking him up, he wasn't going to give her a kiss! We laughed and enjoyed the honesty of his response. In his defiance, he was not ugly, or cruel, or outraged. He simply shook his head no. In the limited language of a 17-month-old, he remained honest to himself.

How many times do we find ourselves in situations when honesty is avoided for fear of the anger or hurt it may bring? Now, I am not talking about cruel or hateful honesty delivered in a manner that tears apart or destroys trust and relationships. I am talking about honest communication for the purpose of building for the good of the kingdom. This passage is an ideal to strive toward: ***"Even in darkness light dawns for the upright, for those who are gracious and compassionate and righteous." -- Psalms 112:4 (NIV)*** In any difficult situation we need to face what is real and what is doable. We need to be honest without being cruel or spiteful. We need to be open to hear both sides of any issue. And the final conclusion may be to agree to disagree, but to respect one another despite the differing issues.

Just as Mom continues to love her son even though he told her no, and son continues to love his Mom even though she would not pick him up, we need to air our differences in a positive honest manner, keeping Christ in the midst. Let us focus on the blessings in our life, focus on those who enrich our life, and focus on our God who gave us Jesus to teach us by example.

### *I. D. D.*

I heard a new phrase, Intention Deficit Disorder. ***"Peter and the apostles replied, 'We must obey God rather than people.' " -- Acts 5:29 (CSB)***

Intention Deficit Disorder is a church or person with no purpose other than to meet each week with no ministry outside the walls of the building. God's intentions are left undone. Is Peter saying the intention of the church is to make God happy? How we go about doing that is what the Holy Spirit calls us to do. Peter had the power of the Holy Spirit to lead him to obey God.

As a parent, I can identify with what it takes for a child to make a parent happy. Perhaps I need to expand that then to what it takes for a child of God to make God happy. If I claim, like Peter, to have the Holy Spirit alive in me, then perhaps I need to obey what the Spirit leads me to do. Good intentions are easy to list, to discuss, and to make known to others. Putting action behind those good intentions is always a different story.

Many churches/people have plans, goals, and mission statements that are full of good intentions. Does fulfilling our good intentions open us up to taking risks? Life is full of risks. Doing anything that is new or different is a risk. What if I fail? Well, then, you have learned something about what you like/don't like or need more help with how to proceed. Not taking the risk means no growth or learning will happen. All risks need to be considered for their safety elements to life or death, but most risks do not fall under those elements. Prayers for direction always help! Seek God's direction.

Do you have Intention Deficit Disorder? Perhaps, in some areas, we all do to some extent. What might we do about it? What might God be calling us to do that would make God happy? Come to Him with open arms and an open heart.

### Handling Crisis

Our nation faces great obstacles. We individually face obstacles. Some obstacles occur daily; other obstacles occur perhaps once in a lifetime.

Scripture is full of stories of God's people facing obstacles and with God's help, overcoming them. The David and Goliath story is one such story. 1 Samuel 17 tells that wonderful story, and this verse sums up his faith. ***"Then David said, 'The Lord who rescued me from the paw of the lion and the paw of the bear will rescue me from the hand of this Philistine.' " -- 1 Samuel 17:37 (CSB)***

David's life was spent as a shepherd protecting his father's sheep. With the help of God, he defended the flock from the lion and the bear. David called on God to protect and guide him always. His time alone with the sheep gave him many opportunities for conversations with God. When the crisis came to face the giant Goliath, he did as he did everyday by calling on God to enable him to defeat the giant. The giant and his people were defying God. David was obeying God. To David this victory was assured! How do we face crisis in our life? Do we call on God throughout the day! Practicing our continuing conversations with God reaps huge rewards when crisis comes. We spend much time standing in line, waiting for others, or stopped at traffic lights. Those are wonderful times for prayer, for conversations with God, or for listening for God's message to us. Continued reading of scriptures also keeps us prepared for life.

Preparations for handling crisis begin long before the crisis ever hits! How we live our lives daily with God enables us to go through any difficulty that comes our way. Enjoy your moments with God!

### God's Thoughts

I share a love for Psalms 139. It is long enough that I leave it for your personal reading. As I reread it again this week, one verse stuck out for me. *"God, how precious your thoughts are to me; how vast their sum is!" -- Psalms 139:17 (CSB)*

Over the years of my life, God's thoughts have come to me in so many ways and through so many people. As a child, the message I heard at church told me of God's love and forgiveness that stuck with me. My mother-in-law witnessed God's love for me through her actions. Later on, her witness came through sharing scriptures. Bible studies and prayer groups helped me to focus on God's thoughts concerning many issues. Sunday worship provided and continues to provide fresh thoughts to lead me through each day. Praise music and hymns always speak to me in a way that allows a phrase or thought to ring in my head for days, repeating its message over and over.

Leading bible studies, children's classes, and youth groups required me to dig into the message and learn it for myself in a way to explain it. Developing materials for others to use in vacation church school required me to understand the purpose and meaning of God's thoughts to bring them to life. Selecting pictures of human behavior to illustrate messages or certain thoughts enabled me to see God at work.

This process is ongoing and has been going on a long time for me, as I know it has for many of you. What precious thoughts of God helped you through this week? Where do you look for and find God's thoughts? How do you connect God's thoughts to your daily life?

While we were in Salt Lake City area, Rudy did genealogy work while I stayed at the motorhome sewing prayer cloths. As I sewed, I played praise music CD's praising God for all the precious thoughts shared over the years and for those of you who share your thoughts with me. Blessings to all of you.

### Remembering

God used a simple song to stir a memory and thought for me to ponder. Often, we play a CD of hymns while dressing for church. While listening to a hymn about eagles, images of Rudy's Dad filled my mind, for we sang that hymn at his funeral. He loved the Lord and sang many hymns during his life. He was blessed with a tenor voice and was a 50 plus year member of his choir in Arkansas. His final years were filled with joy at being near us in Ohio, yet filled with failing health that limited his activities and his strength. He was weary and tired. His wife and daughter had passed on eight years earlier, and we were all the family left for him.

These words from Isaiah gave him hope as we read them together in those last days. *"Do you not know? Have you not heard? The Lord is the everlasting God, the Creator of the whole earth. He never becomes faint or weary; there is no limit to his understanding. He gives strength to the faint and strengthens the powerless. Youths may become faint and weary, and young men stumble and fall, but those who trust in the Lord will renew their strength; they will soar on wings like eagles; they will run and not become weary, they will walk and not faint." -- Isaiah 40:28-31 (CSB)*

I imagine him now soaring on the wings of eagles, running and walking! I remember him as a younger man, vital and full of energy, knowing that his strength came from the Lord. I hear him in prayer seeking God's guidance. I see him taking me fishing, and then taking his grandsons fishing. I hear him singing a solo in church. His guilt for things left undone or unsaid he offered to the Lord, once again placing his hope in the Lord for renewal.

Why did these memories come to me today? I don't know, but I value the journey. Perhaps there are days I feel weary and tired. Perhaps it was a day to renew my own dependency on the Lord. Perhaps Christ wants me to run and not grow weary, to walk with Him and not be faint. Perhaps I needed to spend some time remembering my father-in-law. Perhaps some of you need a similar reminder.

### Your Enemy

Who is your enemy? Is it time, money, certain friends, a job or lack of a job, the economy, health, disease, weight, a difficult relationship, or marriage? Is your enemy taking all your energy to fight? Where do we find comfort?

*"I love you, Lord, my strength. The Lord is my rock, my fortress, and my deliverer, my God, my rock where I seek refuge, my shield and the horn of my salvation, my stronghold. I called to the Lord, who is worthy of praise, and I was saved from my enemies." -- Psalms 18:1-3 (CSB)*

I spent time with a friend recently who is taking chemotherapy treatments (36 of them over 10 months). When we called to say we could come and spend the night, we had no idea she was taking chemotherapy. She insisted that we come and come in time for supper. When we arrived, she made no apologies for the store-bought ready-made pop-in-the-oven supper. She merely enjoyed the simplicity of the meal and the joy of our presence. The food was great, and the company was even better.

She was very upbeat, cheerful, full of laughter and leading a busy life. She knows who her enemy is and gives the enemy no room to rise to the surface! Her faith allows her to concentrate on the joys of life. Her attitude allows her to laugh, and her spunk keeps her on the go.

What a witness she is not only to me, but also to those she encounters daily and at the clinic while receiving her treatments. She is saved from her enemy, and she knows who saves her! Do you know your enemy and how to defeat them? Read all of David's words in Psalms 18 and examine your situation.

### Raising a Child

*"When Jesus saw it, he was indignant and said to them, 'Let the little children come to me. Don't stop them, because the kingdom of God belongs to such as these.' -- After taking them in his arms, he laid his hands on them and blessed them." -- Mark 10:14, 16 (CSB)* Many years ago, I looked at my children and thanked God for loaning them to me. For you see, I considered them His children and I was merely the person chosen to care for them until such time as they became adults. What an awesome task God gave me! My plea then was for God's guidance and wisdom in caring for His children.

Today the news is full of stories about abused children and the effects that years of abuse have had on them. Apparently, some people believe that children are their property, void of feelings and identity. Clearly there are those people who read the scriptures that talk about using a rod on children to punish them and believe literally a rod is used to beat. In the footnotes of my biblical translation the rod is talked about as a figure of speech probably meaning discipline.

The book *"Help! I'm a Parent"** by a Christian psychologist, Dr. Bruce Narramore, helped me to understand the difference between punishment and discipline many years ago. Punishment is revenge for an action, done in anger, often unrelated to the offending event. Discipline, on the other hand, is defined as action taken to correct for future behavior, done in love and void of anger, with action related to the event needing correction. As I prayed for guidance and wisdom, I saw this clearly as answered prayer.

Training God's children in the way they should go is a very big responsibility and one we should not take lightly! Parents need training from a Christian perspective. Even with training we don't always get it right, but with no preparation for parenting, chances are much greater for dysfunctional results. Parents who know the Lord are headed in the right direction, but still need instruction. *"A house is built by wisdom, and it is established by understanding; by knowledge the rooms are filled with every precious and beautiful treasure." -- Proverbs 24:3-4 (CSB)* I see one of our goals as parents is to offer to our children the rare and beautiful treasure of Christ in our lives. By seeking God's wisdom, we come closer to building a house designed according to God's plan.

*"Help! I'm A Parent," by Dr. Bruce Narramore, 1995, published by Zondervan

### Boldly Proclaim

God's answers to prayers never cease to amaze me! Our daughter-in-law was concerned about the lack of movement for the baby she carried (at 38+ weeks out of 40) and went to the hospital, where they monitored her all day. The result was a decision for a C-section. That decision came after prayers for discernment and a very good doctor. Once again, God led all involved correctly as the cord was wrapped around the baby's neck three times, once around the body, once around his leg, and he was positioned face first, making for an impossible natural delivery. Now a healthy 7 lb. 6 oz. baby boy graces our lives. Peter and John told many about Jesus and they replied to those around them, *"for we are unable to stop speaking about what we have seen and heard." -- Acts 4:20 (CSB)*

Another friend has prayed for her husband who needed a kidney transplant and her sister who was donating the much-needed kidney. A long and precious e-mail arrived this week describing the many ways God answered her prayers and more! She must speak about her experiences with our living Lord!

A woman diagnosed with terminal cancer is now responding to her treatment and the tumors are shrinking. She and her parents are proclaiming the glory of our Lord with answers of healing and peace.

Many years ago, God brought a dramatic instantaneous answer to my prayer with my son who was only seven at the time. The story of that event gets told whenever God leads me to share it.

Just as God used Peter and John, humble fishermen, to proclaim the good news of Jesus, God uses us to tell our stories of answered prayer. New stories or old stories, they all are worthy of telling and retelling. These are the stories that enable us to grow in our relationship with God. Lord, enable us to be like Peter and John and boldly proclaim the good news of Jesus Christ!

### *Relationships*

When my computer quit working, panic set in! All my contacts are on it, and I got to thinking about my relationship with my computer!

This "relationship" I, and many of you, have with our computers is a strong one. To many it is a lifeline, it is a means of income, it is an outlet for creativity, and you fill in the blank for what it is to you. When something happens to that relationship, we who have a strong dependency on our computers notice it right away. It doesn't take long to recognize something is wrong. Depending on how strong the "relationship," we rush to fix it since life needs to go on and we can't go on without it. If our dependence is so-so, then we can go weeks without even recognizing the problem and much longer before even wanting to fix it.

In Colossians, Paul repeatedly talks about the believer's close relationship with Christ as a living union. ***"So then, just as you have received Christ Jesus as Lord, continue to walk in him, being rooted and built up in him and established in the faith, just as you were taught, and overflowing with gratitude." -- Colossians 2:6-7 (CSB)***

Is our relationship with Christ one that we would recognize when a break, or some distance, occurs? Would we be aware that we had not spent time with our friend recently? Would we miss our Savior's presence in our life quickly and try to figure out what happened, then fix it? Or would it take us a while to even know something was amiss? Perhaps the broken link to my computer is a reminder of my need to keep my relationship with Christ in good repair day-to-day, moment-to-moment. It always feels good to have my link reestablished once again to Christ, the Internet, and to my friends!

### Heavenly Home

I remember as a teen wondering what I would do in 5 or 10 years. What direction would my life take? Where would I be? What was my purpose for living? As I watched my mother enter a new life in a new place with new people, I heard her asking the same questions at age 82. Why am I here? Is there anything I can still do with my life? What purpose does God have for me to still be on this earth? What do I have to offer that anyone would want? Valid questions for any age really. We all have experienced times of asking these questions throughout our lives.

A wonderful passage about our heavenly dwelling and our earthly body is: *"So we are always confident and know that while we are at home in the body we are away from the Lord. For we walk by faith, not by sight. In fact, we are confident, and we would prefer to be away from the body and at home with the Lord. Therefore, whether we are at home or away, we make it our aim to be pleasing to him. For we must all appear before the judgment seat of Christ, so that each may be repaid for what he has done in the body, whether good or evil." -- 2 Corinthians 5:6-10 (CSB)*

What gifts and skills do you possess that can benefit others? Helping others is good. Add to those actions words such as, "God loves you," "I serve you in the name of Jesus," "I pray for your needs," "God's grace and guidance enable me to be here with you." Perhaps future contacts can lead to prayers together and opportunities to share scriptures that speak to the heart of the one in need. Perhaps studying with others can help you find the direction you seek.

No matter our age, this question of purpose seems important for giving our life meaning. Scripture is full of verses directed toward helping us find value, meaning, and purpose for our lives. God gave us life, and each of us is unique. How can my life at each age and stage help others to come to know the Giver of all life?

### *Snow Coming*

Our grandsons had a treat with four inches of snow in Denton, Texas! The weatherman on TV predicts snow occasionally, but it rarely happens. This time it was predicted, and their parents tried to tell them the night before that it might not happen. When the morning came and the kids saw the snow, they rejoiced over the weather predictions being correct! Soon, every yard in their neighborhood had snowmen beginning to melt in the warmth of the sun.

How many times in our life is something predicted, and it never comes about? What about our dreams? Do our dreams remain dreams or do they become real? Is trust sometimes given only to have it betrayed? Of course, all of the above happens. Failure and disappointment are a part of our lives every bit as much as success and joy. How do we deal with each? I know that my failures and disappointments caused me pain and perhaps embarrassment. They also caused me to ponder and think about what needed to be done. Successes and joy often leave you with a sense of accomplishment, perhaps a feeling of humility but warmth within. Not all of life though is clearly cut into either a success or a failure.

I think of the disciples who were called to follow Jesus. They heard the predictions of Jesus about His being the Son of Man such as found in: ***"For he was teaching his disciples and telling them, 'The Son of Man is going to be betrayed into the hands of men. They will kill him, and after he is killed, he will rise three days later.' But they did not understand this statement, and they were afraid to ask him." -- Mark 9:31-32 (CSB)*** The disciples' sense of direction did not come until the Holy Spirit came to dwell within them after Jesus ascension. Much appears before us that we do not understand. Predictions come and go, and some come true. When the Holy Spirit enters, expect action, expect the unexpected, and expect the ability to serve beyond your wildest dreams.

Lord, allow me to make room for the Holy Spirit to freely enter. May my response to the Spirit be even better than the joy that children experience when they see a four-inch snow in central Texas!

### *Instructions*

What joy to visit with our grandsons once again. Their hugs and kisses, smiles, and laughter delight this grandma (and grandpa) immensely! Of course, being young, normal, and active, they often want what isn't theirs, or they want to behave in a manner that is not pleasing to others. It brings a smile to my face to watch their parents provide boundaries and discipline designed to encourage their children's ability to listen and make choices.

Yet we all know that as children grow, they make choices that often bring about unhappy consequences. On Saturday, five underage teenage boys made some bad decisions. They were out in the middle of the night, without their parents' permission, and with a car that none were legally allowed to drive. Their night ended with a terrible crash that ended the lives of two, left two in critical condition and the driver, with the least serious injury, facing charges.

***"If you stop listening to correction, my son, you will stray from the words of knowledge." -- Proverbs 19:27 (CSB)*** What a sad day when we stop listening to instruction! Even adults need to listen to instructions! God's word in the Bible is important for us to read, to know, and to continue to study. This is one of the ways God speaks to us. Straying from the wisdom provided invites us to make poor choices. Perhaps the consequences won't be as dire as those encountered by the teens mentioned above, but they could be.

Help us as parents and grandparents to have the confidence, the courage, and the wisdom to provide boundaries for our children. Help us to allow our young children to make mistakes and suffer the consequences, while teaching them to think before they act. Help us to learn those lessons for ourselves as well. Help us to pray with and for our children, to teach them about your word, to model for them a life with Christ at the center of everything. Help us to seek the power of the Holy Spirit to be our guide as well as the guide of our children. Then be with us and our children through whatever comes our way.

## Suffering

Suffering. How can suffering be a good thing? No one likes to suffer or to see others suffer. As in many aspects of life, suffering comes in many shapes and sizes.

Some suffer illnesses that threaten the longevity of life. Some illnesses threaten the quality of life. Some suffer the loss of a loved one, a friendship, a job, or you name the loss. Disappointment or delays create a sense of suffering. Stress is a form of suffering in that it is an absence of peace and calm. Addictions cause suffering, not only in those who have the addictions, but also in those around them. Anger creates suffering for the angry person as well as those witnessing or receiving the anger. Perhaps you can add your own description of suffering.

Paul's description of the usefulness of suffering is: ***"We have also obtained access through him by faith into this grace in which we stand, and we boast in the hope of the glory of God. And not only that, but we also boast in our afflictions, because we know that affliction produces endurance, endurance produces proven character, and proven character produces hope. This hope will not disappoint us, because God's love has been poured out in our hearts through the Holy Spirit who was given to us." -- Romans 5:2-5 (CSB)***

His words, ***"we also boast in our afflictions"*** tells us in the suffering, not because of the suffering, we find God present with us. How do we handle suffering of any kind when it comes our way? Do we take the time to thank God for His presence with us through it all? I know at times in my life I have simply wallowed in the suffering -- at least for a while! It is only when I am able to sit back in the midst of the suffering and give God permission to care for me, to guide me, to bring others to my aid, to allow wisdom to prevail, that I find hope restored.

May each of us rejoice in our suffering this week as we give God permission to be with us always. Help us to find the hope, through Jesus our Lord, no matter what!

### *Inconveniences*

Do your days go just as you think they should? In our world of conveniences, how do we react when our conveniences are not available to us as we are accustomed to having them? Often, as we traveled in our modern motorhome, we pondered the experiences of the pioneers who discovered this country, and who tromped out the paths that became roads that became highways. I marveled how they navigated through the mountains without a map, rest stops with facilities, fast food places to eat, or stores to make purchases!

Paul traveled through many countries on foot, often not knowing where he would eat or sleep, but trusting God to provide. He was aware of his mission, his purpose, and the grace and mercy of God that allowed him to carry the good news to many.

Paul tells us: ***"Therefore, so that I would not exalt myself, a thorn in the flesh was given to me, a messenger of Satan to torment me so that I would not exalt myself. Concerning this, I pleaded with the Lord three times that it would leave me. But he said to me, 'My grace is sufficient for you, for my power is perfected in weakness.' Therefore, I will most gladly boast all the more about my weaknesses, so that Christ's power may reside in me. So I take pleasure in weaknesses, insults, hardships, persecutions, and in***

***difficulties, for the sake of Christ. For when I am weak, then I am strong." -- 2 Corinthians 12:7-10 (CSB)***

When we stayed in the mountains, our RV electrical hookups were not updated for today's RV's. The roads are either mud or dust. For the next two months we could complain about this inconvenience, or we could make do and enjoy the joy of the place, the people, and the opportunity to serve. We knew that Christ had brought us to this place. So, as scripture tells us, we delight in the weakness so that we can continue to depend on Christ to remind us of why we are here.

What weakness is present for you to live through with the grace of our Lord? Help us to be grateful for what we have and to find ways and words to tell others of God's grace.

## *Keeping On*

"There is just one more hill!" Words meant to encourage a struggling bicyclist! However, repeating that phrase for the next hill and the next one makes one wonder how many more hills are really there! Can I make it up "one more?"

How do we keep on going during difficulty or adversity? A report about an Olympic swimmer told of how she overcame the desire to quit several years ago. Many of us want to quit or change course when we get tired or discouraged.

Philippians provides encouragement toward our Christian journey: ***"I give thanks to my God for every remembrance of you, always praying with joy for all of you in my every prayer, because of your partnership in the gospel from the first day until now. I am sure of this, that he who started a good work in you will carry it on to completion until the day of Christ Jesus." -- Philippians 1:3-6 (CSB)*** As Christians trying to carry our message to those around us, we find obstacles and defeats that discourage us. For the many years I served as a Director of Christian Education, I faced excuses upon excuses as to why people couldn't or wouldn't serve. I also found many who would, praise God! Even serving on the road presents obstacles, but I know that God is leading and will bring to completion that which He started.

It is important for us to keep on keeping on with the task at hand to share the gospel of Jesus Christ. We might need to alter tactics and methods, but the goal of bringing others to Christ remains the same. Let us keep praying for one another and for Christ to lead us. There may be more than one more hill to climb, but our encouragement is: *"... He who started a good work in you will carry it on to completion." -- Philippians 1:6 (CSB)*

## Calling on God

We were parked and settled for a month before traveling once again. Many of our RV motorhome's ailments were now repaired and it was running much better. Another ailment was scheduled for repair at the end of our stay here, and the list of minor things was scheduled for repair at the factory, our next major stop. How we prayed for relief. How we pursued our resources, and we praise God for the results, even the ones to come.

I think of our RV problems, and then I think of those suffering from hurricanes, wildfires, floods, other natural disasters! I think of those involved in our military wars and defense, and our first responders. I remember those who have lost sons, daughters, spouses, other relatives, and friends. Then about those whose health is causing agony and suffering. Each of us has some form of agony, frustration, pain, or suffering, but in varying amounts.

Everything is worthy of calling on Him for guidance or help. *"God is our refuge and strength, a helper who is always found in times of trouble. Therefore we will not be afraid, though the earth trembles and the mountains topple into the depths of the seas, though its water roars and foams and the mountains quake with its turmoil." -- Psalms 46:1-3 (CSB)*

God wants us to call on Him for all our troubles, not just the ones we consider biggies! He wants us to rejoice over the victories as well. He wants our praise for all the help He sends our way.

What troubles your heart today? Will you allow God to be a part of those troubles? Call on Him now to guide and assist you. Be open to those around you willing to listen, as they may be that angel that God sent your way. Remember to praise Him for each little step of progress, even if you still feel overwhelmed. God is there for our protection and our strength. Let us remember to call on Him each day, each hour, each moment!

## Differing Opinions

As I watched political debates, I observed, as have many others, the differences in the two candidates and their parties. If you look at most any issue you can find at least two different opinions, each trying to persuade others to join with their side, or at least trying to explain their side of the issues. Wars are fought over differing opinions. Families split over issues that they can't reconcile. Christians and Jews fought and still fight. Even Christian and Christian disagree over issues.

Here is what Paul tells us: *"Christ is our peace. He made both Jews and Gentiles into one group. With his body, he broke down the barrier of hatred that divided us. He canceled the detailed rules of the Law so that he could create one new person out of the two groups, making peace. He reconciled them both as one body to God by the cross, which ended the hostility to God. When he came, he announced the good news of peace to you who were far away from God and to those who were near. We both have access to the Father through Christ by the one Spirit." -- Ephesians 2:14-18 (CEB)*

Christ came to do away with the law that binds us. Many of us hang on to the "law," which might be our opinion over issues. Do we ask what Jesus would have us do or think? Do we seek His purpose in our differences? How do we know or evaluate? Do we separate our daily life from our spiritual life to make choices easier? Do we try to interpret the issues to suit our desires?

Can we make peace in all areas of our life? This scripture tells me that only through Christ can peace come in our own life, and in our inner thoughts and feelings. Lord, I pray for peace to come to me as I focus on You. I pray that others can find Your peace as they examine issues in their own lives. I pray that You guide us as a country and as a world to find peace as we try to live with one another.

## Hello Strangers

While at an RV service center, we enjoyed meeting many others and comparing notes about lifestyle and coaches. I shared information about prayer quilts as I did some handwork. The staff was helpful and a NOMAD couple who lived nearby made us feel very welcome in the area. Despite the inconvenience of getting repairs and having to be out of the coach every day, the folks around us made it a bearable situation. I listened to a story about how a small-town general store catered to you as a customer. The owner or one of the employees listened to your request during conversation and took action to assist you with whatever he could to satisfy your needs. My mind drifted off to my years of church work. How many strangers come into a church or new community wanting to be needed? To what extent do we try to make others feel welcome in whatever situation is present? Is the church or community merely our social center for us to visit with our friends? How do we address someone we do not know?

Our life on the road has us in many places where we are strangers. True, we must do something to show interest, but some churches or communities go out of their way to make you feel welcome and others do not. Jesus instructed the disciples how to respond in such situations: ***"If the household is worthy, let your peace be on it; but if it is unworthy, let your peace return to you. If anyone does not welcome you or listen to your words, shake the dust off your feet when you leave that house or town." -- Matthew 10:13-14 (CSB)***

What do you do to make strangers feel comfortable? Do we ask about their families or what brings them to this place? Some people feel that asking questions is prying into their lives. Is that just an excuse? What are the kinds of things you want others to know about you? Try to look for indicators of their interest, tell them what your church offers, and invite them! What kind of community, church, or home is yours? Would the disciples shake the dust off their feet if they appeared on your doorstep? Meet a stranger and do what you can to make them feel welcome or important.

### *Coping With Fear*

One of my grandsons did not like to watch scary shows because he saw monsters in his room at night. He reminded me of a time in my life when the darkness brought fear in my life. Now that I am supposed to be more mature, I find that other things bring fear. Such things as loss of health, potential accidents, and financial resources depleting are among the biggest fears.

Hearing about the 10-year boy with a rare cancer and meeting a lady with breast cancer that, after six years, has metastasized to her spine caused me to think about fear.

The words in Isaiah are powerful: ***"Now this is what the Lord says — the one who created you, Jacob, and the one who formed you, Israel — 'Do not fear, for I have redeemed you; I have called you by your name; you are mine. When you pass through the waters, I will be with you, and the rivers will not overwhelm you. When you walk through the fire, you will not be scorched, and the flame will not burn you.' " -- Isaiah 43:1-2 (CSB)***

These words clearly state that God remains with you no matter what. Our fears can become our strength when we call upon God. Keeping our eyes upon God's love and care for us prevents us from concentrating on unhealthy fear. Yes, we need to recognize danger and health difficulties by seeking the medical resources God provides for us. We do not need to dwell on the fear of possible outcomes. Yes, sometimes the worst happens, but we must always remember that God is with us even in the worst moments or events. He carries us through those times.

Let us remember these words from Isaiah as we face whatever may come our way. Let us encourage others who face difficulties with these words from above: ***"Do not fear, for I have redeemed you."***

## *Peace Within*

At the airport to pick up our son, we saw many people in uniform coming and going. As I watched them hurrying, I prayed for each of them to have a safe journey, not only on the plane, but also in their continuing journeys.

A scripture that appears on the front of many church bulletins this time of year is from: ***"Glory to God in the highest heaven, and peace on earth to people he favors!" -- Luke 2:14 (CSB)*** I thought of those men and women in uniform. How can these men and women find peace on earth during the war? How can people of a warring country find peace on earth? The only possible answer I can accept is that during any crisis, God gives us inner peace to know that He is with us no matter what. We must give all glory to our Lord in the highest form possible.

From what I hear from folks with family and friends stationed in other countries, military personnel appreciate hearing from and receiving care packages from the US.

Let us do our part in supporting those serving during constant danger by praying for them by name, if possible, and by finding ways to send them tokens of our care for them and their service. Regardless of our stance on the ethics of war, wars around the world exist. Our men and women deserve our support and our prayers for their well-being. Let us also pray for the civilians in those warring countries, both those who support and those who oppose the conflict. Help us to find peace on earth and to exhibit good will toward men and women. How I pray for peace to come, not only the inner peace, but also the external peace that brings us to some harmony. To God be all the glory for that peace.

### *Inside/Outside*

When I see the outside of a home that is lovely, I expect that the inside is every bit as lovely. Often the outside deceives us, and the inside is cluttered and in need of some housecleaning. Or perhaps the inside is filled with a family full of anger. Or a family who selfishly exists to meet their own needs. Or a divided family living under one roof. The outside of the house leaves the neighborhood with the idea that all must be in order inside!

Some days, I can see in the mirror that I pulled it together and managed to have the hair, the clothes and the face all looking good. Is the inside as together as the outside? Occasionally, the answer is NO!

At a church we attended, the pastor led a class on the difference in religion and relationship. Do you practice a religion, or do you practice a relationship with Jesus? Is your faith as vibrant on the inside as on the outside?

From the scripture text found in Luke: *"But the Lord said to him, 'Now you Pharisees clean the outside of the cup and dish, but inside you are full of greed and evil. Fools! Didn't he who made the outside make the inside too? But give from what is within to the poor, and then everything is clean for you." -- Luke 11:39-41 (CSB)*

What does your heart treasure? Lord, help me to pay attention to where my thoughts dwell. Help me to pay attention not only to how I look, but also to how I feel on the inside. Help me to keep You close inside so that You may cleanse me from the inside out. Forgive me for those moments of separation from You. Thank You for Your grace. May all who know You rejoice in telling others of Your love and grace.

### *Love Comes First*

Love comes first. I remember a little eight-year-old girl whose heart was overflowing with love. She was a cancer survivor, and her wish was to make over the hospital ward for children being treated for cancer. What a show of love for others as her wish became reality. The story did not tell you about her faith or if she even knows of our Lord and Savior, Jesus. But the statement "Love comes first" stuck with me. Jesus is love and yes, He comes first. His life on earth taught us by His examples about love for one another. He healed those in need who came to Him in faith. The stories He told challenged our thinking about the everyday ways we exhibit our faith. Traditional rituals were not as traditional for Jesus. Love was first with Jesus. He loved first, and that love brought about change.

- *"Love your neighbor, -- love your enemies." -- Matthew 5:43-44 (CSB)*

- *"Love your neighbor as yourself." -- Matthew 19:19 (CSB)*

- *"You know that the rulers of the Gentiles lord it over them, and those in high positions act as tyrants over them. --... whoever wants to become great among you must be your servant." -- Matthew 20:25-27 (CSB)*

- *"Love the Lord your God with all your heart, with all your soul, and with all your mind. -- Love your neighbor as yourself." -- Matthew 22:37, 39 (CSB)*

- *"Because lawlessness will multiply, the love of many will grow cold." -- Matthew 24:12 (CSB)*

- *"I give you a new command: Love one another. Just as I have loved you, you are also to love one another. By this everyone will know that you are my disciples, if you love one another." -- John 13:34-35 (CSB)*

Yes, Jesus showed us how to love and love does come first with Him and through Him. How can we show love this week? Who might we meet that especially needs love, the kind of love offered by Jesus? When we are not capable of loving, Jesus in us enables us to offer His love to others. That love can express itself in many ways. Just listening to a friend. Taking a meal to one in need. Spending time with someone who is lonely. Create your own list of ways to serve in love.

### Dread to Joy

This week began as a trial of patience waiting for the repair work to begin on our motorhome. Since we had to be here and sitting in the motorhome gets old, we decided to see what might be around and found three special things!

At a bookstore, I found a copy of *"My Descent into Death, A Second Chance at Life"* by Howard Storm*. His near-death experience was like none other, and all I can say is read the book! What a witness he is to life with God. His testimony is encouraging to all.

The next day, we stumbled upon a nature center and read about a bird walk for Friday and Saturday. What delightful and informative people we met at each of the events. It was mostly the same folks both days, but at different private ranches. They told us about the conservations efforts to save the acreage from development and to preserve the habitats for a couple of bird species that only come to the south-central region of Texas for three months of the year. Our time together made our unpleasant reason for being here take on a different light.

We walked into a church in town and gazed in wonder at the beauty of the striking stained-glass windows set in against the white stone of the area. The cross is made of stained glass in the front of the sanctuary and is about 15 to 20 feet in height, with sunlight pouring in through the deep blues and dark reds. Viewing this brings me to Psalms : *"Let the whole earth shout to the Lord; be jubilant, shout for joy, and sing." -- Psalms 98:4 (CSB)* What is there about your week to shout praises to God?

*"The whole crowd of the disciples began to praise God joyfully with a loud voice for all the miracles they had seen: Blessed is the King who comes in the name of the Lord." -- Luke 19:37-38 (CSB)*

As we go into a week of dreaded repairs, the events of the weekend helped us to find some joy with birding friends, in a book, and in worshipful praise.

*\*"My Descent into Death, A Second Chance at Life"* by Howard Storm,
Published by Doubleday a division of Randon House, INC, 2005

### Too Busy!

Sometimes we get so busy that we find ourselves wondering how to get out of some obligations and free up some of our time! I overlooked doing two important things that normally I would not overlook. Both cases caused someone else to wait or work extra because of my neglect. After apologizing, then getting done what needed doing, I felt tired. I couldn't help but wonder how I got so involved in some things. God, what is it that You want me doing?

*"Save me, God, for the water has risen to my neck. I have sunk in deep mud, and there is no footing; I have come into deep water, and a flood sweeps over me. I am weary from my crying; my throat is parched. My eyes fail, looking for my God." -- Psalms 69:1-3 (CSB)* The waters here are the activities I have said yes to doing. Which ones are the ones you really want me to do? It made me ponder with another lady, how we can get so caught up in doing (make your own list...). This even applies for our list of church or Christian activities for the Lord's work. God will lead us to do the things He wants us to do. We can say yes to other's requests

without waiting to ask God if that is what He wants us to do. Doing so might find us struggling to fit that activity into our life.

Lord, I feel myself saying yes too often and failing to come to You before saying yes. Forgive me for jumping into activities that are for Your glory, but perhaps not for me to do according to Your will for me. Help me to use wisely the time that You give me. Yet help me not to ignore requests that come from others, since it might really be You sending someone to seek my assistance. Help me to discern the difference. Enable me to be Your servant effectively. Restore my energy to serve You. And may all the praise and glory go to You!

## Value of Old

For years, old barns have fascinated us as we drive through country areas. The weathered wood, the degree of lean (making us wonder how long it will stand), the design, and the landscape near the barn all become points of interest. What stories can that barn tell us? What animals resided inside? How many children romped through the stalls and areas within? What lessons did parents pass on to their children while doing chores inside? What life lessons were learned while observing the livestock housed there? Today we find that old barns and other such buildings are sought for the wood and or items contained. These items find places in new homes as rafters, fireplace mantels, stairway railings, and decorations to add character. What can these old buildings and barns teach us? As I pondered this thought, I pictured many older men who sang to us at an RV Rally. The weathered faces, the need for some to sit on stools, the white hair and beards, and the western clothing brought a smile to my face. Then they began to sing. The joy that exploded on their faces and the energy that exuded from their bodies communicated to us how much they must share.

The scriptures teach: *"Only be on your guard and diligently watch yourselves, so that you don't forget the things your eyes have seen and so that they don't slip from your mind as long as you live. Teach them to your children and your grandchildren." -- Deuteronomy 4:9 (CSB)*

A couple of chapters later: *"Listen, Israel: The Lord our God, the Lord is one. Love the Lord your God with all your heart, with all your soul, and with all your strength. These words that I am giving you today are to be in your heart. Repeat them to your children. Talk about them when you sit in your house and when you walk along the road, when you lie down and when you get up." -- Deuteronomy 6:4-7 (CSB)*

We have stories to tell. Many of these stories involved bits and pieces of how our faith developed. We need to share those stories with our children and our grandchildren, especially those parts about our faith. We need to offer them in both visual form and audio form to become mantels of the next generations, foundations for young lives, and cornerstones to point the way for others to our Lord. As we travel each day, let us discover our strengths and stories to share. Let our lives be like the weathered barn, waiting to reappear in new homes as objects of value.

### Self-Examination

As I prepared to teach again, I ran across some scriptures about self-examination. Sometimes it is hard to do an honest self-examination because we are so biased about our thoughts and actions. God knows us, and we cannot hide from Him, so though it might be painful, we need to give ourselves a good self-exam occasionally.

*"For if anyone considers himself to be something when he is nothing, he deceives himself. Let each person examine his own work, and then he can take pride in himself alone, and not compare himself with someone else. For each person will have to carry his own load." -- Galatians 6:3-5 (CSB)*

*"Search me, God, and know my heart; test me and know my concerns. See if there is any offensive way in me; lead me in the everlasting way." -- Psalms 139:23-24 (CSB)*

*"How many iniquities and sins have I committed? Reveal to me my transgression and sin. Why do you hide your face and consider me your enemy?" -- Job 13:23-24 (CSB)*

These scriptures always point back to everyone as being responsible for oneself. Yes, we help one another, but ultimately each of us must make decisions for ourselves. Even in marriage, each spouse must make their own decisions. The other spouse can only help with or make comments concerning that decision from their perspective. Families too must wait and watch as members make decisions that perhaps cause concern among the others. Each of us must do what is right by our own relationship with God for those times.

Self-examination is important for us to truly understand ourselves. What is our relationship with God? How do we nurture that relationship? How do we deal with issues we can't control?

## Children at VBS

A Vacation Bible School program prepared a musical production for the Sunday morning worship service. About 30 children participated in the production. As I listened and watched, I had to reflect upon the years of doing those programs with children as well as teens. The words for many of the songs were familiar. New beats and tunes refreshed the sounds. The scriptures were presented as musical messages rather than readings. What a great way to teach scriptures to children.

Though the content was different, the children were the same. Their facial expressions and body language told other stories. As always, you have those children who sing and take their roles very seriously. Then, of course, there are those children who stand up there and watch the crowd, never moving their lips! Yes, I saved the best for last! The three boys in the front row, who were in their own world, singing and making up their own motions, keeping the rhythm of the music, but really enjoying themselves. They were not being disrespectful, they were responding to the moment, the music, the audience, and feeding off each other's spontaneous joy. The audience loved the boys and all around you could see people chuckling with pleasure at the exuberance of the boys. I enjoyed all the children, the cute and pretty ones, the serious and conscientious ones, the slightly interested participants and the uninhibited exuberant boys!

The final scripture they put to music was from Matthew: ***"So go and make followers of all people in the world." -- Matthew 28:19 (NCV)*** Their community was doing just that and I applaud:

- the many adults it takes to work with the children to put together any production.

- the parents who take their children each day to church.

- the audience for attending the service and encouraging the children with their applause.

- those who developed the music and their educational materials for keeping it current to the styles of the day without diluting the message.

Each day, as we journey through the week, think about the facial expressions that we carry, as well as other body language that we exhibit. What does that language say about us? What do we communicate to others? Are we standoffish, friendly, judging, disapproving, or what? What messages do we receive from others through their expressions and body language? How do we honor Jesus through our posture and expressions? Lord, lead us to allow your love to be visible to others around us, not only through our words, but through our actions.

### *Walk for Cancer* ·

We happened upon an annual Relay for Life at a state park where we came for other purposes. For those of you, like me, who had never heard of this event, it is an event to raise funds for fighting cancer. Sponsored by the American Cancer Society, Relay for Life is a volunteer event that raises funds for fighting cancer. The event usually runs on a weekend and involves one overnight where participants walk a route in a park or on a track at a field. Some walkers are cancer survivors, some are friends and family of survivors, some are currently in the cancer battle, and some are defenders in medical research. As you walk or mingle, you hear many stories of courage, joy, compassion, and sorrow. The event represents hope for those lost that they will not be forgotten. It represents hope for a cure for those currently, or will be, in the battle. It also brings together those who need one another's support for the fight.

We wondered where the walk would take place, so we ambled over to the registration and music area. Just as we arrived, the speaker introduced a survivor who told her amazing story. This part of the park was in a picnic area with the road making a large loop. The walkers were to walk laps of the loop all night long! The first lap was for survivors only. It was amazing to see their courage as they walked the loop. I stood there with tears of admiration for courage for all that they have endured in their individual battles against this disease. My tears were also tears of thankfulness that my own breast cancer was found so early that I never had to endure treatments other than a simple mastectomy.

*"Listen, Israel: Today you are about to engage in battle with your enemies. Do not be cowardly. Do not be afraid, alarmed, or terrified because of them. For the Lord your God is the one who goes with you to fight for you against your enemies to give you victory." -- Deuteronomy 20:3-4 (CSB)* Cancer is an enemy with battles raging all over the world. Some battles are over quickly with victory, but other battles are ongoing, ravaging the body and those giving care.

*"Be alert, stand firm in the faith, be courageous, be strong. Do everything in love." -- 1 Corinthians 16:13-14 (CSB)* Yes, many battles occur every day. Some have nothing to do with cancer. Who is your enemy? God can enable you to walk each day in battle against the enemy that tries to hold onto your life. You must merely invite God to be a part of that journey. How grateful I am for being at this location for this event.

## Waiting Is Hard

How many times have we waited for something? As children, we waited for Christmas to come so we could get all those presents, or for summer to come so school would be over for another year. Adults wait for other things. We wait for payday to replenish our financial accounts. We wait for the right job to come around. Perhaps the waiting is for a relationship to develop with a special someone, or for a relationship to be renewed after a time of separation. Waiting for forgiveness to be offered or received may be a long wait in some instances. Others wait for a baby that they desperately want but things happen to prevent the development of that life. Some wait for food, shelter, and safety. Some wait for a tour of duty to end safely. Many wait for peace around the world, or peace in families, even with our church families.

The disciples waited as instructed by Jesus, but were not sure what would happen or when. During the time Jesus spent with the disciples after His resurrection is recalled in Acts: ***"While he was with them, he commanded them not to leave Jerusalem, but to wait for the Father's promise. 'Which,' he said, 'you have heard me speak about; for John baptized with water, but you will be baptized with the Holy Spirit in a few days.' "*** *-- Acts 1:4-5 (CSB)*

The disciples knew that something was coming! What? When? How? We also know in our own situations that something is coming, but what, when, or how. Often, we must wait, and most of us don't like to wait! We want everything now or very soon. We want answers to our prayers ASAP!

How do we wait? Filling our time with practical activity keeps us busy while we wait. God's answer will come in His time, not in our time. We need to pray for guidance, investigate alternatives, learn more about our situation, and use the time for reflection. Reading scriptures also provides wisdom and comfort.

I overheard someone say (while talking about forgiveness) that anger is to the soul as cancer is to the body. Waiting for that anger to dissipate and evolve into forgiveness can eat away at you. Anxiously waiting for solutions to problems, or trying to hurry answers that are not God's answers, can eat away at us as well. Lord, grant us the ability to wait for You to send Your Holy Spirit to help us know the decisions/paths that You want us to follow.

## Road Signs

As I opened my bible this morning, the first words that I saw were: ***"Set up road markers for yourself; establish signposts!" -- Jeremiah 31:21 (CSB)*** Of course, this grabbed my attention. Tell me more. Reading on, I found that Jeremiah had a dream about Israel's exile and future return to Judah. The text goes on to say: ***"Keep the highway in mind, the way you have traveled. Return, Virgin Israel! Return to these cities of yours. How long will you turn here and there, faithless daughter? For the Lord creates something new in the land — a female will shelter a man." -- Jeremiah 31:21-22 (CSB)***

Skipping down a few verses, Jeremiah goes on to explain his dream: ***" 'Look, the days are coming' — this is the Lord's declaration — 'when I will sow the house of Israel and the house of Judah with the seed of people and the seed of animals. Just as I watched over them to uproot and to tear them down, to demolish and to destroy, and to cause disaster, so will I watch over them to build and to plant them' — this is the Lord's declaration." -- Jeremiah 31:27-28 (CSB)***

Reflecting on my life, I know this to be true. The Lord watched as I chose the path I took. Sometimes He was happy, other times He put up road signs for me to find my way back. The Lord allows me to make my choices. Yet His love for me never leaves, never fails, and He waits patiently for my return. He keeps the road signs available for me to see and follow.

Sometimes those road signs are in the form of a person that does something to remind me of the Lord's presence. Or maybe it is a message in a song, hymn, or reading that grabs my attention and brings me back to the Lord.

The Israelites were physically in exile; something that we may not experience in its literal form. We do experience exile in small ways when we fail to see the Lord's way each day. Those times of exile or separation may be short or long, but we each have those experiences.

How I praise the Lord for showing me the way back to Him so many times during my life. My prayer for each of you (and for me) is that the Lord will keep His road signs and guideposts ever present before us and our country so that we may always know our way to Him.

### A Service Center

Where is the Service Center? Each of us looks for Service Centers to help us with various problems. Each appliance or gadget comes with a list of where to get service or who to call. But where is the Service Center for a broken heart, or other emotional issues of the body? Can we be a Service Center?

Joshua gathered the 12 tribes and gave them a choice: ***"But if it doesn't please you to worship the Lord, choose for yourselves today: Which will you worship — the gods your ancestors worshiped beyond the Euphrates River or the gods of the Amorites in whose land you are living? As for me and my family, we will worship the Lord." -- Joshua 24:15 (CSB)***

Perhaps a Service Center is not just a place. I think of the many times in my life that I sought out others to share burdens to find solace and comfort. Through them God sends His help. I found God's solace and comfort through reading the scriptures and praying as well.

Service happens as we reach out to those in need to meet them at their points of pain. It might be nothing more than a phone call, or a note, or an e-mail. Perhaps a hot meal, an hour of listening, an extra hand during the day or night. It might be volunteering with many organizations as we sacrifice our time or money for others.

At the end of a bulletin for a Sunday Worship Service, the following line appeared: *"Worship is over, the service begins."* What would happen if everyone who attended worship set out to tithe their time during the week to help others. For a week at 168 hours, that comes to 16.8 hours a week for service. Now if we took only our waking hours for a week, 16 hours a day equals 11.2 hours a week for service. Some of us get these hours in (plus more) when we factor in the type of job we hold. However, let's try to make it more personal. What are we doing that directly affects the lives of others? Not just the material parts of life, but the soulful parts of life. Being a stay-at-home Mother gets lots of hours since you are caring for the future development of their souls. Even those parents who are working, who spend soulful time with their children, probably get their time in for service. The model that you exhibit for them develops their soul. As they see you pray, study God's word, help others, and help them be involved in those activities, you directly help with future behavior of your children. What service does your internal Service Center provide?

### *Ongoing Suffering*

While remembering what happened on 9/11, we learned about the children of those who died that terrible day. Years later, they still grieve. Their comments were important to hear, though difficult to watch. A couple of the children expressed their anger at continually having to watch the buildings collapse, knowing their parent died in that event.

As I read through some Psalms , I found these words describing how I feel sometimes. *"God, listen to my prayer and do not hide from my plea for help. Pay attention to me and answer me. I am restless and in turmoil with my complaint, because of the enemy's words, because of the pressure of the wicked. For they bring down disaster on me and harass me in anger. My heart shudders within me; terrors of death sweep over me. Fear and trembling grip me; horror has overwhelmed me. I said, "If only I had wings like a dove! I would fly away and find rest. How far away I would flee; I would stay in the wilderness. I would hurry to my shelter from the raging wind and the storm." -- Psalms 55:1-8 (CSB)*

Yes, the events of 9/11 directly affected the lives of many people, not only through the lives lost of loved ones, but for those who worked in the area for rescue and then recovery. Those effects are surfacing daily through health issues. Our military families who serve to defend our freedoms face the fears of 9/11 daily.

This scripture spoke to me because those days come when, like David, I would like to escape and find a cave to enjoy by myself and forget the stresses or events of daily living. Naturally, putting my stresses into the same category as those of 9/11 is no comparison. The point is we all have days when stress gets to us. We want to escape and hide from the source. We want to run like David. David also had his faith and tells us to: *"Cast your burden on the Lord, and he will sustain you..." -- Psalms 55:22 (CSB)* and David ends the prayer with the last line: *"But I will trust in you." -- Psalms 55:23 (CSB)* Let us allow God to carry our burdens, sustain us through all suffering, and let us trust Him for our protection and comfort.

### *Hope and Cure*

The Relay for Life was an amazing event. This time I experienced it as a participant in Arizona during our winter stay. I ended up not needing to spend the entire night, but stayed until nearly midnight and went back at 6 am to help with tearing down and some last hour walking.

The energy and enthusiasm of the 700+ people who filled the old football field was electric. I sat at the survivor's dinner table for 8 while 250 survivors were served. I sensed tremendous thankfulness at being present together. Some had simpler treatment early, others much more aggressive treatment.

Why is something like this important? It was not so much about the money raised, but about the fellowship of being with others who have heard those words, "You have cancer." Those who were there for family members were there to honor the battles their loved ones fought or are fighting. This gathering was focused on Hope and Cure.

An extended family of 4 teams brought their children, their grandchildren and their tents and spent the night together walking, resting, eating, and playing in honor of the father, who for 15 years, has waged war on his disease. He walked a few paces ahead of me. He, for me, was a picture of Hope.

During the walk, I met a lady who had lost her husband two years ago to lung cancer. What caused his cancer wasn't the important thing. He was gone and she missed him. As we stood together for the presentation of the names of those being honored or being remembered, she spoke softly as his name appeared on the screen. As we walked around the track, the luminaries for the honorees ringed the track. The lights in the stadium were off. She quietly showed me his candle. I prayed for many whose names were given to me. The words Hope and Cure were lit with luminaries. Yes, we were there to raise money for research that leads to Cures. The other part of our reason for being there was the Hope we give one another.

Jesus gave us these words: ***"The second is like it: Love your neighbor as yourself." -- Matthew 22:39 (CSB)*** I saw and felt a lot of love for your neighbors last night.

### Waiting

One of my grandsons is awaiting his birthday. Waiting is so hard for a great day to arrive. Yet waiting is what we must do many times. All week long those working Monday through Friday wait for the weekend. Just add for yourself all the ways you wait and wait.

Aren't we an impatient society normally! We want our photos instantly or at least in one hour. We want our food fast even if we go to a sit-down restaurant. If the service takes too long, we get anxious. Think of all the ways you want things done quickly.

Scripture gives us these instructions: ***"Wait for the Lord and keep his way."* -- *Psalms 37:34 (CSB)*** How many times do we want to know what God's direction is for us? We want it now!

Think of the characters from the Old Testament who had to wait for God's direction or action. Moses fled to the desert and waited many years for God to lead him back to Egypt. Abraham waited even longer for a son. Sarah laughed when she heard God say she would have a son. Imagine the years she had longed to give Abraham a son. Joseph waited in prison for a crime he never committed until God used the King's dreams to get him out of prison and onto Pharaoh's staff. Quite a switch but he had to wait!

For what in your life are you awaiting an answer from God? Sometimes our prayers take years to have answers. While we wait, we keep our faith, remain close in God's word, trust that God is in charge, and continue our daily activities with as much direction as we have for the moment.

Lord, we ask for Your help in waiting for Your direction. Help us to wait and watch for the people that You might use to guide us or read the messages You might have for us. Your wisdom comes to us in many ways, and we praise You for helping us to wait and to keep Your ways while we wait.

### 40th Anniversary

What a celebration! Seems like we have enjoyed the 40th anniversary to the fullest this year! As I reflect on the events that have transpired since that wonderful day, I am in awe of God's grace, mercy, and sense of humor!

His grace has taken me from someone who barely knew God (and was perhaps somewhat defiant) to someone who loves God with all my heart and soul! His mercy allowed me to be spared from consequences that I deserved at times. His sense of humor allowed me to learn to laugh at and with myself more often than I had in my earlier life. His guidance helped me to become a wiser wife, mother, and woman. That doesn't mean I have it all down pat yet either! He still has much to teach me (perhaps some of that defiance still resides in there).

Throughout scripture, reference is made about two becoming one in marriage. I chose the Ephesians passage: ***"For this reason a man will leave his father and mother and be joined to his wife, and the two will become one flesh. This mystery is profound, but I am talking about Christ and the church. To sum up,*** *each one of you is to love his wife as himself, and the wife is to respect her husband." -- Ephesians 5:31-33 (CSB)*

Living together for 40 years was never easy all the time, but it was most of the time! When you consider the instructions we have for "two to become one," then you commit to overcome those difficult times. Would we each like to make changes in the other? Probably, but we've learned to accept each other for who we are. Working together as a team takes effort, but the rewards are great!

It is easy to reflect on the problems that exist in any relationship, but once we do that, we begin to undermine our strengths. Let us all concentrate on the positives of our relationships, not the weaknesses. Let us expect to find blessings in our marriages and in those of our kids. Let us celebrate God working in our lives to keep us together with one another and with Him.

### Physical Care

Keeping our bodies in shape is a challenge! I've tried many things that always last a few days before the consistency just dies away. Excuses cover "I'm too busy," "We aren't in a good spot for walking safely," "The weather is too hot or cold, too windy or too humid," "My leg hurts when I do...," "I don't have someone to do it with me." I guess you could add to the list of excuses as well.

This year I am determined to do something. Our park has a walking in place group that walks one to three miles each day. I tried it and liked the routine, but found going to their spot at a certain time each day was too confining and did not allow me to do other things at that time of day. Yep, another excuse. A friend told me about buying the DVD and doing it in your own home. Worth a try. Oh yes, I had done that before as well, only to have it die away after a couple of days.

I found the DVD for this routine since I liked the exercises. They suit me and I am capable of doing it well. As soon as I started doing them, I became an advocate for their program. It fits all the needs I have for doing a consistent routine. Now for Lent, I added another level of accountability by making a chart to hang on the refrigerator to chart which of the four routines I do each day, how long, and my weight (ugh).

*"Don't you yourselves know that you are God's temple and that the Spirit of God lives in you? If anyone destroys God's temple, God will destroy him; for God's temple is holy, and that is what you are." -- 1 Corinthians 3:16-17 (CSB)* Yes, our bodies are important vessels, and we need to treat them well. God's Spirit resides in us, and we need to provide a wholesome home. It is too easy for us to put off taking care of our bodies as we justify it by saying we have more important things to do! Providing God's Spirit a wholesome residence within is important. Exercise is a good way to help take care of our bodies.

Find your method, fit it into your day, choose a way to be accountable, and get started! Let us praise God for the wonderful bodies created for us. Let us begin or continue to care for them, keeping them trim and fit for whatever comes our way. We try to care for our spiritual lives through prayer and study, let us care for our bodies with some form of exercise and better eating habits.

### Using Our Blessings

I am amazed at how blessed we are to be able to travel as we wish. Our material blessings are everywhere around us. Many of us own a home to entertain, to provide shelter! Transportation is available by cars or public transport. Clothes and food are abundant, between department stores, grocery stores and restaurants. Yes, we are blessed. Jesus gives us lots of choices to come to Him through worship. We have the knowledge of Jesus. We have the promises of Jesus. We've heard the Good News! That is a tremendous blessing without even mentioning the food, shelter, and transportation! How do we use our blessings?

*"For this very reason, make every effort to supplement your faith with goodness, goodness with knowledge, knowledge with self-control, self-control with endurance, endurance with godliness, godliness with brotherly affection, and brotherly affection with love. For if you possess these qualities in increasing measure, they will keep you from being useless or unfruitful in the knowledge of our Lord Jesus Christ. The person who lacks these things is blind and shortsighted and has forgotten the cleansing from his past sins." -- 2 Peter 1:5-9 (CSB)*

Is our home open for others to come and study the bible, or to share a concern, or to plan for a service project? Does our car allow us to take others in need someplace they need to go? How important is worship in our daily, weekly life? How often do we complain about things not being as we want? How often do we criticize others for the same weaknesses we know exist in our own lives? Do we watch for opportunities to help one another, or are we so immersed in our own activities that we fail to see needs around us?

Yes, we have an abundance of blessings. I praise God for everything in my life both the good and not-so-good. The not-so-good things help to teach me more about myself and about my need for God. Those things help to teach me self-control and patience.

What are you doing with the blessings in your life? How are you sharing, growing, and praising God because of your blessings? Don't forget that just knowing God is the greatest blessing!

### Special Music

We all remember the songs of our high school days. The dances that we went to with a particular person seem cemented in our memory. Young children often want you to sing a special song at bedtime. Play time might also be associated with songs. Singing seems to lighten the heart and allow us a way to enjoy time together. Just listening to music can have the same effects.

*"Amazing Grace"** will never be sung by me again without thinking of my mother-in-law because we sang it at her funeral. How I wished we'd had more days and years to have her with us.

*"Here I am Lord"* by Dan Schutte* culminated 18 months of planning, organizing, and training for a mid-week children's program at our church. During this time, I also had a mastectomy for very early stage breast cancer that needed no treatment afterwards. We sang it as we dedicated the new program and all the volunteers who stepped forward to put the program in motion.

Words to hymns become a means of worship when we connect with their message. Ephesians emphasizes that message: **"Speaking to one another in Psalms , hymns, and spiritual songs, singing and making music with your heart to the Lord." -- Ephesians 5:19 (CSB)**

Another hymn, *"Awake, My Soul, and with the Sun"* by Thomas Ken*, became a prayer I hung on my kitchen window over the sink and read every time I stood there washing, cooking, etc. The words are as follow:

*"Awake, my soul, and with the sun thy daily stage of duty run; shake off dull sloth, and joyful rise to pay thy morning sacrifice! Lord, I my vows to thee renew; disperse my sins as morning dew; Guard my first springs of thought and will, And with thyself my spirit fill. Direct, control, suggest this day all I design or do or say, that all my powers, with all their might, In thy soul glory may unite."*\*

Songs help us with hard times, prepare us for the end of our lives, allow us to celebrate joy with one another, and lift our spirits when nothing else seems right in our life. Think about those songs that feed your soul this week. Perhaps find the words and put them out for you to read throughout the day. Share the message of a song with a friend. Allow music to help you worship and praise our Lord.

\*"*Amazing Grace*," by John Newton, 1772, Public Domain
\*"*Here I am Lord*" by Dan Schutte, Published by OCP Publications in 1981
\*"*Awake, My Soul, and with the Sun*," by Thomas Ken, (1637-1711) Public Doman

### Helping Others

At this point in the life of my mother, others must do things for her that she can no longer do for herself. Those of you who have either young children or young grandchildren find that you must do things for them that they cannot do right now. Some of you even have spouses that require you to do things for them that they cannot do for a variety of reasons.

Sometimes the one needing the help must ask for the help and other times, the caregiver must notice that help is needed. Asking for help is something we may not be good at doing! Occasionally the situation is such that we are compelled to ask for help!

Matthew was telling about Jesus healing Peter's mother and many others who came to him for healing. Some healing involved driving out evil spirits. But this verse sums up Jesus' activity: ***"So that what was spoken through the prophet Isaiah might be fulfilled: He himself took our weaknesses and carried our diseases." -- Matthew 8:17 (CSB)*** Read that again: ***"He himself took our weaknesses and carried our diseases."***

What a powerful image of Jesus! It is easy for us to say, "Jesus is with you," when talking to a friend in need. To picture Him literally taking up our problem and carrying it in His arms is more than we usually will do.

When I learned back in 1991 that I had breast cancer and needed a mastectomy, a friend told me that she visualized Jesus grabbing hold of her cancer cells one by one much like you would visualize counting sheep. That visualization brought her a great deal of comfort and to me as well.

How much energy is spent worried over what will happen? What would our journey be like if we were to put into action the image of Jesus taking up our infirmities and carrying our problems? Would solutions and answers come to us sooner? Would peace surround us, allowing healing to take place quicker? I, for one, believe Jesus brings us peace, comfort, and healing when we keep Him in the center of any dilemma.

What visualization can help you this week? What prayer allows you to bring Jesus into the center of your life? Who can you turn to who might assist you with allowing Jesus to carry you? Lord, we give to You all that we are and ask You to make us new inside and out.

## Evidence of God

It is fun to watch the working of the wind. Can you see the wind? Or are you seeing the evidence of the wind? Today we were driving the car in a strong wind. We could feel the effects of the wind in the car, and outside the car, we could feel the wind! As we drove past the soybean fields in Iowa, the short plants were blowing. The color of the leaves changed from the darker green to the lighter green on the underside of the leaves as the wind waved through the field. Waves of color rippled quickly over the fields, moving fast as the wind blew.

Can you see God? Or can you see the evidence of God? Just as we cannot see the wind, we cannot see God. The evidence of God's presence is around us daily, moment by moment. This week, I have needed to know that God's presence is with us constantly.

Our motorhome is a love/hate relationship. We love the freedom it brings us, the convenience it gives us with its floorplan and accessories. It is comfortable, roomy, and meets the needs of our lifestyle. We hate the consistency of the things that keep needing repair, the delays to our schedule due to down time for repairs, the aggravation and stress of keeping track of its problems. This past week we stopped to have two simple repairs done and, in the process, a major breakdown happened! Our hydraulic jacks and slide outs quit working as the system shorted out, burning the board and other parts of the system. No fire, just electrical burning and the possibility of fire. For four nights we lived in the motorhome with not much room to move around

God's evidence was around us! It happened at the coach factory rather than while we were on the road, and the service staff worked us right in, but it extended over the weekend! We had other NOMADS getting work done and preparing to attend the factory's annual rally. All the repairs to the system were covered by the manufacturer.

***"He is the image of the invisible God, the firstborn over all creation. For everything was created by him, in heaven and on earth, the visible and the invisible, whether thrones or dominions or rulers or authorities — all things have been created through him and for him." -- Colossians 1:15-16 (CSB)*** As we went to visit with our friends after all the repairs were finished, got our hugs, had our laughs, commiserated with one another, (as we all have had repairs), one of the ladies reminded me that we still have our health, we still have our families intact, and on and on about the blessings that still remain in our lives. Perspective is important! All things considered, God is evident around us. We all need to focus on the blessings that remain even during trials. What evidence of the wind and of God do you see in your life? What evidence of God do others see in you? Our friends helped us to feel God's evidence around us this week!

### Two Words

"*Thank you.*" Two very short words. Two very powerful words. Everyone likes to be appreciated for something. It doesn't have to be a big something. Children loved to be told "*Thank you*" for the simple deeds they do right. Parents loved to be told "*Thank you*" by their children when they do something special for them. They don't expect it, but it sure feels good to hear. Friends and co-workers relish the "*Thank you*" that often goes unsaid to one another.

We can all remember times when a "*Thank you*" never came for something that we went out of our way to do. It is not that we expect or demand a "*Thank you,*" but it is like the icing on the cake! God too loves our "*Thank you!*" He gives us so much that we often take for granted. The air we breathe, the water we drink, the earth we walk upon, the people on this earth for us to love, and you can certainly add to the list.

Find time for rest and relaxation and reflect on who you need to "*Thank.*" Is it a friend, a family member, a fellow worker, a teacher, your pastor, or a spouse? Perhaps a "*Thank you*" to our employer is appropriate, even if we don't agree with everything about the job. At least it is a job. (And if it is that bad, perhaps it is time to look elsewhere.)

Perhaps it is time to spend time praising our Lord for His companionship. An example of a "*Thank you*" to God is: ***"It is good to give thanks to the Lord, to sing praise to your name, Most High, to declare your faithful love in the morning and your faithfulness at night, with a ten-stringed harp and the music of a lyre. For you have made me rejoice, Lord, by what you have done; I will shout for joy because of the works of your hands. How magnificent are your works, Lord, how profound your thoughts!" -- Psalms 92:1-5 (CSB)***

The book of Psalms is full of many such verses, all laid out for our benefit. When we can't think of the right words, turn to Psalms , and read until you find one that relates to your situation. Think of others who have had positive influences on your life, who perhaps never knew they had done so and "*Thank*" them. Also let us sing our praises to God for sending not only Jesus to us, but those many other people in our lives who help us to stay connected to God.

### *Shout With Joy*

I read a story in the newspaper about a mother whose daughter is in her second battle with leukemia and the life the mother is living to inspire her daughter to live. I was struck by the dedication of this mother for her four children and the sacrifices she is willing to make for them. I praised God for letting this story be told in the local paper so that others could find courage and hope. Then I watched another story of a family tragedy that would devastate most families. This family chose to praise God for what they had left and to continue to help others in need, even though they had lost everything.

***"Let the whole earth shout joyfully to God! Sing about the glory of his name; make his praise glorious. Say to God, 'How awe-inspiring are your works! Your enemies will cringe before you because of your great strength.' " -- Psalms 66:1-3 (CSB)*** We each have much to praise God for and perhaps we do send out that praise quietly to Him. But the text tells us to ***"Shout joyfully to God!"*** Most of us feel too reserved to really get into that kind of model I was again reminded of our several experiences in congregations that literally do ***"Shout joyfully to God."*** Their joy was refreshing. I have attended Christian concerts that had the crowd praising God with clapping of hands and singing! The joy is contagious and refreshing.

One of the concerts I attended many years ago came at a time when I felt drained spiritually, even though I worked at the church. A new friend invited Rudy and me to attend this concert with them, and we had a hard time saying no, so we went. God knew how much I needed that evening to renew my batteries and restore my soul. The joy of the music, the message, and the crowd brought tears to my eyes as

I realized what was missing – my praising of God through music and clapping and singing the glory of His name.

Music is important to praise, but praise comes in many ways. Seek out how best you can praise God. Find ways to give God praise throughout your day. Let those around you know of your praise to God. Don't keep it to yourself! Shout it out! Hallelujah!

### Hard to Love

Our society is one where we feel comfortable sharing time with friends and people whom we consider like ourselves. We find it fun to spend days or evenings with certain folks. Then some event lands in our schedule as a must attend event. We don't particularly care for the folks hosting the event or attending the event, but our attendance is required.

Any number of reasons account for our not wanting to go. Perhaps some disagreement has occurred. Or do they simply share different values? Maybe they are loud and obnoxious. They may have even said or done things that caused us embarrassment or humiliation. Even family members can say or do things that hurt one another deeply.

Jesus tells us: *"But I say to you who listen: Love your enemies, do what is good to those who hate you, bless those who curse you, pray for those who mistreat you." -- Luke 6:27-28 (CSB)*

November is the beginning of many holiday parties, events, and family functions. To many, this is a very difficult time of year. Sometimes we find it hard to follow God's words to us. Perhaps now, in the days ahead of the holidays, we need to ponder Jesus' message to us. Who are we to help during this season to come? How do we seek God's help in dealing with certain people?

Let us pray for wisdom, for guidance, and for those who have mistreated us, or cursed us, or for those who find fault with us. Let us also pray that God will show us our own areas where we have mistreated others, or cursed others, or have found fault with others.

Forgiveness is a powerful gift to give and to accept. God will enable us to do what He wishes for us to do. God bless you!

## Remain Faithful

In the RV park where we live in the winters, we purchased a park model home which is similar to a mobile home but much smaller, 40' long by 11" wide and is registered as a recreational vehicle. It sits on wheels like a trailer, but the wheels come off and it sits above the ground on supports. We were adding a room onto our park model that is 21'x17' in size and connects to the park model giving us more space.

We hoped to have it finished before I left to await the arrival of our newest grandchild. You see, that was my plan. My other plan was for that precious baby to wait for my arrival, but once again that was my plan! How many times have we had plans that went totally whacky? Or never came about at all. What about how well we wait for God to show us the way He wants us to follow Him? Do we recognize God's guidance or try to force our way as the best way? How impatient are we for answers?

David (in the Psalms ) endured 17 years of fleeing and hiding from King Saul, who wanted to kill him. During those years, David never lost his faith that God would guide and protect him from his enemies. That doesn't mean David lived a safe, comfortable life. Far from it. God never left him during any of those years. David always stayed close to God even in his lowest moments. Psalms 27 is a testimony to David's suffering, need and love for God. The last two verses tell us: ***"I am certain that I will see the Lord's goodness in the land of the living. Wait for the Lord; be strong, and let your heart be courageous. Wait for the Lord." -- Psalms 27:13-14 (CSB)*** Notice that David states that he "will see the Lord's goodness in the land of the living." He has hope and faith that all of God's promises will occur while he is still alive. He knows the value of waiting for the Lord.

We too must wait, but continue serving and watching for God's answer each day. We try different avenues which perhaps are the ones God plans for us to follow, but when we find a closed door, we realize that path is not the one. God was with us as we journeyed.

Surely, we must have plans, but we must always know that God may have other ideas that will sidetrack our plans. We must be okay with that. I guess if the room didn't get finished as I expected, it would eventually happen. The baby would come when it is time, regardless of where I am. Once again, that is ok since God would care for mother and child (and papa too). For those of you struggling with illnesses, depression, financial difficulties, or whatever, know that God's plan for you will come to pass in God's time if you remain faithful and expectant. We must remain with God, just as David remained God's faithful servant for all those years.

## *Our Hope*

I visited a man in the hospital who had his entire family around him. He was facing a difficult day of surgery from which he might not wake. He was not alone with life's difficulties. Many others on the planet share in life's misery. Yet hope exists within some of their lives. Hope for a better today and tomorrow.

The news was full of the suffering of humankind all over the world. Our local news stations bring us stories of the good and bad things happening to people everywhere. Yet, according to the commercials this is the season to be jolly. Perhaps it is a season to focus on the source of our hope. That hope came in the form of a baby named Jesus. He didn't promise us life without problems, but eternal life with Him. He promises to be with us during our problems. He promises us comfort amid sorrow or hardships.

Paul suffered much during his life as a Christian. *"I don't say this out of need, for I have learned to be content in whatever circumstances I find myself. I know how to make do with little, and I know how to make do with a lot. In any and all circumstances I have learned the secret of being content — whether well fed or hungry, whether in abundance or in need. I am able to do all things through him who strengthens me." -- Philippians 4:11-13 (CSB)* The secret for Paul was allowing Christ to live in him, allowing Christ to strengthen him to do whatever Christ needed him to do. During this season of parties, celebrations, gift giving, pain and suffering, we need to allow Christ to minister to us through others. Those of us with plenty need to share ourselves with those in need. Those of us in need must focus on Christ's presence in our lives and allow others to minister to us. Those who do not know Christ need to feel His presence brought to them through others.

Are you a vessel willing to minister to others? Can you bring a gift of love to someone in need? Perhaps that gift is merely your time and your presence for a visit. Did your visit make a difference? We leave that for God to complete. We are not responsible for results in others, but we are responsible for being available for others.

God can give you the courage to visit someone. He gave me courage to visit the man that I did not know in the hospital. I was so glad I went. My heart was heavy for him. I prayed he would awaken to see his family since that was his wish for now. For him, the alternative is to awaken to eternal life with Christ, and what a wonderful alternative! For now, he wants to be with his family. May God be with him and his family.

## Flying Is Safe

God surely has a sense of humor! He knows how I hate to fly, yet he keeps putting me in situations where flying is the only way to get to where I need to be in a practical time frame. I had to fly to Denver for that newest grandson. It was very special to be there for his birth! I had to fly to Texas for a NOMADS special task force meeting that I agreed to help coordinate. Never in my wildest dreams did I envision having to fly somewhere for a committee meeting! I still had to fly back to Arizona! God and many of you must be laughing right now, knowing how much safer it is to fly than to drive the same distances!

Many of you also might remember how special music is in my life. On the plane, my ancient CD player, my headphones, and Christian CD accompany me to fill my mind with songs of faith and strength. They also drown out the noise of the plane. If I could just find some way to smooth out the bumpy turbulence! Any suggestions?

And thank God for wonderful drugs! I confided my anxieties to the doctor who prescribed a wonderful pill that relaxes me for a couple of hours and helps me endure the entire ordeal.

Intellectually I know that flying is safe, but emotionally I don't like it. Why? I haven't a clue! I know that my focus on God allows me to get on that plane! I imagine holding His hand the whole way. I cling to the words of the songs about faith. Yep, those are all crutches, but they enable me to do what I don't want to do!

David (in the Old Testament) had his crutches by composing many of the Psalms to carry him through the 17 years of being on the run from King Saul. Moses had Aaron to speak for him and his staff to be a symbol of God's power.

*"Protect me, God, for I take refuge in you. I said to the Lord, 'You are my Lord; I have nothing good besides you.'" -- Psalms 16:1-2 (CSB)* Each of us has something in life that really doesn't appeal to us, but is necessary to go through. What crutches enable you to focus on God? Yes, I got on that plane with pill, CD player, headphones, and my Christian CD and returned to Arizona, knowing that God laughs while He holds my hand! For that I praise Him with all my heart!

## *Needing Attention*

I did something that often gets put off until another day - cleaning out files! We have a new room built; it is time to move all the files from the motorhome into the house. While under construction, I've had files in the motorhome, in a traveling file case in the park model, and then when I was in Denver, I kept things in large envelopes until I got home. So, this task is nearly overwhelming. Files were everywhere!

That said, there is joy in the process! First, it is all coming together faster than I imagined. The shredder is busy and often needs to be emptied! And last, I am finding some fun memories and reminders of events over the past years. How easily we forget many of the things that happened to us over the years. I've reread cards from folks who received prayer cloths for various reasons. The photos of people with their grandchildren (and we watched the children grow up) let me know of the years that have passed.

Going through the health care folder reminded me how our expenses rose so sharply, affecting our ability to travel as much as we wanted. Also, seeing what we paid for fuel only a few years ago compared to now, explained why our funds simply don't buy what they did several years ago.

I reread some of the stories I wrote years ago for church bulletins, for classes, for other reasons, and relived the days that influenced those stories. How blessed my life is. The dreaded activity of cleaning out files has brought me joy! For it has shown me the moments of joy in our life, the reasons that I continue to sew and pray, and the richness that family brings to our life. It shows me how God has guided me and how I have relied on Him, especially in the hard times. It reminded me how many others have touched my life and made it better.

*"Above all, maintain constant love for one another, since love covers a multitude of sins. Be hospitable to one another without complaining. Just as each one has received a gift, use it to serve others, as good stewards of the varied grace of God." -- 1 Peter 4:8-10 (CSB)*

Yes, God has touched my life and, though I did not look forward to cleaning out my files, God rewarded me with the memories uncovered when I finally got to the task. What task are you putting off? Does God have a reason for you to pursue an activity? Perhaps you are missing out on a great adventure by procrastinating! May God bless you richly!

## Seek Obedience

We have all seen pictures of children doing all kinds of things that make parents cringe and say, "Oh no, not today, not my child"! As a grandmother it is much easier for me to laugh when I see these photos since my kids are now past all of that! Of course, my grandchildren are right in there becoming the new photos.

In fact, we have a photo of our youngest twins caught in the middle of having just emptied two full boxes of tissues and redecorating the living room with lovely white tissues all over everything! As soon as they were discovered, they immediately began stuffing them back into the boxes. (Kids know right from wrong). At age two they were simply doing a fun activity. However, the activity provided a moment for teaching. Rather than spank, yell or attack the kids, their mother simply brought out the trash can and encouraged them to clean up their mess until all the tissues were in the trash. We did not help them! They did not get to go play until they picked up all the tissues. Yes, it took time to let them do it, but it also teaches them to clean up after themselves.

All of us like to try doing things and sometimes, even as adults, we do things that we know are not right, but we do them anyway. Those are the very times that we need to seek forgiveness for going against our conscience. As they grew older, I used to tell my kids they had to live with whatever decisions they made. Don't do anything your conscience won't allow you to live with. That is a statement that works for people with a conscience, but for those who have already severed their ability to experience their conscience, it is wasted instruction. Teaching obedience is a time-consuming part of parenting but one well worth the time.

God's word teaches us in Ephesians and in Colossians: *"Children, obey your parents in everything, for this pleases the Lord. Fathers, do not exasperate your children, so that they won't become discouraged." -- Colossians 3:20-21 (CSB)* As adults we are still children of God, and we also need to learn to obey God's word. God does not inflect trials on us to punish us for being disobedient. Often our own decisions, or simply the forces of this world, create chaos in our lives. Seeking forgiveness when we are the ones who created our own chaos, allows us to restore the joy in our life with God. Let us remember the power of obedience at whatever age we are. Help us to seek forgiveness when we fail to be obedient to God's word.

## Body and Soul

Scripture has many references to running races and my favorite is: ***"Don't you know that the runners in a stadium all race, but only one receives the prize? Run in such a way to win the prize. Now everyone who competes exercises self-control in everything. They do it to receive a perishable crown, but we an imperishable crown. So I do not run like one who runs aimlessly or box like one beating the air. Instead, I discipline my body and bring it under strict control, so that after preaching to others, I myself will not be disqualified." -- 1 Corinthians 9:24-27 (CSB)***

As splendid and spectacular as the athletes in the Olympic Games are, the opening ceremonies leave me wondering how many people could have been helped with even half of the money used to create and produce that event. What are we becoming? Why do we feel that we must top everyone else with our next presentation? Where does it end? I am so much more impressed with the hard work and the stories of the athletes who have worked to achieve their goals.

- To see the love of mothers and fathers with their sons and daughters.

- To hear of the sacrifices they each have made to help accomplish their goals.

- To be privileged to watch as they struggle to do whatever they do for their event.

- To feel their joy or heartbreak at the finish line.

- To a few of the athletes the prize is gold, silver, or bronze.

- To most athletes the prize is merely getting to participate in an event.

In life, the prize Paul talks about is life with Christ. We all can win that prize. We must want it though! Christ has the prize available for all of us, but how badly do we want the prize? Are we willing to go into strict training and what does that mean? Do we want to be spectators watching others seek the prize? Or do we want to be participants in life with Christ? Are we willing to make the sacrifices to have Christ as our Lord? Will we take the time to read scripture, study Jesus life, pray with others, or attend bible studies? Just as the athletes have a different training regimen for their event, we each have different gifts and talents to offer and different sacrifices to make as we make Christ our Lord.

As we remember the Olympic races, let us think about the race that we run making and keeping Christ the prize in our lives.

## *Pray, Trust, Help*

Today I watched some young ladies climb an Alpine Tower. It was my job to take pictures of them. It ended up being my privilege to cheer them on and celebrate their success. One of the young ladies was very afraid of this 50' tall tower. As she approached it with her harness on and ready to start climbing it, she stopped, put her head on her hands, and froze. The two young men who were holding the ropes started to encourage her to go, but the leader of the lady's team quietly told them she was praying. So, all allowed her the time to pray. Then she began her assent up the pole.

Now she did not just run up that pole. She reached a couple of points where she really wanted to get down, but all encouraged her to take one more step. If she had still insisted on coming down, she could have – another young lady did just that. She listened to the encouragement and continued. I could feel her fear of falling. At one point she needed to rest, and the handler told her to sit down in the harness and it would allow her to rest. Reluctantly she did so, but briefly. Finally, she found another way to go up by following the suggestions of the guy helping her. Once she found the top and pulled herself onto the top platform, she could not even stand up. Her victory yell included us seeing her hands and feet up wiggling in victory. Now she had to come down! It took about 10 more minutes to get her to sit on the edge, then another 5 minutes to get her to come off the edge and allow the harness to hold her. She did it, still terrified, but relieved once she slowly began her journey back to the ground.

***"Those who know your name trust in you because you have not abandoned those who seek you, Lord." -- Psalms 9:10 (CSB)*** Her prayers were answered despite her fear! Sometimes we find ourselves in situations where our fears can immobilize us. Perhaps prayer at that time is the knot at the end of the rope that helps us to hang on and let God use those around us to guide us through the situation. As an add-on, the guys asked me if I wanted to go up and, of course, I said, "NO," not today! Maybe I need to say that prayer...

## *Inspiration*

Sometimes I wonder why God leads us to a certain place, especially before we get there! Two things confirmed to me why we are in Potosi, Missouri. First, we were less than two hundred miles from our dear friends who were working a NOMADS project near Springfield, IL. She became very ill and, after many tests, learned she had three spots of infection in her brain requiring three holes drilled in her skull to drain them. Her husband, being a retired minister, wrote some amazingly powerful messages to report her condition as well as what specifically for us to include in our prayers. His messages of hope touched many people. Because we were so close geographically, we were able to drive up for the day and visit with them. Praise God for her continued healing and though, she was not out of the woods entirely, we know that is coming. *(She fully recovered over a period of time!)*

The second reason we are here is a group that comes each year. It is a camp weekend for families fighting cancer which affects one of their children. This camp represents a time for 41 families to get away from the hospital and get out into nature and play! I was asked to take pictures for the camp!

The last two days, I watched and photographed their fun. The children with their shaved heads, (and Dads who had also shaved theirs) and scars from their surgeries, had smiles and awe on their faces as they participated in sheer fun! I fell in love with their faces, with their effort on the tough Alpine Tower as they conquered their fear, with their eagerness to be kids having fun, with the brothers and sisters who obviously cared for one another as they shared in the many activities, and with the parents who participated earnestly just to see their kids smile and have fun. I made photos available for one family who hasn't had a vacation in three years because of their young son's chemotherapy treatments (he is now in remission) and Mom had no camera.

Jesus offers us hope when we turn to Him. *"Humble yourselves, therefore, under the mighty hand of God, so that he may exalt you at the proper time, casting all your cares on him, because he cares about you." -- 1 Peter 5:6-7 (CSB)* Yes, I shall carry with me the images of their hope as I continue to hold them in prayer for healing and for them to cast their cares on Jesus as He cares for them. What is God showing you about why you are in a certain place? Sometimes the answer does not come right away, but it will come. I praise God for allowing me the time I got to spend with our friends and the families that spent their weekend here. Who is your inspiration? What examples surround you that perhaps you haven't noticed?

### Making Amends

A friend was lamenting over the regrets of her life, things she would have done differently had she only known or understood better when she was younger. Her compassion apparently failed to surface many years ago on many occasions. Since I've known her a long time, I was aware of her past failures. As I listened, I heard remorse, sadness, and longing to change. Her health is not good right now, causing her to reflect upon what her life has meant. Now she merely wants to make a difference with her life, but feels that there is nothing she can do until her health returns and she gets physically stronger.

The scripture that came to me as I listened was from Ecclesiastes 3 which talks about time for everything. Perhaps this is the time in her life to make amends, to make changes in her life, and to seek wisdom. As I read more of Ecclesiastes, the text led me to: *"When all has been heard, the conclusion of the matter is this: fear God and keep his commands, because this is for all humanity. For God will bring every act to judgment, including every hidden thing, whether good or evil." -- Ecclesiastes 12:13-14 (CSB)*

My place is not to judge her, though over the years, I probably have! I encouraged her to make amends with those she feels she has hurt, to pray for wisdom, to seek the forgiveness she seems to want and finally, not to wait until she is physically stronger. Even in her weakened condition, she can pray for others. She can write notes to others encouraging them to have faith and she can read inspirational materials to help her own faith grow.

My heart aches for those who live long lives without Jesus as their friend. Yet, I rejoice knowing that those same people can still come around and find some peace as they establish a relationship with God and His son, Jesus. Even though my friend woke me up very early in the morning with her phone call, I praise God for making me available. I pray that He continues to touch her life in ways that make His presence in her life very visible to her. I pray she will know beyond a shadow of a doubt that God's forgiveness and grace covers her and will enable her to heal emotionally, physically, and spiritually. That may take time, but I shall continue to pray for her.

### Beautiful Scraps

A year or so ago I found a little wooden sign with these words printed on it, *"When life gives you scraps, make quilts!"* Of course, I bought it, and it now sits on my fabric cabinet. Yesterday, I participated in a quilting class for making (and designing) a scrappy quilt. For months now I have cut scraps from my prayer cloth fabrics into the small pieces needed for this class.

For me, putting odd pieces together is hard since it goes against my sense of color coordination. Our instructor encouraged us to just grab the pieces and put

them together. As I followed the instructions, I found it hard to like the blocks that I made since the colors simply didn't work together. But I kept going. As the day went on, she gave us additional instructions that enabled me to start thinking about overall design. By the end of the day, I had a design in mind and suddenly the colors began to make sense and came together in a way I had not expected. The beauty of the quilt came into view as I completed the center portion.

The experience reminded me that God takes the scraps of our lives and weaves them into very interesting paths for our life's journey. The older I get, the more scraps get woven into the project that makes me the person that I am. And I am still in the process of being made whole.

*"The eyes of the Lord are on the righteous, and his ears are open to their cry for help. The face of the Lord is set against those who do what is evil, to remove all memory of them from the earth. The righteous cry out, and the Lord hears, and rescues them from all their troubles. The Lord is near the brokenhearted; he saves those crushed in spirit. One who is righteous has many adversities, but the Lord rescues him from them all. He protects all his bones; not one of them is broken." -- Psalms 34:15-20 (CSB)*

Yes, our Lord carries us through many events in our lives. He hears our prayers, knows our hearts, and cares for us very much. I can only be in awe of how much He loves us, of how great is His grace, and of how He meets our needs. He takes the scraps that we give Him and makes something beautiful of our lives. My scrappy quilt will forever remind me of His interaction in the weaving of my life. Praise be to God.

### Events Overlap

Life gets interesting when several unrelated events find ways of overlapping with a theme. Rudy and I went out again looking for a specific bird, a Rufus Capped Warbler, a Mexican bird that rarely comes into the US. Rudy researched the area, and we took off. We knew the area would be rigorous since we had to walk up a wash that comes down a mountain. We had our hiking boots and took lunch and drinks with us. The wash had just a small amount of water running through it as we walked up the rocks, crossing the stream many times for the easiest way up. After stopping for lunch, a couple told us they had seen the birds further up. So off we went! We never saw, but heard the birds. However, during our hike, we observed beautiful butterflies flittering everywhere. We were disappointed that we hadn't seen the bird, but were satisfied with a great hike and the butterflies.

That night at dinner, the entertainer, Kenny Hess, from Canada sang many songs. He is also a songwriter and great family man. Between songs, he told a lot of stories about his father who was a preacher and musician, and about other family members. One was about his daughter at age five. He observed her talking to an imaginary friend, and the conversation with that friend became a new song for him. It is called *"Beeca Fly."* * She believed at that time that Mommy and Daddy could have made her anything they wanted – a boy, a girl, or a puppy dog, etc. The words even talked about making her a butterfly that could fly over the mountains. The images of the butterflies we saw earlier in the day came to mind doing just exactly what she had said to her imaginary friend, flying over the mountains and soaring through the sky.

That same weekend's sermon was about being a committed Christian and doing your best for Christ. Once again, the words to another song from Kenny Hess overlapped some points in the sermon. ***"For no one can lay any foundation other than what has been laid down. That foundation is Jesus Christ."* -- *1 Corinthians 3:11 (CSB)*** Does my world include Jesus? Is my life built on the solid foundation of Jesus? Am I being the best I can for Jesus?

How I praise God for bringing three events together to help me see more of Him each day. I know there is more that I miss simply because I get caught up in my own thoughts or desires. I love those days when God brings meaning to various events, causing me to keep my eyes upon Him. Watch for ways that God brings meaning to your life through the events taking place around you.

*"Beeca Fly," by Kenny Hess, 2001, published by Kate and Beeca Records/Royality Records, Inc.

### *Important in Life*

*"Life is..."* Wow, so many ways to finish those two words! I could start with busy, fulfilling, scary, wonderful, fragile or add your own favorite! It is also a gift. With my Mom's situation this summer, I often reflect on not only her life, but mine. Without her, my life would not be. The same is true for any of us; without our mother or our father none of us would be just as we are. My oldest son has often said to me that his birthday is a time to say, "thank you," to me (his mother) for without me or his dad, he would not have a birthday to celebrate.

**"Do not be conformed to this age, but be transformed by the renewing of your mind, so that you may discern what is the good, pleasing, and perfect will of God." -- Romans 12:2 (CSB)** This message has many applications. Much like "*Life is...*" Our minds can be renewed over many subjects and in many ways. Transformation is a process and many of us want instant results.

What are the things we currently hold as important in our lives? Are those the same things that God wants for us? There is much corruption, greed, and immorality present in today's world. These are some of the things that God wants us to rid ourselves of. Each of us holds on to a certain amount of greed. I must admit that I am greedy over my time and how it is spent. Sometimes the shows I watch and the books I read might promote some immorality. That is watching and reading not living and I make that difference. We all are guilty of similar transgressions, but how do we live out our lives? Do these shows, books, etc., affect how we live? What about reading scripture? Does reading this material affect how we live? Reading scripture, yes, because those are the words of life.

Renewal of our minds to align with Christ is radical! Christ certainly lived a radical lifestyle compared to the Pharisees. Our world teaches us that radicals in the world are not people that you want to associate with. Perhaps we need to consider what is a good radical versus a bad or destructive radical. Which radicals try to make life better versus making lives dependent on welfare? I wonder how much of this scripture relates to the world we are living in today.

Yes, this scripture is challenging. One that we really need to ponder for how it applies to us.

### Wants Me to Be

This scripture is very familiar and doesn't always make me think about it very much. But because of some other issues going on in my life about serving, I've pondered it in a different light. ***"So God created man in his own image; he created him in the image of God; he created them male and female." -- Genesis 1:27 (CSB)*** Yes, God made me who I am. He gave me my gifts and personality. Then the Holy Spirit filled me with His presence. God gave me the potential to be all that He wants me to be. Now I must make use of all that He gave me. Sometimes I do that better than other times.

I've struggled with how God wants me to function within our local worship services. Can my participation be revamped, or do I simply quit my service? My first thoughts were to simply quit and let someone else do the job. After meeting with others, suggestions arose that perhaps allow for the service of others to blend with my gifts and talents. We are currently praying for direction and wisdom.

All of us, at some time in our lives, ponder such decisions. Do we just say "no," or do we say "yes"? Sometimes a "no" is the best decision for us at that given time. Sometimes a "yes" isn't the right decision either. Often when I worked in the church recruiting volunteers for a job, I would go to someone for one job and end up giving them another job more suited to their personality and talents. We can't let others decide what we are to do. Where God is calling us to go and our own knowledge of ourselves takes precedence on those decisions.

Others may be critical of us for our choice, but if God is truly leading us, He will take us where He wants us to go. There are so many ways to serve you simply can't count them! God created each of us in His image. Yet each of us is unique and has different parts of His character and personality.

How I praise Him for creating me the way I am. Now I pray for the Holy Spirit to fulfill the promises God created for my life. May you each find the direction that He has created for you to follow and still be the unique person that He made you to be.

### Love in Action

Ice cream is such a fun food! Especially when you top it with chocolate syrup, caramel, or strawberry, then top it off with some whipped cream! In some parts of the country, you may think it is too cold for ice cream, but here in Arizona ice cream is good just about any time!

***"Little children, let us not love in word or speech, but in action and in truth." -- 1
John 3:18 (CSB)*** Saying "I love you" in words conveys one message. Do your actions
support your words? Our actions of love vary so much during life. Let me try to stir
your memory. What do young parents do for their children? Everything! Why do
they do those things? Because the children can't do some things for themselves,
because it is the parent's responsibility, because they love their children, or all the
above. With young children it is easier to see love in action. That is until they reach
the terrible twos, or until they become teenagers! Then perhaps we might wonder
occasionally... I could digress! We love them regardless of their behavior, and we
need to make sure they know that, not only with our words, but with our actions.

Husbands and wives show loving actions for one another frequently without
necessarily thinking of the action as a way of saying "I love you." However, we may
reach a stage in marriage where we take one another for granted and assume too
much. Rudy came in every night when I washed our daily dishes and picked up the
towel to dry them without me asking. That told me he loves me! Whoever poured
the coffee in the morning, if we are both up, pours it for both of us. That says, "I love
you." Granted, those are simple illustrations, but you get the idea.

We have all the mission projects done in the name of Jesus! How many ways do
we tell Jesus we love Him? Donating money is always a good, fast, and easy way,
and sometimes that is all we can do. What about ways to reach out to help others?
Volunteering knows no limits! Pick your interest, your geographic area, and find
the need. Pray that God leads you to what you can do.

Remember the ice cream I mentioned? Our church group had an ice cream social
and served about 90 people either a sundae or a root beer float. Those people
donated $2300 to the pastor that comes to our park each week so that he can get
a new roof for the physical church that he serves. And we did have fun doing it.
Handing Pastor the money and seeing the joy on his face was our way of saying
to him how much we love him and his ministry to us. Now we know that he can
contact the contractor to plan the work.

### *Joyful In Hope*

Wonderful insights surround us that we might never know of or see. Often, they
seem to be insignificant items or pieces of knowledge that we either take for
granted or fail to observe. Perhaps that is because we are assaulted (and often
overwhelmed) with visual images daily. As we helped move our son and his family
in Texas to a bigger house this week, Rudy discovered our son's business card

141

which we had never seen before. He grabbed two of them and gave one to me. Since I sometimes design or layout business cards for folks, I like to examine all the content - graphics and text. Down near the bottom in small font was "Rom 12:12." I knew right away it was a reference to Romans 12:12 but could not remember exactly what it said.

When I looked it up, I found a new text to embroidery on my prayer cloths. The verse is, *"Be joyful in hope, patient in affliction, faithful in prayer." -- Romans 12:12 (NIV)* I had an opportunity to learn more about this scripture as part of the story of his life from his wife.

Being joyful in hope reminds me that, as we hope for something, keep a smile on, keep laughter alive, and remain positive while you wait. Patient in affliction requires us to wait since it can take a while to resolve, but to do so patiently. No need to fret, worry or constantly replay the affliction. Just keep living in a positive manner. Faithful in prayer keeps me on my knees, aware in my mind, active in thoughts, vocal with song, words, and praise, with a prayer life that happens all day!

The words here are simple, but the power behind them brings comfort, peace, and strength when we can apply them in our lives. Each of us can think of situations where at least one of these phrases affected our lives. Paul wrote many words about living in such a way to allow Christ to lead us through each day. What if we were to fill our minds with these simple words each morning, ponder them during the day, and reflect upon how they helped us at the end of each day. By keeping our eyes upon Jesus, we will see life in new ways.

I praise You Lord for giving us new insights each day. Help us to recognize them for how they can strengthen our walk with You. Thank You for the friends we have here in Texas and for being able to help our son's family relocate into a new home which will be used for serving You as well.

### Ripple Effect

When we throw a rock in a lake, we can see how the ripples continue in what seems to be an unending circle. Most of us do not know the ripple effects that we leave around us. Do we even give much thought to any ripples that are created by what we say or do? I can think of many ripples from others' lives that crossed my path in a very positive manner. Some of those people perhaps don't even know the impact they made on my life.

While I was in college and in a sorority, my alumni Mother (an alumni living in town was my mom away from home) became a role model for me as I watched her interact with her husband and her children. She took me to church with them some Sundays and out to lunch with their family. She cared about me in such a positive and supportive way. Years later, I was able to thank her for allowing me to be a part of their family during some years that I needed to be with them. The ripple effects stayed with me, making me want what she had.

When our second son was born, a young couple's class brought meals to us for several weeks just because! You can't repay those folks, but the ripple effect caused me to then aid others with meals.

A pastor at our church in New Jersey, had faith in me when I was a very young Christian, encouraging me to walk in faith on a big community project. His faith in me created a ripple effect that enabled me to learn more about the power of faith in God.

Another pastor encouraged me to believe that God had a job for me to fulfill in our church. My response to him was "Who me?" His faith rippled over to me, allowing me to step out into a new direction I felt totally inadequately prepared for. ***"In every way I've shown you that it is necessary to help the weak by laboring like this and to remember the words of the Lord Jesus, because he said, 'It is more blessed to give than to receive.' " -- Acts 20:35 (CSB)*** How very grateful I am for those who gave encouragement to me over the years, who offered acts of kindness during times of trials, who gave of their time when I needed help, and those whose faithful lives rippled through to mine.

We attended a church that we had not attended for three years, since our last visit to Washington. A lady thanked me for helping them start their prayer cloth ministry years earlier. She went on to tell me of a lady with needs who had received a prayer cloth. It had a tremendous impact on her life. She recovered from her illness and was a quilter herself. To do an act of kindness for them, she made them a quilt for a raffle to raise funds for their prayer cloth ministry. The lady telling me the story was so glad to see me again to thank me for sharing the ministry idea with them. My response was to praise God, for He is the one I give the credit for their results. Later in the day, we were at our son's house, and I shared the story with my daughter-in-law. As I told her the story, she explained that she knew the story because she bought a raffle ticket for the quilt. She knew it was me they were talking about. I tell these stories to give praise to God for the work He does once the prayer cloths are distributed. What kind of ripples are you creating with your acts of kindness? Let God lead you!

## Special People

There are times in our life when we don't know what to say or how to respond. One of those times is when a friend or loved one appears to be in a losing battle with life through whatever events have taken place. I say "appears to be" because I know the power of our God to provide miracles that we simply don't understand. I also know that all of us will lose our battle with life at some point in time. That fact is a given, and the miracle God gives to us is eternal life at that point.

How do we minister to someone appearing to be close to passing on in the journey from this life to eternal life? We take meals, send cards, emails, flowers. Visits become something we hesitate doing because of immunity issues that make visits not practical. Visits are wonderful when planned for through family.

Recently I got an update about a friend whose cancer was terminal with little time left. I can't go to visit because of the distance. I wanted her to know how she touched my life. Sending her an email allowed me to tell her that I am praying for her and her husband. Also, I included stories of the times when we met, when our lives intersected, and how those times affected me as a person. To me, she had great worth in her life, and I wanted to tell her a story. She came to me via a phone call one day that really touched my life with a simple question, "Have you prayed about it?" She called me out of my anger, and she was right on! I thanked her for that and other things too. Her husband later told me how much that meant to her. Lesson: don't wait to tell someone how special they are. When someone dies suddenly, we can only tell their families those kinds of stories.

It seems we can always put off even thinking about how special folks are to us. What if we share those thoughts, even before someone gets ill or before tragedy strikes? Perhaps your comment at the right time just might be a spark that brightens a dark or down day for them. Even when the person is ill, to hear something positive about their life can mean more than we can even fathom.

The parable of the Ten Virgins in Matthew teaches us to be ready when Christ returns. *"Therefore be alert, because you don't know either the day or the hour." -- Matthew 25:13 (CSB)* Don't wait or procrastinate your preparations for Christ's second coming. We also don't know when our time is to end. That also tells me to not wait to tell others how special they are, at least to you. Everyone needs to know that their life matters. Find something worth sharing with a friend or loved one or even an acquaintance.

## WWII Veteran

We stopped in Flagstaff, Arizona at Cracker Barrel for an afternoon snack. An older gentleman was seated a couple of tables away from us by himself. He was laughing and enjoying conversing with the waitress. After she left, I spied his cap that said, "Gen. Patton, 4th Inf." and had a pin on it that I thought was a Purple Heart. He just seemed lonely. She brought his meal to him, and he removed his cap, bowed his head, closed his eyes, and said a prayer. Since Rudy and I only ordered dessert, we finished quickly. I walked right up to his table and asked him if he served with Gen. Patton.

I wish I had had a camera with me, as his face just sparkled! After telling me he really served with Omar Bradley, but when the 3rd Infantry was combined with the 4th, Gen. Patton was then the overall commander. He asked me if I also saw the Purple Heart, confirming to me what it was. Then he began telling us how he faced the Germans, bullets coming in from everywhere and then grenades. Finally, one grenade landed next to him. He had heard the trigger and knew it was going to blow. He did a back flip which saved his life, but took his leg. That was the end of the war for him. He laughed as he spoke of all the prosthesis he had. At 91 nearly 92, he is still active, drives, and misses his wife who died five years ago. They had 64 years together.

We didn't have a lot of time, but we each thanked him for his service to this country and for sharing his story with us. We also told him how impressed we were with his prayer time in the restaurant. He was so grateful and seemed to want us to stay. There aren't too many of his generation still living and able to get out in public as easily as he does. Seeing him today was a very special treat for me and I don't really know why except for his attitude, his smile, his love for life, country, and God. I only pray that he is not as lonely as some are at his age. Yes, we have been blessed to travel this country, but he has been blessed with a long life filled with memories that appear to fuel his longevity. His faith sustained him in the foxhole when he prayed for rescue and safety just as his faith continues to sustain him today.

***"This is why, since I heard about your faith in the Lord Jesus and your love for all the saints, I never stop giving thanks for you as I remember you in my prayers." -- Ephesians 1:15-16 (CSB)*** I will remember this man for years to come and thank God for allowing me the moments I had with him. I also pray for him and for the years he has left on this earth. May his spirit, love, and positive attitude be shared with others. Watch for the serendipities of life that happen around you. Praise God for them and store up those memories for the grey days of life.

## Prayers, Prayer Cloths

### Tragedies

Tragedy seems to be all around us over the last few decades: from 9/11, to school shootings, other mass shootings, wars in Iraq and Afghanistan, political upheaval, the Pandemic, and to all the personal issues we go through. Finding words, thoughts, and scripture to cope with the tragic events takes me to Psalms 56, among others. As you read change the singular to plural to encompass us all.

*"Be gracious to me, God, for a man is trampling me; he fights and oppresses me all day long. My adversaries trample me all day, for many arrogantly fight against me. When I am afraid, I will trust in you. In God, whose word I praise, in God I trust; I will not be afraid. What can mere mortals do to me?" -- Psalms 56:1-4 (CSB)*

In our prayers, let us keep the families directly affected by these events and the ones yet to come. Guide the leaders of our country as they prepare responses, the rescue workers and medical personnel who attend to the many needs, and the countless others who assist in the investigations involved. May God's grace and comfort enable us to move on toward justice and peace.

### Lorna

I need to tell you about a friend named Lorna. She was 80 years old, with failing eyesight, unable to drive at night, and no family nearby. This same lady had a gift that she shared, providing inspiration to many. She loved Jesus and she loved to sew and to pray. People brought her scraps of fabric and she made prayer quilts. They were simple and only about 16" square, but beautiful. Then she faithfully brought them to her Sunday School class for them to be blessed before sending them on to someone in need. She prayed for whomever would receive it even though they might be strangers.

The basis for this ministry is found in Acts, but of course the cloth holds no power. The power is in the prayers that accompany the cloth. **"God was performing**

extraordinary miracles by Paul's hands, so that even facecloths or aprons that had touched his skin were brought to the sick, and the diseases left them, and the evil spirits came out of them." -- Acts 19:11-12 (CSB)

In my nomadic lifestyle on the road, it occurred to me that I could also sew prayer quilts and tell others about her ministry. I made prayer quilts for some special people and prayed either with them or for them. I wrote this prayer to be attached to them for the people who receive them. I pass this on to you in honor of Lorna, her life, her love, her Lord, and her ministry. She is now with Jesus in all glory!

*Lorna's Prayer*

*O Lord, my questions and my fears often overcome me.*

*Doubts hang like a shadow keeping me in the dark.*

*Pain dwells in my body clouding my thinking.*

*Guilt and sorrows sometimes engulf my daily thoughts*

*Until I consciously bring you into my mind and heart.*

*Then you bring comfort to my soul.*

*You restore the life within me and*

*Enable me to dwell in your warmth and embrace.*

*Allow the simplicity of this symbolic quilt to remind me*

*That you are with me, that you offer me warmth, peace,*

*Comfort, love, grace, wholeness, forgiveness, joy, and life.*

*Let it remind me of the prayers being said for me by others,*

*And of the hope I need for each day.*

*Lord, thank you for always being here*

*to hold my hand no matter what happens.*

*All my praise goes to you, O Lord.*

Do you know someone who might join in the making of prayer quilts to enable others to find strength during times of trouble? Have them contact me, or simply continue this ministry.

### *Scraps of Life*

As I sewed together the quilt squares of various fabrics, colors, and designs, I pondered how life resembles those patches. There are the plain moments, the clear sky days, the splotchy moments of indecision, the brilliant days of excitement and joy, the days of indecision and of uncertainty, the days of busyness and of plans gone awry, and finally, the days with the hand of God touching my life.

Surround these scrap squares with a border and then add a piece for backing. It all comes together to complete the story of that quilt. As I wandered through the bolts of fabric looking for just the right backing, I wondered how God decides whom to call. As I selected different fabrics, I started with the sale table. I knew I could find beautiful fabrics on the expensive tables, but they wouldn't tell the story the same way! Besides they would outshine the scraps. Perhaps He has the same dilemma that I experience, I want to buy pieces of all the fabrics!

*"Brothers and sisters, consider your calling: Not many were wise from a human perspective, not many powerful, not many of noble birth. Instead, God has chosen what is foolish in the world to shame the wise, and God has chosen what is weak in the world to shame the strong. God has chosen what is insignificant and despised in the world — what is viewed as nothing — to bring to nothing what is viewed as something, so that no one may boast in his presence. It is from him that you are in Christ Jesus, who became wisdom from God for us — our righteousness, sanctification, and redemption,— in order that, as it is written: Let the one who boasts, boast in the Lord." -- 1 Corinthians 1:26-31 (CSB)*

My selections made; the sewing continued to completion. Now scraps become something gorgeous, beautiful, and useful.

Have you given the scraps of your life to God for Him to make you His child? Do you believe He is pulling your pieces together? Do you want Him to take your confusion and use it to make something beautiful in your life? Open the door and let Him in to do His work.

### *Pray for Others*

Nine miners finally emerged from a flooded mine. How many prayers were said on their behalf? During the past few weeks of listening to stories of abducted children with both tragic and joyful results, I know that once again many prayers were prayed.

The people affected by the tragic events of abduction and the mine flood depended heavily on prayers to strengthen them during their ordeals. Did God help with the placement of the airshaft to give the men a chance for fresher air and some warmth? Did God help with knowing where to place the 30" rescue shaft? Now that those events have come to some conclusion, the people involved still need prayers for dealing with lives forever changed by the events they endured.

*"Pray at all times in the Spirit with every prayer and request, and stay alert with all perseverance and intercession for all the saints." -- Ephesians 6:18 (CSB)* Even though we do not know the people involved directly, we can still follow the instructions from Ephesians.

We must also spend time talking to God on a personal level by giving Him our thoughts, fears, and joys during the day from waking, through working, and on into the evening. He is there waiting for us! What parts of your life do you allow God to share? Have a cup of coffee and a chat with God frequently throughout your day!

### Intercessory

An email is circulating about the need for prayers for our country. Rather than ask for a specific direction that we want God to take, we need to pray for guidance for our leaders, the leaders of other countries, and anyone else involved in the decisions that affect our world right now.

James talks about the prayer of faith. *"The prayer of faith will save the sick person, and the Lord will raise him up; if he has committed sins, he will be forgiven. Therefore, confess your sins to one another and pray for one another, so that you may be healed. The prayer of a righteous person is very powerful in its effect." -- James 5:15-16 (CSB)*

Intercessory prayer (those prayers said on behalf of someone else) are powerful. I spoke with Rudy's cousin, who is several years older and suffering from many physical health problems. Her husband is very ill as well. A year ago, I gave them one of the quilted prayer cloths that I make, and she reminded me of it and how much it means to her. Her physical problems remain, but her spirit remains close to God knowing that others continue to pray for her and Bill.

Healing comes in many ways. The outcome to our world problems may be resolved in ways we cannot fathom at this moment. We must pray as directed in the letter from James. Our collective prayers need to be for guidance for those making decisions. Allow circumstances to indicate answers to those prayers. May we also pray for all the military personnel, men and women, mothers and fathers, sons and daughters, wives and husbands, brothers and sisters, affected by those decisions.

### *Spirit Intercedes*

As I wrote some additional prayers for my prayer cloth ministry, I found myself reading Romans 8 once again. So many memories come to me when I read this chapter. While writing these prayers, I often think of the many situations that lead us to pray. These words spoke so well of our needs at times. *"In the same way the Spirit also helps us in our weakness, because we do not know what to pray for as we should, but the Spirit himself intercedes for us with inexpressible groanings." -- Romans 8:26 (CSB)*

How many times do we feel weak or speechless? I remember once being so mad and upset with a situation, but I cannot recall the reason why. What I do remember is a phone call from a friend. I sat at my desk wallowing in my anger when the phone rang. As I explained the situation to my friend, her first response was to ask me if I had prayed about it yet! She also wanted to know if I had read in the scripture anything helpful for this event. Of course, all I could say was "no." She was not a person to call me very often, so it seemed to be God's way of meeting my need even when I could not remember what to do. As soon as I hung up, I grabbed my bible and began reading, and once again, God seemed to guide me in my selection for reading. Though I don't remember the details of what or why, I do remember vividly the process of God intervening on my behalf through my friend. By the end of that day, my anger subsided, my focus once again was on God, and the events no longer threatened me.

Each of us has the responsibility to help focus our friends on what God would have us do when we seem to be off course. When you feel an urge to call someone or even write them a note, you could very well be feeling God nudging you into action. Seems as though every time I read Romans 8, another important message retouches my life. May God lead you to your important message for this week.

### *Serendipities Await*

One of the joys of our lifestyle allows us to renew friendships across the country and to make new friends as well. Visiting friends at their home church, we enjoyed breakfast, and a tour of their church led me to appreciate the beautiful, quilted altar cloths and wall hangings in the sanctuary. Later, we enjoyed the wonderful hospitality of friends who are blessed with a home overlooking the majesty of the San Juan Islands. Their witness for Christ extends outward to many people through their many activities and contacts. This scripture became even more evident after our evening serendipity: *"There is one body and one Spirit — just as you were called to one hope at your calling — one Lord, one faith, one baptism, one God and Father of all, who is above all and through all and in all." -- Ephesians 4:4-6 (CSB)*

Rudy and I took an evening walk and came across a group from a local church. Suddenly, we remembered that they were having a special singing group, but we missed it by over an hour! One of their folks invited us to eat supper, or at least have dessert! As he insisted, we came over, inquired about the singing group, and learned they were still there! The pastor asked them if they would sing a song for US! They had packed their instruments already, but all six of them agreed to sing a cappella. Their voices blended in glorious harmony, filling the air with joy, praise, and a testimony to their love of our Lord! Because of their gift to us, I asked them to wait while I got them a gift. I returned with my prayer cloths and gathered the pastor and a couple of others standing by to join in a prayer of thanksgiving for their ministry.

How I praise God for those who open their homes to friends and strangers; for leading us toward that group site tonight even though we were late; for the man who invited us to share their abundance even after we said we had already eaten; for his persistence in bringing us to his table; and for His message in worship about our being one body, united in faith, hope and love!

Where were the serendipities in your past week? What serendipities await you this week? May we all keep our eyes on Jesus as we watch for the serendipities, He brings our way.

### *A Tool to Use*

*"Honey, I need a certain size drill bit to complete this job. Could you go get me one at the store while I work on this problem?"* Sounds like a simple request, but we all know that the types and numbers of tools available can instantly overwhelm you in a place like Home Depot.

Tools are needed in any field. Doctors, engineers, teachers, construction workers, journalists, lecturers, artists, musicians, and all others have their own unique tools. As we toured the museum in Victoria, we viewed the tools used by people many centuries ago. They were very crude compared to today's efficiently manufactured ones.

There is one tool that I know of that is very much like it was centuries ago and little has changed over time. Paul talked about it: ***"Pray at all times in the Spirit with every prayer and request, and stay alert with all perseverance and intercession for all the saints. Pray also for me, that the message may be given to me when I open my mouth to make known with boldness the mystery of the gospel. For this I am an ambassador in chains. Pray that I might be bold enough to speak about it as I should." -- Ephesians 6:18-20 (CSB)*** In my bible some time ago, I wrote this note about verse 18: "In every battle we fight to win, prayer is the power for the battle, it gives us the strength."

Yes, we have formal prayers and books of written prayers, but prayers are also those words from the heart shared with God. They can take the form of a request, a plea, a statement of concern, a burst of joy, thanksgiving or awe, a question, an expression of confusion or doubt, or any other emotion felt and experienced. Anyone can say a prayer since God requires no level of experience to participate. Prayers are those utterances and thoughts shared in private or in public between us and God.

We, as Christians, have a mighty tool called prayer. May Paul's words in Ephesians encourage us to use the tool of prayer to accomplish the work God gives to us.

### *Seed Planters*

I wrote something for some special youths as they graduate from high school. A few of these special young people may not actually graduate for various reasons. I do not know who will and who won't, but all are special regardless. I made them prayer cloths after working at their school in New Mexico. Why did I bother to put that much effort into a gift for them that they might not appreciate or even understand? I guess for the same reason many of you do service projects like teach Sunday School, lead youth groups, lead bible studies, help with Vacation Bible School and on goes the list. We are seed planters! Not the harvesters, but seed planters. Others provide water, sun, and fertilizer while God comes along and gathers the harvest. Sometimes our seed planting is part of the watering or the nurturing that helps bring the harvest closer. All the parts are important to the cycle.

Paul tells us in: ***"What then is Apollos? What is Paul? They are servants through whom you believed, and each has the role the Lord has given. I planted, Apollos watered, but God gave the growth. So, then, neither the one who plants nor the one who waters is anything, but only God who gives the growth. Now he who plants and he who waters are one, and each will receive his own reward according to his own labor." -- 1 Corinthians 3:5-8 (CSB)***

With this in mind, I wrote to those special youths. Your quilted prayer cloth is inscribed with a quote about life being a gift and what will you do with that gift. Today is a time to remember those who brought you to this day: those people who care for you, who share their faith with you, who try to inspire you to be all you can be, and those who love you no matter what. Tomorrow is your step into the rest of your life. Is your journey one you intend to make with Jesus as your guide? You must make decisions to follow where Jesus leads you, or to follow the ways of the world. Jesus uses His sheep as they live in the world. His flock around the world prays for you to make your life a gift to God. May this cloth be a visual reminder of the many prayers said for you today and always.

Why do I plant seeds? Because God leads me to do so. Let us all watch for what God leads us to do.

### Thankful Always

Some days are a challenge. I remember the insurance commercials that show one disaster creating another disaster that leads to yet another disaster and on it goes! It reminds me of a domino setup that allows one domino to knock over another domino in a chain reaction. Once started, it cannot be stopped. This commercial is such an unhappy scenario! Perhaps we can relate to the utter devastation followed by the frustration in coping with the aftereffects.

Some of my quilted prayer cloths have similar words embroidered on them: *"Give thanks in all circumstances; for this is God's will for you in Christ Jesus." -- 1 Thessalonians 5:18 (NIV)* Many of my cloths go to those with health concerns, or grieving the loss of a loved one, or celebrating a special event. This scripture speaks to us about many different times in life, both difficult and enjoyable.

One lady received one at a memorial for her husband. Why would one give thanks for losing a husband? Perhaps the thanks are for allowing the relationship to bring fulfillment for many years. Perhaps an illness took away so much of the life that death brings relief. Perhaps the thanks are for the many friends who surrounded her in her time of need.

Another man received one as a reminder of the chaos that often exists in his office. Even during chaos, the Holy Spirit brings grace and solutions about on a continual basis.

Paul knew the benefits of following his advice: *"Rejoice always, pray continually, give thanks in all circumstances; for this is God's will for you in Christ Jesus." -- 1 Thessalonians 5:16-18 (NIV)*

So, the next time things seem to fall apart, and the day feels like a line of dominoes falling all around you, take time to "Give thanks in all circumstances."

### Jesus, Peace

How do we explain the unexplainable? How do we console when consolation seems impossible? How do we understand that which has no reason? Many of us have received news of someone's death that simply does not seem real. How could it happen? My friend is with our Lord, suddenly and without warning. It all started with a bee sting. Three days later, after never regaining consciousness, she died. Being far away and not being able to attend her memorial service, I made her husband a prayer cloth to allow him to know of the many prayers being said for him. What scripture would I embroider on it? So many came to mind and yet, the struggle ensued. Without much time to ponder, I prayed for peace and guidance.

In other difficult times of my life, I sought peace, inner peace, peace that allows me to think, to move forward. John said it all, ***"Peace I leave with you. My peace I give to you. I do not give to you as the world gives. Don't let your heart be troubled or fearful." -- John 14:27 (CSB)*** Since that was too long for the cloth itself, I shortened it to, "Jesus gives you peace. John 14:27." Jesus did give peace to my friend. For her husband and adult children peace is available, yet claiming that peace and owning it, comes through the grief process as he allows the Holy Spirit to minister to him. That often takes time. My prayer for him is for the peace of Jesus to lift the troubles of his broken heart. That is a prayer others and I pray for him. None of us can ever explain why this happened.

As fellow Christians, we can provide support through our prayers, our deeds, and our love for those in similar positions. Along with the prayer cloth I sent to him, I included this prayer:

*The loss of a loved one always leaves a void.*
*But what a time for memories to flood my mind.*
*Lord, allow me to listen to others as they relate their stories.*
*Enable me to focus on the joys of life gone by.*
*Allow this simple quilt to remind me of your comfort*
*and peace as I go through the days to come.*
*Help me to vision the quilt wrapped around my loved one*
*just as the arms of the Savior enfold me.*
*Grant me rest in the knowledge that our Lord Jesus*
*cares, understands, and is available anytime.*

Who do you know that needs a similar prayer? Is it you, or a friend, or perhaps a family member?

### *Change, Grow*

Remember when you were a teenager? Some things are very clear to us from that time in our lives. One is clear for me. I remember having the thought that I would never discuss my opinions on sex, politics, or religion with others, since it was just too risky. Oh, how God molds and shapes us as we mature! Imagine me becoming a Director of Christian Education in a church! That certainly wiped out all my teenage thoughts. Religious beliefs dominated my life. I even organized and helped teach sex education at the church to middle school kids. Anyone who has ever worked anywhere, especially in the church, deals with political issues constantly.

This scripture from Paul: *"Therefore, I remind you to rekindle the gift of God that is in you through the laying on of my hands. For God has not given us a spirit of fear, but one of power, love, and sound judgment. So don't be ashamed of the testimony about our Lord, or of me his prisoner. Instead, share in suffering for the gospel, relying on the power of God. He has saved us and called us with a holy calling, not according to our works, but according to his own purpose and grace, which was given to us in Christ Jesus before time began. This has now been made evident through the appearing of our Savior Christ Jesus, who has abolished death and has brought life and immortality to light through the gospel." -- 2 Timothy 1:6-10 (CSB)*

God certainly took me places I never intended to go and continues to do so. I was in a store buying fabric for my prayer cloths. The clerk asked me what I was making and naturally, when I told her, she asked me more questions. I was able to tell her about the power of prayer and how God honors our prayers. Several other customers were waiting their turn to get fabric cut and could not help but overhear our conversation. Did they agree or disagree? I don't know, but they heard and perhaps God used our conversation to influence their lives. That isn't for me to know. The clerk gave me her phone number to make a couple of cloths for her, and another customer asked me many questions since she wanted to make some.

Years ago, I would not have answered her question as I did, and I most assuredly would not be writing devotionals! God gave me my gifts, taught me how to use them, and because of God's grace and love, finds ways for me to exercise those gifts. My praise and adoration for God's work in my life is something I must tell others about. I am not worthy of God's saving grace, but God gives it to me anyway. His Son Jesus died on that cross for all of us. If we are loved that much, can't we at least share our story of what God does for us with others? Try it, you'll like it!

### *Treasures*

Dreams. Nightmares. Voices. Ideas. Things that make noise in the dark. Ever wake up and wonder what was going through your mind? Or better yet, try to tell someone about it and suddenly what seemed so clear is now a jumble. Occasionally in the past, I got out of bed and made a note of that which occurred to me in my sleep. Sometimes it is just too weird and disoriented. Other times, logic happens to bring my wakeful stress into shape. One morning before daylight, I awoke with an idea for a new prayer cloth. It even came with a scripture. It was so clear, vivid, logical, and meaningful. As I lay awake in bed marveling at the wonder of having such a great thought in my sleep, I knew I would remember it the next morning.

Two days later as we were driving from Kansas to Oklahoma, it suddenly dawned on me that I had forgotten to write down my new idea. What scripture was it? Oh, please Lord let me remember it! Part of the idea, a vision of the finished product was clearly retained in memory. Finally, after several miles, it came to me! I grabbed my bible to look up the location of the scripture. I pondered: ***"Don't store up for yourselves treasures on earth, where moth and rust destroy and where thieves break in and steal. But store up for yourselves treasures in heaven, where neither moth nor rust destroys, and where thieves don't break in and steal. For where your treasure is, there your heart will be also." -- Matthew 6:19-21 (CSB)*** Two separate messages came for me to consider embroidering into the design. *"Store up for yourself treasures in heaven."* *"Your treasure is where your ♡ is."*

As I meditated on this passage, I tried listing treasures and came up with some of the following treasures in my life: freedom to pray to my Lord, a life centered in Christ, a desire to perform acts of kindness in Christ's name, ability to forgive because Christ forgave me, and a sense of peace that comes from knowing Christ. What are the differences in the blessings in our life and our treasures? My family and my home (be it on wheels or firmly planted on the ground) are blessings. Having a relationship with Christ is a treasure! I invite you to ponder your treasures in heaven and praise God for them. I know that my list is only a beginning. What do you add to the list?

### God's Plan

A privilege came my way to meet a young boy via his web page. He has a very rare form of bone cancer. Yet, he is an inspiration to many because of his faith in God. A friend of his asked me to make him a prayer cloth. His web site is filled with his love for his Lord.

One scripture that his family clings to is: " *'For I know the plans I have for you' — this is the Lord's declaration — 'plans for your well-being, not for disaster, to give you a future and a hope. You will call to me and come and pray to me, and I will listen to you. You will seek me and find me when you search for me with all your heart. I will be found by you' — this is the Lord's declaration — 'and I will restore your fortunes and gather you from all the nations and places where I banished you' — this is the Lord's declaration. 'I will restore you to the place from which I deported you.' " -- Jeremiah 29:11-14 (CSB)* What a jewel to cling to! This young man is very fortunate to have a family so filled with faith to guide him this way.

I look ahead to a new year for Rudy and me, knowing it will be financially the tightest year we have yet encountered for several reasons. What awaits us? What plans does God have for us? When will He reveal his plans for us?

Yes, our situation in no way parallels to the enormity of bone cancer in a 10-year-old. However, God has plans for us no matter what the situation is in our lives. Our tendency is to negate God's plans for us because our situation is not important enough. How could He spend time on something so unimportant in the scope of life? God wants to be involved in all the details of our lives. He does have a plan, but we need to allow His plan to evolve. That doesn't mean we sit still and wait for the doorbell to ring. Just as the boy and his family seek medical care, we need to seek solutions through resources that God sends our way. What is God's plan for you?

### God's Nudge

In our RV park, a motorhome was parked across from us in a spot only for overnight, but it had been there for over a month. We observed two women come and go and occasionally someone else would show up for a night and then leave. We learned the husband had had a heart attack and was in the hospital.

I considered giving them a prayer cloth but hardly ever saw them and knew nothing about them. For several days, I wondered if I should step out and approach them. I knew prayers had to be important for them. I know that others had reached out to me during my times of trouble. The power of having others offer support in the name of Jesus is amazing. *"And not only that, but we also boast in our afflictions, because we know that affliction produces endurance, endurance produces proven character, and proven character produces hope. This hope will not disappoint us, because God's love has been poured out in our hearts through the Holy Spirit who was given to us." -- Romans 5:3-5 (CSB)*

One afternoon, I saw two women return to the motorhome. Do I impose on them and take them a prayer cloth? The nudge would not go away. Finally, I grabbed a card that I had ready, wrote them a note, took a prayer cloth and found myself knocking on their door. After telling them who I was and that the prayer cloth represented many prayers being said for them, the sister-in-law began telling me of the traumas. He had not only had a severe heart attack, but also four open-heart surgeries during 11 weeks in ICU. At 65 years of age, the doctors did not give him much hope for survival in the early weeks. He was moved to a rehab center that week. Then one morning a week or so later, the wife and another woman came over from their motorhome. Their joy was obvious! They were going home on Saturday with her husband. He still had lots of healing to do. She told me how much the prayer cloth meant to her husband and how she displayed it at the rehab center to share with others who were also healing. She attributed her husband's survival to God's grace and all the many prayers said for him. Thank You, Lord, for this man and his family. Thank You for nudging me to follow Your leading. I await Your next nudge.

### Life Journeys

I spoke with a lady whose friend has Lou Gehrig's disease. She was selecting a prayer cloth to send to her. The colors in one cloth appealed to her while the message on another brought comfort for her friend. Of course, I would make her one that included the two in one cloth.

Once again, I began sewing and pondering this scripture that I have seen many times. *"Then Jacob made a vow: 'If God will be with me and watch over me during this journey I'm making, if he provides me with food to eat and clothing to wear, and if I return safely to my father's family, then the Lord will be my God.' " -- Genesis 28:20-21 (CSB)* Jacob said this after his dream of climbing Jacob's ladder and his night of struggling with God. Now, Jacob was speaking of the journey he was embarking on, not really knowing what he was going toward. Isn't that like many of us? Don't we often see ourselves heading off and not really knowing where this journey would take us? Oh yes, we usually have ideas about what we hope to find when we arrive at our destination. We even have ideas of what the journey might be like!

There are those occasions that we don't know what awaits us. Cancer patients, upon first learning of their diagnosis, don't have any idea what is to come. Most people who are suddenly diagnosed with some diseases are filled with concern simply because they are embarking on a journey about which they know nothing. Those high school and college graduates are also embarking on a new direction in their lives. They have heard stories and read books, but those are others' stories. They simply do not know how their journey will progress. What about the families who have a loved one heading off to military duty overseas? All the family members embark on new journeys. Perhaps you are starting a new job or a new career. Much uncertainty surrounds new working relationships.

As I embroidered *"God be with and protect me on this journey"* on her cloth, I prayed that prayer for her and for others. God stayed with Jacob and many others who journeyed with God through scripture just as God will with us during our journeys. Where are you and God going today? Be sure to take Him with you!

### *Prayer Power*

The RV park where we are staying had a Country Store each month. I got a table to show my prayer cloths, which are only visual reminders of the power of prayers. Usually when I do this, I know that I won't sell many, which is ok! I do this to share the concept of praying for others. Sales are always nice since it allows me to continue giving prayer cloths away to those God leads me to.

As I sat and talked to many folks, I couldn't help but wonder if my time here was being used wisely. Late in the morning, a lady came by and paused. I explained what I was making, and she still didn't say anything, but her eyes were fixed on the cloths as she gently touched them. As her eyes moistened, I knew that something was happening within her, so I prayed for God's comfort to be with her.

Finally, she said, "These are biblical." She began to tell me of her church's ministry with prayer handkerchiefs. One lady had cancer in five locations of her body and was not expected to live. Several from the church brought in handkerchiefs and laid hands on them and prayed for her healing. One person from the group took the blessed handkerchiefs to her and she put them on her pillow in her bed for her to lay upon, others beside her bed and others to drape on her arms as she lay. That was five years ago and now she is still alive. My new friend was so thrilled to find my ministry that she ordered several. As I tell all who buy one, they enable me to give more away.

*"Blessed be the God and Father of our Lord Jesus Christ, the Father of mercies and the God of all comfort. He comforts us in all our affliction, so that we may be able to comfort those who are in any kind of affliction, through the comfort we ourselves receive from God." -- 2 Corinthians 1:3-4 (CSB)* Each of us can bring comfort to others in many ways. I pray that we each can find at least one someone, if not more, to share the good news and comfort of Christ. God bless you.

### God's In Control

Ever tried to get out of doing something? You feel you have overcommitted yourself; can someone else do this! I am leading a bible study at our RV Park, and I didn't feel that I was giving enough time to preparing the lesson. I wanted a better lesson for the folks attending and somehow, I didn't think I could give them what they deserved. Ok, Lord, guess it is up to You and me! Somehow, someway Lord, enable me to do what needs doing. Dragging my feet all the way, I pulled out the material and began plodding through it. Suddenly I realized that Rudy was giving a Power Point presentation on Wi-Fi immediately preceding the bible study in the same room and he was using the projector with his computer. I could put my bible study in a Power Point presentation and make it easier to lead and help me with remembering where I am! The content began to flow and quickly it was done.

One of the ladies in the bible study came by my home asking me to bring one of my prayer cloths to bible study, but didn't tell me why. I set up my computer, but before I could start the lesson, the lady who got the prayer cloth asked if we could pray for a relative's family that had suffered two tragedies within a week. First, their house had burnt to the ground and then, the 19-year-old daughter was in a near fatal auto accident suffering severe head trauma. Not knowing if she would live, we began praying for her. We needed to pray for her complete recovery.

By the time we finished, I knew the program I planned was not appropriate for that day. However, recently I had done a program for a church's prayer volunteers that was on my computer! Quickly I switched gears and shared this program. We spent the hour reading scriptures about prayers, sharing ideas, and sharing answers we receive to prayers. God heard my prayer and not only gave me the program, but I also have the next week's program done! *"Ask, and it will be given to you. Seek, and you will find. Knock, and the door will be opened to you. For everyone who asks receives, and the one who seeks finds, and to the one who knocks, the door will be opened." -- Matthew 7:7-8 (CSB)*

## Moses, God, Me

Over the years, I have led a couple of programs on prayer. The joy of doing something like this always opens me to others' ideas and reminders that either I forgot or simply didn't make the connection to until someone pointed it out.

Such is the verse: *"But Moses sought the favor of the Lord his God: 'Lord, why does your anger burn against your people you brought out of the land of Egypt with great power and a strong hand? Why should the Egyptians say, 'He brought them out with an evil intent to kill them in the mountains and eliminate them from the face of the earth'? Turn from your fierce anger and relent concerning this disaster planned for your people. Remember your servants Abraham, Isaac, and Israel — you swore to them by yourself and declared, 'I will make your offspring as numerous as the stars of the sky and will give your offspring all this land that I have promised, and they will inherit it forever.' So the Lord relented concerning the disaster he had said he would bring on his people." -- Exodus 32:11-14 (CSB)*

I had not made the connection of this conversation between Moses and God as a prayer! But it is. What a wonderful example of the power of prayer from Moses, who had followed God reluctantly. This from the man who had stood up to Pharaoh as he followed God's instructions. From the man who had risked the anger, frustration, fear of millions of people who followed him daily in the desert. Through it all Moses maintained his dependency, trust and faith in God who led him. Moses had nurtured his relationship with God, dedicated his life to doing God's will, sought God's guidance, and encouraged others to do the same.

That day came when Moses saw God's anger toward the same people God saved using Moses as the front person to do the work. What a wonderful display of Moses' conversation/prayer with God that allowed Moses the privilege of speaking boldly to God. And God listened! How can this example apply to me today? We can follow Moses' example through our conversations and prayers with God.

### Watch Over You

Daily occurrences are but a mere beginning of the ways we see God at work in our days. In the western sky, the sun, clouds, and atmosphere combined for a gorgeous sunset. A walk at Boyce Thompson Arboretum east of Phoenix revealed beauty as God had arranged it in the birds' feather combinations as well as the flower petal arrangements in the plants growing in the desert environment. In church this morning, we lit candles in memory of the saints in our lives. The display of the small candles all lit warmed my heart and evoked loving memories.

While talking to our twin grandsons, they began to giggle and giggle. We had no idea what brought about the giggles until their Mother described what was happening in their living room. The joy of the giggles lightened our day. As I remember their giggles, I smile. My mail contained a note from a friend that reinforced why I continue to make prayer cloths. The story in the book I am reading describes relationships that exhibit both joy and suffering. Without the sufferings how do we know joy?

*"I lift my eyes toward the mountains. Where will my help come from? My help comes from the Lord, the Maker of heaven and earth. He will not allow your foot to slip; your Protector will not slumber. Indeed, the Protector of Israel does not slumber or sleep. The Lord protects you; the Lord is a shelter right by your side. The sun will not strike you by day or the moon by night. The Lord will protect you from all harm; he will protect your life. The Lord will protect your coming and going both now and forever." -- Psalms 121:1-8 (CSB)*

If God is watching over me so well, then I am free to enjoy all that surrounds me as a blessing from God. No matter what surrounds me, God is with me. That assurance of God presence always with me allows me to watch for Him in everything each day. Open my eyes each day to see God, open my ears to hear Him, open my heart to accept Him. What will I see next? What will you see next?

### Storytelling

We hear in the news everyday about people who encounter evil events which totally disrupt their lives. From each other, we hear stories about God's mercy and grace that fill us with awe and joy. In magazines, stories remind us of how fortunate we are and of how God helps others in need. Cards often carry inspiring messages that direct us to trust in God's grace and seek His protection.

Sometimes we find ourselves around others who don't walk with God, or at least their words and actions lead us to that conclusion. Yet some people make their faith obvious without offending or judging others. Always we find people who we don't know how important God is or isn't in their lives. I find myself listening for telltale clues in their conversational choices or their actions toward others.

When I am not sure about someone's reception of conversation about God or about serving others, I often decide to test the water so to speak.

Scriptural thoughts pass through my mind as I contemplate some conversation with others: *"Protect me, God, because I trust in you. I said to the LORD, 'You are my Lord. Every good thing I have comes from you.' As for the godly people in the world, they are the wonderful ones I enjoy." -- Psalms 16:1-3 (NCV)*

It is easy to then proceed with talking about, for example, my prayer cloth ministry. Response ranges for no interest at all to a long warm conversation about prayers. God then leads me as to where to go next with the conversation. It means I must risk their rejection of what is important to me. I learned not to take it as a personal affront! Their lack of interest is not my concern. I have proceeded as directed by God. Their response is their own responsibility.

This past week was one of those conversations as we attended an event we don't normally attend. Yes, we found some Godly folks, but we also found some who had no interest. Was the time worth spending at the event? Yes, even though we had little in common with many. Two conversations may result in fruit for God. We may never know, but we got to plant seeds. And we did not experience personal rejection. We did avoid some people because all God showed us was closed doors.

Lord, allow us to see open doors for us to tell others of Your comfort, grace and mercy. Help us to risk rejection for You, knowing that You are there to protect us.

### Heavy Burdens

Some of us carry heavy burdens. I just finished making a prayer cloth for a 6-year-old boy who is to have brain surgery this month. I can only imagine what concerns his parents have. A long-time friend just celebrated the life of her husband who passed away far too early. Many families are separated from one another due to military service overseas with dangers looming daily. A young woman I know searches for direction in her life and relationships. Another lady still hurts after losing her husband a year ago after 52 years of marriage.

We all know folks who carry very heavy burdens. Sometimes knowing others' burdens make our burdens seem so inconsequential. Our burdens are burdens. How do we deal with the load?

When we traveled in Guatemala with our son many years ago, I remember seeing many people carrying heavy loads on their heads, walking for miles that way. To me, it seemed impossible to accomplish the task. Those people learned to carry loads like that as children and the loads got larger and heavier as they got older. So, they grew up with their ability to carry loads.

Often, we find burdens thrust upon us unexpectedly while other burdens creep up on us gradually and perhaps, we don't see (or want to see them) until the load gets too big. David cried out to the Lord about the burdens that weigh him down. ***"Cast your burden on the Lord, and he will sustain you; he will never allow the righteous to be shaken." -- Psalms 55:22 (CSB)***

This seems impossible to do, just like the people who carry heavy loads on their head. We must begin somewhere, and the ability to cast those cares on the Lord gets easier the more we do it. That doesn't mean that we never think about the issue again or ponder options for resolutions. It means, for me, that we allow the worry to rest with God. This frees our thinking to consider our role, our options, and our responsibilities to examine through prayers what is God's direction for us. We keep our eyes open for signs of that direction in the circumstances that exist around us.

Let us start with the small burdens of our life, casting those cares upon the Lord so that when the heavy burdens occur (and they will), we can go into automatic casting of cares upon the Lord. What burden small or large are you willing to give to God? Lord, help us to recognize our burdens and allow You to carry them for us while we follow Your leading on the journey.

### Build a Snowman

Hope. Laughter. Fun. Illness. Humor. Despair. Faith. What do these words have in common? I made some prayer cloths using fabric created by a friend. It had printed on it *"We can build a snowman."* Yes, it is a seasonal type of fabric, and I pondered a long time as to how appropriate it might be for my prayer cloths. My first impression was one of fun and cold temperatures. I remember building snowmen with the kids when they were little. The joy of watching them frolic in the snow, listening to their voices, and hearing such happy sounds that represented joyful times, fun times. The thought brought a smile to my face.

What do I embroidery on them as a scripture or comment to tie into the purpose of the prayer cloths? Many medical professionals have validated the importance of humor and laughter in the healing process. Sometimes the best medicine is a good laugh with others, or even at our own situations, or at the difficulties that we face. Laughter seems to lighten the load. Memories of good times in our lives also provide reflective thinking that can bring a smile to our face. Memories of the laughter in our lives may not bring up the exact joke or event, but it will bring up the feelings of the moment. When we are dealing with an illness of our own or of a loved one, our focus can center entirely on despair, the illness, the problems involved with the situation. Perhaps this focus on snowmen can help stir up memories of better days and bring a smile!

*"Finally brothers and sisters, whatever is true, whatever is honorable, whatever is just, whatever is pure, whatever is lovely, whatever is commendable — if there is any moral excellence and if there is anything praiseworthy — dwell on these things. Do what you have learned and received and heard from me, and seen in me, and the God of peace will be with you." -- Philippians 4:8-9 (CSB)*

A snowman causes a child to hope it snows enough to go outside and play in it. A snowman brings out the child in us to use our creativity to create the biggest, the most unusual, and the best dressed one we can build. As I pondered all of these thoughts, these words finally came to me, "With God's Angels..." we can build a snowman. Yes, with God's angels, we can do most anything. Our faith can guide us through the most difficult of days. These prayer cloths can hopefully bring a smile as they deal with illness, loss, grief, pain, or the many other struggles that we endure. May each of you remember a snowman that brought you a smile and praise God for the snow that allowed you to build it.

Thank you to the designer, Terri Degenkolb of *Whimsicals* by Terri, for the challenge your fabric brought my way. Terri's mother, Jackie Conaway (in her heavenly home now) was one of my quilting mentors and fellow NOMADS member. She and Terri started a fabric/pattern/book design company, *Whimsicals* at *https:// whimsicalquilts.com/*.

## Light Guides Us

While making one of my prayer cloths, I wanted to use a lighthouse embroidery pattern on it. What scripture would I use to go with it? I found the following three that got me thinking.

*"Lord, you light my lamp; my God illuminates my darkness." -- Psalms 18:28 (CSB)* I thought of ships at sea coming toward shore, perhaps in the dark or in the fog, praying for a sign that shore is near. They glide through the water, surrounded by darkness, only to see this flashing light from the lighthouse. For them, that becomes the knot at the end of the rope so to speak! Of course, with the radar that most ships have, lighthouses don't provide as much service as they once did. Suddenly with the presence of the light, hope springs to life as the light guides them safely through the perilous waters.

*"Give light to my eyes" -- Psalms 13:3 (NIV)* As I was sewing, the light at the needle on the machine was not as bright as I needed since I was sewing on black fabric. It was hard to see where I was going. My eyes needed more light to keep my stitching on the correct line. How often do we find ourselves needing more light on a subject to understand what the situation requires of us? We ask, "God give light to my eyes" or perhaps understanding to my soul. This scripture tells me we depend on God for the guidance to go where He wants us to go.

*"Send your light and your truth; let them lead me." -- Psalms 43:3 (CSB)* I used this one on the prayer cloth as it struck me as the request we seek from God often. Help us to know what You want us to do, where You want us to go. The image of the lighthouse sending forth its light, guiding the ships and crews into safe waters, reminded me of how God helps send me light to guide me into safe places of my life. We still might have to encounter some rough water along the way, but the light is guiding us wherever we go.

May God provide light for our eyes, helping us go the direction that He wants for us to go. May we all give our praises to God for that guidance.

## Compassion

On our way to Texas from Casa Grande, Arizona, we stopped in Tucson, when a telephone call took us back to Casa Grande to show someone our motorhome (it was for sale). He was flying down from Spokane, Washington, so we figured it was worth going back to show. He chose not to buy anything for now, meaning we could continue our trip.

 Now you might think that the time was wasted and our trip back to our park was not important, but let me tell you the rest of the story. In talking to one of the residents, I learned about several people who were still in the park and having major health problems which were keeping them in Casa Grande for now. Had we not gone back, I might not have known this information for some time.

 As I sat at my computer, I open the scriptures that I read on my calendar and found this scripture: *"Therefore, as God's chosen ones, holy and dearly loved, put on compassion, kindness, humility, gentleness, and patience." -- Colossians 3:12 (CSB)*

There were moments after I heard about the folks needing treatments that I pondered which ones I should give a prayer cloth. I didn't know all of them very well, but knew who they were. I only had a few available and nothing appropriate for one of the ladies. I knew what God wanted me to do. I pulled out some prayer cloths, made one quickly for one lady and took them to all these folks. I had no idea where they are spiritually, but knew that God did know. Several times since then, they have come to mind, and I send up a prayer for the procedures they have coming up.

The scripture also comes with a comment on my calendar that reminded me of how important sharing acts of kindness are to all. How I praise God for nudging me into remembering all these folks then and in the days to come as they face surgery, treatments, and recovery.

Each of us has opportunities to share kindnesses, compassion, and patience with others. Sometimes we get it right and do what God's wants and sometimes we fail to act because we are distracted by our own lives. Let us each look for opportunities to follow God's nudging in touching someone else's life.

### *FROG*

Over the weekend, our RV park was involved in the Relay for Life event to raise money for cancer research. I made a Hope prayer cloth to include in the raffle for our park at the event. It went to a friend of mine who told me her story!

I went to her RV to give her the prayer cloth. When I got inside, I saw many frogs! Not live ones but stuffed, soft ones of many sizes that she could collect. I've seen a lot of collections that folks carry with them as they travel, but I had not seen frogs as a collection.

I gave her the prayer cloth and learned that she plans to give it to a lady who recently found out that she had a treatable pancreatic cancer and had just started her treatment. I asked her about her frogs and their significance to her. Then she told me about her frogs. As she travels, she collects the frogs. As she meets folks in need, she gives them a frog, telling them it is to remind them to "Fully Rely On God" - FROG. What a great visual reminder of relying on God. A frog has already gone to her friend with pancreatic cancer. My friend is also a cancer survivor and believes that God gave her the peace to go through her ordeal.

That phrase reminds me of Paul's instructions: ***"Rejoice in the Lord always. I will say it again: Rejoice! Let your gentleness be evident to all. The Lord is near. Do not be anxious about anything, but in every situation, by prayer and petition, with thanksgiving, present your requests to God. And the peace of God, which transcends all understanding, will guard your hearts and your minds in Christ Jesus." -- Philippians 4:4-7 (NIV)*** Perhaps all of us need to keep frogs around to remind us to Fully Rely on God! I'll never look at a frog the same way again!

## Scripture Inspired

### Many Trials

Reading scripture usually leads me to looking at footnotes and other related scriptures. One such search this week led me to: ***"Consider it a great joy, my brothers and sisters, whenever you experience various trials, because you know that the testing of your faith produces endurance. And let endurance have its full effect, so that you may be mature and complete, lacking nothing."*** *-- James 1:2-4 (CSB)*

Each of us is shaped and developed by the journey of our life. At times our path seems smooth and pleasant. Sometimes the journey is rough, with lots of boulders and problems in the way. How do we handle those bumps along the way? We can choose to be bitter, annoyed, angry, or frustrated about having the problem OR we can choose to direct our thoughts and actions toward solutions, assistance, growth and prayer, trusting Christ to lead us in all ways through the situation.

Looking back over my life allows me to see where God was developing my ability to trust in Him more. Trials allowed me to develop patience, compassion, understanding, empathy, etc., but only as I allow Christ to walk with me in those trials. The ones that I tried to fix, solve, and ignore on my own left me frustrated, angry, and stressed. Asking Christ to be my guide, my comforter, my teacher, and my savior enabled me to find solutions, understanding, and acceptance, not only of myself, but also of others. This scripture reminds me that this development process goes on and on and my work is still not complete.

Fortunately, I can see improvement periodically and I praise God for His guidance in my life. The pure joy of trials for me comes in knowing that, with Christ's help, I have another opportunity to learn something new about myself that will make me stronger, wiser and even more trusting in Him. With His help I can do whatever He leads me to do. My journey with Him is enjoyed as He walks beside me during good times and recognized as carrying me through the tough times. Ask Him to be your savior, your companion, your guide, and your friend always.

## Taming the Tongue

*"So too, though the tongue is a small part of the body, it boasts great things. Consider how a small fire sets ablaze a large forest. -- With the tongue we bless our Lord and Father, and with it we curse people who are made in God's likeness." -- James 3:5, 9 (CSB)* The whole text for James 3:1-12 is titled "Taming the Tongue" and is not a new one for me. I stumbled across it this week, probably because God knew I needed to refresh my memory about the dangers of the using the tongue inappropriately. Certain situations and certain people tend to put me, and perhaps others, into a mindset that triggers words and thoughts that are not edifying. Those words can be so destructive and hurtful, far more than we realize. All of us have memories of words said to us or about us that caused us great pain or sorrow. Often, we do not even realize that our words sometimes do the same to those around us, especially when we say them in a kidding manner.

How often do the words used when teasing someone reflect our real thoughts of judgment, rather than the fun and fellowship of laughing with one another about individual quirky habits? I hear people say, "Well, it's the truth," "I'm just being honest," "Would you rather I lie?" Communication deals with such delicate issues with fine lines of distinction. Correction, truth, and honesty are important, but so are timing, manner of delivery, tone of voice, and our attitude and follow up. Even when driving, angry words said to other drivers hurt those in the car with me as well as myself. Perhaps a prayer said for their safety and the safety of those around them is more edifying.

Lord, help me to be wise and think before allowing my tongue to spew out words that hurt, criticize bitterly, and judge others. Help me to remember to pray silently for someone rather than to verbally attack. Help me to seek forgiveness when I do spew out words inappropriately. Help me to choose words wisely when needing to confront or correct someone.

## Our Security

As I reread the Psalm, I saw a celebration of security found in life as viewed by a believer in our Lord Jesus Christ. Verse 8 is the center: *"As we have heard..."* from our fathers, *"...so have we seen..."* with our own eyes *"...in the city of the Lord Almighty, in the city of our God: God makes her secure forever." -- Psalms 48:8 (NIV)*

Christ views me as His own just as God views Zion as His City; therefore, I am secure in Christ forever by yielding Him as my Savior. Other verses show Zion to be protected from outside evil forces, strong in belief, and able to ward off attacks, all because of faith in their Lord and Savior Jesus. Read this last section from the Psalms as though you are Zion: ***"Walk about Zion, go around her, count her towers, consider well her ramparts, view her citadels, that you may tell of them to the next generation. For this God is our God for ever and ever; he will be our guide even to the end." -- Psalms 48:12-14 (NIV)***

What are your strengths (count them), how strong is your Godly defense system, where are the high points of your Christian life, and what stories do you tell to your children about your life with Christ? How can I improve my relationship with Christ? These thoughts for me are so special. My prayer is for you to also seek and find comfort in a close relationship with Christ. For me, Christ is my ***"God for ever and ever; he will be my guide even to the end."***

## Soothing Words

At times I need to be reminded of thoughts found abundantly in Psalms such as, ***"I will keep watch for you, my strength, because God is my stronghold." -- Psalms 59:9 (CSB) I am at rest in God alone; my salvation comes from him. He alone is my rock and my salvation, my stronghold; I will never be shaken." -- Psalms 62:1-2 (CSB)***

These words:

- are like ointment on a sore, they soothe the soul.

- create a confidence that gives me courage to step out in faith to follow God.

- create a sense of calmness that allows clear thought.

- help me understand how important God is in my life, and why I should keep reading and studying God's word.

- bring the joy and praise of God within me to expression.

True, not every day finds me so upbeat and confident, but taking time to read these words certainly improve the chances of me seeing God at work in the events of each day. How often does God appear in the events of my life and I fail to notice His presence? The more that I look for Him each day, the more I find Him. He is the fortress that surrounds me with His protection, the savior that fills me with His love, the loving friend that enables me to experience His comfort, and the rock that keeps me focused on His world. How can you see God as your fortress, savior, loving friend, and rock today?

## Scripture Helps

Every now and then I manage to have fun with one of my faults and today I found scripture that really allowed me to stretch a bit, but have some fun with a serious subject – eating too much!!! Knowing my cholesterol is slightly high and weight gain since retiring is not good, I decided to begin praying for help. Then I read a Psalms and the humor hit. Allow me to share with you the actual reading.

> *"Save me, O God, for the <u>waters</u> have come up to my neck. I sink in the <u>miry depths,</u> where there is no foothold. I have come into the <u>deep waters</u>; the <u>floods</u> engulf me. I am worn out calling for help; my throat is parched. My eyes fail looking for my God. <u>Those who</u> hate me without reason outnumber the hairs of my head; <u>many</u> are my enemies without cause, those who seek to destroy me. I am forced to <u>restore</u> what I did not <u>steal</u>. You, God, know my folly; my guilt is not hidden from you." -- Psalms 69:1-5 (NIV)*

For any of you who have similar feelings, may we all pray together for strength to just say no to our enemy. Now my playful version to help with overeating and changing only the underlined words to post on the refrigerator:

> *"Save me, O God for the* food *has come up to my neck. I sink in the* fatty *depths, where there is no foothold. I have come into the* local restaurants*; and the* aromas *engulf me. I am worn out calling for help; my throat is parched. My eyes fail looking for God.* The fat grams *that hate me without reason outnumber the hairs of my head;* desserts *are my enemies without cause, they seek to destroy me. I am forced to* reject *what I did not* say no *to* consuming. *You, God, know my folly; my guilt is not hidden from you." Psalms 69:1-5* (Carolyn's adaptation)

## Rare Treasures

*"A house is built by wisdom, and it is established by understanding; by knowledge the rooms are filled with every precious and beautiful treasure." -- Proverbs 24:3-4 (CSB)* My first image was of a house, or perhaps a home. Yes, a lot of wisdom needs to go into the building of a house. Is the house used for a couple, a small family, a large family, or for single adults? Is it in a hot or cold climate, rainy or dry? What is the terrain like for the foundation? And a million other questions, it seems, go into making a wise decision about the house. As these questions are considered, an understanding of their purpose comes to focus. Studying the construction, the features offered, and learning about the details of the rooms in the house, allows for filling the rooms with precious possessions.

What about a child instead of a house? The development of our children begins before birth with careful thought about what the mother eats, the exercise she can achieve, the love in her heart for that child. The father, even though not carrying the child, contributes to that development in how he cares for the mother. As the child grows, wise discipline, a loving environment, praise, and encouragement all contribute positively to the child's understanding concerning responsibility, self-esteem, creativity, and love. The rooms of the child's heart and soul become filled with rare and beautiful treasures.

What about relationships with fellow workers, friends, other Christians, other family members, and any number of other situations? What kind of wise thought goes into considering how we speak to or about others? Do we care enough to learn about the cares and concerns of those around us? Do we care enough to pray for their salvation and their needs and share those prayers with them? Can we visualize their hearts and souls filled with rare and beautiful treasures? My prayer is for God to help me look for and find the rare and beautiful treasures in the people I meet. May you also wisely consider what it takes to find the rare and beautiful treasures around you.

## Spread The News

Ever wonder how the early church grew? The early Christians endured more persecution than we can even imagine. In watching a video about the lives of Peter and Paul, the words of scripture became more vivid while watching actors try and portray the accounts from Acts. I was struck by the loneliness, the rejection, the discouragement, and the fear they must have encountered going from town to town, never knowing how people would respond to their message. Yet, they continued to press on with just what they had on their backs to the next town, knowing that God was with them. The confidence in their message was astonishing even in the face of death. Communities of Christians developed, leaders emerged, and the gospel spread through the work of the Holy Spirit touching the lives of the disciples. The people in the Christian communities who had only heard about Jesus and never met Him, sometimes found themselves arguing and imposing their own rules causing the disciples, especially Paul, to write many letters of encouragement and correction to them.

I was struck by these verses in the concluding chapter of Hebrews: *"Keep your life free from the love of money. Be satisfied with what you have, for he himself has said, I will never leave you or abandon you. Therefore, we may boldly say, The Lord is my helper; I will not be afraid. What can man do to me? Remember your leaders who have spoken God's word to you. As you carefully observe the outcome of their lives, imitate their faith. Jesus Christ is the same yesterday, today, and forever." -- Hebrews 13:5-8 (CSB)*

These words are as true for us today as for the early Christian communities. In this time of economic uncertainty, layoffs, stocks declining, school shootings, disrespect for teachers, policemen, authority, parents, children, and laws, we need to unify in the spreading of the gospel. We Christians need to claim for ourselves the fullness of life with Christ, and then tell all around us about the availability of Jesus' saving grace and love. Who can you share the good news with today?

### *Parched Places*

A friend had a string of difficult years, months, days, or moments. *"The Lord will always lead you, satisfy you in a parched land, and strengthen your bones. You will be like a watered garden and like a spring whose water never runs dry." -- Isaiah 58:11 (CSB)*

According to Galatians 1:18 through 2:1, Paul spent many years in preparation for his ministry after his conversion experience. He used that time to learn and to become strong in his understanding of Jesus as his Lord and Savior. I can only imagine the degree of discouragement, loneliness, fatigue, and rejection he experienced as he traveled in foreign lands. Yet, at each desperate moment, some event would occur to renew him and enable him to continue with his journeys. A strong foundation was needed for his journeys to enable him to endure the persecution and hardship of traveling that came to him from all directions. Yet even during his trials and hardships, God sent the living water needed for a garden to flourish. Paul saw the garden blooming through the people's lives that he touched. He felt his soul renewed by witnessing faith develop in others. Paul survived many parched places.

Though many of us are not called to travel and witness in the manner that Paul did, we often encounter difficulties like Paul did. Just as Paul needed the strength of the Holy Spirit to guide and sustain him, we also need the Holy Spirit. Isaiah's message is as vital to us today as it was during his life. Knowing that Christ is my foundation enables me to continue doing, living, and serving just as a watered garden continues to grow, flower, and reseed. God provides His Son, Jesus, as the living water, the spring of water that never ceases to refresh me, to cleanse me, to heal my heart and mind.

Living life with Christ does not promise a life free of problems or parched places, but it does promise a way of living with and through our problems as victors instead of victims.

### In His Presence

*"He will revive us after two days, and on the third day he will raise us up so we can live in his presence. Let's strive to know the Lord. His appearance is as sure as the dawn. He will come to us like the rain, like the spring showers that water the land." -- Hosea 6:2-3 (CSB)*

A couple came to mind because they are retiring suddenly when a good company offer became available. The future is suddenly different, uncertain, and everything is changing. They face selling the home and relocating to an unknown location. So many unknowns, yet the one constant is the presence of the Lord. He is with us always; it doesn't matter where that place is. That place often changes because the Lord's presence is everywhere. The Israelites were extremely anxious as they fled Egypt, and they spent 40 years wandering in the desert. Yet, God was with them, guiding them, providing for food and water, protection from enemies, and giving them a path. Ruth left her homeland to travel with her mother-in-law Naomi and found peace and satisfaction in her life through the presence of the Lord. Abram left Haran with his wife Sarai to go to a new land. All these people, and many more, experienced hardships, but they also experienced great events that they had not expected. Some of the people they came across touched their lives in unexpected ways because the Lord is available to us in all places.

All these people had difficult transitions, but the common denominator was the presence of the Lord with each. As we take new directions in our life, we also take the presence of the Lord with us to each new place. No matter where we go, God goes with us. We merely need to acknowledge that our journey includes His presence. Request His presence to be with you wherever you go today and every day.

### A God-Incidence

Have you ever received a phone call followed by a series of events that caused you to wonder about the timing, the impact it had on your life, and was it a coincidence or a God-incidence? The night before we left for New Orleans, I received a telephone call from a stranger. She was, however, a member of NOMADS which we also support doing mission work. We soon learned that, on our drive, we would pass by her location within one mile. We stopped, and as we sat in her living room as strangers, our sharing made us feel more like family.

After we left, I couldn't help but ponder the family of God. *"To those chosen, living as exiles dispersed abroad in Pontus, Galatia, Cappadocia, Asia, and Bithynia, chosen according to the foreknowledge of God the Father, through the sanctifying work of the Spirit, to be obedient and to be sprinkled with the blood of Jesus Christ. May grace and peace be multiplied to you." -- 1 Peter 1:1-2 (CSB)* As the disciples traveled through their world, they meet many strangers, yet they also meet other believers who shared their love for Christ. That shared love for Christ is important for us to seek as we travel. Some of us can travel great distances, others travel within smaller boundaries, yet all of us encounter strangers every day. I always wondered how Paul found the Christians in the new cities he entered. Some he found by going to the synagogues, some by speaking on the street corners, some through mutual acquaintances that he sought by name, and some by risking speaking of his faith to strangers.

I discover Christians among strangers when I speak of prayer, wear my cross necklace, or when I listen for content in conversation that offers opportunities to either ask or share. Why do I do this? God has accepted me into the most wonderful family in the world and I feel so humbled to be worthy of His acceptance. If I can be accepted, then so can anyone else. I know that my God-incidence on our trip is leading me on another part of my faith journey, and I praise Him for that phone call. What strangers are in your path today?

### *Your Mentors*

Paul's letters were, of course, written to specific people such as the Colossians in 1:3-14 & 4:18. The letter was from Paul, but his writing includes Timothy as they traveled together – thus the use of the "we." At one point in this text, I am leaving a blank space for you to fill in the name of your mentor or mentors. Allow the "you" (referring to the Colossians) used throughout this text to mean you.

*"We always thank God, the Father of our Lord Jesus Christ, when we pray for you, for we have heard of your faith in Christ Jesus and of the love you have for all the saints because of the hope reserved for you in heaven. You have already heard about this hope in the word of truth, the gospel that has come to you. It is bearing fruit and growing all over the world, just as it has among you since the day you heard it and came to truly appreciate God's grace. You learned this from Epaphras,(_____) our dearly loved fellow servant. He is a faithful minister of Christ on your behalf, and he has told us about your love in the Spirit." -- Colossians 1:3-8 (CSB)*

*"For this reason also, since the day we heard this, we haven't stopped praying for you. We are asking that you may be filled with the knowledge of his will in all wisdom and spiritual understanding, so that you may walk worthy of the Lord, fully pleasing to him: bearing fruit in every good work and growing in the knowledge of God, being strengthened with all power, according to his glorious might, so that you may have great endurance and patience, joyfully giving thanks to the Father, who has enabled you to share in the saints' inheritance in the light. He has rescued us from the domain of darkness and transferred us into the kingdom of the Son he loves. In him we have redemption, the forgiveness of sins." -- Colossians 1:9-14 (CSB)*

*"... I, Paul, am writing this greeting with my own hand. Remember my chains. Grace be with you." -- Colossians 4:18 (CSB)*

Is the Holy Spirit leading you to remember the mentor for whom you might "fill in the blank" by thanking them or praying for their work? Is the Spirit leading you to pray for someone who needs an open heart and soul to receive the love of Christ, or to perhaps open your own heart? May this personalized greeting from Paul, a mighty saint of old, add meaning to your week.

### Showing Mercy

*"And who is my neighbor? " -- Luke 10:29 (CSB)* is the question asked of Jesus which led to the telling of the good Samaritan parable. Jesus concluded the parable with a question: *"Which of these three do you think proved to be a neighbor to the man who fell into the hands of the robbers? " -- Luke 10:36 (CSB)* The answer was, *" 'The one who showed mercy to him,' he said." -- Luke 10:37 (CSB)*

Neighbors – who are they? Is it just the person next door? Doesn't that title include our co-workers – all of them, not just the ones we like. Are strangers our neighbors? Must our neighbors dress in certain ways, speak certain languages, or behave in a manner similar to our own?

Mercy – must we earn it? Is mercy a reward for certain behavior or a gift unearned? Who deserves mercy? Is mercy merely something we receive? How do we show mercy? What situations require mercy?

Challenging questions, when applied considering the relationships, acquaintances, and strangers in our lives today. Jesus, allow us to watch for our neighbors and look for ways to show mercy during the coming week.

### The Outsiders

*"Act wisely toward outsiders, making the most of the time. Let your speech always be gracious, seasoned with salt, so that you may know how you should answer each person." -- Colossians 4:5-6 (CSB)* The scripture above kept coming back to me even when I tried to disregard it. So apparently God wants me to use this one!

These are difficult words. Are outsiders and strangers the same? Perhaps, but outsiders can be people we know, but who are different than we are. In many states, an outsider is anyone who has not lived in the area for generations. In high school, an outsider might be a new kid in school, a kid with out-of-date clothing, nerdy glasses, or any number of other out of sync characteristics. In the New Testament, outsiders were Gentiles, Samaritans, Romans - those who did not keep the Jewish laws, to name a few.

The scripture tells us to be wise. Careless words or actions speak loudly and are not forgotten. They also cause those same outsiders to form opinions of us. If they know that we claim to be Christian, how does our treatment of them affect their image of a Christian?

It is so easy to dislike people or even to just be apathetic toward them when they fit the mold of an outsider. Yet Jesus sought out the outsider continuously. But He challenged and encouraged them to change in a manner that allowed them to want to follow Him. If He is our example, then shouldn't we consider how we treat outsiders?

## Path to Follow

*"In their hearts humans plan their course, but the LORD establishes their steps." -- Proverbs 16:9 (NIV)* No matter what journey we find ourselves taking, roadblocks appear which often make us wonder if we should have followed another path. Perhaps dreams seem to be unfulfilled.

Whose plan are we following, ours or God's? Do our prayers reflect the desire to recognize God's plan? In expressing our desires, do we leave room for God to mold and shape our desires into the plan He has for us?

Is our tunnel vision oriented toward one particular goal obtained through one specific plan? Is our vision scanning all around us for what God is providing every step of the way?

We can claim hope and future through the words in Jeremiah. Lord, help me to live my life following the plans You have for me. Continue to reveal to me each day the path You have for me, allow me to recognize it, and especially to have the confidence to follow You.

## Seeing Hope

As I observe the news, conversations among different groups of people, prayer requests and individual contacts, I see hope amidst our daily stresses and trials. Sometimes hope is not very visible. Scripture brings visibility to hope with this text: *"Humble yourselves, therefore, under the mighty hand of God, so that he may exalt you at the proper time, casting all your cares on him, because he cares about you. Be sober-minded, be alert. Your adversary the devil is prowling around like a roaring lion, looking for anyone he can devour. Resist*

**him, firm in the faith, knowing that the same kind of sufferings are being experienced by your fellow believers throughout the world. The God of all grace, who called you to his eternal glory in Christ, will himself restore, establish, strengthen, and support you after you have suffered a little while."
-- 1 Peter 5:6-10 (CSB)**

Suffering sometimes is a part of His plan! During that period of time, seek more of God as growth can happen even during and through the suffering. Scriptures can help us see hope and trust when all else around us is bleak.

The devil appears to us in many forms – temptations, money, material goods, food, alcohol, drugs, sex, sports, judgments of others and you add to the list. Any of these things can be good parts of life, but when they control our life or are used in a manner out of God's plan for us, then they are like the roaring lion trying to devour us.

Let us keep our eyes on God's grace and the path He wants us to follow so that we too can share daily in the glory in Christ. His grace will lead us to those persons necessary to help us in our daily walks.

### Temptations

According to Matthew 4:1-11 Jesus faced his temptations from the devil. **"Then Jesus was led up by the Spirit into the wilderness to be tempted by the devil. -- Then Jesus told him, 'Go away, Satan! For it is written: Worship the Lord your God, and serve only him.' " -- Matthew 4:1, 10 (CSB)**

Isn't everyday filled with temptation, or even several temptations? Whether the temptation is overeating, gossiping, judging others, swearing, drinking too much, sitting in front of the TV or computer too long, spending too much money, allowing our fears to rule, ignoring others, taking advantage of others, cheating, lying, etc., we find ourselves up against something every day.

How reassuring that Jesus faced temptations as He lived and walked this earth. His ability to face temptations gives me hope that I can also name my temptations "Satan" and tell them to go away in the name of Jesus. What are my temptations? What keeps me from living life as God wants?

Once I recognize my temptations, then I must learn how to call upon the strength of Jesus to overcome them. Jesus used the above scripture during His temptation and is an example for us to use. Should I leave myself notes around the house as reminders? Should I discuss my temptations with someone else to gain their support? Should I seek medical advice or support? Should I read up about any products, technology, or other avenues available to assist me? Should I pray for strength of overcome temptations? Yes, yes, and yes - all the above are tools for climbing out of the pit into which our temptations throw us. Let's keep our toolbox open and our bible close by.

### Simple Belief

From childhood we are programmed to work hard, do our best, study hard and make good grades, etc. As a parent, I too wanted my children to do all the above, plus more! Our parents gave us a work ethic of earning your own way in the world; there is no free lunch. So we strive, we labor, we persevere and we carry the weight of our own troubles and those of others as well. After many years the load gets heavy, and we get tired. Depression may set in. Discouragement allows a heaviness to settle over us. The picture of Atlas with the world on his shoulders is our image. He is bent over from the weight.

Jesus has a message for us: ***"Come to me, all of you who are weary and burdened, and I will give you rest." -- Matthew 11:28 (CSB)*** Now the question becomes, HOW? John finds the people asking the same question *" 'What can we do to perform the works of God?' they asked. Jesus replied, 'This is the work of God — that you believe in the one he has sent.' " -- John 6:28-29 (CSB)*

That seems so simple! Too simple! After all, nothing in life is free! Yet, God sent us Jesus to teach us about faith, love, and hope. Our new life begins with simple belief, yielding to His Lordship, and repentance. Our journey with God revolves around our trusting, believing, seeking, and being open to His presence. He carries our loads, He guides our paths, He soothes our pain, He cares for us, His sheep.

Why do we make it so hard? Yes, we still have jobs, responsibilities, and duties to fulfill, but having Jesus as our companion makes the loads lighter, the decisions easier, the directions clearer and the way more joyful.

### Our Light Shines

In our travels we occasionally stay overnight in the parking lot of a Wal-Mart. The first few times we stayed, we had a hard time sleeping because of the bright lights illuminating the lot. I finally made us some "boondocking" curtains from black cotton fabric to cover the bedroom windows. The front of the coach is still lighted, but the bedroom is darker. That intense light is one we want on the outside, but we want to cover it for sleeping. But do we want to cover all light?

*"No one lights a lamp and puts it under a basket, but rather on a lampstand, and it gives light for all who are in the house. In the same way, let your light shine before others, so that they may see your good works and give glory to your Father in heaven." -- Matthew 5:15-16 (CSB)*

A story was on TV about a clown leading a class for other clowns to teach them some lessons for doing hospital ministry. Their *"light"* through humor brings smiles, possibly laughter, and a brief respite from pain and suffering. Even thoughts of their visit renew the *"light"* for the sick.

A pastor at the church we attended is certainly a light! His love of God, Jesus, and the Holy Spirit shone and glistened. His message was one you experienced, not just heard. Why? He allowed the Holy Spirit to work in and through him to touch the congregation. The message he brought was about the light and there was no doubt the light lived in him and was part of all he believed. There was no putting "boondocking" curtains on his message!

How do we let our light shine? Do others see our *"light"* and know it is the light of Jesus? Or is our light a reflection of our personality, deeds, and talents for which we take personal credit? What praise goes to our Lord for what we do and who we are so that others know the source of our light? Perhaps our *"light"* needs the intensity of the Wal-Mart parking lot lights where even curtains have a hard time dimming it!

### Your Ways

Memories, memories, memories! We all have them good or bad, painful or joyous. Glancing backward allowed me to see some of the times when these words from Psalms spoke to me. *"Make your ways known to me, Lord; teach me your paths. Guide me in your truth and teach me, for you are the God of my salvation; I wait for you all day long." -- Psalms 25:4-5 (CSB)*

Writing a story found me reflecting on how the Lord once showed me the importance of finding peace from Him. There was the time of how His path of prayer enabled me to find resolution to a situation I could not control. On many occasions during a bible study, I gained understanding about myself from the lessons studied about some bible character. From the beginning of my conscious walk with my Lord, the awareness of the length, the variety, and sometimes the wandering of my journey, gives me hope for the future.

The hope comes not from learning so much, but from His grace and patience with my repeated omissions, my stumbles along the path of life, my judgments of others, my words that come before thinking and so on. My search for more of His truth continues. My hope is in knowing He will continue to walk with me over the hills and through the valleys of today and tomorrow – all I need to do is take His hand.

### The Raging Fire

Which way do we go? What do we do? How do we know if it's right? Many of us face questions and decisions on a daily basis. Some of the questions and decisions have tremendous impact on our life. Those are usually the ones that we wonder what God's will for our life is. We all want to do the right thing, make the best decision, and go the direction that takes us to the most successful use of our talents.

Even David in the Psalms wrote about his feelings on the subject: ***"I desire to do your will, my God; your law is within my heart." -- Psalms 40:8 (NIV)***

Max Lucado identifies knowing God's will for your life as *"The Fire of Your Heart"* with the following comment, *"As a young man I felt the call to preach. Unsure if I was correct in my reading of God's will for me, I sought the counsel of a minister I admired. His counsel still rings true. 'Don't preach,' he said, 'unless you have to.' As I pondered his words I found my answer: 'I have to. If I don't, the fire will consume me.' "* *

What fire rages in your heart? What gifts of the Spirit do you possess? Is God calling you to use your gifts in a new job, occupation, a new location for living, or a change to retirement? Is He calling you to a new relationship or a renewed relationship with family or friends? What talent lives in you that must be used? Are you a good administrator, manager, teacher, listener, companion, diagnostician, writer, problem solver, advisor, builder, organizer, thinker, parent, supporter, or ... Is God calling you first to Him? Ponder the fire raging in your heart.

*\**"The Great House of God"* by Max Lucado, Copyright 1997 Max Lucado, used by permission of HarperCollins Christian Publishing. www.harpercollinschristian.com*

### Amazing Grace

As we sang that good old favorite "*Amazing Grace*,"* it had an odd effect on me at that moment. It was as though the Holy Spirit descended once again on me as I remembered those times when God's grace was what kept me going.

Once again, this scripture found its way into my path: ***"But he said to me, 'My grace is sufficient for you, for my power is perfected in weakness.' Therefore, I will most gladly boast all the more about my weaknesses, so that Christ's power may reside in me." -- 2 Corinthians 12:9 (CSB)***

All of us watch children, adolescents, and young adults struggle to find their own path in life. I remember so well the conflicts, the struggles, the desire for independence, and the feelings of doing things my own way that usually led me through rough waters. I also remember reaching very low spots of feeling "lost" and being the "wretch" described in "*Amazing Grace*."

God's grace is always available for accepting just as easily as accepting a graduation or birthday gift. But we must ask. I remember that first time of really asking and wanting, knowing that a loving God existed, but knowing how undeserving I was. My weaknesses lead me to Him. My weakness keeps me with Him.

As I lay on a table having an MRI done on my neck to check the bone spurs growing there, my weakness of fear tried to surface, but again I sought out my friend, Jesus. For the 15 to 20 minutes of lying in that tube with the surface a mere 4 inches from my face, He and I took journeys together and all the mental pictures of that walk kept the fear away.

"*Amazing grace! How sweet the sound that saved a wretch like me! I once was lost but now am found; was blind but now I see*."* Praise God for His all-sufficient grace.

*"*Amazing Grace*," by John Newton, 1623, Public Domain

### Protect the Soul

***"What I tell you in the dark, speak in the light. What you hear in a whisper, proclaim on the housetops. Don't fear those who kill the body but are not able to kill the soul; rather, fear him who is able to destroy both soul and body in***

*hell." -- Matthew 10:27-28 (CSB)* As I read this scripture, the images of many people came to me. The stories of those people from 9/11 keep us aware of their last-minute conversations and decisions. The prayers said, the love expressed, and the pain involved are examples of this scripture. What a great gift their examples of faith are to a nation and a world. Protecting our soul is paramount. Helping a loved one protect their soul is equally important.

How many stories of strong faith and courage never make the news? Most stories seem mundane compared to 9/11, or other disasters but many people are afraid of such a variety of events, people, and things. Jesus wants us to trust in Him. Yes, our bodies will pass away; it is inevitable, and we cannot stop that process. But our souls live on forever and Jesus wants our souls with Him.

Can we possibly learn from those who told their heart wrenching stories of life lived and lost while holding the hand of Jesus? Let all those people not only from 9/11, or other disasters but from our own lives be examples for us to remember as we prepare our souls daily for that inevitable unknown day.

### Always Be Ready

I find my emotions on a roller coaster of sadness for lives lost; anger for the destruction of peace; uncertainty for what lies ahead; fear for those in harm's way; and hope for each to find inner peace. Jesus speaks words that enable me to focus on the historic events of the past and of those to come: *"But know this: If the homeowner had known what time the thief was coming, he would have stayed alert and not let his house be broken into. This is why you are also to be ready, because the Son of Man is coming at an hour you do not expect." -- Matthew 24:43-44 (CSB)*

Questions of non-violence versus violence and retaliation versus turn the other cheek seem to be prevalent currently and throughout all of history. We live in a world that struggles to know perfect peace. But each has his or her definition of peace and what it takes to bring it about for all. Christ came to bring us peace within, which allows us to live in a violent world. Look at the lives of the disciples who all except one died violent deaths in the name of Christ.

For me, I hope that all may come to know our Lord and Savior in a way that helps them to find the inner peace that allows us:

- to walk through whatever happens in this world.

- to prepare for that day when either He comes to live in our world again or

- to go to live in His kingdom.

Help us to know the importance of always being ready.

### Heal, Don't Tell

This scripture has intrigued me on more than one occasion! Mark 1:21-45 finds Jesus healing many people at the beginning of His ministry. After healing a man, Jesus: *"telling him, 'See that you say nothing to anyone; but go and show yourself to the priest, and offer what Moses commanded for your cleansing, as a testimony to them.' Yet he went out and began to proclaim it widely and to spread the news, with the result that Jesus could no longer enter a town openly. But he was out in deserted places, and they came to him from everywhere." -- Mark 1:44-45 (CSB)*

Why would Jesus tell the man not to tell anyone? According to Lev. 14:1-32, upon healing, someone with an infectious skin disease needed to see the priest for a cleansing ritual to validate his healing. Sacrifices were a part of that ritual. Jesus wanted the priest's validation of the healing not only to testify to the authorities about His ministry, but also to allow the person healed to reenter society.

The people Jesus healed brought in crowds of people interested in physical healing, thus causing a distraction to His message. It brought attention toward Him that hindered His real ministry, so He moved on to other cities and out to the hillsides. But the people followed Him, wanting what He offered for selfish reasons. Yet, He never failed to show compassion to those in need. And, of course, some actually came to really know Him as the Son of God after their physical healing. Today is no different than those days.

Since the sacrificial system is no longer practiced today, perhaps today's sacrifices might involve other kinds of offerings to God. Perhaps a giving of our time to prayer rather than watching more TV, a giving of our services in Jesus' name to others in need rather than another afternoon of our leisure, or a giving of our wealth to enable ministries in Jesus' name rather than buying ourselves another gadget. Or is the sacrifice one of giving up selfish desires for more time in relationships with our children and spouse? What sacrifices do we make in Jesus' name to proclaim the healing of our soul to the world?

## Ears to Hear

The Parable of the Sower is found in Mark 4:1-20. Jesus speaks: ***"Let anyone who has ears to hear listen." -- Mark 4:9 (CSB)*** The first image that came to mind was a conversation between a teen and a parent! Somehow the words and the message lose something as "communication" transmits between them. How many parents try to teach, tell, or advise a teen about any issue only to see that look, experience that sigh, or listen to rebuttal? How many teens try to explain something from their viewpoint, only to have the parent either jump to conclusions or issue orders without allowing the teen to finish their thought?

The second image that stirred my mind was one of two adults talking about faith coming from different viewpoints. Usually not much listening is taking place. Too often we try to prove our point without really hearing the unspoken questions or roadblocks that exist in good communication.

Jesus taught using everyday situations to try to get a point across to others. Often people recognized the situation, but did not understand the meaning in the story. Just as the two images described above leave parties to the communication wondering what the other was trying to say, Jesus' disciples left wondering what the parable meant. When Jesus was alone with His disciples, they asked Him to explain the meaning of the parable.

Wonder what life would be like if we all took the time to ask, "Help me to understand your point of view?" Now I realize that we won't all come to agree with each other, especially in some teen parent conversations. The fact that we heard one another out on an issue goes a long way toward understanding or acceptance. Just as it took time and patience for Jesus to spell out for the disciples the meaning of what appeared to be an obvious story, we need to take time to seek the meaning in our conversations. At that point "good seeds" can begin to grow, perhaps even the "seeds" that lead us toward an understanding of our Lord and life with Him. How may Jesus touch your ears for hearing the conversations of those around us, as well as His messages to us?

## My Steps

With many years yet to live (according to my calculations!) I find myself always seeking some way to stay active and productive in my walk with God.

*"A person's heart plans his way, but the Lord determines his steps." -- Proverbs*

*16:9 (CSB)* Yes, my heart leads me in a direction that fits what I enjoy doing, fits my skills, and appears to fill a need. Now I need the Lord to determine my steps. But I want Him to do that right now, today, this minute! I'm ready. Let's get going. What is the delay?

Can you see how patient I am? But aren't we all very much like that? Surely, I can't be the only person looking for the steps that the Lord wants me to follow. My prayer at this point is to channel my eagerness, to allow the Lord to prepare the way, and to keep me tuned into His frequency, ready to recognize the steps He prepares. Yes, I have many questions about the steps to follow.

Why can't I just do what I want without following rules and regulations? Seems as though society and government help determine some of my steps as well! Yes, I must jump through some of society's rules, but the Lord will help with the steps by bringing the right people in my path to help with the process.

This process I find myself in is one all of us experience every day just by living! We know in our heart what we want to do, but we also need to seek God's counsel and await His guidance and blessings. Lord, be with us as we await Your steps.

### *Risk and Faith*

I once heard a speaker begin with words such as, risk great things for God. Step out and use the full talents with which you have been given. Then the speaker went on to ask questions similar to: but where can we find the courage? Do we have the strength? I think of Moses at the burning bush being told by God to lead the people out of Egypt. How he argued with God, claiming all the reasons he could not do what God was calling him to do. *"But Moses asked God, "Who am I that I should go to Pharaoh and that I should bring the Israelites out of Egypt?" -- Exodus 3:11 (CSB)* His rebuttals continued throughout chapter 3 and the beginning of chapter 4 until God provided no other way out.

Can you think of a time you argued with God about something you did not want to do or did not feel qualified to do? Just as Moses was empowered by God to fulfill his leadership role, we are empowered when God seeks us to do a job. Aren't we also empowered to walk with courage through rocky parts of our life's journey? When we wonder where the strength comes to endure unknowns about tomorrow, God sends angels in the form of people, or perhaps sends messages in books, songs, or thoughts.

Faith in Christ helps us to step forward to risk doing what we are daring to accomplish. Knowing that directs our steps. God enables us to develop, gives us the courage and confidence to take the next step.

God gives us the talents, the will and the desire to use for His creative purposes here on earth. What talent has God placed in you that calls you to share? Is the desire present to use that talent? Can you have faith that God will lead you where you need to go to use your talents for His creative purposes? Seems like much to ponder as you go through your life.

### *Into The Pool*

Let us begin at John 5:5 with the story about the man at the pool of Bethesda. A cripple, for 38 years, tried to get into the pool when the water stirred for healing. He could never get there soon enough by himself. Jesus came to him by the pool and asked: ***"Do you want to get well? " -- John 5:6 (CSB)*** The man responded to Jesus' question: ***"I have no one to put me into the pool when the water is stirred up, but while I'm coming, someone goes down ahead of me." -- John 5:7 (CSB)*** Jesus is telling him and us not to wait for someone to take him or us to the pool. The pool though is only an image for trusting Christ to save you, or heal you. God had a vision for wholeness for this man, and Jesus enabled him to have the courage to pick up his mat and walk. Why did it take him 38 years? He spent all those years depending on someone else that never showed up. He never asked for help. He just tried to do it himself, and he couldn't get there on his own fast enough.

What vision does God give us? What keeps us from "getting into the pool" (or having life with Christ)? What are our hopes and dreams? Now what keeps our hopes and dreams simply hopes and dreams as opposed to reality, action, and service. Just like the man who could not "get to the pool" because others got in the way or no one was there to help him, we could keep our hopes and dreams from fulfillment by waiting for someone else to do the work for us.

I don't know about you, but this message spoke to me. To "get into the pool," all I need to do is ask Jesus. Am I willing to ask for help? How might I pray for help? What excuses do we have for our neglect at "getting into the pool?"

Prayer is the option for us. God hears our requests, help will come. It might be a quick response, in an unexpected way, or delayed for other reasons. God's time is not our time so sometimes patience is required!

### Tragedy Strikes

Another tragedy struck our hearts when the Space Shuttle Columbia shattered the lives of seven persons and their immediate and extended families. One of the reports I heard quoted a well-known scripture that caused me to ponder the many issues facing us today. See where this scripture takes you!

> *"There is an occasion for everything,*
> *and a time for every activity under heaven:*
> *a time to give birth and a time to die;*
> *a time to plant and a time to uproot;*
> *a time to kill and a time to heal;*
> *a time to tear down and a time to build;*
> *a time to weep and a time to laugh;*
> *a time to mourn and a time to dance;*
> *a time to throw stones and a time to gather stones;*
> *a time to embrace and a time to avoid embracing;*
> *a time to search and a time to count as lost;*
> *a time to keep and a time to throw away;*
> *a time to tear and a time to sew;*
> *a time to be silent and a time to speak;*
> *a time to love and a time to hate;*
> *a time for war and a time for peace."*
> *-- Ecclesiastes 3:1-8 (CSB)*

*"I know that everything God does will last forever; there is no adding to it or taking from it. God works so that people will be in awe of him. Whatever is, has already been, and whatever will be, already is. However, God seeks justice for the persecuted." -- Ecclesiastes 3:14-15 (CSB)*

What is the time for you? What is the time for our country? I think of all the troops building up in other places and if war comes, if deaths of our troops come, will we hear much about them? Will their deaths be remembered like those of the seven astronauts? Astronauts know about the risks that they (and military personnel and other first responders) take to do their jobs, yet they go anyway. Will they be missed, of course. Exploration (and defense of our country) continues but investigate what happened, correct the problems, and move on to the next mission. Any astronaut would gladly fly the next mission. Lord, be with those in mourning of a lost loved one. Lord, grant us the wisdom, and the direction to follow Your lead as we explore the universe that You created.

## What Is Best?

"Be the best you can be." "Do your best!" "May the best person win." At one time or another, we have all heard or said these words to one another or to ourselves. I am reading the book, *"My American Journey"* by Colin Powell,* and several comments in the book made me think of Jesus choosing His disciples and many others He called to serve. Only choosing the right or best people for the job gets the work done. That doesn't mean the smartest or most popular but those who have the skills and temperament to give the job their all, their best.

For several days this stuck with me, causing me to ponder God's take on this concept. How do we determine who is best? I thought of the many people called by God in the Bible. Many were simple, ordinary people, some uneducated, yet each gave their best for God and excelled in the work God called them to do. Think of Moses, David, Ruth, Mary, Joseph, the twelve Disciples, Jonah, and your favorite. They still had their human flaws and imperfections, but their faith in God was mighty!

*"I am the Lord your God, who teaches you for your benefit, who leads you in the way you should go." -- Isaiah 48:17 (CSB)*

To God, it appears the "best" were those who excelled in faith and trust in God. Throughout the bible are scriptures about giving from our best fruits, giving the best land, putting on our best clothes, doing our best, and others.

Yes, this idea of using the best people for a job applies to many venues, not just the military. "Best" doesn't always mean the smartest, the strongest, or the quickest wit. For me when pertaining to God's people, "best" describes those most focused on doing what God calls them to do. The most organized, thoroughly planned activities could fall flat if the people involved are only going through the motions of managing those planned activities. Is an event or an organization filled with the "best" people? Do we merely go through the motions of making plans, studying theories of leadership and management, and getting our organization structure just right? Let us not forget the people and find ways to call forth their "best." Let us also call forth the "best" that God enables us to give.

*"My American Journey," by Colin Powell with Joseph E Persico, A Ballentine Book published by The Random House Publishing Group, 1995

### Healing Needed

We see many people in need of healing of some kind or another. As you read through the New Testament, you find many encounters of people coming to Jesus for healing. ***"When he went ashore, he saw a large crowd, had compassion on them, and healed their sick." -- Matthew 14:14 (CSB)*** Max Lucado, in his devotional book, *"Grace for the Moment,"** brought new light to this text for me. Jesus never asked if they deserved the healing. He even knew which ones the healing would forever change, and which ones would have no appreciation for what Jesus did for them. Knowing this, Jesus chose to heal them anyway. Some were not physically healed, and we question, why? But Jesus had His reasons. Perhaps the faith of that person was enough, and allowed others with infirmities to see that faith is more important than healing!

How many of us make judgments before deciding to help others. If they appear to deserve the help, then we proceed. For others, though we think "Why, help them? They are out to get whatever they can get!"

Yet Jesus is our example and, if He had compassion and healed many, aren't we also to seek to help many who are in need? Our role as a minister of Jesus is to have compassion for all, just as He did. His compassion for all did not equate with physical healing for all.

*"Grace for the Moment,"* by Max Lucado, 2000,
Published by J. Countryman, a division of Thomas Nelson, Inc.

### Know My Heart

Have you ever been misunderstood? Of course! Have you ever wondered about your own motives in a given situation? Probably. Perhaps the process of wondering and contemplating your own decisions helps to understand how others might misunderstand or question your motives. Sometimes, just the passing of time and allowing yourself more time to reflect allows for reasonable deductions to filter through to your consciousness.

***"Search me, God, and know my heart; test me and know my concerns." -- Psalms 139:23 (CSB)***

Yes, God does know my heart! God is so patient to allow me that time to know my own heart and find ways to wisely express ideas meant to bring glory and praise to God. This verse assures me that God knows me! All scripture assures me that God helps to guide me through the anxious thoughts and concerns that occur as a part of my humanness. I just need to trust God's word to be my guide. How grateful I am for the constant love and forgiveness made available to me through Jesus, my Lord and Savior.

I pray for all of us to continue to encourage God to search our hearts and minds and help us to serve the Kingdom wisely.

## Source of Peace

*"Now he came near the path down the Mount of Olives, and the whole crowd of the disciples began to praise God joyfully with a loud voice for all the miracles they had seen: Blessed is the King who comes in the name of the Lord. Peace in heaven and glory in the highest heaven!" -- Luke 19:37-38 (CSB)*

How excited the people and the disciples were for this moment! We are so like the disciples ready to cheer when conditions seem favorable to do so. Now seemed to be their moment to welcome Jesus into Jerusalem. But reading on gives us Jesus' view on the moment.

*"Some of the Pharisees from the crowd told him, 'Teacher, rebuke your disciples.' He answered, 'I tell you, if they were to keep silent, the stones would cry out.' As he approached and saw the city, he wept for it, 42 saying, 'If you knew this day what would bring peace — but now it is hidden from your eyes.' " -- Luke 19:39-42 (CSB)*

While the disciples shouted praises, Jesus wept over those who did not recognize Him as the Son of God. Yet He praised His disciples for their joy. Jesus, the risen Lord, is who brings me peace. Ultimately only through Jesus does true peace come. My family, my friends, circumstances can bring me temporary peace, but Jesus brings me peace always. The miracle in my life is having Jesus at the center. That does not imply that I always do everything the way I should. I know that when I stumble, when I speak rather than listen, or act before praying, that Jesus is there to guide me back. He helps me to see my way, forgives me, and embraces me once again.

I celebrate the miracle of my acceptance into God's Kingdom, even though I do not deserve it! How I praise Jesus for giving of His life for me and for you. This is a glorious day!

### Promise of Hope

Hope is something that fills us all for various reasons. We hope for good weather, for the right job to come along, for the man or woman of our dreams, for healthy children, for the best buy, and the list goes on!

Is our hope for events to turn out as we think they should? Is our hope only for our own needs? Is hope futile? How do we explain hope when all seems hopeless? Does hope exist when doctors declare a situation that seems beyond hope? When reason and experience tell us "no hope exists," why do we still hope, and for what do we hope?

*"This saying is trustworthy and deserves full acceptance. For this reason we labor and strive, because we have put our hope in the living God, who is the Savior of all people, especially of those who believe." -- 1 Timothy 4:9-10 (CSB)*

Our hope is for God to be with us through whatever comes our way. During a year we know that spring follows winter, summer follows spring, then comes fall and winter again. It is a life cycle! We know that whatever happens, we have no choice. It is built into our world. We have seen it over and over. Seasonal changes are only one way that God shows us His presence always! He is with us in that cycle of life and time, and He is with us no matter what happens every day in our lives. Our hope eternal is in God.

When we take God with us into every aspect of our life, hope abounds. Perhaps it is not the hope of our eyes, but the hope of our hearts. God is our rock, our solid foundation, to be with us no matter what else happens. Let us claim that promise of hope as we face our faith, our economy, our fears, our uncertainties, and all our todays and tomorrows.

### God Is With Us

The sun was trying to break through after several days of spotty storms and even seven inches of snow overnight. Several breaks in the cloud cover allowed the late afternoon sun to beam down through to the ground. It was a comforting sight as I was reminded of how God reaches out to us through difficult times.

Tornados come and go and occasionally hit the same area again. I can only imagine losing my home twice to tornados. How grateful people are when the storm is over, even if they must rebuild. Somehow when the sun returns, hope seems to find a foothold. Others gather around to help. God's army of followers go into action.

Psalms 107 talks about our ups and downs in our relationship with God. It always seems to be amid storms (difficulties) in our life that we especially reach out to God. ***"He stilled the storm to a whisper, and the waves of the sea were hushed. They rejoiced when the waves grew quiet. Then he guided them to the harbor they longed for." -- Psalms 107:29-30 (CSB)*** Just as the sun's rays reached to touch the ground and the next morning finds the sky clear and the sun bright, people seemed to rejoice and come out of their homes to bask in the warmth. Yet, God never left. During the storm, scripture helps direct us with reminders of who God is. Perhaps during the storm, we get so focused on the events that we fail to see the ways God is present.

When I looked toward the mountains during the rain, the snow, and the bad days, I could not see the mountains, but they were still there! When the clouds lifted, my eyes could once again take in the splendor of their beauty. I knew the mountains were still there (even though not visible) just as I know that God is with me even when I cannot see or feel His presence.

How grateful I am for the ability to picture scenes in my mind and to picture God's love and grace embracing me. It is that assurance of faith that leads me day by day.

### *Chosen Friends*

The word "friend" takes on many meanings. Perhaps a friend is an acquaintance, or a close confidant that you enjoy spending time with, or a person you have known for a very long time, or someone who shares an activity you enjoy.

Jesus tells us about friends: ***"I have called you friends, because I have made known to you everything I have heard from my Father. You did not choose me, but I chose you. I appointed you to go and produce fruit and that your fruit should remain, so that whatever you ask the Father in my name, he will give you. 'This is what I command you: Love one another.' " -- John 15:15-17 (CSB)***

Jesus set the example for us by choosing us as His friends. There was nothing we could do about it; He simply chose us! We choose others to be our friends and we need to choose them with the same conviction as Jesus chose us.

As chosen friends of Jesus, we must bear fruit by loving others unconditionally. Each of us has a different way of fulfilling that command. Some love by protecting our country, some by protecting our rights, some by doing medical research to find cures to diseases, some by visiting prisons, some by preparing meals for others, some by opening their homes, some by fighting or warning us of disasters like fires or weather, some by teaching, some by preaching, some by simply listening or sitting with us, and the list goes on.

What does it mean for me to hear Jesus telling us to love one another? We each have a special way to love one another. Finding our way to bear fruit for Jesus is our task. May our eyes be opened as we allow the Holy Spirit to help us.

## Always With You

*"Jesus came near and said to them, 'All authority has been given to me in heaven and on earth. Go, therefore, and make disciples of all nations, baptizing them in the name of the Father and of the Son and of the Holy Spirit, teaching them to observe everything I have commanded you. And remember, I am with you always, to the end of the age.' " -- Matthew 28:18-20 (CSB)*

From this wonderful text can come many important thoughts, but one phrase rang over and over with me, *"...I am with you always..."* For those who endure tragic events perhaps it is hard to see that God is with you always. We pray for God to make events turn out the way we want but that doesn't always happen. Is God to blame? Is God turning His back on us?

We don't know why events turn out the way they do! It is easy to give God the credit when we like the outcome, saying His angels watched over us. But what about the tragic loss of a loved one, sudden economic upheaval, health problems that bring burdens to many, or name your own situation?

I believe that Jesus is still there watching over us to bring us comfort through others, to lead us toward a new dependency on Him, and perhaps to help us walk a new path that we didn't want to take, to increase our compassion, to open our eyes, hearts, and minds to life we would never have known. Living life as an imperfect being allows stuff to happen. Jesus and God, His Father, are there to enable us to move on and to care for us in our suffering and pain.

It is my privilege to pray each day for God to help me through whatever happens. Yes, each day I pray for our safety, our well-being and that of our children. I thank God for all our blessings for I know that if tragic events happen, He is there always to help me through it. Keep those words close in your heart and mind, trust them to be true and watch for how Jesus is surely with you always.

### I Do It Myself

A two-year-old states emphatically *"I do it myself!"* As adults we can relate to this spirit of independence, this statement of control. How many times do we make this statement in various ways? At work, we want to appear confident and capable of accomplishing any task, so we turn down or do not seek assistance from others. As parents, we think we know all there is to know about parenting just because we perceive that we turned out ok.

Our need for God can so easily be relegated to Sunday mornings during worship. We do just fine during the week making our own decisions. But what happens when we get stuck with problems, bad relationships, ill health, or no job. We want God to fix it. Suddenly we can't do it ourselves! Things happen that can't be reversed, but God can help us deal with the aftereffects.

**"He said to me, 'My grace is sufficient for you, for my power is perfected in weakness.' " -- 2 Corinthians 12:9 (CSB)** That verse reminds me that the bad, difficult, and sorrowful times in my life are often the very aspects driving me toward God. His grace is sufficient to take me through the unknowns, the losses, the rejection, and the failures of my life. All I must do is to seek and ask for His grace.

In my weakness, His power becomes my strength to go through any ordeal. What ordeal is the grace of God carrying you through this week? How is His grace making a difference in a week filled with blessings or even just an average week? How is His power making you strong? Have you asked Him into your struggle or kept Him at a distance? Do you consider yourself undeserving of His grace and power?

Jesus considered you important enough to give up His life on the cross. Yes, you are important, and His grace and power can and will carry you through all situations in your life. His grace can help you to see the positives in each day. How I praise God for being here for you and me!

### How Full is Full

How full is full? As I measured the water to fill my coffee pot this morning, I filled the pot to the top. Anymore and it would spill out! When the coffee was ready, I filled my drinking cup to the top as I wanted to enjoy all of it. Yesterday, I bought some more fabric and filled my containers holding the fabric in the motorhome to the brim and squeezed the lids shut! Things are easy to see when full.

Paul prays a prayer for the Ephesians: ***"I pray that you, being rooted and firmly established in love, may be able to comprehend with all the saints what is the length and width, height and depth of God's love, and to know Christ's love that surpasses knowledge, so that you may be filled with all the fullness of God." -- Ephesians 3:17-19 (CSB)*** It would be nice to have a measuring guide like those on measuring cups to show us when we are filled to the measure of God's love! How do we gage the fullness of God?

Paul says we must be rooted. For me, being rooted means that I must actively and continually focus on God through faith, conversation in prayer, worship, and study. Even being rooted does not grant us the ability to fully understand the magnitude of God's love as it surpasses knowledge. Fortunately, God does not limit the fullness of His love to just those who are rooted! How many of us come to Him out of desperation, as a last resort? Perhaps the person has only heard of a loving, powerful God and in desperation reaches out to that unknown God! God comes to them in their desperation with the fullness of His love. His peace fills them regardless of the outcome to their physical state. We must be open to recognizing His love, since it may not come in the form we expect.

Being filled to the fullness of God is a concept hard to visualize, but if briefly experienced, it is hard to describe. Jesus is the ultimate example of the depth of God's love as Jesus gave His life for us on the cross, that we might be made pure in the eyes of God. Paul's prayer is one I pray for all of us today! May God's love fill you to overflowing!

### *Life and Death*

Our son recently wrote a story for the daily paper about a soldier who was killed in war. Several prayer requests recently were for people who passed away. The news is full of stories of those who died for various reasons.

***"Those who walk uprightly enter into peace; they find rest as they lie in death." -- Isaish 57:2 (NIV)***

Paul tells us in Philippians: ***"For me, to live is Christ and to die is gain. Now if I live on in the flesh, this means fruitful work for me; and I don't know which one I should choose. I am torn between the two. I long to depart and be with Christ — which is far better — but to remain in the flesh is more necessary for your sake." -- Philippians 1:21-24 (CSB)*** Death is never an easy subject to think or to write about. It seems to be an issue we would rather avoid, but it is inevitable for all. Perhaps the mysteries of the unknown for ourselves, and the feelings of loss for those we love, make it difficult to contemplate.

Fortunately, the decision about when or how our life ends is unknown to most of us. Even illnesses which appear to be headed in a given direction can change course and take a different path from bad to good or from good to bad. The reasons for the different directions may remain unknown to us or to our loved ones.

Yet, Paul's words offer much wisdom about his personal feelings and help me to form my own. How wonderful life will be with Christ! But while I am here, there is abundant life to live and many opportunities to continue ministry for Christ. Death is much harder on those left behind. Those living with that person missing now have choices to make to continue their life.

How do we deal with that void? As I look at Paul's statement, I infer that he would want others to celebrate his new life with Christ! He would want them to continue his ministry by telling others of the good news of life with Christ.

How do we live each day until our life ends? For Christ. Praise God for life both in this world and with Him.

### *Decisions - Action*

*"Bartimaeus (the son of Timaeus), a blind beggar, was sitting by the road. When he heard that it was Jesus of Nazareth, he began to cry out, 'Jesus, Son of David, have mercy on me!' Many warned him to keep quiet, but he was crying out all the more, 'Have mercy on me, Son of David!' " -- Mark 10:46-48 (CSB)*
Bartimaeus decided to ask Jesus for mercy. After being rebuked by others, he took the action to continue shouting out for Jesus to grant him mercy. How many of us make decisions, then fail to act upon them? Especially our decisions about our faith. Do we ask our neighbor to join us at church? What about asking others to pray for our concerns? Or joining a bible study that requires homework and other preparations? Perhaps the decision is to volunteer to teach a Sunday School class, do we make the call to offer our services or wait for someone to call us? How about the really risky decision to share our faith with a friend when we do not know where they stand on faith or we know the friend does not believe in Jesus? Is our decision to give more time and/or money to the church? Do we wait for someone to seek us out or step forward to offer?

Faith is certainly not earned through good works, but good works are a necessary byproduct of our faith. My faith allows me to step out in action knowing, claiming, and expecting Jesus to be with me each step of the way. Those risky steps take me deeper into my faith as I experience the promise of Jesus to walk with me as my guide and comforter.

As Bartimaeus shouted to Jesus for His aid, let us shout to Jesus to go with us on our journeys. Let us not just make decisions, but let us take the next step of action toward that goal. What decision rests with you today that now requires action? Invite Jesus to lead you to act on your faith.

### *True Accounts*

What is the difference between a tattletale and a whistleblower? I often think of children as tattletales running to mom or dad with some tale of what a sibling has done to them. Whistle-blower seems to be a name used for adults telling stories of wrongdoing within companies or government agencies.

In chapter 18 of Matthew, the parable of the Unmerciful Servant is about a master with a servant who owed him a great debt. When the master called for payment, the servant begged for mercy and patience on the part of the master. The master had mercy and forgave the entire debt, which was apparently a very large sum. Then the servant found someone who was in debt to him and did not forgive his debt but demanded payment. *"When the other servants saw what had taken place, they were deeply distressed and went and reported to their master everything that had happened." -- Matthew 18:31 (CSB)*

These servants could easily appear to be tattletales running to the master out of envy. The servants took a risk knowing that, if the master chose not to believe them or did not do any investigation himself, they could be in trouble! If the master saw them as passing on a true account of events, perhaps he would consider them as whistleblowers.

Either way, those who throw light upon true accounts are generally not popular folks with everyone. When Jesus went into the temple and cleaned out the moneychangers and merchants, He certainly was not liked by many! Yet, others approved greatly of His actions.

Often in our jobs, our work in our churches, or in our families, we find times when events happen that are not right. What to do? Who to talk to? Is the event worthy of bringing to light? Is my view realistic? Do I know all the facts? Do I need to know all the facts, or do I report merely what I observe? What would Jesus do? Prayers for guidance are a must! Lord, give us the courage, the wisdom, and the discernment necessary to follow You in all we do.

### Called, Enabled

I love watching people and gaining insights from their words, their behaviors, or both! During the weeks we have attended church in New Orleans, I have quietly studied the pastor as he delivers his sermons each week. It is obvious that he is called by God to preach.

This scripture reminded me of him and others whose lives have intersected my journey. Paul says: *"Brothers and sisters, consider your calling: Not many were wise from a human perspective, not many powerful, not many of noble birth. Instead, God has chosen what is foolish in the world to shame the wise, and God has chosen what is weak in the world to shame the strong. God has chosen what is insignificant and despised in the world — what is viewed as nothing — to bring to nothing what is viewed as something, so that no one may boast in his presence." -- 1 Corinthians 1:26-29 (CSB)*

God called many characters from all walks of life throughout scripture to carry His message to the world. In my life, the special people called included:

- my mother-in-law.

- a visiting pastor I didn't know who enabled me to ask Christ into my life.

- a neighbor who encouraged me to step out in faith.

- a friend who helped me to pray.

- children who relied on me when I didn't know how to be what God wanted.

- a Christian psychologist's book about parenting that changed me forever.

- a pastor who believed in me and encouraged me to take risks.

- all the women in Bible Study Fellowship who shared and taught.

- church members who humbly lived as servants of Christ.

- so many more called by God.

Most of these people were simple folks trying to live as Christ called them to live. God took the weak moments of their lives to teach them how to be strong so they could reach and teach others. Most never sought attention or fame. They never boasted of their knowledge. They simply shared what God had called them to share. Why? Probably because they were compelled by the Holy Spirit to do so!

As I thank the pastor for his insightful sermons, he merely passes the praise on to Christ saying something like, "No one comes to hear what I have to say. I merely say what God wants me to say." What is God calling you to do today? This week? This month? This year? When He calls you, He enables you! All praise to Christ, our Lord!

### Giving You Rest

Fatigue is upon me. Duties seem overwhelming at times. What happened to leisure time? How easy it becomes to complain and whine about having too much to do! Even my retired friends are often overbooked with meetings, volunteering, and other activities. Our world today wants us to fill all our time with something to do. But what is it that God wants for us?

I have a new friend recovering from TB who has been in isolation for three months in a trailer parked next to us. She cannot work, go anywhere, or have friends over (unless they stay outside). All her meals are brought to her. Her family is in Uganda. She faces possible isolation for another five months.

Many of us think it would be wonderful to have some quiet time like that! She spends it studying and reading God's word. She prays and listens to music. God is carrying her through a very difficult time and she sees His hand on her life daily.

*"Come to me, all of you who are weary and burdened, and I will give you rest. Take my yoke upon you and learn from me, because I am lowly and humble in heart, and you will find rest for your souls. For my yoke is easy and my burden is light." -- Matthew 11:28-30 (CSB)*

Through Christ we find peace, even in the middle of dreadful situations. May you find rest today. Look for it, expect it, pray for it, praise God for that rest and peace.

### Share the Gospel

All of us struggle with certain tasks! Our youngest grandson struggled at eight months old to put everything in his mouth, or to coordinate the hands and knees for an effective crawling motion. Obstacles seemed to be everywhere he went.

Paul had obstacles all the time! He tells the Ephesians: *"And now I am on my way to Jerusalem, compelled by the Spirit, not knowing what I will encounter there, except that in every town the Holy Spirit warns me that chains and afflictions are waiting for me. But I consider my life of no value to myself; my purpose is to finish my course and the ministry I received from the Lord Jesus, to testify to the gospel of God's grace." -- Acts 20:22-24 (CSB)*

What about the task of sharing the gospel of God's grace with others? I know without a doubt that God's grace has brought me to where I am today. I also know that I could always do more when it comes to sharing what God has done for me. Why don't I?

Sometimes my daily activities take precedence over sharing God. Sleep often wins over study. TV programs win over reading and meditation. Occasionally, I simply feel overwhelmed by trying. Is anybody listening? Does anyone care about how God's grace can change his or her life? Many people ask about the details in testifying to the gospel of God's grace.

Lee C. Camp, *"Mere Discipleship"** in his book describes a way of life filled with action, not only words. Discipleship involves not only words that tell about Jesus, but it involves our actions in how we live our life. Each individual needs to discover a way to proceed as they pray, study, read scripture, and remain open to the leadership of the Holy Spirit.

*"Mere Discipleship," by Lee C. Camp, 2008, Published by Brazos Press
a division of Baker Publishing Group, Grand Rapids, Michigan

### Promises

Following a thunderstorm, I saw a full double rainbow! It was absolutely splendid! The vibrant colors shone with the dark clouds of the passing storm behind them. The sun behind us blazed in to bring out the color particles in the sky.

Immediately I thought of God's promise to Noah: *"And God said, 'This is the sign of the covenant I am making between me and you and every living creature with you, a covenant for all future generations: I have placed my bow in the clouds,*

**and it will be a sign of the covenant between me and the earth. Whenever I form clouds over the earth and the bow appears in the clouds, I will remember my covenant between me and you and all the living creatures: water will never again become a flood to destroy every creature.' " -- Genesis 9:12-15 (CSB)** How wonderful to have a physical sign from God! Of course, a rainbow is easy to see!

I remember one day being very angry when I was at home by myself. A big pity party ensued as well! The phone rang and it was a friend who normally did not call. After asking the normal, "How are you," and getting my blunt answer, she listened to me rant and rave for a few minutes. Finally, when I paused, she asked me if I had prayed about the situation. Well, I had not! I was too occupied by my anger! She became the rainbow I needed from God to put the situation into a better perspective and show me that His grace was available for me to claim.

How do we handle not having a sign from God about His promises? Or do we miss seeing the signs of His promises because we aren't really looking or because the signs might be subtler? God's grace and love is available for us always through Jesus Christ! He offers that to us through scripture, through others, through music, and perhaps through nature. The rainbow, as described in scripture, (and my friend) reminded me of God's many promises and gifts.

### Giving All

Have you accomplished all you hoped to do in life? Have you thought about all you want to do in life? Good questions. Many of us can say that we have thought about it, but perhaps not done anything about it. Some can say they never give those questions a thought at all! Others perhaps have thought about and done something about what they want to accomplish.

If we did think about these questions, would they be a list of what we consider successes in life? Do we hope to be a good parent, hope to have a nice house, car, job and a good amount of money to enjoy life? What are the things we spend lots of time doing or thinking about?

After the Holy Spirit descended upon the disciples and others, Peter begins preaching boldly to the crowd. **"With many other words he testified and strongly urged them, saying, 'Be saved from this corrupt generation!' So those who accepted his message were baptized, and that day about three thousand people were added to them. They devoted themselves to the apostles' teaching, to the fellowship, to the breaking of bread, and to prayer." -- Acts 2:40-42 (CSB)**

As a Christian professing Jesus as my Lord and Savior, would I answer the questions I posed to you earlier differently? I hope so! Do I allow God to use me to live the life He wants me to live? Often, but not always. Do I stand in the way of God working through me by putting obstacles in the way of action? Sometimes, yes.

Do I give Jesus all my life or just parts of it on Sunday? More than just Sunday, but probably not all. He certainly gave all His life for me when He died on the cross. Success for me is being a servant for God, allowing Him to lead me wherever He wants me to go. My prayer is for all of us to ponder these questions. Do not put it off. We all can relate stories of those who were taken from this life suddenly. Jesus wants us to be ready and our life needs to serve a purpose for Him.

### *Our Blessings*

Blessings are in a couple of categories – material and spiritual. Yes, our material blessings are abundant. We have housing (even if it is on wheels!). We have food and the ability to eat out as well. Our health is good, clothing overflows in the closets and drawers, electronic gadgets adorn our space around us, and the list goes on! Some people have very limited material blessings and seem to thrive on spiritual blessings. Then there are those who need more of each.

Freedom allows us many privileges in the United States. Yet the elements of crime and evil exist and require us to exercise caution. The ratio of freedom to evil in our country is heavy on the freedom side for most of us. In certain areas, of course, the ratio is heavy on the evil side. Freedom to worship is basic to our country's rights. Our spiritual blessings are abundant and open to us always.

Peter gives us some specific instructions concerning our spiritual blessings: ***"For this very reason, make every effort to supplement your faith with goodness, goodness with knowledge, knowledge with self-control, self-control with endurance, endurance with godliness, godliness with brotherly affection, and brotherly affection with love. For if you possess these qualities in increasing measure, they will keep you from being useless or unfruitful in the knowledge of our Lord Jesus Christ. The person who lacks these things is blind and shortsighted and has forgotten the cleansing from his past sins." -- 2 Peter 1:5-9 (CSB)***

Scripture gives us direction, but we must study and follow. This formula in 2 Peter perhaps is one we need to print out and read frequently, until it becomes as natural as breathing. What can you add to your blessings? Which ingredient do you need? Lord, lead us toward Your love each day.

### Shepherd's Voice

I was reflecting upon role models which shape our lives. The story about the good shepherd mentions the sheep listening to His voice. ***"The one who enters by the gate is the shepherd of the sheep. The gatekeeper opens it for him, and the sheep hear his voice. He calls his own sheep by name and leads them out. When he has brought all his own outside, he goes ahead of them. The sheep follow him because they know his voice." -- John 10:2-4 (CSB)*** The Good Shepherd knows His sheep.

My mother left me a voice message on the cell phone, "*This is Catherine Traylor, I am Carolyn's mother. I am not sure if you will recognize my voice.*" She has Alzheimer's disease. Of course, I recognize her voice! Her voice was with me before I was born!

Jesus is a wonderful example of the best role model that enables us to lead productive and positive lives. He raised His voice only once when He cleansed the temple. He saved His righteous indignation for a just cause, not for the daily annoyances. Complaining and keeping lists of mistakes was not a part of His life. He challenged folks to change their ways or pay the consequences of their own actions. He led people with consistency, encouragement, and caring.

A good shepherd (or good role model) uses a pleasant, firm, and confident tone of voice rather than a commanding, demeaning one. Are we good role models for others to follow or are we providing poor examples that may cause others to stray? Have we had poor role models that we copied and now need to change? Perhaps only one aspect of our life needs a new model, perhaps more. Is it time for us to recognize the voice of our Lord as we read the scriptures and seek role models more like Him?

Praying always brings us face to face with God to seek forgiveness, ask for direction, and praise God for everything. What kind of shepherd are you? How does your voice affect the sheep around you? Lord, lead us each day, and thank You for the examples of Jesus for us to follow as His sheep

### *Joyous Times*

Celebrate - a happy occasion with festive activities. We all enjoy times of celebration. Most often we recognize those times. Anniversaries, birthdays, births of new children and births of animals in nature, joys of recognition for a job well done, accomplishment of a hard project, normal findings from health testing, and the list goes on. What makes the celebration so sweet?

The journey that led to the accomplishment or occasion holds many clues. The story of the Prodigal Son, found in Luke15:11-32 offers us a look at the journey. After asking for and receiving his inheritance from his father, the son goes out and lives life in the fast lane, spending all he has. Life was grand for a while, but when the money ran out, his journey found him wanting for even the daily needs of housing and food. Life at his father's home was better for the servants than what he had now. His return home and his request for forgiveness gave way for his father's words: *" 'For this son of mine was dead and is alive again; he was lost and is found.' So they began to celebrate." -- Luke 15:24 (NIV)*

Some people experience the joy of birth only to discover the child cannot survive a normal life span. What journey lies ahead for them? A wedding seems to be a most happy and joyous occasion and perhaps years later the couple struggles to find joy at any moment. What obstacles came into their journey? Our health appears good one day, and suddenly a bump appears, a pain erupts, or blood surfaces unexpectedly. Testing ensues. What emotions accompany us during the waiting for results?

My journeys in this life seem to go best when I invite Jesus to walk with me. It doesn't mean the outcome is always what I want, but the journey goes by more smoothly and with less anxiety when I feel His presence with me. By inviting others to join me in prayer over matters of concern, I feel His support through them. Sometimes our celebration is about how God stayed the course with us rather than the actual outcome. That can be a daily celebration! Yes, the Psalms are full of praise poems. Find them and read to fill that void on those days you simply feel no sense of celebration. The Prodigal Son repented and returned to a joyous, forgiving father! With Jesus in your life, there is much to celebrate.

## *Our Gifts to Offer*

Many sermons are preached about Jesus feeding the 5,000. This text has many good messages. Over the years, I am sure we have all heard so many we often say, "I've heard that before" and begin our daydreaming. Maybe God had me pay attention to something a pastor said that triggered my pondering. Imagine Jesus sitting on the mountain with His arms outstretched and, in His hands, He held the five loaves and the two fish, and the text says: ***"Then he commanded the crowds to sit down on the grass. He took the five loaves and the two fish, and looking up to heaven, he blessed them." -- Matthew 14:19 (CSB)***

Now imagine us sitting in our favorite spot with our arms outstretched and, in our hands, we hold... What is that small gift that you have that you can give to someone else? The size and importance are of no particular significance. Yet it is all you have. You offer it to God, thanking Him for it. Now, the significance of the gift is something of value to offer.

If you are housebound, perhaps all you have to offer is the ability to pray for others. Your income is small, fixed, and barely enough to cover your own expenses, but you have time to share. Creativity is not high on your list, but you can follow directions quite well. Teaching a class scares you, but childcare is fun. God blessed you with finances and the ability to help fund activities. This list could go on!!!

God wants us to feed the "5,000" in need around us with whatever gift we have. By offering our gift to God in advance and thanking Him for that gift, He will expand our gift to reach far more than we ever dreamed.

Lord, encourage us to offer to You our gifts for Your use and Your glory. We thank You for giving us the gifts to offer and for giving us the wisdom to use them for Your glory.

## *Seeds for Growth*

As I read scriptures, my attention once again focused on what kind of ground I am on right now. Jesus explains the meaning of the parable about the sowing of the seeds. ***"This is the meaning of the parable: The seed is the word of God. The seed along the path are those who have heard and then the devil comes and takes away the word from their hearts, so that they may not believe and be saved." -- Luke 8:11-12 (CSB)*** Yes, there was a time that God's message hit the ground around me, but the devil found his way back into my life and encouraged me to live life his way. Fortunately, I always knew the difference, but made some bad choices.

The next verse goes on to say: *"And the seed on the rock are those who, when they hear, receive the word with joy. Having no root, these believe for a while and fall away in a time of testing." -- Luke 8:13 (CSB)* Many events in my life found me allowing the teaching to seep in and find root, and I praise God for those times. Currently though, I find one issue that keeps coming back to me that perhaps I am giving up on rather than doing as God would have me do. Am I giving up and taking the easy way around the issue?

*"As for the seed that fell among thorns, these are the ones who, when they have heard, go on their way and are choked with worries, riches, and pleasures of life, and produce no mature fruit." -- Luke 8:14 (CSB)* Living life on the road does bring us pleasure, but is it allowing me to neglect another part of my life?

*"But the seed in the good ground — these are the ones who, having heard the word with an honest and good heart, hold on to it and by enduring, produce fruit." -- Luke 8:15 (CSB)* Would paying attention to this verse bring about a peace that seems to elude me? I so often wonder what God wants me to do. I continue to pray and sometimes the answer seems to be to continue as I am. Then I begin to wonder... Lord, we want to do what you lead us to do, but sometimes it seems to take so long to understand exactly what we are to do. Once again, I come to you seeking that answer. Allow your seeds to fall on fertile ground. *(Years later this book is fulfilling that which I put aside and left undone.)*

### Jesus Today

Ever wonder what life would be like if Jesus appeared for the first time today, rather than 2000 years ago? With our instant media coverage of everything, Jesus' message would be available for many more folks. However, the critics would also multiply. A fictional book, *"Eli"* by Bill Myers,* is such a book. Eli is Jesus. His disciples included varied types of folks that normally would not have much to do with each other but who became a group following him by giving up other things much as Jesus did in scripture. Try to imagine who Jesus might call in today's society that were the equivalents to the disciples in scripture. *"Then Jesus said to his disciples, 'If anyone wants to follow after me, let him deny himself, take up his cross, and follow me.'" -- Matthew 16:24 (CSB)* The events in the book follow the scriptural events of Jesus' walk, but using modern day examples and situations. Very thought provoking.

How would Jesus feel about many of our elaborate worship centers? Let us remember His reaction when He entered the temple grounds and found all the things for sale. How would He respond today to a Christian bookstore? I love browsing through bookstores, in fact, that is where I found the book I am reading! What about the many evangelistic ministries that seem to be money hungry in such a way as to make you think you are buying goods you need to help you know God? What about the grand Christmas and Easter pageants? The ones done by the children made with simple costumes are in a different category. Some pageants have so much grandeur, they charge fees for admission.

How much have we commercialized our Lord? The comment to those things in the book is that God wants a relationship with you and me. He wants our obedience. He does not want us using His name to promote business. Often a fine line exists between serving God and exploiting God. Help us, Lord, to examine our lives to see where we exploit rather than serve. Help us to make changes so that we may follow you in all that we do and say.

*"Eli,"* by Bill Myers, 2003, Published by Zondervan

### Faith Journey

One of my favorite chapters in the Bible is Hebrews, which is about faith. Hebrews 11 starts with: ***"Now faith is confidence in what we hope for and assurance about what we do not see." -- Hebrews 11:1 (NIV)***

I have a lot of hope for:

- Numerous places suffering from destruction.

- Many people lost and not sure what tomorrow holds.

- Families separated from one another by either distance or disagreements.

- Those feeling lost in the world.

- Those seeking cures for diseases which devastate our bodies.

Often, I do not see the answers for these situations. I know that God can and does bring comfort and aid. The rest of the Hebrews 11 talks about many whose faith was used to help others in their life. He used the most unlikely of people. For example, God used Rahab: ***"By faith Rahab the prostitute welcomed the spies in peace and didn't perish with those who disobeyed." -- Hebrews 11:31 (CSB)***

Even though she was a prostitute, God granted her grace and redemption as she sought a better life by helping Joshua's men.

Early in my faith journey, I sought out a bible study so I could learn, and our pastor asked me to start one! Who, me? I decided to invite others to join me, hoping leadership would come about! I took that step of faith and God provided some mature ladies to meet with me. My growth began and that step of faith encouraged me to take another step, baby steps to grow toward the next step. Faith in how God can lead you enables you to do things you never thought you could. His grace frees you to be who He wants you to be. Are you ready to take the first step or the next step?

## Forgiveness

Have you been mad, angry, or irritated with someone recently? I know I have. Pardon me if I don't go into the details. Trust me, it isn't pretty or something I am proud of! But the results caused me to act out in a manner not pleasing to my Lord nor to the person who received my anger. Yes, I went to each person and requested forgiveness for my actions and words. But it is not for me to grant forgiveness. *"Then Peter approached him and asked, 'Lord, how many times must I forgive my brother or sister who sins against me? As many as seven times?' 'I tell you, not as many as seven,' Jesus replied, 'but seventy times seven.' " -- Matthew 18:21-22 (CSB)*

This verse gives me great hope for forgiveness to come. I often must remind myself that Christians are not perfect, just forgiven. Gratefulness doesn't begin to describe my feelings at how glad I am that Jesus paid the price for the sins I have committed and for those I have yet to commit! No matter how hard I try to live as Jesus wants me to live, I can't seem to be that good every day, every moment. Sometimes I recognize my error right away and other times it takes much longer for that recognition to occur.

I often think of Peter, one of Jesus' disciples who claimed he would never deny his Lord. And yet, a short time later, he did deny Jesus three times, just as Jesus predicted he would. The fact that Jesus told Peter what he would do, and Jesus still allowed Peter to continue following Him is such a strong example of how the love of Jesus overpowers the sin we do to Him. Later, when Peter realized his error, he sought and received Jesus' forgiveness. Look at what a strong follower he became when the Holy Spirit filled his life. Even then though, he erred in judgment at times, but found forgiveness each time.

Sin and forgiveness go hand in hand. Yes, we shall all sin at some time or another and the love of Jesus is still there for us, along with His forgiveness. I pray for each of us to recognize our sins and then seek the forgiveness that is available.

## *Saints in Life*

Who are the saints in your life? The Catholic church has a much stronger category of sainthood which is beyond my definition. A saint, to me, is someone who is extraordinarily patient, loving, and giving of time and service because of their faith in Christ. I know of several people whose paths have crossed my life that, to me, are saints. What was it about them that touched my life?

A man who had a high position in the state, member of the same church, a friend, humble enough to clean the toilet of an immigrant family we sponsored when the family had to move. A mature lady who taught me the power of prayers through her examples of praying. A friend whose life dealt with a sin same as mine and we experienced forgiveness through Christ. Their examples taught me! The descriptions that come to mind are compassionate, dedicated to learning, teaching, and studying; with the ability to listen, to accept, to encourage, to lead; able to guide you to grow, and to forgive; and the gentleness to comfort.

Romans tells of the qualities of a true Christian, one who can: ***"Bless those who persecute you; bless and do not curse. Rejoice with those who rejoice; weep with those who weep. Live in harmony with one another. Do not be proud; instead, associate with the humble. Do not be wise in your own estimation. Do not repay anyone evil for evil. Give careful thought to do what is honorable in everyone's eyes. If possible, as far as it depends on you, live at peace with everyone." -- Romans 12:14-18 (CSB)***

This week is a time to ponder those who have been and are the Christ-like examples in your life. How can you be to others as Christ is to you? Lord, allow us to love one another as You love us. Thank you for the many people You have sent my way over the years and for those yet to come.

### Treasure Chest

A treasure chest filled with… Now how would you finish that statement? What kinds of things would you want to find in a treasure chest? I ran into a lady this week who has a very wonderful way of using a treasure chest. Each year she collects items to put in a treasure chest for her three daughters/daughters-in-law. Then at Christmas it becomes one of their gifts. Her mother did it for her all her life and now she is doing it for the three women in her life. She told them that, this coming year, she could only give them one gift. All three said to keep the treasure boxes coming and no other gift is needed. She purchased three prayer cloths for their treasure box! I felt very honored to have an item worthy of such a gift. But the cloths represent her prayers for her three special family members.

*"By knowledge the rooms are filled with every precious and beautiful treasure." -- Proverbs 24:4 (CSB)* My friend very carefully selected those items she wanted to share with her daughters. Each was selected specifically with a purpose for that person.

Jesus tells us: *"Don't store up for yourselves treasures on earth, where moth and rust destroy and where thieves break in and steal. But store up for yourselves treasures in heaven, where neither moth nor rust destroys, and where thieves don't break in and steal. For where your treasure is, there your heart will be also." -- Matthew 6:19-21 (CSB)* The treasures she gives to them are more about the relationship than the items selected. She shows them how much she cares through her efforts all year long.

Jesus wants us to care for Him that way. He wants us to be in a relationship with Him daily, storing up the treasures of that relationship. A treasure chest filled with… Now how would you finish that statement? May God's grace and peace abide with you.

### Understanding

A few verses from Mark 4 pertain to the parables and how some did not understand the stories. *"When he was alone, those around him with the Twelve asked him about the parables. He answered them, 'The secret of the kingdom of God has been given to you, but to those outside, everything comes in parables so that they may indeed look, and yet not perceive; they may indeed listen, and yet not understand; otherwise, they might turn back and be forgiven.' " -- Mark 4:10-12 (CSB)* Of course, we all thought of Pharaoh and how God gave him many chances to believe, but each time Pharaoh seemed to become even harder in his heart to God's message. But didn't God know that would be the case?

Jonah was sure the people of Nineveh would not ever repent. He was bound and determine to not go there to proclaim God's message. Jonah also knew that if they repented, God would forgive them. He did not like those people, so he went the opposite direction by boat. A storm on the sea, led to him being thrown overboard and was swallowed by a whale After three days in the belly of a whale, he was saved because God had other plans for him. Jonah decided to do as God asked and went to Nineveh. We know that he was reluctant, but God used him anyway. Though Jonah started out in the wrong direction, he eventually followed God which Pharaoh did not do.

Those two stories show very different sides of God – one side very forgiving and the other that accepts being rejected repeatedly by hardening hearts. But did God harden Pharaoh's heart, or did Pharaoh harden his own heart? The Parables that Jesus told have meaning about spiritual issues. Many people fail to see those issues and only see the surface meanings of the stories. Jesus knew that many would not hear or see, nor would they try to understand.

What this tells me is that we have a role in trying to understand the messages of God's spiritual truths in the stories Jesus told. God is waiting for us to come to Him. His forgiveness for our sins is available. Our lack of understanding can be overcome by our coming to Him requesting understanding. What a joy to know that, as we seek understanding, God opens doors for us. Does God harden the hearts of people? For me, it seems that we choose to harden our hearts to Him instead. He just happens to know which way we will choose to go.

### Not of This Pen

I love it when I find something new in a familiar scripture! Then I wonder why I hadn't seen that before. Perhaps I had, but perhaps I forgot it was there all along. John 10:11-18 is the complete text, but verse 16 contained the "new" material for me. *"I am the good shepherd. I know my own, and my own know me, just as the Father knows me, and I know the Father. I lay down my life for the sheep. But I have other sheep that are not from this sheep pen; I must bring them also, and they will listen to my voice. Then there will be one flock, one shepherd." -- John 10:14-16 (CSB)*

Jesus was already telling us that others outside Judaism are meant to be a part of His family. As I pondered this, I couldn't help but realize that the disciples also missed it. Paul, on the other hand, knew that Jesus wanted the Gentiles included in the Christian church and defended his position many times with the disciples. If those closest to Jesus missed that part of the message, then my missing it is not so different. Actually, it gives me a lot of encouragement to continue reading and studying the bible for other parts of messages that I have either missed, overlooked, or simply forgotten.

In the meantime, what "sheep" around us are lost or merely struggling along? What "sheep" have wandered away and need to be gathered back into the herd? Are we not also shepherds who aid in the gathering of the sheep? Just as a head shepherd had helpers, Jesus also wants us to aid in ministering to the flock. Jesus is the lead shepherd that we all follow. We even need the Shepherd's staff gently nudging us to follow Him and to not fall asleep during our watch.

Where are you in the flock? Who do you feel led to welcome back into the flock? What other messages in the Bible are waiting for you and me to discover? Lord, grant us wisdom each day as we read, pray, and study.

### *Food That Endures*

What a fun-filled celebration we had with lots of food, laughs and visits with friends. Most of us, when we plan parties, plan way too much food! Yep, so did we and we have it still hanging around in the refrigerator, waiting to be eaten or thrown away. Yes, the food will spoil and must go!

Jesus feed the 5,000 in John and people followed him afterward to get more bread because they were astonished at how he feed them. ***"Jesus answered, 'Truly I tell you, you are looking for me, not because you saw the signs, but because you ate the loaves and were filled. Don't work for the food that perishes but for the food that lasts for eternal life, which the Son of Man will give you, because God the Father has set his seal of approval on him.' 'What can we do to perform the works of God' they asked. Jesus replied, 'This is the work of God — that you believe in the one he has sent.' " -- John 6:26-29 (CSB)***

I can't help but think that Jesus and His disciples laughed a lot with one another reflecting on the events of their three years together. Yes, they probably had other moments of sadness, fear, and pain also associated with their time together. That is so typical of our friendships today. Jesus stands with us through the good and bad of our lives. We recognize Jesus standing with us when we believe that He is

We need to go for the food that endures – life with Jesus. That is a big one for us since we seem to have insatiable appetites for literal food and stuff. The guilty feelings of taking too much, rob me of time allowing Jesus to help me be strong and not take more than I need. I need to focus more on my dependency on Jesus to keep me dependent on His food and not the world's food.

Reflecting on the events of the weekend, I remember the love, the laughter, and the friendships that exist through our relationships with Jesus. Jesus is the food that needs the focus, not the literal food on the table. Help me, Lord, to keep You as the food for all that I do or say.

### Bread for The Soul

What is the constant in your life? Your spouse, as much as you love one another, is not a guaranteed constant. Death, separation, or everyday issues might keep you away from one another on occasions. Food is constant to a degree, but too much is not good, the wrong foods are not good for long term. Our jobs often become a constant for us, but once again that is usually for a period of our life (not its entirety) and jobs can't be counted on to meet all our needs.

*" 'I am the bread of life,' Jesus told them. 'No one who comes to me will ever be hungry, and no one who believes in me will ever be thirsty again.' -- Therefore the Jews started grumbling about him because he said, 'I am the bread that came down from heaven.' They were saying, 'Isn't this Jesus the son of Joseph, whose father and mother we know? How can he now say, 'I have come down from heaven' ? " -- John 6:35, 41-43 (CSB)*

Jesus compared Himself to bread which has been a staple of life for centuries, long before Jesus was born. Of course, He is so much more than just bread. Bread merely feeds our body. Jesus feeds our souls and is our constant companion.

As the Jews of Jesus' day viewed him, He was merely the son of Joseph and Mary. How could He be the Son of God? That was too much to comprehend. Even today, many people have a hard time comprehending the life of Jesus and His role as the Son of God.

When I review my life and look for the constant in my life, the only one I can come up with is Jesus. He was with me as a child, as a young adult (even though I hardly recognized Him except in times of need), and as an adult. Jesus meets my needs in the ways He knows they need to be met. I probably have other ideas about what meets my needs, but Jesus knows what I need much more than even I do. He

217

walks with me through the good and the bad. Even when I make bad choices, Jesus is there to bring me comfort, to redirect my path, to stand with me through the consequences of my actions. He doesn't take away the consequences, but He stays with me, enabling me to grow and to keep going. Yes, Jesus is the constant of my life...He is the bread of the life.

### *On a Bike Ride*

Rudy and I got new foldable bikes. Many years ago, we rode recumbent bikes, but we couldn't take them with us when we moved into our motorhome. For two weeks now, we have adjusted, tweaked, and tested, trying to get them as comfortable as possible. Going from a recumbent to an upright foldable is quite a change.

Where we are parked, we have access to extensive bike trails that allow us to ride for as many miles as we want. We finally began stretching our rides to new directions. The result is that we now require our bodies to use muscles that have lain dormant for several years. The return trip back to our motorhome includes a moderate uphill that we have walked many times without our bikes. By the time we get back from over six miles of riding, the muscles in our legs are screaming as we climb that very moderate rise. Why do we do this? Despite the agony of the last climb, the joy of the ride makes it worth that last bit of agony.

Jesus taught in the synagogue in Capernaum about Him being the bread of life and: *"The one who eats my flesh and drinks my blood has eternal life, and I will raise him up on the last day." -- John 6:54 (CSB)* Followed by: *"Therefore, when many of his disciples heard this, they said, 'This teaching is hard. Who can accept it?" -- John 6:60 (CSB)*

Though Jesus' statement was not a literal command to eat His flesh and drink His blood, it was the background for our sacrament of communion. Partaking of the elements of communion is a reminder of our relationship with Jesus and our constant need for grace and forgiveness.

As I work to climb that upgrade with the bike (or any other upgrade in life), Jesus makes the way easier by the sacrifice He made for all of us. Following Him is not easy, but worth any agony in the journey. As I remember to take Jesus on those rides with me, the tough spots are bearable. He helps me keep my sights on the goal. It is Jesus who makes each day worthwhile. He truly is the bread of life. Let us remember to thank Him each time we hold bread and prepare to consume it.

### Come as You Are

I remember many years ago being picked up for a pajama-come-as-you-are party. What fun we high school girls had arriving at a party in various nighties. We literally had to go at that moment with no warning it was coming. Pajamas, hair curlers, and all kinds of outfits showed up.

What would happen if Jesus suddenly came, knocked on our door and said "Come, now." Would we recognize Him? Would we believe Him? Would we want to say goodbye to others? Would we say to Jesus, "Give me a minute, ok?" Easy to say "Yes," we would recognize Him and that we would go with Him. But what happened to the people who saw Him the first time He came to earth? Most rejected Him and did not recognize who He was.

Are we prepared for Him to come again? *"About the times and the seasons: Brothers and sisters, you do not need anything to be written to you. For you yourselves know very well that the day of the Lord will come just like a thief in the night." -- 1 Thessalonians 5:1-2 (CSB)* A thief does not make an appointment with you; he simply comes on his own timetable. Is your house ready to protect against a thief? Is your life ready to recognize and go with Jesus when He comes? Is everything settled with your loved ones? Of course, you'll always have some items left undone, but are your relationships healthy? Do you have some issues that need to be settled or forgiven?

Perhaps this week we need to ponder our readiness for Jesus' second coming. It could be anytime; we simply do not know, thus making the point that we just need to be ready no matter when. Is it time to forgive someone? Is it time to tell someone how special they are? Is it time to repay the debt? Is it time to say, "I'm sorry?" Is it time to write a letter? Well, let's get it done and be ready in case Jesus comes to take us to that "pajama-come-as-you-are party" in eternity!

### Self-Discipline

Discipline. Boundaries. Sounds like something we associate with what parents should do. But what about self-discipline? Whoa! Let's not go there. I like who I am, and I have a right to live as I want. Maybe. Sort of. But not really. God gave us life. After all, He created us. He created the reproductive process. We are His children. We can choose to be rebellious children or obedient children. Sometimes we vacillate between the two. We can also choose to defy the Creator. God gave us that right.

Hebrews 12:1-12 is one of my favorite passages about discipline and our relationship with God. It is a model for parenting, mentoring, or leadership of any kind. As you read be sure to include daughters wherever sons are mentioned! *"And have you completely forgotten this word of encouragement that addresses you as a father addresses his son? It says, 'My son, do not make light of the Lord's discipline, and do not lose heart when he rebukes you, because the Lord disciplines the one he loves, and he chastens everyone he accepts as his son.' Endure hardship as discipline; God is treating you as his children. For what children are not disciplined by their father?" -- Hebrews 12:5-7 (NIV)*

Dr. Bruce Narramore, in his book, *"Help! I'm A Parent"** taught me about being a better parent. I learned that discipline is aimed at helping one to remember next time to behave in a more correct manner. Therefore, discipline needs to be related to the kind of misbehavior in some manner and to the individual. Factors such as the number of times an event happens, response to previous discipline, and seriousness of the event affect what discipline is used. The consequences of our actions teach us effectively when applied with thought. Supervisors, parents, teachers, and pastors all need to consider many factors in determining a course of action to apply to a person. But all that applies to others. What about self-discipline once again? Most of us can resist major temptations of decent living. But what about the temptations of overeating, eating the wrong foods, talking about negative aspects of other people, neglecting regular exercise, focusing on the negative in others rather than recognizing their positives, and you can fill in your own temptation. How do we establish self-discipline to do better?

Prayer is a good place to start. Pray to recognize the temptation. Pray for direction and a plan. For me, having some accountability is necessary to someone or something other than myself. Implement the plan. Use it for a while and evaluate what needs to change, then revise it as needed. For improving my exercise non-habit, I found that a good DVD routine which I could do inside was good. But then to help my accountability, I made a chart for the refrigerator to post my accomplishments. Finally, I added a column for weight! And anyone who comes in the motorhome can see it! But most of all I can see it! Writing this weekly message helps me because I needed to be accountable for my continued bible study and meditative life. Prayer led me to writing these messages and prayer led me to my DVD and chart. Prayer keeps me there as well when the temptation to quit arises.

In what area(s) of your life do you need someone to help you be accountable for your own self-discipline? God holds us accountable, and we can band together in holding one another accountable for growth. Learn to hold yourself accountable for your actions. Allow others to partner with you to find the self-discipline that we all need.

*"Help! I'm A Parent,"* by Dr. Bruce Narramore, 1995, published by Zondervan

### Building Process

Construction is a constant activity at our home. Drywall is the next step. As I reflect on this process of building a room onto our tiny home, I see many parallels to life with Christ. There is an order (of sorts) to the process.

We know we need or want something. With life we know something is missing. An emptiness or void is present. In construction, we develop a plan for meeting our need. In life with Christ, He has the plan, and we simply ask to have the plan applied to our life. Once the building permit is issued, we start with the foundation – from the bottom first! Christ is our foundation, but we still start from the bottom to learn more about our life with Christ. We start with simple concepts in scripture to grasp more understanding of God, Jesus, and the Holy Spirit.

Now the work is underway! To continue building the walls and add the ceiling requires hard work. Certain things must be in place to hold the walls and then the ceiling. We can't put the ceiling in until we have walls. Life with Christ requires that we grow spiritually through study, through experience, through prayer, and through searching.

1 Corinthians 3 paints for us a very good picture: ***"For my part, brothers and sisters, I was not able to speak to you as spiritual people but as people of the flesh, as babies in Christ. I gave you milk to drink, not solid food, since you were not yet ready for it. In fact, you are still not ready, because you are still worldly. For since there is envy and strife among you, are you not worldly and behaving like mere humans? For whenever someone says, 'I belong to Paul,' and another, 'I belong to Apollos' are you not acting like mere humans? What then is Apollos? What is Paul? They are servants through whom you believed, and each has the role the Lord has given. I planted, Apollos watered, but God gave the growth. So, then, neither the one who plants nor the one who waters is anything, but only God who gives the growth. Now he who plants and he who waters are one, and each will receive his own reward according to his own labor. For we are God's coworkers. You are God's field, God's building. According to God's grace that was given to me, I have laid a foundation as a skilled master***

*builder, and another builds on it. But each one is to be careful how he builds on it. For no one can lay any foundation other than what has been laid down. That foundation is Jesus Christ. If anyone builds on the foundation with gold, silver, costly stones, wood, hay, or straw, each one's work will become obvious. For the day will disclose it, because it will be revealed by fire; the fire will test the quality of each one's work. If anyone's work that he has built survives, he will receive a reward. If anyone's work is burned up, he will experience loss, but he himself will be saved — but only as through fire." -- 1 Corinthians 3:1-15 (CSB)*

Yes, we build from worldly to spiritual in our life. As our new room continues to progress, I pray that my spiritual life continues its journey onward toward perfection to culminate in my eternal life with Christ. Let the building continue!

### Care for Our Body

How is the spiritual building of your inner life progressing? What about the building of your physical body which scripture tells us: ***"Don't you know that your body is a temple of the Holy Spirit who is in you, whom you have from God? You are not your own, for you were bought at a price. So glorify God with your body." -- 1 Corinthians 6:19-20 (CSB)***

What fills our time? How are our lives making a difference to someone else? In our world of instant gratification, we eat/drink too much and/or eat/drink the wrong foods. We give way too much attention to our clothing and our wages. But how do we use these aspects of our lives for the benefit of others? How do we build our lives so that others see and feel our praises and thanks to God?

I heard a doctor talk about the liver and how it affects all aspects of our physical lives. It filters everything we take in. Just as air filters in cars or our air conditioning units become clogged with pollutants, our livers become clogged and affected by the pollutants that we eat. Medications, both prescription and over the counter ones, interact in the liver and can cause problems. Lack of exercise also allows our excesses to remain in the body and allows the body to lose the vitality of function. ***"Now, the Lord of Armies says this: 'Think carefully about your ways: You have planted much but harvested little. You eat but never have enough to be satisfied. You drink but never have enough to be happy. You put on clothes but never have enough to get warm. The wage earner puts his wages into a bag with a hole in it.' " -- Haggai 1:5-6 (CSB)***

The instructions from God tell us to ***"Think carefully about your ways."*** Let us give careful thought to our ways to bring praise and thanks to God who gave us our bodies and wants us to be the best we can be. Feed your spiritual life as carefully as we feed our bodies. Eat and drink healthily. Read, watch, and listen to God's word which edifies your soul. Then share with others the harvest of God's blessings and grace.

### Guideposts in Life

Asking for directions is an action many of us find we must do during our lives. Comedians get lots of laughs describing how some people do and don't do that act! Age old legends exist about how a man will drive around forever before stopping to ask for directions.

Wonderful GPS technology makes it possible for us to find our way! When we lived in New England, finding our way around was quite different. In Maine (*in very small towns only*) you find a post with perhaps 15 or more signs with points on them and the name of a place on each sign telling you which way to go for each place. It was not possible to read them, though, while driving. If you were walking or able to stop, then the signs were helpful. Fortunately, I never depended on those signs to help me, but I loved them for their historical purposes.

In life, what do we look to for direction in our lives? What guideposts does God gives us? My list would include Jesus, the Holy Spirit, God's word in the Bible, my family and friends in the Lord, experiences that show me the way, and the intricate beauty and balance of nature created by God. Each of those parts can also be broken down into detailed lists of guideposts. *"When the day of Pentecost had arrived, they were all together in one place. Suddenly a sound like that of a violent rushing wind came from heaven, and it filled the whole house where they were staying. They saw tongues like flames of fire that separated and rested on each one of them. Then they were all filled with the Holy Spirit and began to speak in different tongues, as the Spirit enabled them." -- Acts 2:1-4 (CSB)*

From then on, the disciples were changed people. Their lives took on a new meaning and direction. Their personalities were changed. Peter became bold and unafraid, speaking out confidently about Jesus.

Many guideposts exist in our lives, with great impact at each point. We need to identify those posts. We too are a guidepost for our children and grandchildren and others around us. Are we pointing others toward God? Consider this week the guideposts in your life and what kind of a guidepost you are to others. Praise God for sending us those waypoints that send us in the right direction.

## Separation

Separation from God. Ah, yes, those are moments, days, or longer times of our lives that we perhaps would not like to remember. Each of us has experienced some event or time when we felt our lives or actions were not honoring our relationship with God.

Those events occur often during our youth and young adult days, perhaps because we were in the process of finding our way in this world. For me, I learned from the school of hard knocks, but I finally got the message. Separation from God seems to still occur, just on a different scale and for various reasons.

The Parable of the Lost Son centers on the young man who asked for his inheritance from his father, got it, and then proceeded to spend it recklessly until it was all gone. Seeing the error of his ways and realizing how much better his father treated his servants, he decided to go home and work for his father. He went home a repentant and changed son. His father welcomed him with a feast and great celebration. The story is found in Luke 15:11-32.

My thoughts drifted off toward those times we choose to strike out in directions that we know God does not want us to go. Yet we do so anyway, only to find defeat, isolation, and loneliness. Once there, remorse sets in and again, I knew that I have abandoned God. How unworthy I felt during those moments. He has not abandoned me, but awaits my return no matter how long it takes.

*"May your hand be ready to help me, for I have chosen your precepts. I long for your salvation, Lord, and your instruction is my delight. Let me live, and I will praise you; may your judgments help me. I wander like a lost sheep; seek your servant, for I do not forget your commands." -- Psalms 119:173-176 (CSB)*

We all experience being separated from God at times, but God awaits our return like the father awaited the return of his lost son in the parable. How very grateful I am for the unconditional love that God provides for us. That doesn't mean we don't suffer consequences for our actions or that the event is erased from our memory, but God's love, grace, and forgiveness await our return.

Lord, forgive me when I fail to live up to what You want for me. Help me to recognize those failures and to seek Your forgiveness and the forgiveness of those whose lives were affected by my actions or words.

### *Seek Forgiveness*

At times in our life, when things are going along without much stress or trauma, we may feel that our lives are in line with God's teachings for us. Perhaps we feel content with our faith. Yes, all is right, and God is good. We live in His peace. As I read the following Psalm, I had some doubts.

Here is a challenge to ponder: *"Lord, who can dwell in your tent? Who can live on your holy mountain? The one who lives blamelessly, practices righteousness, and acknowledges the truth in his heart — who does not slander with his tongue, who does not harm his friend or discredit his neighbor, who despises the one rejected by the Lord but honors those who fear the Lord, who keeps his word whatever the cost, who does not lend his silver at interest or take a bribe against the innocent — the one who does these things will never be shaken."*
*-- Psalms 15:1-5 (CSB)*

Much in our society makes us wonder where are God's people? Perhaps even in our daily lives, we offend God with some of our thoughts, words, or deeds. If only some of our thoughts, words or deeds are offensive, does that mean we do not live with God? Well, it means we have need for forgiveness!

For me, it means that each day I need to examine my day and recognize those moments needing forgiveness. Some days I am not able to make that recognition, at least not at that moment. I pray for the ability to see, the ability to understand, and the ability to acknowledge what needs forgiving. Is it easy to do? No! Is it necessary to do? Yes.

Fortunately, our Lord Jesus came to pay the price for the sins we commit, and I rejoice in that forgiveness. This Psalms gives us a standard to try and achieve. Yet humanity makes it impossible to do it all perfectly! Praise God for sending us Jesus so that we may know we are forgiven and loved by God. In the days to come, let us reflect upon this passage as to how we respond to our world, our families, and our faith.

### *Still Learning*

Amazing how our perspective influences us! Years ago, when I was in my 20's, 65 seemed old! People quit working at that age because they just can't work that hard anymore or the brains get tired and they can't think straight anymore. It is time to sit and read all the time. Having reached that age and more, the brain seems to still be working, or at least fools me into thinking it is working! I don't think life has slowed down much as the days fly by with all our activities. Each time I make another prayer cloth, I must test my math skills in adding, subtracting, using fractions, division, and multiplication to figure how many strips I can cut from a length of fabric for the maximum cuts.

Yes, perspective does influence our lives. That also goes for my spiritual life. When I was younger, I knew how much I didn't know about God, Jesus, and the Holy Spirit. After years of study and life experiences, I occasionally find a moment of complacency settling in as though I know all of that. But there is always so much more to learn!

Hebrews 5 has a subtitle: *"THE PROBLEM OF IMMATURITY -- We have a great deal to say about this, and it is difficult to explain, since you have become too lazy to understand. Although by this time you ought to be teachers, you need someone to teach you the basic principles of God's revelation again. You need milk, not solid food. Now everyone who lives on milk is inexperienced with the message about righteousness, because he is an infant. But solid food is for the mature — for those whose senses have been trained to distinguish between good and evil." -- Hebrews 5:11-14 (CSB)*

Our bodies make a good analogy. We must continually eat to stay alive. If we miss one meal, we'll do ok. If we miss meals for several days, we can still survive. If we merely nibble and drink, our bodies still function, but our energy levels can suffer. If certain vitamins and minerals are missing from what we take in, judgment can be affected. But if we miss meals for several weeks, our organs begin to suffer and shrivel, causing systems of the body to begin shutting down, and leading to death. Food is essential to our daily life. Good food, not junk food, ensures that our mental capacities and energy levels remain at a peak.

Our spiritual life is much the same. If we feed our spiritual life with reading, praying, and worship with others, our spiritual life can grow and remain strong. If we neglect those aspects of our spiritual life, we waste away. You get the picture...

I simply cannot rest upon the knowledge of the past, but must continue to read, pray, worship, and stay active in my spiritual life as well as my physical life. Learning sometimes now is relearning! Here's to another 65 years... Well maybe by then, I'll enjoy that eternal life with Jesus, and I won't write anymore!

### *Mistakes*

At our winter park, I agreed to edit and publish the newsletter for the park. Along with quilting, this is something I enjoy doing. As in anything in life, mistakes happen! A newsletter is certainly open territory for making them! This week once again taught me about the power of sincere apologies and the humbleness of being wrong.

I forgot to include the article about Worship and the December families we were supporting! The day 550 copies of the newsletter went out she called to remind me that I had received and acknowledged her email! Instantly, since I was already on my computer, I began looking for her article, found it and realized how I missed it. I won't bore you with those details. With her still on the phone, I, of course, apologized since I felt bad. I also made the decision to put out another page immediately to get her message to the folks in the park by the next day. When she first called, I could hear the anger in her voice, and I didn't blame her at all. By the time we finished, I could hear the relief in her voice.

*"For the Lord gives wisdom; from his mouth come knowledge and understanding. He stores up success for the upright; He is a shield for those who live with integrity so that he may guard the paths of justice and protect the way of his faithful followers. Then you will understand righteousness, justice, and integrity — every good path. For wisdom will enter your heart, and knowledge will delight you. Discretion will watch over you, and understanding will guard you." -- Proverbs 2:6-11 (CSB)*

None of us like being wrong or forgetting to do something we said we would do, but mistakes and forgetfulness happen. That is part of living this life. It becomes, then, what we do with the mistakes and forgetfulness afterwards that matters. That is where God's wisdom needs to surface for us. We need to immediately take the steps necessary to make amends.

How many politicians have we seen make mistakes and try to cover them up, only later to be pushed to the point of having to admit they were wrong. Some are even prosecuted by the law for the cover-up! They might save themselves lots of press coverage and further prosecution if they admit their failings up front.

What wisdom from God do we need to connect with? Even if our mistake is not something seen in 550 copies, what can we do to make amends? How can God guide us to correct something forgotten, something neglected, or someone we perhaps have hurt? Let us pray...

## Hearts Warmed

God presents Himself to us in many ways. John Wesley, the founder of the Methodist Church, felt his heart warmed and filled by the Holy Spirit. Perhaps many of us have had heartwarming times, knowing without a doubt that God's presence accounted for that feeling. Perhaps we felt God's presence in a different way, but again, without a doubt, we knew it was God working. Then there are those times that, only on reflection of the past, can we see where God was at work in our lives as we simply couldn't or didn't see it at the time. Did God use another person to help us with the event? Who was it? What influence did they have on our lives? Was that person someone who was an intricate part of our lives or merely someone passing by at a particular time in our lives?

Change comes and goes in our lives brought on by many events, places, and people. Do we embrace that change as important to our lives whether it is a good change or a difficult change? Often, for me, the difficult changes helped more to shape my life by how God used those events to get my attention.

*"Teach me, Lord, the meaning of your statutes, and I will always keep them. Help me understand your instruction, and I will obey it and follow it with all my heart. Help me stay on the path of your commands, for I take pleasure in it."*
*-- Psalms 119:33-35 (CSB)*

*"Teach me your way, LORD; lead me in a straight path because of my oppressors."*
*-- Psalms 27:11 (NIV)*

Our military personnel serve our country to protect our freedom. Also, our first responders serve us in ways that allow us to know others care. Let us not forget the sacrifices they make for us. Their families and loved ones also serve by supporting one another through periods of separation and fear. I pray for their families. May they find their hearts strangely warmed by God as they walk the paths laid out for them.

## Things to Ponder

Looking ahead to some scripture readings, I came across one in Jeremiah that made me ponder the following questions: Where do you put your trust? Who do you blame when things go wrong? What is the state of your heart (and not its physical state)? What thoughts linger in your mind? When stuff happens each day, how do you view the situation? Are you thirsty? Is your life fulfilling?

*" 'But blessed is the one who trusts in the LORD, whose confidence is in him. They will be like a tree planted by the water that sends out its roots by the stream. It does not fear when heat comes; its leaves are always green. It has no worries in a year of drought and never fails to bear fruit.' The heart is deceitful above all things and beyond cure. Who can understand it? 'I the LORD search the heart and examine the mind, to reward each person according to their conduct, according to what their deeds deserve.' " – Jeremiah 17:7-10 (NIV)*

Now ponder the questions again. Where do you put your trust? Who do you blame when things go wrong? What is the state of your heart (and not its physical state!)? What thoughts linger in your mind? When stuff happens each day, how do you view the situation? Are you thirsty? Is your life fulfilling?

The image of a tree by the river reminds me of many trees I have seen on our hikes. Some look weather beaten and crooked, but the leaves are strong and abundant. Isn't that like our lives? We have had rough days with emotional scars, or even physical scars, but remain strong in our faith. As Christians, we are not perfect, just forgiven. The living water of Christ sustains us and helps keep our heart pure and our steps in the right direction.

Perhaps we can find at least one thing in this scripture to ponder. Write it down and see how your life goes. I am trusting that God will bring peace to my Mom. I am starting to see the peace come about in her new place and I trust that this will continue for her. God had us here for reasons that go beyond helping Mom. Let us each look for the blessings that come every day. O Lord, I praise You for Your guidance, for Your comfort, and for Your gifts of other people that cross our paths.

### Defending Faith

For many years, centuries even, we have enjoyed the freedom in this country to share our faith without the worry of persecution. In my lifetime, I have watched slow changes happening to Christians. When did it start? How did it start? That might be hard to pinpoint because much of it was so gradual. Perhaps the most obvious first change was when prayer was banned from schools. But perhaps apathy allowed that one to creep in on us. No one ever believed that law would pass!

I don't have to enumerate the many ways we see our Christian freedoms being challenged or just plain taken away. Change is inevitable. But we need to be awake to that change and do whatever is necessary to protect our Christian freedoms.

*"For I am not ashamed of the gospel, because it is the power of God that brings salvation to everyone who believes: first to the Jew, then to the Gentile. For in the gospel the righteousness of God is revealed—a righteousness that is by faith from first to last, just as it is written: 'The righteous will live by faith.' "*
*-- Romans 1:16-17 (NIV)*

How willing are we to defend our faith? How willing are we to share the gospel news about Christ? Do we know what that involves? How do we find out? Scripture is there for us to read, learn, and share. Yes, questions arise as we read and thus arises the purpose of bible study groups where we have opportunities to share, question, and learn. Even for those who are on their computers a lot, much information to help explain passages from scripture is easily accessed. Human interaction is still important. As I look back over my life, I cannot begin to tell you the value of the hours spent discussing scripture, reading scripture, and praying for wisdom. Worship with music and sermons feed my soul.

Though all my years of study have helped me in the past, it is not enough. For each time I study or discuss with others, I constantly get new insight. Life changes as we grow older, but Christ is the foundation that salvation is built around. Scripture tells us that story. Let us not be ashamed of the gospel as Paul preached to the Romans.

### Restore My Soul

*"He renews my life;" -- Psalms 23:3 (CSB)*

*"I will never leave you or abandon you." -- Hebrews 13:5 (CSB)*

*"I have told you that I am going to prepare a place for you?" -- John 14:2 (CSB)*

Words of comfort available for all. Over the past few weeks, I read several books by Karen Kingsbury that are fictional, but could be stories about real people in real situations. Most of the characters are Christians, but Christians going through life with difficulties crossing their paths. The author masterfully reveals their struggles, shows their faith being questioned and tested, describes emotions found in everyday life, and leads you down the journey of everyday living. The value of knowing scripture comes alive as the author takes you through the characters' thoughts and words. The importance of family and friends for support when difficulties occur jump off the pages, as does the importance of celebrations of even the small parts of daily life.

Each of us needs to take the time to allow our souls and bodies to be restored. What in your life enables this to happen for you? Is it an early morning walk or run, a cup of coffee with a good book, a day spent with a friend or spouse, some quiet time with your Bible, or music to direct your thoughts. Yes, for me it can be all the above. As I was working on a quilt, I played some Christian music on my computer and the messages allowed me to sing along and ponder the messages. Reading the books by Karen led me into the lives of the characters. As I read, I thought of people in my life who were like the characters. I reminisced over friends whose lives have crossed my journey and how God was shared.

As I learned of friends enduring health changes, I was strengthened by knowing that Jesus will never leave us or forsake us. Jesus does go to prepare a place for us, but none of us know when we'll go to that special place!

All three of these concepts are so closely connected. Knowing that Jesus will never leave me restores my soul! Knowing that He prepared a place for me restores my soul! No matter what awaits me tomorrow or even later today, I take comfort in knowing that Jesus is my Savior. Let me live each day with His joy in my soul regardless of what is happening around me. How I praise You, Lord! For You are mighty, gentle, caring, and forgiving. You are who restores me. Your promises to be with me always and in everything makes me know You truly have a place prepared for me. Thank You.

### Idols Around Us

The Bible has a lot of passages about how idols wrongly influence our lives. It often seems that, when God is silent in our lives, we reach out to the visible things around us. Perhaps we even make idols out of parts of our lives simply because it feels good.

In scripture, idols appeared to be other gods that the people worshipped. What in our society today are our idols? I can name a few, but I'm sure each of you can think of additional ones. Things like money, status, power in work titles, sports figures, political figures, entertainment people, exceptional talent within oneself, food, exercise...Each of these things in and of themselves does not make them idols. What we do with them is what makes them idols. How much importance or how much time do we spend dedicated to it? Do thoughts of these things overpower our thoughts of God?

Isaiah 46:1-2 talks about the idols the Babylonians carried around. Then, in the next two verses, Isaiah writes: ***"Listen to me, house of Jacob, all the remnant of the house of Israel, who have been sustained from the womb, carried along since birth. I will be the same until your old age, and I will bear you up when you turn gray. I have made you, and I will carry you; I will bear and rescue you."*** -- *Isaiah 46:3-4 (CSB)*

Will the other people or things listed above come close to the type of relationship God promises us? Money might provide physical comfort, but what about inner comfort and peace of mind for eternity? Status brings about other issues which can drag us down, as others begin to find things to criticize (whether valid or not). Work titles come and go and outside that realm, they mean nothing. For all the others listed, they are things that come and go. Yes, celebrities can be inspirational, but they should not become our idols. Our God is the only one who will carry us from birth to death into eternity. None of the other important people or things will carry us into eternity. That may not mean we give up the activity, but we change the attitude about the hold it has on our lives.

Even when God is silent in our lives for a period, He is still with us. Perhaps His silence is only about one issue, but He never leaves us. For now, the focus is on idols and how God is the only God we need. We worship Him and no other person or thing. Let us ponder our lives and see if we carry any other idols around that perhaps we need to relinquish in favor of our Lord, who is with us always. Yes, even to my old age and with my gray hairs, God sustains me and rescues me often from myself. How I praise Him for His mercy, grace, constancy, and love.

### Comfort, Protect

As we drive past several fields near us or in the Phoenix area north of us, we often see sheep grazing on the alfalfa. Their shepherd moves them from field to field as they eat up all the alfalfa. Then the field is flooded to allow the alfalfa to regrow. There are always many young sheep in the herds. You can often see them running together and playing with each other, or they might be near their mother nursing, resting, or just being near her.

I get many requests for my quilted prayer cloths. Seems lots of folks need God's comfort. ***"He protects his flock like a shepherd; he gathers the lambs in his arms and carries them in the fold of his garment. He gently leads those that are nursing."*** -- *Isaiah 40:11 (CSB)*

How much we all need comfort! Not just the comfort of a warm and safe home, but the comfort of someone who cares for us. Burdens are easier to carry when someone helps you carry them. Sorrows are easier to work through in the comfort of a good friend or family member. But God offers the ultimate in comfort! He is available 24/7 for us to lean on in times of trouble. He is patient with us, giving us time and space to reach out to Him. Some come quickly into His arms, while others try to work out their need for comfort in other ways. Just as a shepherd keeps track of each sheep, God knows everything about us.

As I sew, I know the comfort each cloth brings, not because of the cloth, but because it represents our God who loves us so much. I feel God's comfort surround me even as I sew; I know that God continues to provide the comfort the person needs. Each of us can bring comfort to others. Some take meals to those in need, some simply sit with them and listen, others offer help with daily tasks that need to be done, while some offer funding to help with extra expenses involved. Each of these activities bring comfort to those in need. God is the motivator for us to do the deeds that we do. Let's praise Him for creating us with the love for one another to be instruments of His work.

Jesus is our shepherd, and a shepherd knows everything about His sheep so that He can take care of them. How wonderful to play in His field and enjoy our lives, knowing that His comfort is always there for us to claim, depend on, and enjoy.

### Live Sacrificially

The Winter Olympics have started. Some incredible stories will unfold as we watch the athletes compete. The world holds these young men and women in very high esteem. Our media does not usually tell us about any spiritual journeys that they take as a part of their preparations for these events.

Some of our celebrity sports figures are very good at getting their spiritual lives out to the public. Some of them even live out their spiritual lives as they speak about their faith. But regardless, the world still holds them all in high esteem. So many young people want to grow up to be stars, players, or musicians. They want glamour, money, fame, and prestige. How often have we watched a talented/beautiful/handsome teenager succeed in the eyes of the world only to grow a little older and descend into the grips of sin for all the world to see.

Romans 12 talks about living your life for Christ. *"Therefore, brothers and sisters, in view of the mercies of God, I urge you to present your bodies as a living sacrifice, holy and pleasing to God; this is your true worship. Do not be*

**conformed to this age, but be transformed by the renewing of your mind, so that you may discern what is the good, pleasing, and perfect will of God." -- Romans 12:1-2 (CSB)** This challenge of living sacrificially a life that is holy and pleasing to God, goes with us into any vocation or journey that we undertake. What compromises are we willing to make between serving God and living in the world? Do we even ponder this question as we walk into each day? How do we recognize a compromise in our life to the values that God wants for us? Staying in tune to God's word helps us to recognize detours in life.

I wonder if I were to serve God with the same fervor and concentration that an athlete puts into their training, where would I be? Some of us do put that kind of energy into our service and we see the results of their work. We see the love of God in the quality of their life. That quality has nothing to do with material possessions either. It is an inner quality of life that shines through everything else in their lives. May we consider how we live out this scripture in Romans.

### Praise With Songs

Have you ever noticed some of the aspects that we use to make selections of gifts? When we pick a wrapped package from a pile of packages, how do we decide which one? Some people want the biggest one, or perhaps the fanciest one. We usually equate the contents with the packaging.

What about people? How do we determine whether a person (namely those we don't know) is worthy of conversation? Is it by their looks, their actions, or their voice tones, or the clothes they wear? We all make judgments about people based on some observations. Yet, how often are those initial observations that reliable? We all know at times we were wrong with initial judgments!

Sometimes we sit in church and hear someone singing near us so loud and off key. Oh, the thoughts that can come to mind: can't they sing softer; surely, they know how bad they sound; why do they insist on singing so loudly; and other such comments.

Many of the Psalms tell us to sing to the Lord! The scriptures don't say only if you can sing on key, or if you have a great voice. The scriptures simply tell us to sing our praise to the Lord.

*"God, I will sing a new song to you; I will play on a ten-stringed harp for you."*
*-- Psalms 144:9 (CSB)*

*"I will praise the Lord all my life; I will sing to my God as long as I live."* -- *Psalms 146:2 (CSB)*

*"Sing to the Lord with thanksgiving; play the lyre to our God"* -- *Psalms 147:7 (CSB)*

*"Hallelujah! Sing to the Lord a new song, his praise in the assembly of the faithful...-- Let them praise his name with dancing and make music to him with tambourine and lyre. For the Lord takes pleasure in his people; he adorns the humble with salvation. Let the faithful celebrate in triumphal glory; let them shout for joy on their beds."* -- *Psalms 149:1-5 (CSB)*

And the best for last! *"Praise him with the blast of a ram's horn; praise him with harp and lyre. Praise him with tambourine and dance; praise him with strings and flute. Praise him with resounding cymbals; praise him with clashing cymbals. Let everything that breathes praise the Lord. Hallelujah!"* -- *Psalms 150:3-6 (CSB)*

Yep, that seems to include all of us, no conditions! Now when I hear someone in the congregation singing with joy, I praise God for their joy, even if they are off key! Perhaps the next time I must select a gift from a pile of many, I'll seek the least of those in the pile. Perhaps I need to look beyond the surface just as, I pray, Jesus does for me!


### Do Your Best


How many times as parents do (or did) we tell our children, "*Do your best.*" How many of our children heard it as, "Don't fail" or "Be perfect" or perhaps "Get busy and study so you'll ace that test." We want that phrase to be encouraging and perhaps at times it is. I guess it depends upon the rest of the relationship that we have with each child or person, or the tone of voice used to deliver the phrase.

*"Whatever you do, do it from the heart, as something done for the Lord and not for people." -- Colossians 3:23 (CSB)* Wow, what a big order! Yet it is such a simple task. No matter what your job is for the day, do it well as though the Lord is the friend coming to spend the day with you. I know that if I have company coming, I try harder to have the house picked up and cleaned. If I have a responsibility to fulfill for others, I try to do it well. However, things don't always happen that way. When I allow my schedule to get overloaded, my attention to quality suffers. My attention to the Lord suffers as well. When I'm at home I tend to put off tasks. I let things lay undone.

We can become task masters for ourselves, demanding the best all the time! What about God? He wants us to be in a relationship with Him. As humans though, we can't be all that God wants us to be. Thanks to Jesus, His death on the cross became the sacrifice that enables us to be made right before God. Jesus extends His grace and forgiveness to us.

The quality of what we achieve is not as important as the attitude of our heart toward God. If we are doing our best for God, even though it is not perfect, we have lived well that day! The pictures my young grandchildren make for me are precious, but not perfect. Given their talent, age and skills, the projects are gifts of love, treasured and enjoyed. The brownies I make for my husband may not be the best in the world, but I make them for him out of the love I have for God giving him to me.

The ladies that gather at my house on Thursdays come for the discussion, the laughter, the fellowship, and the prayers. My preparations are such to make everyone comfortable so that we can share God's word with one another rather than to have a show house for all to praise my cleaning ability! That cleaning ability falls under Jesus' grace and forgiveness!

How can each of us live out this scripture in Colossians: *"Whatever you do, do it from the heart, as something done for the Lord and not for people." -- Colossians 3:23 (CSB)* May we consider as we approach our days, the attitude of our heart toward God and give God our best.

### You Want Healing

Let's have a party! Oh, how I love parties! Will you come to my party? By the way, it is pity party! We'll have so much fun empathizing with each other over the limitations of our lives. I wonder which of us will have the greatest pity issue! Remember the story of the woman who bleed for 12 years? She probably had many well-earned pity parties! Even though she had tried everything to help her, she always believed she would be healed sometime! She kept searching for help. She heard about Jesus.

*"Just then, a woman who had suffered from bleeding for twelve years approached from behind and touched the end of his robe, for she said to herself, 'If I can just touch his robe, I'll be made well.' Jesus turned and saw her. 'Have courage, daughter,' he said. 'Your faith has saved you.' And the woman was made well from that moment." -- Matthew 9:20-22 (CSB)*

Each of us carries around some weakness or limitation that we can't seem to delete. Or perhaps it is a physical problem that prevents us from doing things we want to do. Maybe we have dreams left unfulfilled, and we can list excuses as to why we aren't able to fulfill them. In our own minds we can conjure up some good pity parties about those issues. Have those issues resulted in damaged relationships over the years? What effect do those limitations have upon our self-esteem?

Jesus often asked if someone wanted to be healed. Then sometimes He just recognized their desires to be healed. Often when asked if we want healing or help, our answer usually is, "Yes," but do we really mean it? Sometimes wallowing in excuses and unfulfillment is easier than the work or faith needed to be healed. Jesus healed this woman immediately, but then remarked that her faith was enough, and she was healed.

We have the option of asking Jesus to help us with our weaknesses, to seek forgiveness, to walk in faith regardless of the limitations which might surround us. Paul, throughout his ministry, suffered an affliction, but never allowed that to limit his ministry. We need to see beyond our suffering, our weakness, or our limitations and live for Christ, despite the difficulties of our lives. Let us have a party together in spirit, but not a pity party. Let us have a celebration of all that Christ does for us so that we can shine for Him. May we help one another in some way to experience the love of Jesus.

### Mary or Martha

Are you a Mary or a Martha? If you're a guy you probably said "neither!" Guys, you can be like one or the other!

The story of Mary and Martha is one many of us know: "***While they were traveling, he entered a village, and a woman named Martha welcomed him into her home. She had a sister named Mary, who also sat at the Lord's feet and was listening to what he said. But Martha was distracted by her many tasks, and she came up and asked, 'Lord, don't you care that my sister has left me to serve alone? So tell her to give me a hand.' The Lord answered her, 'Martha, Martha, you are worried and upset about many things, but one thing is necessary. Mary has made the right choice, and it will not be taken away from her.' " -- Luke 10:38-42 (CSB)***

Now, back to my original question, are you a Mary or a Martha type? Jesus' answer to the question indicates that Mary is best, so let's consider our options. When it comes to listening to Jesus, yep, she is hard to beat. As I ponder my own life, as I hope you will ponder yours, I find some of both types alive in me.

As a young mother of three children many years ago, I felt like Martha most of the time. Or at least on the surface that is what I saw. What about the times I would sit and listen as each of them told me about events of the day, or asked questions that they had to find answers to? Did my Mary type of listening help them discover things? Did the example of my listening in worship enable them to model anything for their lives? Did the time I spent going to Bible Studies while they were in school enable me to enjoy the Mary role? Yet my Martha role was essential at home to provide for their physical life.

During the years of working as a church staff person, I spent a lot of time doing Martha type work. It was essential to allow others to spend time listening to words and programs that allowed them to be Mary types. Yet, I found during those years that it was equally important for me to find places to be a Mary and sit at the feet of Jesus filling my soul with His love, grace, and His teachings. Those sessions enabled me to continue being a hard-working Martha so that others could be served in Jesus' name.

Now as a mother of grown adults, they teach me. They are Martha's for me on many occasions and tell me to let them do the work. They want me to go be with their children. I love sitting at the feet of Jesus and learn what He has for me, and I appreciate every Martha at work that allows me the privilege of just sitting. But I also love being the Martha that allows others to sit at the feet of Jesus and grow closer to Him. May we allow ourselves to find the Mary and the Martha times in our daily lives.

### Words We Speak

I love the book of James! It has so many wonderful instructions for living a life of faith and prayer. *"Not many should become teachers, my brothers, because you know that we will receive a stricter judgment. For we all stumble in many ways. If anyone does not stumble in what he says, he is mature, able also to control the whole body." -- James 3:1-2 (CSB)* Fortunately, forgiveness helps all of us who stumble and are not perfect!

*"Now if we put bits into the mouths of horses so that they obey us, we direct their whole bodies. And consider ships: Though very large and driven by fierce winds, they are guided by a very small rudder wherever the will of the pilot directs. So too, though the tongue is a small part of the body, it boasts great things. Consider how a small fire sets ablaze a large forest. And the tongue is a fire. The tongue, a world of unrighteousness, is placed among our members.*

*It stains the whole body, sets the course of life on fire, and is itself set on fire by hell." -- James 3:3-6 (CSB)* How very powerful is our tongue! How many times have I said something before putting the mind in gear only to find I said something offensive or hurtful unintentionally. Help me to think before I speak. Once again, I praise God for grace and forgiveness!

*"Every kind of animal, bird, reptile, and fish is tamed and has been tamed by humankind, but no one can tame the tongue. It is a restless evil, full of deadly poison. With the tongue we bless our Lord and Father, and with it we curse people who are made in God's likeness. Blessing and cursing come out of the same mouth. My brothers and sisters, these things should not be this way. Does a spring pour out sweet and bitter water from the same opening? Can a fig tree produce olives, my brothers and sisters, or a grapevine produce figs? Neither can a saltwater spring yield fresh water." -- James 3:7-12 (CSB)* This scripture hits home for many of us! I find much offensive language used on TV today and in other media. Not just offensive, but sarcastic and disrespectful language which subjects our children to behavior that teaches disrespect for one another. Yes, it is funny sometimes, but the disrespect is so overdone now that I question what we are teaching our younger generations. Words that come off our tongues are powerful in both good and bad ways. I would hope that we could see more praiseworthy language being shared on the media, in our homes, workplaces, schools, and in our world today. What can each of us do to tame our tongues and to encourage others to also be aware of what words they use?

### God Equips You

How many of us have been asked to do something and immediately think of a dozen reasons why we can't? Some of us nearly always say yes because we simply can't refuse, while some always say no. My favorite example of God giving you something to do is in Exodus 3 where Moses meets the burning bush which certainly gets Moses' attention! Then God explains to Moses the nature of the mission - to rescue the Israelites from Pharaoh in Egypt. For the rest of this chapter and into chapter four Moses negotiates with God. Hum, that sounds like something I would do and perhaps you might do also! I love the excuses that Moses uses to try and get God to choose someone else. Let's look at them.

*"But Moses asked God, 'Who am I that I should go to Pharaoh and that I should bring the Israelites out of Egypt?' " -- Exodus 3:11 (CSB)* When I was a very infant Christian, I asked our Pastor if he would start a women's bible study and he

encouraged me to do it. How could I do that as I knew nothing about the bible, but I proceeded to gather a group of ladies. God brought to the group a couple of very mature Christians, who started my growth and faith journey.

*"Then Moses asked God, 'If I go to the Israelites and say to them, 'The God of your ancestors has sent me to you,' and they ask me, 'What is his name?' what should I tell them?' God replied to Moses, 'AM WHO I AM. This is what you are to say to the Israelites: I AM has sent me to you.' " -- Exodus 3:13-14 (CSB)* Again, Moses did not think anyone would believe him! When I taught Parenting classes, I wondered "Who do I think I am?" I had studied material that I found worked for me at home, and I had prayed about what God wanted me to do. Others asked me to teach them what I had learned. God made me qualified.

Here is another expression of reluctance. *"But Moses replied to the Lord, 'Please, Lord, I have never been eloquent — either in the past or recently or since you have been speaking to your servant — because my mouth and my tongue are sluggish.' " -- Exodus 4:10 (CSB)* God answered that He would help Moses speak and teach him what to say. My first day in my office as the Director of Christian Education, I sat there praying and said, "Ok, God, you got me here, now what do I do?" God answered every day!

*"Moses said, 'Please, Lord, send someone else.' " -- Exodus 4:13 (CSB)* God gave Moses Aaron to be his spokesperson. When I applied for the job of Director of Christian Education at my church, I told everyone, even God, let them find someone else better equipped for the job. I was only applying because I wanted to be obedient to any call that God might have given to me, but if He wanted someone else for the job it was OK with me!

I have learned over the years that God equips us for the jobs He calls us to do. Sometimes though, it is not God calling us and no is a good answer. If I simply don't know if it is God calling, prayers and time become important in following God's leading. What is God calling you to do?

### Spiritual Growth

Instead of attending a formal worship service on Sunday, I had a personal time of retreat. Rudy was off for the weekend, with our only car, at a photography workshop at Mt. Rainier. As I sat in our motorhome alone enjoying the quiet, many thoughts were dancing through my mind and soul. After reading some scripture, some commentary, some questions, the one that struck me was: *"Additionally then, brothers and sisters, we ask and encourage you in the Lord Jesus, that as you have received instruction from us on how you should live and please God — as you are doing — do this even more." -- 1 Thessalonians 4:1 (CSB)*

As a mature Christian who has walked with God for more than 40 years, how do I increase my walk? It is so comfortable being with my regular habits with God. But am I really growing? What more do I have to give to God? These are the thoughts that are rattling around in my mind. Is coasting enough? Not according to these passages in 1 Thessalonians. God is never finished with our growth. We should also be seeking ways to move on toward perfection!

Our bodies need to constantly be stretched, used, exercised, rested, fed, and groomed. Our spiritual lives must also meet these goals. How do we stretch, exercise, and feed our spiritual life? The answer for each of us is different since the answer considers the spiritual gifts we were given. Do we know what those spiritual gifts are? Perhaps that is a place to start. Read Romans 12 and 1 Corinthians 12 for more information on spiritual gifts. Also, many books are available to help you discern your gifts. May you find some "retreat" time alone to ponder and seek God's direction for your growth. I know that I shall be in the process of praying for direction, seeking information related to my gifts, and discussing with others. At the same time, I plan to listen and watch for signs from God as to where He wants me to stretch my growth. Perhaps the answers may be the subject of a future thought...Update: That future thought is now this book of devotionals! Writing them between 2000-2011, I am finally being obedient and getting them published! Yes, I am still growing spiritually as I turn 80 this year(2023)! For years, I have been "too busy," "not sure how to proceed," "what have I got to say that anyone wants to read," but God keeps sending me notes, people and even a self-publisher guide! I met the

lady four years ago, but just met with her and her husband this year with my questions about self-publishing. My sewing machine has been put aside until I can complete this task. My bible study ladies and other friends are also encouraging me to get the book done! Finally, I am saying "YES" to God, and "forgive me for taking so long." I'm not a bible scholar, but I am still, and always will be, a bible student. All I write is to give praise to God!

## *Travel, Trips*

### *Pacific Ocean*

Standing on the edge of a cliff on the coast of Oregon, I watched in awe the breakers rolling in from the Pacific Ocean, splashing against the rocks. The mist from the water thrown into the air carried up and hung suspended over the trees and roadway like haze. The gulls sat sunning themselves or swooping in search of food. Warblers and wrens chatted as they scurried from tree to tree. Such a peaceful setting. Was it really so peaceful?

One sign we read spoke of the constant turbulence of the force of the water pounding and shaping the rock. Rockslides occur to change the scenes. Trees fall, taking whatever is in the way, down with them. Messages on all the beaches warn about "sneaker waves" that are bigger than others. They can come unexpectedly washing away whatever is in the way.

Our lives are like that nature scene, in constant change from the situations around us. Jesus, amid His last hours on earth, cried out in the garden, *"And he said, 'Abba,' Father! All things are possible for you. Take this cup away from me. Nevertheless, not what I will, but what you will.' " -- Mark 14:36 (CSB)* Abba speaks of an especially close relationship to God.

As I stood on the cliff, I said thank you, Abba Father, for creating all the beauty I enjoyed, even amid the turmoil that nature brings. I said thank you for being with us in the turmoil of uncertainty that exists so prevalently today. How grateful I am to know that God embraces all who seek that Abba relationship. May we seek God's will and allow it to prevail through the peace and the turmoil in our lives and in nature.

### Seeking the Way

We made our first trip to the desert this week! It looked barren, with little in the way of vegetation. As we studied the map looking for someplace to go, we set out for KOFA National Wildlife Refuge, Palm Canyon, Arizona. As we drove miles down a dirt road, still seeing nothing but getting closer to the mountains, we entered the refuge only to find a sign that didn't tell us much. Spotting a bird, we stopped. While looking at the bird, a couple in a Jeep stopped to ask about what we saw. Quickly it became evident to them that this was our first trip and we needed guidance!

Thanks to their ability to see our need, they guided us for the next two days, taking us deep into the canyons in river washouts in our cars and then by foot up into the hills. They shared with us the locations for some new birds, the footpaths used by Indians many years ago. They also showed us the pictographs left on the hills, told us about the survival ability of the plants, and shared their love for the desert.

*"Dear friend, you are acting faithfully in whatever you do for the brothers and sisters, especially when they are strangers." -- 3 John 1:5 (CSB)*

How do we recognize a seeker of faith? Are we looking? Are we watching for those opportunities that God leads us to for sharing? Are we prepared for sharing? Are our prayers daily allowing us to center enough on Christ to recognize a seeker? I pray that God keeps my eyes, ears, and heart open to those seeking His love and grace. May I be just as open to them as our new friends were to us in the desert.

### God or Our Plans

We are about to embark on another journey. Questions about our destinations often arise. Is the distance more than we want to travel? With the economy in the uncertain, do we want to incur the traveling expenses associated with being on the go? What people and places do we choose to see? How can God use our availability along the way?

As we struggled with these and other questions, we came across: *"Come now, you who say, 'Today or tomorrow we will travel to such and such a city and spend a year there and do business and make a profit.' Yet you do not know what tomorrow will bring — what your life will be! For you are like vapor that appears for a little while, then vanishes. Instead, you should say, 'If the Lord wills, we will live and do this or that.' But as it is, you boast in your arrogance. All such boasting is evil. So it is sin to know the good and yet not do it." -- James*

***4:13-17 (CSB)*** As any of us go about planning our days, even if it just includes our daily trip to work, do we let God's plan enter our plans? What kind of time do we spend trying to recognize what God wants for us? How flexible are we for making changes as we recognize opportunities for service that arise? Thinking about God's teachings certainly influences our plans. May we seek God's direction in all our thoughts and plans.

### The Space Station

We had the opportunity to experience a wonderful treat. Space Station 3D is showing at the IMAX Theater. Just sitting in the theater waiting for the movie to begin, we laughed as we looked at one another with the head goggles on that allowed us to see 3D. We even documented the spectacle with our digital camera in the room lighting making it all look very red with weird faces! Then the show began!!!!

Pictures from space looking back on the earth are awesome. Seeing the Space Station being built in the vastness of outer space, and trying to comprehend all the elements necessary for that building to take place, overwhelms me. I found myself just sitting and staring like an awestruck child seeing something for the first time. Yet, I have watched my share of NASA's missions, from the first flight into outer space, to orbiting the earth, to circling the moon, to landing on the moon, and on! Perhaps it was the size of the screen and the 3D that added to this experience.

David's words here are still true today: ***"The heavens declare the glory of God, and the expanse proclaims the work of his hands. Day after day they pour out speech; night after night they communicate knowledge. There is no speech; there are no words; their voice is not heard. Their message has gone out to the whole earth, and their words to the ends of the world." -- Psalms 19:1-4 (CSB)***

With the Space Station being a project of many nations, perhaps it is also a symbol of how we can work together to accomplish a task. What other projects encourage us to come together for peaceful purposes? Few other projects can fill the heavens quite literally like this one. Perhaps we need to add to the perspective of other projects, allowing God to expand our vision to experience the awesome in any of His works.

Stories abound of His awesome work in magazines and books. Within our Christian communities, within our lives, our awesome God is also at work.

We watched an awesome sunset last night, but God's awesome work exists even within the smallest, darkest most unlikely area of our lives when we open our eyes to see, our ears to hear, and our hearts to feel. Where do you experience our awesome God today?

### Pillars of Fire

God finds a way to get my attention on so many occasions! We traveled with our son and family to see Mt. Baker, a 10,780' volcano in Washington state that still emits steam from the heat deep within the mountain. We spotted a very unusual rock formation which was featured at the visitor center where we found a description and explanation.

Imagine hundreds of approximately 6"x 6" "posts" (hardened lava) standing on end with definite vertical lines visibly defining each "timber." Then have the tops of each "timber" stop at different lengths from each other. Now picture them curving without losing any of their width. These three-dimensional walls of rock were named "Pillars of Fire" since fire was one ingredient responsible for their development.

The term "Pillars of Fire" always reminds me of God leading the Israelites in the wilderness after leaving Egypt. The Pillar of Fire led them at night and the Pillar of Clouds led them by day. Sometimes life feels like wandering in the desert, always seeking direction. Do I take this job? Do I move to a new location? Do I join this church? Do I start another project? Where do I use my energies? Is this a relationship to pursue? How do we spend our disposable income? Where do I follow my "pillar of fire"?

Nehemiah reviews the blessings of the Israelites: ***"You did not abandon them in the wilderness because of your great compassion. During the day the pillar of cloud never turned away from them, guiding them on their journey. And during the night the pillar of fire illuminated the way they should go." -- Nehemiah 9:19 (CSB)***

Out of His great mercy for us, God will not leave us in the desert. He may not take away our pain, our suffering, the consequences of our actions, or our disease, just as He did not lead the Israelites out for 40 years. Yet He will stay with us in the desert and offer us His comfort and welcome us into His arms. Thank you, God, for showing me the "Pillars of Fire" to remind me once again of your presence.

### Along Steep Slopes

We traveled with friends in the Rocky Mountains. All along the way, the mountain peaks awed us with the beauty of the snow, the ruggedness, and the sheer steep sides. As we drove, I noticed the animal trails going horizontally along the steep slopes. Once, we watched eight mule deer walking along one of these paths in a single row. I was amazed how agile they were as they walked so precariously along the path which appeared to be so dangerous. We rode the tram up the side of one of the mountains. At the top, the view was awesome! Getting up to that site without the help of the tram would not be easy.

This verse connected for me our journeys in life: *"He makes my feet like the feet of a deer and sets me securely on the heights." -- Psalms 18:33 (CSB)*

One of the people with us for the weekend is awaiting a medical diagnosis next week and feels she is on a steep mountain awaiting the outcome. But her faith is strong and enabling her to enjoy each day, knowing that God is in control.

What "mountain" are you traversing currently? How is God making you like the deer that does not stumble? My prayer for all of us is that we will allow God to help us to stand strong as we encounter whatever is difficult in our life right now.

### Plans Revised

Our plans are in place, every detail is arranged, anticipation of the event is great, and eagerness to get going abounds. Finally ready to go, we drive off, asking for God's protection and guidance in making decisions. The skies were beautiful and mountain views breathtaking as we drove to Steamboat Springs. As we reviewed the plans for the next day, going over the route for the half marathon run for our daughter and her husband, our excitement grew.

Morning came with a clear sky, cool temperatures. As we drove the car toward our goal, we began to see dark clouds that stretched far and thick. Rain loomed in the distance with the temperatures in the mid 40's. At our destination for the marathon start, the rain and lightning boomed! Sitting in the car, deciding do they battle the elements of the present and jeopardize the hopes of tomorrow? Decisions came though disappointment hung around, no run today for my daughter and her husband. They decided it was not worth the risks.

The rest of the day, as we worked our way back in the car, we endured the rain, the cold, almost got ourselves stuck in mud (which is another story), until we finally arrived back at the motorhome. The rain was finally letting up, but much too late to continue our plans. The trip home the next day in the motorhome was again under beautiful skies which revealed fabulous scenery, a stop at the ice cream store, and hope restored for the next outing.

Once home, I began reflecting on our beginning prayer as we left asking for God's guidance and protection. *"A person's heart plans his way, but the Lord determines his steps." -- Proverbs 16:9 (CSB)* God did protect us and enabled us to see beyond the moment, allowing us to follow another course of action that differed from our plans.

How many times does life alter our plans? Asking for God's guidance and protection always enables us to follow the path we did not want to follow. Reflection on events needs to help us find the positives, the influence of God's action, and the hope for tomorrow in His presence.

### Sense of Awe

As we drove into Butchart Gardens in Victoria, B.C. Canada, the beauty greeting me made me want to get into the gardens quickly. With my mouth hanging open in awe, my senses were engulfed with the immensity of beauty. As I stood at several of the overlooks to the Sunken Gardens, all I could think to say was a prayer of thanks to God for creating such beauty. God must have thought some kid was turned

loose in a candy store with all the praise I sent His way! Pictures do not capture the overall beauty of the spot. The fragrance added to the scene. The sounds of water running, of people talking softly, and the sounds of quietness all around amplified the experience. The detail of the colors, the softness of the petals, and the richness of healthy plants was apparent all around.

As I reflected on the experience since leaving the Garden, I likened it to the impression we Christians leave with the world about the life we live with our Lord. Paul spoke of our strengths: ***"Now may the God who gives endurance and encouragement grant you to live in harmony with one another, according to Christ Jesus, so that you may glorify the God and Father of our Lord Jesus Christ with one mind and one voice." -- Romans 15:5-6 (CSB)***

Fifty-five gardeners maintain the Gardens during the summer with a total of about 500 employees. They work for one goal, the beauty and health of the Gardens so that all who come may enjoy their stay. As Christians, we hope for others to see some of Christ in us. Our churches and we as individuals often live our lives in ways that do not reflect our Christian values daily. If we want the world to see the beauty of life in Christ, we need to be competent gardeners of our words, our actions, and our thoughts.

How inviting is our Christian life to the world? Granted, God is the one who leads others to us. He is the one who opens doors in the hearts of men, women, and children. We Christians are His tools and His messengers. We must work toward the same goal of leading all to Him. Wouldn't it be great if all who came into our churches left with the same sense of awe as those who came to a place like Butchart Gardens!

### *Carnival Time*

What is your comfort zone when it comes to worship? Many prefer a traditional service. Then many others prefer a more boisterous sound with a beat. Just feel it, the toe tapping qualities that stir physical movement. Along with the music comes a message that challenges the daily life we live. There are blended options of everything above. While in New Orleans at Mardi Gras time, the locals say, it is Carnival time preparing for Lent.

***"Hallelujah! Praise God in his sanctuary. Praise him in his mighty expanse. Praise him for his powerful acts; praise him for his abundant greatness. Praise him with the blast of a ram's horn; praise him with harp and lyre. Praise him with tambourine and dance; praise him with strings and flute. Praise him with resounding cymbals; praise him with clashing cymbals. Let everything that breathes praise the Lord. Hallelujah!" -- Psalms 150:1-6 (CSB)***

The folks at this church certainly lived up to the Psalm! The music worship team set the stage for the pastor to preach a powerful sermon about our God who gives second chances (and gives those chances repeatedly as we journey through life). Serving our Lord is a joy! Worshipping to jazz renditions of *"Onward Christians*

*Soldiers,"* "'Tis So Sweet to Trust in Jesus,"* "Savior Like a Shepherd Lead Us,"* "What a Friend We Have in Jesus,"* and of course, the finale "When the Saints Go Marchin' In"* stirred the soul, brought the hands together, and kept the toes a tapping. At the breakout of "When the Saints...," the Pastor stood up in the front row with his opened Mardi Gras umbrella with the gold fringe dangling all around and led the crowd in a spontaneous parade up and around the sanctuary! The Psalms tells us how our God loves praise and worship.

God was worshipped and praised with the 3Ms - music, message, and meaning. For those who attended as visitors, we had the opportunity to hear about second chances and to see Christians praising our Lord in mighty style. What a joy to attend worship at this place. What creative ways do you use for praising our Lord?

*"Onward Christian Soldiers," words by Sabine Baring-Gould, 1864; " 'Tis So Sweet to Trust in Jesus," words by Louisa M. R. Stead, 1882; "Savior Like a Shephard Leads Us," words attributed to Dorothy A. Thrupp, 1836; "What a Friend We Have in Jesus," words by Joseph M Scriven, ca. 1855; "When the Saints Go Marchin' In," words by Katharine Purvis, 1896 (many versions authors vary); all songs in Public Domain.*

### *Finding Direction*

At a rally for motorhome owners, we found ourselves among thousands of motorhomes. With our new motorhome, we had appointments for repairs. Some involved troubles which made us wonder if we made the right decision to buy our new coach. Hours were spent in seminars trying to gain knowledge about how to solve some of the problems.

Then one evening, we heard about the death of one of the national officers during the event. I learned that he had bought a new coach one week before he passed away. I can only imagine his wife's list of troubles and concerns compounded by her grief.

As I spent time catching up with friends and new acquaintances, I learned of other troubles that plague their families. Some were consumed by their grief; others were handling their troubles while continuing to live.

*"Consider it a great joy, my brothers and sisters, whenever you experience various trials, because you know that the testing of your faith produces endurance. And let endurance have its full effect, so that you may be mature and complete, lacking nothing. Now if any of you lacks wisdom, he should ask*

**God — who gives to all generously and ungrudgingly — and it will be given to him." -- James 1:2-5 (CSB)**

I praise God for showing me the place of troubles in our life. Solutions are found through patiently seeking the answers. As we ask for wisdom about how to deal with daily or unusual issues, we need to expect answers from God. Perhaps He sends us the right person to help. Yes, God did bring us to several people this week who helped. He also sent us to others to help with their troubles.

Do we give our troubles to God, or do we hang on to them, trying to solve them all ourselves? Let us remember to pray for one another and to pray for wisdom to handle our troubles.

### Needs Around Us

When we attend RV rallies, we always meet lots of new people. Some, of course, are more interesting than others, but we love meeting new folks. At a smaller rally, about half of the folks present had never attended one of these rallies.

A scripture reminded me of a lady I met during those few days. **"Don't neglect to show hospitality, for by doing this some have welcomed angels as guests without knowing it. Remember those in prison, as though you were in prison with them, and the mistreated, as though you yourselves were suffering bodily." -- Hebrews 13:2-3 (CSB)** When I first met this couple, I never would have known the suffering they have endured over the past months. As our conversation progressed, I began to share about the prayer cloths that I make. One thing led to another and soon she was telling me about the needless death of her 22-year-old son.

On another occasion in a small church, we easily stand out as visitors. Several people made it a point to welcome us. As strangers in their midst, we appreciated their warmth. As I listened to their prayer needs and observed their care for one another in the form of prayers, I felt moved to offer several prayer cloths to them. Who will they go to? I do not know, but I do know the pastor will use them and add to them the prayers of the congregation. Those in need want visual reminders of our prayers.

The part of the scripture that is not a part of my life is the part about prison. Suffering and welcoming strangers, I can identify with quite readily! But prison? I have no frame of reference for literal prison confinement. Don't prisons come in various forms? Do we make of ourselves prisoners of certain aspects of life merely out of fear or ignorance? Yes, that form of prison, I can visualize. This scripture expects empathy for others, an ear to listen to others, and a hand to hold. It doesn't expect us to approve of or condone situations, but merely to be available to others with the grace that God offers to us and to others. These situations also offer us opportunities to witness the saving grace of our Lord. How can we welcome strangers, care for those in prison, and comfort those who suffer? Help us to recognize needs around us daily.

### *Risky Journeys*

"You're going to West Chicago, Illinois." "What do you think about Morristown, New Jersey?" "Dublin, Ohio is the home of your next location." "What about southern New Hampshire?" "Retirement, motorhome, full-time, hum." All of these statements, questions and comments are a part of my life's journey. We all have journeys that begin with a comment or statement that carries with it a certain amount of fear, anxiety, uncertainty, anticipation, excitement, and surprise.

Journeys are a common thread in our Christian history. The Lord said to Abram: ***"Go from your land, your relatives, and your father's house to the land that I will show you." -- Genesis 12:1 (CSB)*** Yes, Abram and Sarai must have been filled with a mixture of emotions as they followed the Lord's leading. Doesn't the Lord encourage us to step out in faith in a variety of ways that parallel with the one He gave Abram?

A neighbor needs help, but we don't really know them, so we hesitate, even withdraw for fear of doing the wrong thing or looking foolish. We read about opportunities to go on a mission trip to a place we do not know. Therefore, we wait for others to fill the need, confident that God isn't calling us! We attended the annual NOMADS reunion in Hope, Arkansas. Our administrator addressed us using this scripture and the chapter that followed. God is calling us to go to projects that need help. God isn't listing just the projects that offer the best parking spots, the most convenient destinations, and the spot in the best weather or the easiest work. God is leading us to the places with the greatest needs.

How ready are we to answer God's call? God led many people on difficult journeys through deserts, through battle, through relationships, through choices, and through fear. God continues to lead us daily through the events of each day. We must listen to Him, watch for Him, seek His wisdom, and wait for His guidance. Too often we use these times of listening, watching for, seeking, and waiting as excuses to postpone deciding. Lord, help us to follow Your lead rather than finding our own way. Enable us to trust Your calling rather than evaluating it to death before acting. Lead us to the scripture that helps direct us!

### New Discoveries

We explored Carlsbad Caverns and viewed the Rock of Ages inside the Big Room. All was amazing. Having been there when I was 10-years-old comparisons were inevitable. The truly amazing part for me was the relatively new discovery of Lechuguilla Cave (lay-choo-GEE-uh) in the boundaries of Carlsbad Caverns National Park. We attended a ranger program about the geology of the area and learned about Lechuguilla, discovered in 1986. This cave is protected, and for good reasons. Carlsbad is now 95% a dead cave due to the many visitors that walk through each day. Lechuguilla is alive and researchers intend to keep it that way.

The photographs are spectacular! NASA and other medical researchers are making new discoveries about the findings from deep within our planet. Microorganisms found in Lechuguilla have never been seen on earth and some eat rocks and minerals. Some were put in Petri dishes and put in with breast cancer cells. The new microorganisms ate the cancer cells!!!! This is just one example of life deep within the earth which exists without photosynthesis. What wonders does God still have waiting for us to discover?

Walking through the caverns once again brought my mind to the verses of Psalms 104 that are so descriptive of the beauty of our earth and the majesty of our Lord. *"He waters the mountains from his palace; the earth is satisfied by the fruit of your labor. -- How countless are your works, Lord! In wisdom you have made*

***them all; the earth is full of your creatures." -- Psalms 104:13, 24 (CSB)*** Entry into Lechuguilla is highly restricted. Methods of travel once inside are carefully controlled to protect the natural growths that exist there. Left unprotected, this wonderland would be destroyed by man's greed to see for themselves.

Aren't our lives much like this wondrous new cave? We can destroy them with too much of this world or we can expand them by living as Christ directs us to live. What a joy to know that God is still holding new discoveries for us in our world. Yes, Carlsbad was an awesome experience, yet sad as I realized what mankind has done to this natural beauty over the years. What are we doing with our life that is awesome in some respects and sad in other ways? Lord, show us the way to make all our life a witness to You.

### Snowy Canyons

Most people go to Arizona for the beautiful weather during the winter! Yes, we enjoyed the warm, dry days, all 343 each year of them without any rain. But the rain came for two days. Then we woke to the cleanest, most beautiful day, no haze, no dust, cool and beautiful. We had reservations in early March for the Grand Canyon that evening and were packed and ready to go!

North of Phoenix, the traffic was very heavy with lots of cars all going north! As we climbed a long 5-mile increase in elevation, the snow on the sides of the road began to get deeper from the previous day's storm. At the top was a rest stop and many cars got off, including us, to see what was going on! As we came down the exit ramp, cars were everywhere on the sides of the road, with families out in the snow building snowmen, throwing snowballs, and taking pictures! Those Phoenix folks are not used to that much snow so close to town! As we continued, the traffic also decreased, and the clouds got thicker and darker. We began to see snow blowing, then accumulating, and finally we were in a full-blown snowstorm! We still had about 30 miles to go to reach Flagstaff, which was another 100 miles from the Grand Canyon!

Once in Flagstaff, we learned we had to stay there since the roads to the Grand Canyon were bad. Finally, Monday morning arrived with another beautiful sky, clear and crisp (in fact, very cold!) Off we went to our destination. Our excitement mounted as we got closer, knowing the snow would be all over the Canyon as well. Low hanging clouds covered part of the North Rim as we stood on the South Rim at Desert Viewpoint. Snow rested on the walls a third of the way down into the Canyon. The enormity of the Canyon simply boggles the mind! The layers of type and color of rock make you wonder at the marvels of development over the centuries. The ribbon of river that flows through the bottom seems so insignificant, yet my brain tells me what a powerful river the Colorado is at that location! All I could say as I stood there taking in the magnificent view was "*Praise you, God, for your artistry.*"

*"Mountains rose and valleys sank — to the place you established for them. -- May the glory of the Lord endure forever; may the Lord rejoice in his works. -- I will sing to the Lord all my life; I will sing praise to my God while I live." -- Psalms 104:8, 31, 33 (CSB)*

I think of many of God's creations that have the same effect on me...newborn babies, newborn or newly hatched animals, new blooms on plants, new leaves opening, cloud formations, waterfalls, sunsets, sunrises, people whose love has weathered many storms, people walking hand in hand, a child hugging an elderly person, groups enjoying fellowship, groups engaged in deep conversation, works of art created by people, excellent craftsmanship, and I'm sure you can expand the list. Lord, allow us to look around us to see the marvels of Your creation right where we are.

### Umbrella Tree

I stood under an enormous umbrella shaped tree at Ensenada Lodge in Costa Rica, on the Gulf of Nicoya off the Pacific Ocean. The birds were singing all around us

and the sun was brilliant in the early hours of the day. God showed me a setting that reminded me of what life is like when we live expecting God's blessings. This tree served as protection and home for many of God's creatures. The trunk was massive, with branches reaching out 360 degrees. The shape of the top of the tree was perfectly rounded like an umbrella, providing shade and shelter for all who stood under its branches. The diameter of the umbrella was perhaps 70'to 100'. I felt surrounded by God's cover! Then I noticed the Palm tree that grew straight up about 4' away from the main trunk of the umbrella tree! The Palm tree grew up through the

branches of its companion tree. I saw that tree as the straight path to God that our prayers provide us.

Those few minutes that I stood there absorbing the scene filled me with a peace and joy that warmed my heart. Thanking God for the bit of inspiration was my silent praise. As I sauntered on down toward the others in our group to see the many birds stirring around, I kept looking back at the tree. Before leaving, I got the camera to record the images that inspired me so much.

Psalms has many scripture references about God's protection, but this one applies to me for that moment: *"When I think of you as I lie on my bed, I meditate on you during the night watches because you are my helper; I will rejoice in the shadow of your wings. I follow close to you; your right hand holds on to me."* *-- Psalms 63:6-8 (CSB)*

Our trip was better than we even imagined. God blessed us and I shall continue to praise Him for His magnificent creations. I pray that those images and memories can remain forever embedded in my memory. I pray that God gives me the words to share those blessings. Look around each day and find the beauty that God provides for us everywhere. Picture God in the setting and what message we are to take from each scene.

### Birds, Costa Rica

Our recent venture to Costa Rica to see God's birds reaped generous rewards. *"Then God said, 'Let the water swarm with living creatures, and let birds fly above the earth across the expanse of the sky.' So God created the large sea-creatures and every living creature that moves and swarms in the water, according to their kinds. He also created every winged creature according to its kind. And God saw that it was good." -- Genesis 1:20-21 (CSB)*

Yes, God filled the earth with the most amazing displays of color, size, shape, and behaviors that we can even imagine in the bird kingdom. Pictures in books simply do not capture the limitless beauty of these small to large creatures. Seeing them in their natural habitats brings a thrill to the soul and issues forth praises to God for His mighty creation.

I must admit it helped us to have three experienced, professional birders with us in our small group of seven! Their wisdom, experience, hearing, and spotting abilities aided us in seeing much more. We saw parrots and scarlet macaws in their nests in the mangrove swamps, as well as flying overhead noisily announcing their presence! The Montezuma Oropendola had a whole tree filled with perhaps 8 to 10 long hanging nests that only the female entered. Each male has a harem of many females to which he offers protection by chasing off predators during the nesting season. And yes, we saw a Wood Stork though it was in flight not on a nest.

The colors of the feathers and the patterns formed were breathtaking. As a quilter, I really pay attention to color combinations. God's use of color for so many purposes is an inspiration. Some color is for attracting other birds, some color is defensive to protect and allow the bird to blend into its surroundings. Other birds' color changes during the seasons causing me much trouble in making good identifications! We saw toucans, motmots, parrots, and tanagers that were brilliant. There were also flycatchers of all kinds, five different kingfishers in one day, and king vultures. Three white hawks blessed us by settling in a tree not too far away so we could get excellent views. On one walk we saw birds taking

baths and one small Orange Collared Manakin that did a hopping dance to attract females by leaping from small limb to another small limb making a clicking noise at the same time.

*"The Lord God formed out of the ground every wild animal and every bird of the sky, and brought each to the man to see what he would call it. And whatever the man called a living creature, that was its name." -- Genesis 2:19 (CSB)*
Watching the birds flit and fly, always looking for and finding food, reminded me of how God takes care of His own. God cares even more for us. The blessings in our lives abound all around us. Birds are actively seeking their sustenance. We need to actively seek the blessings around us rather than focus on our problems. Yes, we will always have problems, but God can comfort us more as we focus on the blessings provided. A positive attitude helps lead us to solutions or ways to accept problems.

### Across America

Yes, America is beautiful. Traveling across I-90 from Iowa to Washington state, we've seen many fields of waving grain. The colors of the grains and the colors of the bales from green to gold made us wonder what grains we were seeing. The cattle graze, lie in the fields, or slowly follow one another to the next spot to graze. Some places are green from the rain just as some areas are brown and dry from lack of rain. Forest fires from previous years leave lingering scars to the earth that will take years to remove. Trains wait to continue their journey once an oncoming train makes its passage. Trucks, cars, and RVs rush onward to their destinations, sometimes great in numbers and other times sparse along the highways.

Signs line the Interstate assaulting our senses with clutter and information. Some states have the ad signs back from the highways, while others allow them to be close to the roadways. Visual pollution interferes with the natural beauty of the countryside in many areas. Other areas, however, restrict the visual pollution and we can enjoy the natural beauty. The plains stretch out for long periods as we travel when suddenly small bushes, then trees, begin to appear. The mountainous areas give rise to dramatic rocky outcroppings, and winding roads with steep grades up and down. Volcanic areas show the darker colors of the rock with grasses growing up around the rocks.

Then the cities emerge. Some older towns display old, abandoned buildings from former years of prosperity. What will our current population centers look like a century from now? As generations down the road look back on our life today, what will they ask about our lifestyles? What is happening today that will leave ugly marks on our earth?

*"So God created man in his own image; he created him in the image of God; he created them male and female. God blessed them, and God said to them,*

*'Be fruitful, multiply, fill the earth, and subdue it. Rule the fish of the sea, the birds of the sky, and every creature that crawls on the earth.' " -- Genesis 1:27-28 (CSB)* Yes, we are to rule over the earth, but our sin prevents us from making the best decisions for earth's existence! We see beauty, but it is often hidden by the things of our own creations. Each of us has a role to play in the care and keeping of our planet. It is the home that God gave us. We would not intentionally trash our home, let's not trash our earth. Use less water, recycle more items, use less paper etc., and perhaps live simpler lives. Encourage others to help save our earth! Yes, America is beautiful and so is the rest of the world that our God created.

### Erosion Dangers

We are in Newport, Oregon, at an RV Rally. Our RV Park is right on the coast on a high cliff that overlooks the ocean. The last two nights we've walked over to the cliff to observe the ocean waves rolling onto the shore. The first night had high waves as the last effects of the tropical storm that hit Japan finally arrived here. It was misty, but you could see a good distance. Last night, we walked about half-way down to the beach and the waves were calmer as the weather system continued to move away. The morning fog engulfed us, but the sun was predicted to come out.

While down along the cliff, we noticed several houses along the top of the ridge. One was perilously in danger of losing the ground it sits upon. Over the years, erosion has undermined the ground right up to the base of one part of the house. Our first thought was, "Why did they build so close to the edge?" Probably the erosion has crept up to them over the years until now the house is in peril.

Our Christian walk often faces the same kind of erosions. Storms come our way in various sizes with different lengths of endurance. Several paths emerged because of the storm. The storm can strengthen our faith, it can erode bits and pieces of our faith, or It can make us defiant and bitter toward our faith as we feel abandoned.

*"Therefore, everyone who hears these words of mine and acts on them will be like a wise man who built his house on the rock. The rain fell, the rivers rose, and the winds blew and pounded that house. Yet it didn't collapse, because its foundation was on the rock. But everyone who hears these words of mine and doesn't act on them will be like a foolish man who built his house on the sand.*

## Safety Prayers

Each day that we travel, I start off either right before we drive away or as we are driving away in the motorhome with a prayer. Out loud I ask God to surround us with His angels of protection, for Rudy to have wisdom and clarity as he drives, and for a safe arrival. About 20 miles down the road, we pulled off the Interstate to check on some genealogy material for Rudy, but didn't find a good place to park so headed back to the Interstate. As we turned left onto the entrance ramp, we both heard a pop sound from the back. Rudy looked in the rear TV monitor at the car and sensed something was wrong. As he kept driving slowly on the ramp and wondering, I saw we had enough room to pull off and check the car before getting on the Interstate highway. He immediately pulled off. As I exited the front door, I saw the car off to the right of the coach! It doesn't ride there normally!

Our tow bar broke one of the two arms that attach to the car. It sheared off where it threads into the locked portion. It is a solid piece of aluminum about 1.25" thick. The motorhome was not damaged nor was the car, but the tow bar was trashed! That pop sound we heard was the tow bar breaking! Praise God we were not on the Interstate yet, just the ramp.

We took pictures of everything, unhooked the car, decided on a destination about 50 miles away, and we each drove a vehicle. We stopped in a large city at an exit with everything we needed! God wasn't through with the care He was providing for us. After lunch, I went to get the supplies we needed while Rudy called Blue Ox (the tow bar company). They had just serviced and inspected our nine-year-old tow bar three weeks earlier at their factory in Pender, Nebraska. We arranged to send them the photos. Rudy looked online for Blue Ox dealers in our area and yes, there is one six tenths of a mile from where the motorhome was parked! There were only two dealers in the state, and we were right next to one of them! Blue Ox replaced our tow bar for free since they had just inspected it! The next morning, we were on our way again, starting with our travel prayer.

*"However, God has listened; he has paid attention to the sound of my prayer. Blessed be God! He has not turned away my prayer or turned his faithful love from me." -- Psalms 66:19-20 (CSB)* Yes, God heard my travel prayer that morning and was there to care for us when the need arose.

## Mountain Road

We took a tour up a mountain south of Tucson to see the Whipple Observatory. An unusual weather system moved in that brought 50 to 60 mph winds at the summit of the 7,660', mountain with a temperature of 40 degrees. It reminded me of our trip last year to the Grand Canyon with the same cold temps and high winds. The beauty in the universe and the exploration of man to seek hidden treasures reminded me of God's infinite power and size.

The trip up the mountain was on a very crooked road, traversed by a small bus for the tour group. The view just kept getting better and better as we climbed. When we arrived at the summit, we walked to the edge to see the entire road with all the switchbacks, ups and downs to reach the top. It wasn't always a smooth road either. Isn't that how life goes as well?

Our journey into life is simply miraculous! Not an easy one for a baby or for a mother but one that brings joy most of the time. How else could a baby make that journey unless God designed the process. Any of us can look back over our lives and see the switchbacks when life took an unexpected turn. The valleys we cross and the mountains that we climb help define our faith. Just as that bus took us up the difficult journey on the mountain, God takes us through the difficult journey of life.

The driver of that bus was a very crucial person on our journey much as God is crucial for my life's journey. Perhaps there are many crucial people in our faith journey that God gives to us to help us along the way. Can you identify those folks? Think about the switchbacks, the difficult climbs, the deep valleys, in your life and who was there to help you make your way? Those are the people for me that God sent as angels to help me see His place in my life. Some of them were only in my life for a day or for a short period of time, but their impact was profound. Only God could have sent them.

The other image that came to me today, while I was standing in the observatory was the vastness of God's creation. *"In the beginning God created the heavens and the earth." -- Genesis 1:1 (CSB)* Mankind simply cannot know the vastness of God. The more we learn, the more we see of His work. How I praise God for all that He does for us. The trip up and down the mountain reminded me of so many aspects of my faith journey.

### Clean Up Needed

On the south side of Tucson is a 9,157' mountain named Mt. Lemmon. The day was perfect! We took lots of photos since it is very different than any other mountains that we have seen. Almost at the top, we were told about a place where we could walk in, have our picnic lunch, and see some birds as well.

When we arrived at the picnic area, we found a mixed setting. I climbed up to a table in the sun to help us stay warm, only to find two six packs of beer bottles and the cartons scattered on the ground. Whoever left them also left juice single serving foil packages scattered as well. I watched as Rudy took photos of the trash scattered on the ground beside the trash cans. Trash was left outside the cans, and animals had torn open the bags and scattered the trash all over the area. While waiting for Rudy, I sat there observing the woods around me. If I looked up rather than at the ground, I saw the beauty that God created for us to enjoy and for the animals to use as their home. When I looked down, I saw the trash, the discarded items of others who had visited the woods.

 It came to me that God gives us His best, and we add our trash to what He gives us. Our trash is perhaps the sin that we allow to creep into our daily lives. All of us have sin in our lives since we simply aren't perfect! Most of the time, we choose to see only the beauty in our lives and fail to see the sin that resides in us. Romans 6 talks about being dead to sin and alive to Christ. *"But now, since you have been set free from sin and have become enslaved to God, you have your fruit, which results in sanctification — and the outcome is eternal life! For the wages of sin is death, but the gift of God is eternal life in Christ Jesus our Lord." -- Romans 6:22-23 (CSB)*

Christ gives to us forgiveness and grace, and we give Him our sin and praise. After all, He died on the cross for our sins. When we see the sin in our lives or become aware of its presence, we need, at that time, to clean up the forest floor of all the trash and offer it to Christ for forgiveness so that His grace covers us. Then we can truly see the full beauty of the forest without all the debris cluttering up the place.

How much I enjoyed the trip to Mt. Lemmon and the gentle reminder of what sin looks like in our lives. But mostly, I loved enjoying the great creation that our Lord made for us to walk in, to behold, and to breathe in the aromas all of which are His gifts to us. May we use those gifts as reminders to praise God for all that He has given to us. May we each clean up the sin in our lives by acknowledging it, seeking forgiveness, and praising God for His grace and mercy.

### *Amid Splendors*

How do you explain the majesty of God? Our travels have us in the middle of splendor! From Denver, we went to Flaming Gorge National Recreation Area in northeast Utah. The friends we were visiting took us to see incredible beauty which was created deep within the earth when the ground moved millions of years ago. Geology studies were endless! Our photo opportunities were endless as well!

From there we traveled north to Grand Teton National Park. We exercised our cameras abundantly. For those of you who know we are not early risers, we managed to get up before sunrise and drive to Oxbow Bend to capture the pink color that covers the mountain peaks as the sun gradually comes up. Lunch was eaten beside a side stream of the Snake River with that amazing view of the mountains, birds all around us, beaver lodge (but didn't see the beaver) and a wedding taking place with just the couple, minister, and photographer.

The highlight was at Lake Jackson Lodge on the back balcony where we hoped to see any moose that might be in the area. We did see several female moose and a herd of elk. At supper in the lodge, we heard the tale of an earlier event that day of a wolf pack that now lives in the Willow Flats. They had an attack and kill on an elk that lasted about 60 to 90 minutes in the morning which was witnessed by many from the balcony of the lodge. As we stood on the deck outside, one of the witnesses who had a spotting scope that morning stood next to us describing the event. Rudy had our spotting scope and, as we watched the elk, the wolves came into view for us! At first it was only one, but finally three were playing in the field. From that one spot on the balcony, we watched a herd of elk, three wolves playing, another couple of moose in another spot, and another group of four adult elk and one small calf. Fortunately, that small group of elk with the calf were not close to the wolves. Sunset occurred while we stood on the balcony and, though small in the sky, it was a beautiful strip of color.

This time was filled with praises for God for creating this beauty and for allowing us to behold it. *"His splendor covers the heavens, and the earth is full of his praise. His brilliance is like light; rays are flashing from his hand. This is where his power is hidden." -- Habakkuk 3:3-4 (CSB)* The next evening at sunset, since there were no clouds, the photos were of the sun's rays flooding in over the tops of the mountains as the sun set behind the mountains. God's creative power is excellent, not only in the physical aspects of this earth, but in how He guides our lives.

## NOMADS' Service

### Shining Light

We finished a NOMADS (see the Introduction section for details on NOMADS) three-week project at a church with a day care center and a senior citizens nutritional center. I want to pay a high tribute to the people we worked with, the people who work at the centers, and the members of the congregation. *"If, therefore, your whole body is full of light, with no part of it in darkness, it will be entirely illuminated, as when a lamp shines its light on you." -- Luke 11:36 (CSB)*

We saw light in the eyes of the children being cared for in the center and in the eyes of the seniors as they gathered to eat a meal together every day. The workers all made the day possible for them and for us. We saw light in the joy of the people at the church greeting us each Sunday. They went out of their way to welcome us, to care for us, to speak to us, to feed us, even to telling us goodbye. They also shared the same joy with and for each other. Their faith and love of God shone in their prayers, their singing, their conversations, and their faces.

The couples we worked with showed light through their faith, their stories, their dedication to our task, and through the cooperative way we worked together through a very large and physically demanding task. After removing thousands of staples from walls (preschool hung pictures on the walls with staples), repairing a bathroom floor that was rotten, repainting everything, repairing lighting fixtures, and a multitude of other issues, we left the project feeling tired, yes, but renewed and uplifted in spirit. Where do you see the light of God shining as you go through each day? Look for that light and, in the process, let your light also shine for all to see God through you.

### *Faith Commitment*

We worked in a church for NOMADS which was living on faith. They needed a teacher training session for new people coming into the church from various backgrounds. I pondered how to explain to a mixed language audience (non-English speaking and non-Spanish speaking) about grace and how faith, works, mission, service and being a part of a worshiping community all work together. One of the scripture texts that I used was: ***"What good is it, my brothers and sisters, if someone claims to have faith but does not have works? Can such faith save him? If a brother or sister is without clothes and lacks daily food and one of you says to them, 'Go in peace, stay warm, and be well fed,' but you don't give them what the body needs, what good is it? In the same way faith, if it does not have works, is dead by itself." -- James 2:14-17 (CSB)***

A vision for a dying church with no children and located in a changed neighborhood began a journey in faith that could only be led by God. A year later, 75 children from the surrounding neighborhood attended and some of their parents began to attend. A growing Sunday school program, a mid-week program with supper for children, a 15-passenger van to go pick up the children, an adult Spanish Bible study, a thrift shop, a food pantry, and so many other answers to prayers are tangible evidence of faith at work.

The congregation of older people saw the needs of the community, decided to open their doors and their hearts, and they praise God for all that is happening. Do they get tired, yes; do they get discouraged, yes; do they feel overwhelmed, yes; do they experience tension over funding, yes; do they expect a miracle or two, yes. Are they making a difference, yes; do they still have needs, certainly; is their faith alive, absolutely!! In the training session, I discovered that several of the mothers and their children did not have Spanish Bibles so how can they study? Fortunately, some New Testaments in Spanish immediately appeared to give to them on the spot. They did not have children's Bibles in Spanish. They constantly asked anyone and everyone who would listen for help. Help came.

The congregation took their faith and put it to work so that the community could share in the rewards. Faith without works is dead. Works do not earn faith, for faith is a gift given only by God, through belief in Jesus. Where in your life do you see faith in God at work?

### Adventure in Life

How stuck in our ruts are we? What adventure do we find in our lives? Living our lives with Christ is a life of adventure when we truly give our lives to him.

The simple act of praying sometimes results in a change of plans. For example, read: *"Very early in the morning, while it was still dark, he got up, went out, and made his way to a deserted place; and there he was praying. Simon and his companions searched for him, and when they found him they said, 'Everyone is looking for you.' And he said to them, 'Let's go on to the neighboring villages so that I may preach there too. This is why I have come.' " -- Mark 1:35-38 (CSB)*

Each time we arrive at a new NOMADS work site a new adventure awaits us. Brothers and sisters in Christ come together from different walks of life and different generations, to use and learn different skills for the purpose of completing a task. Our hosting organizations often are walking tight financial lines to fund our work, causing creativity to be a part of the task. After three weeks, we all head in different directions to find the next adventure God has waiting for us, either through rest or work.

*"Let's go somewhere else"* is often a challenge about where God leads us next. Where might we go or what might we do that is different than our normal routine? What might God be trying to have us see in a different light, with a different attitude, with a different heart? What adventures await us if we ask for and listen to guidance from our Lord?

### Strains of Ministry

What a special week! As a visitor to many of the places we go, we have the privilege of observing people at work in a variety of circumstances. While at a NOMADS project, we observed a congregation daring to risk many new ministries. Because Rudy and I find it hard to be casual observers, we found ourselves actively participating in preparations. Our energies were tapped for only a short while, as opposed to those living here who are in the daily, weekly, on-going drama of living out each day. A quote from Oswald Chambers *"My Utmost for His Highest"* is, *"God does not give us overcoming life: He gives us life as we overcome. The strain is the strength. If there is no strain, there is no strength. Are you asking God to give you life and liberty and joy? He cannot, unless you will accept the strain. Immediately you face the strain, you will get the strength."* *

Each congregation, group or individual involved in ministries of service or worship finds strained relationships, drained physical energies, and yes, lapses in our faith. Yet the fruit of the work, the involvement of the Holy Spirit, and the joy experienced as people come together is energizing! The next day always comes and with it is a tiredness, an awareness of our human physical, emotional, and spiritual weariness ready to engulf and overwhelm us.

At that moment these words renew us: ***"He gives strength to the faint and strengthens the powerless." -- Isaiah 40:29 (CSB)***

The worship was a time for praising God for renewing all who gave so much. Chambers goes on the say in the same book, "*God never gives strength for tomorrow or for the next hour, but only for the strain of the minute.*" *

*Taken from *My Utmost for His Highest* by Oswald Chambers. © 1927 in the U. K. by Oswald Chambers Publications Association, Ltd., on behalf of Oswald and Gertrude (Biddy) Chambers. © 1935 in the U. S. by Dodd, Mead & Company, Inc. Copyright renewed 1963 by Oswald Chambers Publications Association, Ltd. All rights reserved.

### Light = Growth

At the annual NOMADS Reunion, as several of us stood outside talking, the sun began its journey down for the day. The clouds provided a setting for hiding the sun, yet allowing the rays to spill out in all directions shedding their brilliance for our enjoyment. What a fitting beginning for the gathering of NOMADS.

The words of Jesus: ***"Jesus spoke to them again: 'I am the light of the world. Anyone who follows me will never walk in the darkness but will have the light of life.' " -- John 8:12 (CSB)***

Light is one of the ingredients for plants to grow. Light often improves our moods and temperaments. Light brings clarity to situations. Light enables us to find our way. Light, even in small amounts, gives us hope, like the light at the end of the tunnel.

As I stood watching the brilliance of the rays, I thanked God for sending us His Son to be our light. As NOMADS, we go out in different directions to do work in Jesus' name. We share the good news of His love with the other workers and with those for whom we work. We pray for the sick and the needy. We try to follow His light as He leads us to various projects.

What life NOMADS have! Though we have not met many of the other NOMADS, we feel like family. Since we all follow the same light, we experience a common bond. Just as the rays went out in different directions, we also went in different directions, providing a form of light to the agencies and the people that we serve. What does the light of God lead you to do? How does light affect the quality of life that you live? Praise God for the sun and its setting as well as its rising.

### Purging the Files

NOMADS come together to assist others in Tucson, AZ. As we worked, we ladies found ourselves doing what some might think very unimportant work - purging files! Now all of us know how we hate doing that work for ourselves. We stuff our file drawers until we can't get another piece of paper inside and then we push harder thinking we can add just one more piece.

At the agency we are assisting, 14,000 people a year find help with housing, food, jobs, utility bills, training, rehab from substance abuse, parenting, etc. As we worked in the office beginning to purge their client files, we listened as the phone rang with often three calls coming in at one time! The staff works constantly assisting those in need! We soon realized why the purging of files gets put off - no one has the time to even consider doing it.

*"'If any of your fellow Israelites become poor and are unable to support themselves among you, help them as you would a foreigner and stranger, so they can continue to live among you." -- Leviticus 25:35 (NIV)* As we reflected on our purging job, we came to see ourselves as performing a valuable service to the staff which in turn allows the staff to spend their time helping the needy to live and work in this area.

What tasks might we do that assist those in need? It is often easy to see ways that we are blessed by God, but what do we see when we look for ways that we participate in the blessing of others in need? Our participation in NOMADS helps us to keep our perspective on life. We can also see ways that others are helping those in need. As we work, we view, as important, all of the tasks we are asked to assist with. How I praise God for all He leads us to do!

### *Judging Others*

As I looked at the house our NOMADS team worked on the past three weeks, I wondered about the people who resided inside. It would be easy to say they do not take care of their home, but then we didn't see it before the hurricane. It would be easy to conclude that they were lazy and did not attend to repairs in a timely way. It would be easy to make all kinds of judgements about them when comparing to how I live. That seems to be typical for most people, they are right, and the other person is in the wrong!

Reading once again reminded me of Jesus' teaching on judging: *"Stop judging according to outward appearances; rather judge according to righteous judgment." -- John 7:24 (CSB)*

The way things look is often deceiving! Many times, we simply do not have enough information to know what is right about a given situation. Making blanket statements which cover someone's action is dangerous. It is so easy to think we know what is "really right." Is it right from God's word? Is it edifying to God? Is it according to the teachings of Jesus? Is it done or said with love? Does it fit in the walk that person has with their Lord?

I know that when I spoke with the owners of the home we worked on, their hearts belong to God. They trust in God's provisions for them. They used God's name with reverence and respect. What else do I need to know? God knows their heart and it is not for me to judge. The same is true for any other friend or acquaintance I encounter. Judgement need not be a part of my relationship with them. Lord, help me to avoid judging others.

### *High to Low*

As we drove toward the NOMADS Reunion in Bowling Green, KY, it occurred to us that our week was one of extremes. One day we drove up the road on Mt. Evans in Colorado to an elevation of 14,179' and now we are driving at an elevation of 450' in Kentucky. I compared the extremes to the highs and lows of life.

At times we feel as though we are on the mountaintop, and everything is great! Then circumstances or our own attitude take us to the valley, the low spot, and everything seems awful or complicated. What a difference in the high and low. Interesting note for those of you who have never been to the top of a mountain that high. It is very rugged terrain, the oxygen is 40% less than what your body is accustomed to breathing, the roads are narrow with steep sides and no trees. But the views are awesome, making the elements less important. The opposite at 450' finds lots of humidity and bugs! Of course, the plant life is much lusher (unless you happen to be in a desert!) So, in either place, the mountain, or the low spots, are advantages and disadvantages.

The commonality of both places though is God. As creator, He made them both. As Psalms tells us in so many places: *"Hallelujah! I will praise the Lord with all my heart -- The Lord's works are great, studied by all who delight in them. All that he does is splendid and majestic; his righteousness endures forever. He has caused his wondrous works to be remembered. The Lord is gracious and compassionate -- The fear of the Lord is the beginning of wisdom; all who follow his instructions have good insight. His praise endures forever." -- Psalms 111:1-4, 10 (CSB)* No matter where we find ourselves, in high spots or low, may we always remember that God is with us, enabling us to experience His presence in every situation. May we keep our eyes, ears, and hearts open to Him.

### *Prayers Supported*

At a NOMADS Reunion, we were renewing friendships and making new ones. A special aspect of this event was the sharing of stories about God's care and comfort. As a part of my prayer cloth ministry, I send cloths to many NOMADS on our prayer list. Meeting them is special and hearing how God touched their life was a privilege. Several occasions arose for immediate prayers, bringing us together to ask for God's peace and comfort.

The words from John came to mind as I listened to their stories: *"I give you a new command: Love one another. Just as I have loved you, you are also to love one another. By this everyone will know that you are my disciples, if you love one another." -- John 13:34-35 (CSB)* What ways do we show our love for one another? I saw examples of people helping strangers stranded from a wreck that totaled a pickup truck and a fifth wheel trailer. I saw people praying together, laughing together, and hugging one another. Some helped with RV repairs, some helped with raising funds for the work of NOMADS, some helped by simply listening. An auction of seven dozen leftover donuts raised over $400! Many other items were auctioned off, raising thousands of dollars, but the donuts were simply fun! The money raised went to the materials fund to help with future projects for people in need.

I listened as others told of prayers supporting them and bringing comfort to them as they went to treatments, to testing, to surgery, to rehab. Something as simple as offering a prayer for someone in need or for someone celebrating a joy is following the command Jesus gave to us to love one another. In our NOMADS community and in our local churches many of us do not know one another, but we pray anyway for we hold the common bond of love for our Lord Jesus. Each of us can find some way to show our love for one another because of the love that Jesus has for us. Find that someone, especially someone that you don't know or perhaps someone you have trouble loving, for you to show the love of Jesus.

### Challenges in Life

Having arrived at our newest location with a team of NOMADS, we face several new challenges. Hard work heads the list with digging into the hard packed New

Mexico soil to pour concrete pads to anchor picnic tables. Another challenge is moving a storage shed on a concrete pad to another location by placing steel rods under the concrete pad and dragging it to the new location with a tractor.

In the sanctuary of the church we attended was a beautiful stained-glass window with the following scripture: ***"Then an angel from heaven appeared to him, strengthening him." -- Luke 22:43-44 (CSB)*** Jesus was in the Garden of Gethsemane praying for His Father's will to be done, rather than His will. None of the challenges I face are comparable to the one Jesus faced, but what hope this scripture gives to me with challenges I have. Yet, God's angels come in many forms to strengthen you and me. I never ceased to be amazed at the many ways God brings comfort to those in need. Some people keep their challenges and needs to themselves; others talk about their challenges and needs. The talking about our needs in a healthy way, allows others to bring comfort in the name of Jesus to us.

As we checked in at an RV Park in New Mexico this week, the owner was telling me about the hectic life they were living with her aunt in ICU. I learned of her life-threatening situation and of the close family's concerns and prayers for her. I assured her that I would pray for her. The next morning, I took a prayer cloth to the office hoping to see the daughter-in-law once again. Instead, I found the sister of the woman in the hospital. It was an opportunity to share hope while bringing a gift symbolizing the prayers of many for this situation.

God uses us to touch the lives of others. How grateful I am for the many of you who have touched my life. I also praise Jesus for bringing me to places that offer me new scriptures to renew my thoughts and spirit. Even as God sent an angel to strengthen His son Jesus in His time of need, He also sends others to touch our lives in the challenges we face.

### *Don't Be Fooled*

Our NOMADS group of 10 traveled to a little town 30 miles away from our RVs' location to attend church. El Rita is a small town in northern New Mexico with a small church. With only 19 people in worship, we hoped for a place to eat and were told of a good place right there in El Rita. The local folks told us it was small, and it didn't look like much, but the food was good!

Yes, we found it. Even knowing it was small, we almost passed on it because it was really small! After checking to make sure it was big enough to seat all of us, we went inside. As our food began to come out, our eyes told us good things! Then we began eating and found the food excellent! Adorning the walls were copies of magazine articles about this hidden eating experience – magazines from Santa Fe and even one from Gourmet. What looked like a place we should pass by turned into a memorable eating spot.

The scripture text from: "the whole crowd of the disciples began to praise God joyfully with a loud voice for all the miracles they had seen: *'Blessed is the King who comes in the name of the Lord.'* " -- *Luke 19:37-38 (CSB)* The people all thought He was their King, coming to save them from the Romans. Even as He rode in on a donkey, their joy at seeing Him arrive did not call them to question His reason for

arriving. Had they really known the reason for His arrival would they have even had the capacity to understand? Yes, He told His disciples that He was to die in Jerusalem, but they could not believe Him. It seemed too impossible. He came for a different reason.

The scripture text and our group's eating experience once again remind me not to judge based on appearances or on what my mind alone tells me. Often, we have to wait, test and possibly wait some more to see the value and reason for events in our life. Yes, Jesus rode into Jerusalem to hear praise and hosannas but the events of the week quickly changed. As we trusted our new friends, we learned the joy of the local restaurant. As unknowns continue to come our way, we need to remember the joy of trusting our Lord to carry us through each day.

### *Why You Came*

In talking to some of the international students working in the mountains, I asked "What brought you to this place?" One student told me, "God brought me here." As I meet people in various spots, I often ask that question. Usually answers have to do with wanting to visit a particular spot, or family lives in the area. When we go to NOMADS projects, I sometimes ask why they came to that spot. The basic answer is to serve the agency sponsoring the project, but the secondary answers also involve location, interest in the type of project, or they knew of others who worked at the spot and liked it. When I served in the local church, I often pondered what makes folks volunteer since I recruited lots of people to help with lots of projects.

As I read in Ephesians, I found this answer: ***"For we are God's handiwork, created in Christ Jesus to do good works, which God prepared in advance for us to do."*** *-- Ephesians 2:10 (NIV)* What is considered "good works"? God wants us to work for Him and I believe that our income earning jobs also give us opportunities for doing God's work as well. Young people often wonder what they should do with their lives. Retirement brings a seeking of how to spend our remaining years of productivity.

God made us to do good works which I assume means for all our life, not just for a few years of it. The question then becomes, "What does God have planned for me in that department?" How I wish for a quick and simple answer for each of us. Sometimes it is not that simple to learn what God's plan is for us. Other times the answers jump out at us! Perhaps, as we keep our focus on Christ, God's plan for us may become more visible. Rather than evaluate the pros and cons according to our terms, evaluate according to Christ's teachings and then see what happens. Does our role involve good work? Does our work help show the love of Christ to others? Does our work involve forgiveness, acceptance, and care for others? Does scripture help you decide?

I pray that each of us may enjoy the search for God's plan for our lives. May the daily living of that plan bring satisfaction in knowing God leads us where He wants us.

### Drive With Jesus

Rudy is the primary driver of our 40' motorhome plus our tow vehicle in the rear. Due to a fall and concussion, he was not to drive until he saw the doctor again; that meant I had to drive! Now the weird part is, before he fell, the thought ran through my mind that if something ever happened to Rudy, I would have to drive the motorhome and I could. Well, it was time. Nearly a week after his fall, he was better, though not cleared to drive due to medication. We needed to get to our NOMADS project a hundred miles away as we were already a week late.

I have driven it short distances on wide-open highways, but never in traffic. Yes, I had all week to consider the trip. My plan was to travel on Sunday morning since the traffic would be lighter. That morning while lying in bed, we listened to the drip, drip of heavy fog falling from the trees onto the roof – that meant wet roads and poor visibility! I tried seeing if Rudy wanted to wait until Monday – that might help! He wanted to leave. I suggested we might as well go to church and leave later in the day once the fog lifted. Ok, that sounded like a good plan. but God had a plan that was even better than mine!

God knew where I needed to be! Instead of leaving, we decided to attend church. The pastor preached a sermon just for me (and a few others). He talked about living with a new perspective. ***"For the kingdom of God is not a matter of talk but of power." -- 1 Corinthians 4:20 (CSB)."*** Jesus promises us peace, joy, and strength. Then one of my favorite scriptures affirmed that: ***"I am able to do all things through him who strengthens me." -- Philippians 4:13 (CSB)***

All the way home from church, I knew I could drive that coach in the afternoon because God would enable me to do that which I feared. Yep, all during the drive, I repeated that verse from Philippians! Thank You, God, for how You arranged the day, for how You prepared me for doing that which I feared. Thank You, God, for encouraging me to live by Your power! Thanks for letting me make the drive without the usual sweaty palms and nervous dread. P.S. - Rudy wanted me to drive more often! Me - Only in emergencies!

## Health Kits

Thirty-six thousand health kits are off to disaster areas. Those kits came about because of many people willing to serve in the name of Christ for the care of those in need. Some sent funds to a relief organization to purchase the items for the kits. Some sent a few health kits weeks or months earlier. Other people volunteer time at the facility in Baldwin, Louisiana to help prepare the kits for shipment. The employees at the facility made the arrangements for shipment, which involved trucking to Maryland to a military base for overseas transport to the disaster area.

As the truck was loaded, those employees and volunteers, including us, gathered to join hands in prayer for the safety of shipment and those involved in the transportation, and for the recipients of the kits.

Peter spoke to me about the disaster, the suffering, and the many people offering help. *"If anyone speaks, let it be as one who speaks God's words; if anyone serves, let it be from the strength God provides, so that God may be glorified through Jesus Christ in everything. To him be the glory and the power forever and ever. Amen." -- 1 Peter 4:11 (CSB)*

This kind of action is taking place all over the world year-round! Many organizations, both secular and religious, are reaching out to those in need. Many of you are involved in supporting organizations with similar disaster relief. Let us also look for those small ways that we can support one another every day. Pain and suffering exist every day, everywhere! Let us not forget to reach out to one another in the name of our Lord, Jesus Christ.

## Birds of the Air

God seems to bring us to such interesting places! For the past week, our home was in Sacramento, New Mexico. It is a town of "38 people plus one old Crab" according to the sign on the rustic Post Office. The church camp is the largest employer in the area. It is also the office for NOMADS, and we came to help with various work for two months.

Many of you know that we love to watch and identify birds. Our life list is growing thanks to our nomadic life style. Upon getting our RV parked, we began to see and hear hummingbirds everywhere. As we sat watching them, suddenly appeared a Western Tanager (a spectacularly beautiful bird not found everywhere). As we waited and watched, we began to see other varieties that are not common to most places.

A favorite Psalms of mine talks about this earth: ***"The birds of the sky live beside the springs; they make their voices heard among the foliage." -- Psalms 104:12 (CSB)*** That first morning, we awoke to the singing of many birds. The hummingbirds are so very territorial, especially the male Rufous Hummingbird. He defends and claims all rights to the feeder that we set out. He proclaims his presence vigorously and is not shy. He is alert, decisive, and boldly makes his wishes known. With his female, he is very tolerant and protective. Some of his traits are ones that serve him well.

We can learn from his behavior, both good and bad. Jesus proclaimed His presence boldly, not boastfully. He stood up for His beliefs and did not back down. With the disciples and His followers, Jesus is protective and tolerant of their behavior and doubt. We are not to run off all who come our way as the Rufous does. Jesus challenged His opponents to change, but did not run them off. God gave us the birds of the air. Much enjoyment can come from watching them and studying their behavior. What about our own behavior? Is it something that we would want others to watch? Is our behavior something that God can watch and find pleasure in so doing? How I thank Him for bringing us to this place and allowing us to observe the birds in the air.

### Teens for Christ

At church camps, groups come and go each week and on weekends. Last week, nearly 100 elementary aged students spent the week enjoying camp where we were. Over the weekend, two different large family reunions roller-skated together, played baseball and volleyball, and threw horseshoes while laughing and enjoying one another. We kept hearing about the 370 teenagers and their counselors that were coming. We envisioned this rowdy, loud group that was to arrive. So, we decided it was a good day for an outing into town.

Returning to our motorhome and sitting with the windows open, I watched as the large group of kids all gathered in the hall about 100 yards from us. Then the music began. Rudy and I walked up to the hall to photograph the group since we needed photos for the work we were doing. God knew we needed to go inside!!!! The room was filled with teens and adults standing and singing praise music. The balcony offered a better vantage point for the picture and for observing what was happening. As I watched them clapping, singing, and enjoying one another and being here, my heart smiled with joy.

The words of Nehemiah. *"Lord, the God of the heavens, the great and awe-*

*inspiring God who keeps his gracious covenant with those who love him and keep his commands, let your eyes be open and your ears be attentive to hear your servant's prayer that I now pray to you day and night for your servants." -- Nehemiah 1:5-6 (CSB)*

So much is said about bad teens, but it is so exciting to see teens seeking God. As the music turned to a prayerful mood, the group began to spontaneously wrap arms around the shoulders of the person next to them. Before long, the entire room had every row connected with arms over shoulders and swaying to the music and the mood. When they began singing, I sang with them and thanked God for allowing me to witness this event. Join with me in prayer for any bunch of teens that they might find Jesus as their Lord and Savior, not just for a moment but for all of life. The prayer of Nehemiah is for the servants of God, just as my prayer is for these and other teens. May the teens in your life find an opportunity to experience our awesome God.

### Hands That Help

The hurricane destruction which our southern states have endured presents us with opportunities for assisting. Yes, many stepped forth with donations of money and goods. Others were able to provide housing, food, and personal assistance with rescues. As the country shifts into clean up and repair mode, many more of us can now see other ways of helping.

Of course, other areas of the country continue to have needs. Long before the hurricanes caused their damage, many denominations had organizations like NOMADS with schedules already established. Habitat for Humanity already had homes it was working on for people counting on those places to live. Yes, the needs were great.

Today's Psalms reminded me: *"Let your work be seen by your servants, and your splendor by their children. Let the favor of the Lord our God be on us; establish for us the work of our hands — establish the work of our hands!" -- Psalms 90:16-1 (CSB)*

Food pantries still need to feed many people as we approach cold weather coming in for much of the country. Children need school supplies, coats, and warm dry shoes. Men and women need jobs to help feed their families.

How can we use our hands to help? Grab a bunch of tools and use them. Go through your closets and examine the good unused items that others need. Guide the steering wheel of your auto or RV to sites needing help. Write a check to do what you cannot physically do. Dial others on the phone or type messages to organize a team to pool resources to help.

If none of these things are doable for you now, then put your hands together and pray. Yes, pray. Pray for others to be moved and others to find help. Pray for God to use us to be His hands and feet in service to others. How does God want you to use your hands?

## Working Together

We are back at the church camp helping the staff work on the house the new director will live in once the updates are finished. This house, which is part of the camp's property, has not had any significant work done in many years, and several directors have resided in it. As I painted, the two staff maintenance guys were laying ceramic tiles on most of the first floor. As they strained and groaned, I kidded them about the hard work. We would all laugh and keep working. But they never complained!!!! They just kept thanking me for doing the last of the painting. (Another group of NOMADS had done most of the painting, but had to leave before they could finish.)

As I flipped open my bible, I came across: ***"Do everything without grumbling and arguing" -- Philippians 2:14 (CSB)*** I immediately thought of the two maintenance guys. What a joy they were to work with. You ask for help; they interrupted their work to help (if they weren't grouting). You ask for a tool; they jumped to help you find it or tell you where it was. When another staff lady's housekeeping schedule allowed for her to help me, she would be right there just doing what needed to be done with a smile and lightness in her spirit, even though the physical pain in her back was present. Never complaining. Yes, we were in each other's way as I painted doorframes and doors right where the guys were going back and forth. Early on I tried working in areas where they weren't, but finally, I just couldn't avoid being where they were unless you quit working. They were so grateful for the help, they never complained about why that door had to be painted right then. We just worked around one another laughing, telling stories, and getting a lot accomplished. When they bumped into my fresh paint accidentally, I simply touched it up, when I dropped a box edge in the fresh grout, we simply patted it down and then laughed.

What a joy to work with others in close quarters, doing hard work with the Holy Spirit flowing all around us. The staff at the camp are committed Christians. I saw their character traits and commitment for making the conference center as nice a place as they can with the limits they have for funding and time. Yes, they probably have times in their lives that they complain since they too are human. While they were working, those complaints never surfaced. What a joy to experience that kind of fellowship and love. Yes, Rudy and I love the staff at this camp and look forward to being a part of their fellowship whenever possible.

What complaints could you revisit in your life that perhaps you could redirect into positive and helpful comments or requests? Obstacles in our lives are merely opportunities to allow the Holy Spirit to take charge and direct our path toward positive solutions. Lord, help us to resist the urge to complain and pause to think of positive responses.

### *Changing Plans*

Surprises come in many packages. Earlier this week, we knew our time in Texas was ending, but we weren't sure exactly which day we would leave. An email arrived telling us about a NOMADS drop-in site needing help in Arkansas at a conference center. It was on our way to our next location; perhaps we could squeeze in a week there. After a couple of phone calls, we decided to leave early to start work the next day.

What a delightful experience God brought our way! Yes, they need lots of help! We can only do so much, but every little bit helps. Imagine eighteen doors with frames needing painting. We could not put them in the house since it was being spray painted. Setting them up in the workshop was a maze. I liked to call it a house of cards because, if you accidentally hit one, they would all fall! We got them primed, sanded, and ready for the final coat. Now the house is painted and ready for electrical, installation of doors, and trim. So much to be done this week. People were leaving and others arriving, but somehow God would bring in the help needed.

I know that God led us here since we would probably have taken another route. Meeting new people, learning about a new agency, and providing service once again is a blessing for us. ***"In every way I've shown you that it is necessary to help the weak by laboring like this and to remember the words of the Lord Jesus, because he said, 'It is more blessed to give than to receive.'" -- Acts 20:35-36 (CSB)*** Yes, we are giving, but we are also receiving.

Giving always brings more back to you in ways you never expect. Most of the time you never expect anything in return, but usually something comes. Perhaps it is only the satisfaction of having done something for someone else. The blessings are there, we merely need the eyes to see and the hearts to feel.

What opportunities present themselves to you that perhaps could take you on a different journey? Is God asking you to give? Each of us has different kinds of opportunities to help according to our abilities. How might God touch your life? Pray for that direction to be clear. Then act upon it in faith knowing *"It is more blessed to give than to receive."*

### Many Blessings

Too much candy at one time makes you sick. My mom always told me to eat just a little! Will too many blessings wear you out? Blessings come in many shapes and sizes and we have experienced many. Have you ever NOT gone somewhere just because you didn't think you would enjoy it that much? Branson, Missouri was one of those places for us. Our caring, good, Christian friends who are working at Silver Dollar City in Branson, invited us to visit. They showed us around with their employee/guest passes. 3 shows, 2 dinner shows, Silver Dollar City, and two minor attractions in 2 days. They helped us to appreciate not only the town of Branson, but the quality of life in that area of the country. I laughed so hard my throat was close to being sore. The inspirational and patriotic music was a wonderful surprise. I left there tired, but feeling very blessed.

We came to Branson from our NOMADS project in Arkansas, where we saw transformation taking place with a large cabin as several of us worked to improve it. We left Branson to go to a church for me to lead a Women's Retreat with the theme, "Live Expecting God's Blessings." With so much awareness about blessings going on within me, I felt overwhelmed at times about how good God is. As I talked to people at the retreat, I know that others carry burdens about loved ones while looking for the blessings around them. I, too, have been in those situations and know that God does bring us blessings, even during pain and suffering. *"But when the kindness of God our Savior and his love for mankind appeared, he saved us —not by works of righteousness that we had done, but according to his mercy — through the washing of regeneration and renewal by the Holy Spirit."* *-- Titus 3:4-5 (CSB)*

God wants us to have faith and work hard. *"God is fair; he will not forget the work you did and the love you showed for him by helping his people. And he will remember that you are still helping them. We want each of you to go on with the same hard work all your lives so you will surely get what you hope for. We do not want you to become lazy. Be like those who through faith and patience will receive what God has promised." -- Hebrews 6:10-12 (NCV)* As we helped others, God provided for us through our friends in the places we went. During our stay to lead the retreat, the wonderful people there cared for us more than we expected. Yes, we are physically tired. Our spirits soar in thankfulness to our Lord for the many blessings we have experienced. Look around you for the blessings that are already there and for the blessings that you can offer to others because God is leading you.

### NOMADS Pray

Why are we amazed when God guides us, and action happens? We pray for something, and when our prayers are answered, we walk around with a sense of awe that God heard our prayer and then answered it immediately. This week simply reinforced my faith in the value of intercessory prayers for one another. The story goes like this...

At the NOMADS reunion, one of our members went to the hospital late our first night together. The next morning, we got word she was in the hospital. By noon we heard that she had had a stroke. I took one of my prayer cloths and went to the microphone and asked the gathering of about 300 people to join hands and pray with me for her recovery. Several of us held the prayer cloth as we prayed. My plan was to have someone else take the cloth to her since I did not know her. I couldn't think of anyone who was going over to the hospital since one pastor had already gone to see her. I had nothing to do for the next hour and felt led to go myself. On the way to the hospital, I prayed for God to enable me to follow through as He wished. As I walked into her room, I introduced myself to her husband and to her. She was aware I was there, but didn't say anything. I told them about our group prayers and asked to pray with them. I laid the cloth on her chest and the three of us joined hands. After I prayed for her recovery, she began to tell me a story about an incident from last year's reunion of the group signing a tote bag to give to a NOMAD who was ill. After she told me the whole story, her husband looked at me with a big smile and said, "That was the first complete sentence she has said since noon yesterday!" It was several sentences! Then she looked at him and uttered her last name. A tear came to her eye!

Later, he told me that she had not been able to remember her last name since coming to the hospital. He and she believe our prayers brought her out of the woods. God heard our collective prayers for her. Why? We don't know! When I returned to the conference, I shared the story with all present and we praised God for hearing our prayers. Later we learned she had suffered three strokes as a clot passed through her brain. She had no visible speech or physical impairments. A couple of days later she was released from the hospital and resumed her travel schedule, though she had to rest while traveling.

James teaches us about the power of prayer: ***"Is anyone among you suffering? He should pray. Is anyone cheerful? He should sing praises. Is anyone among you sick? He should call for the elders of the church, and they are to pray over him, anointing him with oil in the name of the Lord. The prayer of faith will save the sick person, and the Lord will raise him up; if he has committed sins, he will be forgiven. Therefore, confess your sins to one another and pray for one another, so that you may be healed. The prayer of a righteous person is very powerful in its effect." -- James 5:13-16 (CSB)***

God answers prayers according to His will and this appears to be one of those times. Yes, great things happened that we could see immediately, and we sing our praises to God for His grace and compassion. Sometimes answers to our prayers come in much more subtle ways, come much later, or come over a longer period, but this time, God's answer came quickly. Now you could say it was a coincidence that our prayers and her speech coincided at the same moments, but all of us involved believe God acted in response to our prayers. Let us remember the power of prayers and continue to pray for one another and give the praise to God for answers that come for us according to His will.

### Unearned Gifts

We have all heard of the phrase, "pay it forward." Some of you may have even received this kind of gift. At our stop in Cedar Rapids, Iowa, Rudy and I met the NOMADS who were working on the flood disaster restoration work in the downtown district. We were invited to join the NOMADS for brunch together at a restaurant. While all eleven of us stood in the front waiting for our tables, Judy, a local NOMAD, talked to the owner about the group and the work they were doing here in town. As we all sat down, we joked about getting our checks right as we were not sitting next to our spouses! When she returned with drinks, she informed us that one of their regular customers had paid $100 toward our bill as a thank you for the work the teams had done and were doing. Wow! We told the waitress that we would just divide the remainder of the bill between us. We even talked about ways to help others and perhaps some ways we were already doing that for others. After our meal, our waitress informed us that the $100 took care of both the bill and the tip!

*"Teach me to do your will, for you are my God. May your gracious Spirit lead me on level ground." -- Psalms 143:10 (CSB )* Level ground meaning smooth sailing, no ruffles in life at the moment. Often, when our life is on level ground, we tend to put God on the back burner. We tend to roll along on automatic pilot each day without as much prayer, without as much thankfulness. This verse is telling us to be doing God's will even when we are on level ground.

While we are on level ground, it is easier for us to concentrate on things around us. How can each of us find a way to share an act of kindness with someone who needs a lift or deserves a pat on the back? I know that I, for one, will long remember the kindness of a stranger who paid for lunch for eleven strangers as a way of saying thank you. I was even more humbled since we were merely visiting those who had done the work. Yes, we had wanted to work, but our care for Mom this summer prevented us from working with this group.

We felt totally unworthy of this gift! God's grace is given out just as that gift of a free lunch was given to us! We did nothing to deserve the free lunch, but the stranger gave it anyway since we were a part of the group. God's grace is given to all who come to Jesus. *"The righteousness of God is through faith in Jesus Christ to all who believe, since there is no distinction. For all have sinned and fall short of the glory of God; they are justified freely by his grace through the redemption that is in Christ Jesus." -- Romans 3:22-24 (CSB)*

### Random Thoughts

Random thoughts. From here to there. Life takes us through days of random duties and events. What value do we find in them? Peace, simplicity, boredom, rest, catching up, time to think, restlessness, frustration, (add your own words...). Our days are filled with either too much to do or not enough. It seems to me that both are good. The busy days keep us involved in others and in the world around us; the not so busy days allow us rest in peace. I am one who likes to keep busy, but occasionally really enjoy a quiet day. Now that we are back on the road, we fluctuate between active days and quieter days. Yet God is with us in both.

Our repairs were done, so we were slowly making our way over to Columbus, Indiana, to meet with all our NOMADS friends. Each day I thank God for our safety as we travel and the people (strangers as well as old friends) we met along the way (even at the rest stops). The quiet nights we spent in new places have allowed me to plan for projects coming up, make calculations for quilts, and order materials without other interruptions.

Surprises happen too, such as coming to Indiana and showing up for church an hour late wondering why everyone was leaving rather than arriving! Indiana, for the many years we lived in Ohio, was never on Daylight Saving time. But about two or three years ago they changed, and we didn't know that! Since we were staying in a campground, the only clocks we had were those in the motorhome! Oh well! Sorry God, but we tried.

Frustration arises from being in campgrounds that say they have Wi-Fi, but it just didn't work at OUR site! How dependent we had become upon the communication made available through the Internet. Humor when our GPS took us to a laundromat in a residential neighborhood which turned out to be someone's home. I contemplated ringing their doorbell and asking if they were open! We kept searching the GPS and found a legitimate laundry. Praise God since we were out of clean clothes!

Yes, these days have been good for us. God does provide even though our plans changed and changed over the summer because of caring for Mom. It looks like we will be able to stop at most of the places we had hoped to see, but just not with as much time as we had planned.

This sums up our time and my hope for things to come: *"I will bless the Lord who counsels me — even at night when my thoughts trouble me. I always let the Lord guide me. Because he is at my right hand, I will not be shaken. Therefore my heart is glad and my whole being rejoices; my body also rests securely. For you will not abandon me to Sheol; you will not allow your faithful one to see decay. You reveal the path of life to me; in your presence is abundant joy; at your right hand are eternal pleasures." -- Psalms 16:7-11 (CSB)*

### With NOMADS

We shared a joyful week with 376 NOMADS who were gathered in Columbus, Indiana, for our annual meeting! Such a group of Christian servants all together in one place. Hugs abound. Conversations found us catching up on what had been happening since we last saw one another. Old friends met new friends. Prayers flowed in private with one another as well as our group prayers. Laughter was everywhere. Our common bond was and always will be our Lord, Jesus.

A large gathering of RV's pulled into the parking/camping area, and all came from many different places. The folks had gathered early just so we could visit one another! What a privilege to be among these folks. After about ten days, only four for the official meeting, we had our final gathering for worship and a memorial service for those who have passed on to be with Jesus during this year. After being rejuvenated, we all parted and went separate ways across the US to continue our mission work in so many ways.

This was the mountain top experience for me during the summer! I soaked in all the sources of spiritual food to revive and restore. I felt like a squirrel going out to gather all the nuts on the ground so that during the winter the squirrel can have food for survival. Now that I used that analogy, I realize we do have some nuts among the NOMADS too, but they are such joyful nuts!

Walking among us were those we had held in such powerful prayers for physical healing during the past year. How special and meaningful was their ability to be with us. For me, some of the special moments were those shared about how God had attended to our personal needs during the year.

*"Praise is rightfully yours, God, in Zion; vows to you will be fulfilled. All humanity will come to you, the one who hears prayer. Iniquities overwhelm me; only you can atone for our rebellions. How happy is the one you choose and bring near to live in your courts! We will be satisfied with the goodness of your house, the holiness of your temple." -- Psalms 65:1-4 (CSB)*

Yes, I praise God for allowing us to attend this gathering of your servants. I am so honored and humbled to have been there. May this gathering continue to remind me of the special moments that strengthen my love for You and allow me more opportunities for Your service.

## Easter Thoughts

### Entertain Angels

Palm Sunday found us deep in the foothills of North Carolina. The pastor from a local church came to share a message with our RV Rally group of about 250 persons. What a diverse group we were, yet we shared our faith as one of our common bonds. The presence of our worship guests, with their country gospel songs and heavy North Carolina accents, added to our understanding of the message that Jesus has for all of us.

*"Keep on loving one another as brothers and sisters. Do not forget to show hospitality to strangers, for by so doing some people have shown hospitality to angels without knowing it." -- Hebrews 13: 1-2 (NIV)* Now the question was, which group was entertaining angels? They perhaps thought of us as strangers since we were in their land. We perhaps thought of them as strangers among our community!

Jesus came triumphantly into Jerusalem on Palm Sunday. Our guests came triumphantly into our midst, proclaiming the good news of Jesus, salvation, and His death for us as the ultimate gift of love. They came with boldness into our midst, nervous about our response to their message and the size of our group (we were more than three times what they normally have in their services). Their willingness to share their message spoke highly of their commitment, their faith, and their joy in serving their Lord.

Their example is one for us to follow. We need to go boldly into the world, not knowing what awaits us, to share the good news of Jesus with those around us. What and how can each of us be involved in His service? The answer varies for all of us as we each find and understand our gifts. May we learn from one another as we share examples of our service and our testimonies. Let us take those steps of faith to risk the unknown for our Lord, who gave His life on a cross for us out of His deepest love.

### Alive Everyday

Joyous moments are usually easy to remember. A first intentional smile from your child. Finding a treasure you thought lost. Recovery from an illness or accident most thought hopeless. Getting the job you anxiously awaited. Moving into your dream home. The birth of your children, and the list goes on! Think about those joyous moments in your life.

Easter Sunday, I remember the experience of Mary Magdalene as she went to the tomb, filled with sadness. Upon her arrival, fear filled her as she found the tomb open. Questions suddenly flooded her mind as she discovered the body gone. An awesome wave of emotions engulfed her. Then He said her name and she knew, instantly and suddenly, the completeness of His presence. The sadness, the fear, and the anxiety all left her, and she knew He was alive! What joy she felt: ***"Mary Magdalene went and announced to the disciples, 'I have seen the Lord!' And she told them what he had said to her." -- John 20:18 (CSB)***

Can you imagine the look on her face as she said those words, the body language that emphasized her words, the tone of voice as she spoke! The disciples could not dismiss her joy for it was infectious, convincing, and compelling.

Is Easter joy reserved just for Easter Sunday? Jesus gave His life so that all other days we could experience the joy of resurrected life in Him. Just as Mary rushed to share the news and joy with the disciples, we needed to go tell others the news and share the joy! What is that moment in your life when you knew Jesus lives in you? How can you share that moment with others? Do you want Jesus alive in you? Ask, seek, and the door will be open for you, too. Find a Mary or a Peter in your life and talk with them. Pray a prayer asking Jesus into your heart. As Nike advertising says, "Just do it!"

### Path We Travel

During this Holy Week, we remember the way that our Lord traveled for us. It was not an easy path. It was filled with personal suffering, both physical and emotional. The guards took advantage of this opportunity to cause Him pain.

***"After they had mocked him, they stripped him of the purple robe and put his clothes on him. They led him out to crucify him." -- Mark 15:20 (CSB)*** What about the path we travel for the Lord? I know that, for myself, I have never suffered in the way that my Lord suffered for me. I have never suffered in the way those who hunger suffer, or those who are in a war-torn area suffer, or of those in prison suffer. No, I do not know that kind of suffering and how I praise God for my blessings. Have I suffered for my Christian faith? Once again, not in the way that our Lord did. The Christian suffering I can identify with is mostly in the form of rejection from others who listen to my witness of God's work in my life. Does that deter me from wanting to share? No. Does it deter me from sharing with that same person again? Sometimes.

Suffering is something each of us has experienced in some form during our life. Usually, any suffering I experience becomes another opportunity for God and His people to minister to me again. When I think of Holy Week and all that happened during that week to Jesus and His disciples, I find hope knowing that when suffering comes my way, that Jesus is there for me! He can carry me through anything. Praise God for giving us His son Jesus and for loving us so very much.

### He Is Not Here

There is much uncertainty surrounding our lives because of the economy, climate concerns, as well as our own personal issues of health, family, and friends. It seems that every day brings something new on the news front either personally, locally, or around the world.

Easter Sunday is the greatest day of hope, the day of resurrection, the day of new life for Christians. What joy comes amid uncertainty when we witness the resurrection story from scripture!

I think of the disciples as they reflect on the events of the three years serving Jesus - traveling with Him, listening to His stories, wondering what was to come, yet feeling secure around him. Then suddenly, as Jesus had foretold them, events unraveled that shook their very foundation, filled them with fear, sent them into hiding, and caused Peter to renounce his association with Jesus. The angels appeared to the women who had come to the grave to minister to Jesus body. *"So the women were terrified and bowed down to the ground. 'Why are you looking for the living among the dead?' asked the men. 'He is not here, but he has risen!' " -- Luke 24:5-6 (CSB)* On the morning of the third day, the women went to the tomb only to find it empty, to hear of their risen Lord, and to run back to the disciples exclaiming to them the joyous news! Yes, Easter morning began that day. What a day for hope to build, to conquer, to fill us all with knowledge that eternal life conquers death, and for hope to live forever.

My prayer for all of you is that this Easter Day will renew our spirits, refresh our souls, and enable us to see beyond the struggles of each day. As we pray for those we love, let us pray for the Easter experience to surround their situations and bring them a sense of peace and joy, even during struggle. May we carry the Easter experience with us every day of the year, beginning today! Jesus died and rose again for each of us that we may be forgiven and find the inner peace we each seek through Him.

### Accurate Accounts

Police often rely on witnesses to help determine who did what in an accident. A newspaper story disturbed us. Out of 285 murders in a big city, only one brought about a conviction, even though many witnesses existed for most of the acts. Witnesses refused to testify due to intimidation and threats by the perpetrators or their friends.

Parents try to train their children to give accurate accounts of events, i.e., to be reputable witnesses. Witnesses often have conflicting stories as well. Our television programs are filled with dramas about the importance of witnessing what was seen or heard.

Our natural response when seeing something out of the ordinary is to tell someone else as much detail as we can remember about the event. This tendency applies to great moments or events in our lives as well.

The book of Acts contains a message from Peter to Cornelius. *"We ourselves are witnesses of everything he did in both the Judean country and in Jerusalem, and yet they killed him by hanging him on a tree. God raised up this man on the third day and caused him to be seen, not by all the people, but by us whom God appointed as witnesses, who ate and drank with him after he rose from the dead. He commanded us to preach to the people and to testify that he is the one appointed by God to be the judge of the living and the dead. All the prophets testify about him that through his name everyone who believes in him receives forgiveness of sins." -- Acts 10:39-43 (CSB)*

What kind of witness would you have been to the resurrection? What opportunities do we seize upon or pass up? What prevents us from witnessing? What enables us to witness to others about our risen Lord and Savior? Peter came from denying any knowledge of Jesus to be a mighty spokesman for his faith as the Holy Spirit enabled him. Let us allow the Holy Spirit to enable us to tell others about how Jesus blesses our life.

### *Judgements Made*

I found a story about a lady, and she made judgments about folks before she even got to know them. She was set up for a surprise meeting with a big guy with tattoos who arrived to pick her up on a Harley motorcycle! He was known by others to be a caring, compassionate fellow who was sent to spend an afternoon with her. As she got to know him, her opinion of him changed.

Now to Easter morning! John 20:1-18 tells the story of Mary Magdalene arriving at the tomb and of her expectations. When she arrived, she first noticed the stone was rolled away! Who did that? Why is it missing? Did someone take his body? How many of us jump to conclusions based on our first observation, our previous experience, and our preconceived notions about life and others? Guilty. All of us, guilty! At least to some degree. Mary ran to the disciples, told them what she saw, and they all returned to the tomb. Two angels appeared to her and: *"They said to her, 'Woman, why are you crying?'—'Because they've taken away my Lord,' she told them, 'and I don't know where they've put him.' Having said this, she turned around and saw Jesus standing there, but she did not know it was Jesus. 'Woman' Jesus said to her, 'why are you crying? Who is it that you're seeking?' Supposing he was the gardener, she replied, 'Sir, if you've carried him away, tell me where you've put him, and I will take him away.' Jesus said to her, 'Mary.' "* -- John 20:13-16 (CSB)

Second assumption, Mary did not recognize His changed appearance nor His voice and assumed He was someone else! We too fail to recognize changes because we were expecting something or someone else. Do we fail to see Jesus around us just as Mary did? Probably. Just as Jesus came to Mary and to the other disciples during the next week in ways that they did not immediately recognize Him, He also comes to us in various ways. Perhaps we too need to expand our vision of others and, of course, also balance the need for safety today. Allow Jesus to minister to us through scripture but also through other avenues. Look for Jesus around you every day and praise God for His presence.

### *Tearful Reactions*

During worship I found myself pondering some "whys" about myself. Why does some music affect me so profoundly? Why do Hallmark commercials bring tears to my eyes? Why do I feel so loved when I am in a worship service? Why does the suffering of others, even those on TV cause such pain within me? One answer from many praise songs is that Jesus cares for me and for you. He cares so much He willingly gave His life on the cross for us. How can I possibly deserve that kind of love? I don't deserve His love; Jesus just gives it to me.

The disciples (and others) experienced the miracle of His love and acceptance following the resurrection in several events as Jesus appeared to them. Peter had denied Jesus, as predicted, and found forgiveness and love; Thomas doubted the stories of resurrection by his fellow disciples until he witnessed Jesus' hands and side himself; Mary Magdalene did not recognize Jesus until He called her by name. All came to believe, and their faith was solidified by the events.

The next couple of verses in John reminded me once again: *"Jesus performed many other signs in the presence of his disciples that are not written in this book. But these are written so that you may believe that Jesus is the Messiah, the Son of God, and that by believing you may have life in his name." -- John 20:30-31 (CSB)*

Music affects me because of how it reminds me of Jesus abundant love for me. Hallmark commercials bring tears of joy as they once again remind me of the kind of love that Jesus offers all of us through one another. We just need to claim it! Being in worship immerses me completely in His arms so that I can feel the security of His presence. Seeing the suffering of others arouses in me the pain of separation from God and reminds me of how He grieves for us. I feel their pain and pray for their healing and for their reconciliation with God. My tears are my way of experiencing my gratitude for His love for me and for others. Sometimes they are merely tears of joy!

### *A New Normal*

Jesus is risen! Christ the Lord is risen indeed. Such joy to go from so much sorrow on Friday and Saturday to a whole new world on Sunday morning! A moment in time can change all we know and set us in a new direction. Our son and his wife, who have seven boys, had a baby girl. That moment of her birth forever changed our lives. Even another boy would have changed our lives, but in a different way.

Another friend was in a head-on collision that severely injured his wife. Their lives are changed. Normal is no longer as they once knew. Through grace and God's healing power, we pray for a return of as much as possible to the normal they once knew. They are forever changed from this experience.

Any major change in our lives produces a new normal. Christ died a horrendous death. His death produced a temporary new normal for believers, but only for three days! His resurrection suddenly changed everything. ***"The angel told the women, 'Don't be afraid, because I know you are looking for Jesus who was crucified. He is not here. For he has risen, just as he said. Come and see the place where he lay. Then go quickly and tell his disciples, 'He has risen from the dead and indeed he is going ahead of you to Galilee; you will see him there. Listen, I have told you.' " -- Matthew 28:5-7 (CSB)***

Knowing of the resurrection is different than believing in the reality of the resurrection and in our risen Lord Jesus. How does that belief change your normal life? What is the new normal to your life because of what Christ did for you and me? Do we even think about the impact that Jesus' resurrection has on our lives? Perhaps we should. Old Testament and New Testament scriptures come together with the prophecy and the fulfillment of Jesus birth, life, death and resurrection.

Lord, help us to reflect on the new normal that Your resurrection has on our lives. Easter Sunday is a day of rejoicing, but then so is every day after that! Our personal relationship with Jesus pleases God. Living our life so that others can see Christ alive through our actions and our words is a goal. Help us to see how to live out that goal daily.

### Anticipation

We all know about the anticipation of waiting for a loved one to arrive. Our son and his wife were coming soon! I recently saw the photos of our daughter-in-law (in Texas) whose sister and her four children were waiting for her husband and their father to arrive home from deployment. The joy on their faces of reuniting was very special! I'm sure their anticipation of his arrival was great!

During Lent, we anticipate Easter and the joyous resurrection of Christ because we know it is coming. The disciples, however, didn't know, that to get to Easter, they had to go through Good Friday. They faced events and emotions that we only read about. We, also, face daily issues that we have no idea how they will be resolved or evolve.

Geography, jobs, and lifestyles cause separation from kids, other family or friends. Those are issues we learn to deal with. Coming together once again allows for the anticipation for that day. Perhaps it involves great places to visit as we travel to see each other. Families separated by military service deal with many painful issues which they can't control. Yet, they learn to help one another pass the time till reunion happens.

The disciples could not even comprehend what was about to happen to Jesus. When Good Friday came, they went into hiding. Peter even denied knowing Jesus three times. They did not have the ability to anticipate Jesus' resurrection as it was all a new experience, whereas for us, we know the ending to the story. Even though Old Testament prophecy Isaiah 53:3-12 told of the coming events, they simply could not comprehend Jesus resurrection. They found no joy until that Sunday morning, when the women went to the tomb to care for Jesus' body. Then the amazement, the joy, the surprise, the doubt, the questions, all flooded over them while awaiting Jesus' appearances to them. As Jesus walked later that day on the road to Emmaus: *"He said to them, 'How foolish you are, and how slow to believe all that the prophets have spoken! Wasn't it necessary for the Messiah to suffer these things and enter into his glory?' Then beginning with Moses and all the Prophets, he interpreted for them the things concerning himself in all the Scriptures." -- Luke 24:25-27 (CSB)*

What in your life are you anticipating? What struggles go along with the anticipation? Are you waiting for a job, for something lost to be found, for a loved one to get healthy again, for... Add your own phrase to that sentence. How do we deal with the time during the waiting? How do we allow Jesus to be an example for us, a comforter for us, a healer for us, or a companion for us? Read the different versions in Matthew 28 and Luke 24. Find the hope that is there and carry it with you daily.

### Life Changes

Palm Sunday - a time for remembering the celebrations that brought Jesus into Jerusalem. A week that started with such high hopes for the people changed by the end of the week. Life can change quickly!

A couple goes to the doctor for a fairly regular check-up with complaints of dizziness and find themselves hours later in the hospital getting the wife ready for emergency heart surgery. Nine people on motorcycles sit at a red light only to be run over by a dump truck, killing four of the motorcyclists and putting the other five in serious condition in the hospital. A teacher is accused of molesting a student. A boss is accused of harassing an employee. Life can change quickly!

Accusations abound over guilt or innocence when a wrong is committed and proof is vague. Our legal system tries to sort out the right from the wrong, the guilty from the innocent. Sometimes the system gets it wrong. We all hear stories of prisoners released after years of serving a sentence for a crime they really didn't commit. The reasons vary as to how this happens.

Jesus came into Jerusalem being praised as the King of the Jews. He didn't call Himself that, but the people did. Certain people did not like Him or what He was doing. The Pharisees schemed to get Him arrested. Luke 23:1-2, starts the story of His trial with their accusations of Him. *"Then their whole assembly rose up and brought him before Pilate. They began to accuse him, saying, 'We found this man misleading our nation, opposing payment of taxes to Caesar, and saying that he himself is the Messiah, a king.' " -- Luke 23:1-2 (CSB)*

Those three accusations simply don't add up to crucifixion! However, Jesus was greatly feared by the Pharisees, the priests of the Jews. They were so entrenched in their Jewish laws that the message of Jesus could not penetrate their world. They feared Him enough to use the Roman law to demand His crucifixion in place of another criminal, Barabbas.

What lessons can we learn from how the Pharisees viewed the object of their fear, Jesus? Keep an open mind. Read, know, and listen to God's word. Don't seek revenge. Work together for understanding. Pray for guidance from God. Slow down and don't hurry up the process for getting things right.

Let us focus this Holy Week on how we hold Jesus in our lives. What did His death on the cross mean to me or you individually? How can I honor His sacrifice?

### The Empty Tomb

He is risen. He is risen indeed! What joy it is in finding an empty tomb! Of course, the first women to arrive were confused and frightened. Our expectations often prevent us from being open to the surprises that God has for us. God has a way of letting us catch up. He is patient and waits for us to absorb all that is happening around us. It is easy for us to rush to judgments, just as the women who arrived at the tomb. Their first thoughts were that someone had stolen His body.

When events happen in our lives that leave us confused, we jump to conclusions often without obtaining the facts or praying for guidance. Reflection allows God to slowly reveal to us His plan. We are blessed that we have read about and studied the Easter Resurrection story and know it well. That story, though, needs to find a daily place in our lives.

Mary finding the tomb open ran to John and Peter saying: *" 'They've taken the Lord out of the tomb, and we don't know where they've put him!' At that, Peter and the other disciple went out, heading for the tomb. The two were running together, but the other disciple outran Peter and got to the tomb first. Stooping down, he saw the linen cloths lying there, but he did not go in. Then, following him, Simon Peter also came. He entered the tomb and saw the linen cloths lying there. The wrapping that had been on his head was not lying with the linen cloths but was folded up in a separate place by itself. The other disciple, who had reached the tomb first, then also went in, saw, and believed. For they did not yet understand the Scripture that he must rise from the dead. Then the disciples returned to the place where they were staying."* *-- John 20:2-10 (CSB)*

As always on Easter, I reflect upon experiences from the past where God has allowed me to find an "empty tomb," meaning something that wows me with the impact like what the women found that morning when they found the empty tomb of our Lord.

Many years ago, at the church where I worked, I was doing the Children's messages each week. For the first Sunday in Lent, we had a young lady come and dance as though she was a caterpillar. We made a large cocoon for her to dance into and she closed the door behind her. Once the children left the sanctuary, she came out the back and quietly exited. Our plan was for her to come out of the cocoon Easter Sunday morning as a butterfly. That Easter morning as I arrived at church, I learned that we had not followed up with her to make sure she was coming for the second service where the dance was scheduled to happen. Her parents told us that she never heard from us, so she made other plans. Now I had to figure out what to do. In a panic, I retreated to my office, grabbed my bible, found the story of Resurrection morning, praying for guidance about how to handle this situation I had helped create! As I read the story of the empty tomb, it took on a different meaning for me that morning. The cocoon was empty! So, for the children, I explained my error and apologized to all for the error. Then I asked the children about all the paper butterflies around the room taped to the walls. Did they see them get put up there or see them come out of their cocoons? No. Just as we didn't see Jesus come out of the tomb that Resurrection morning either. Just because no one saw Jesus leave the tomb does that mean it didn't happen. All the evidence of the linen clothes, the removed stone, the angels that appeared, and even Jesus speaking to Mary, indicating that Jesus did leave an empty tomb. Perhaps God had a better plan for us than to have a dancer come out of the cocoon that morning, leaving us with an empty tomb story. I'll never forget my emotions of total panic about the cocoon's emptiness that became great joy for its emptiness! How much more the story of the women finding the tomb empty and finding Jesus alive now means to me. Pure joy that Jesus lives! (*I did send the young lady an apology letter.*)

King-size quilt, original design

## Other Holiday Themes

### New Year

For 2002, my resolution is found: ***"Devote yourselves to prayer; stay alert in it with thanksgiving." -- Colossians 4:2 (CSB)*** Busy-ness is easily an interrupter of my prayer time. I can usually manage to continue with my quick-on-the-go prayers every day. It is the reflective, quiet, prayer time that can escape from my day. When I make the time for my study and prayers, my days seem more peaceful.

Paul goes on: ***"At the same time, pray also for us that God may open a door to us for the word, to speak the mystery of Christ, for which I am in chains, so that I may make it known as I should." -- Colossians 4:3-4 (CSB)*** Believers are ministers in some form as we share prayers with others, as we relate to others in daily life, and as we read and study God's word. The quality of my prayer life carries over to opportunities I recognize for proclaiming the mystery of Christ.

Resolutions for a New Year usually drift away after a few days, or weeks, of the New Year. This resolution I plan to be reminded of daily and, with God's help, I plan to fulfill.

What scriptural resolution can you take with you into this New Year? If you need suggestions, investigate Philippians 2 and 4, James 1-5, Ephesians. Of course, you can find suggestions in any book of the Bible. Write it out and put it somewhere so that you can see it each day.

### The Magi Come

How do we know where we are going? Or why? The Magi in Matthew 2 following the star makes me wonder about their journey.

Matthew 2:1-12 for the whole story, but verse 2 says: ***"Where is he who has been born king of the Jews? For we saw his star at its rising and have come to worship him." -- Matthew 2:2 (CSB)*** They did not know where they were going but they went anyway. They followed a star. King Herod gave them directions along the way, but he was trying to use them for his own gain, and they knew it. The star continued to guide them until they found their way to Bethlehem and to a manger holding the baby Jesus.

The Magi were astrologers and learned men. They knew the stars and they knew about the predicted Messiah. Following the signs, they set out on their journey.

God gave us the star to follow also. For us that star is Jesus and our study of biblical scripture. Like the Magi, we have a journey to make in our lives. Where is God leading us today, this week, this month, this year? Is it to places we have never been, or a repeat journey that we need to make again and again? What directions might we receive from others that might perhaps be helpful or harmful? How do we know which they are? Again, scripture helps us recognize the journey.

We need to prepare. Read God's word. Pray for direction. Seek wisdom. Remain open to God's guidance. Follow Jesus all along the way to the destination of His choice for us. When we take our eyes off Him, detours can catch us off guard and deceive us into going another way.

### *Love Each Other*

Valentine's Day, a day to celebrate loving relationships. Hmm. Just one day to celebrate important relationships. Of course, many people have loving relationships not only with spouses but others as well. Those relationships are equally important! Grandparents, friends, brothers, sisters, cousins, other relatives, co-workers, neighbors, and strangers.

Perhaps defining love is part of making the most of Valentine's Day. Colossians gives us a look at relationships: ***"Therefore, as God's chosen ones, holy and dearly loved, put on compassion, kindness, humility, gentleness, and patience, bearing with one another and forgiving one another if anyone has a grievance against another. Just as the Lord has forgiven you, so you are also to forgive. Above all, put on love, which is the perfect bond of unity. And let the peace of Christ, to which you were also called in one body, rule your hearts. And be thankful. Let the word of Christ dwell richly among you, in all wisdom teaching and admonishing one another through Psalms , hymns, and spiritual songs, singing to God with gratitude in your hearts. And whatever you do, in word or in deed, do everything in the name of the Lord Jesus, giving thanks to God the Father through him." -- Colossians 3:12-17 (CSB)***

Shouldn't everyday then be Valentine's Day as outlined in Colossians? Who in my life today needs forgiveness? Who in my life am I thankful for today? Who do I want to tell of my love for them? What songs come to mind that express my joy for Christ and others? Which Psalms inspires me, read it again. What about the strangers around me? Who is in need? How can I help? Is there one thing I can do this week to reach out to others?

Per the last instruction in the previous Colossian's passage: *"do everything in the name of the Lord Jesus, giving thanks to God the Father through him."* Have a wonderful day, week, and year as you celebrate loving relationships all around you!

### *Mary for Me*

On Mother's Day, I heard from two friends who have mothers nearing the end of their lives. Many more of us have already endured that event or are also seeing the end coming. *"For we know that if our earthly tent we live in is destroyed, we have a building from God, an eternal dwelling in the heavens, not made with hands...-- Now the one who prepared us for this very purpose is God, who gave us the Spirit as a down payment. So we are always confident and know that while we are at home in the body we are away from the Lord. For we walk by faith, not by sight." -- 2 Corinthians 5:1, 5-7 (CSB)* Our faith teaches us that the end is only the beginning for those who know and love the Lord.

I treasure the last days with my mother-in-law, Mary. She taught me much about Jesus. She would recommend a course of action that suited her, knowing I would go another way, yet she continued to love me unconditionally. She loved scripture and was the person who gave me my first readable and understandable Bible at a very important point in my life. We talked about living a Christian life together, shared thoughts about what Jesus meant in some of His teachings. She loved our children and wanted to see them grow up, but that was not to be. Breast cancer found her, and she became one of that disease's victims. In the hospital those last weeks, I had the privilege to read scripture to her, to sing and read hymns to her, to witness her last communion and share in that moment when her pastor talked to her about going to be with the Lord. She could not talk by this time, but she nodded her head in acknowledgement of her destiny soon to come. My grief was for myself and for those of us who loved her. My joy was for her destiny, free from the pain in her body, and basking in the warmth of our Lord's home.

The bonds between mothers and children are strong, even when the relationship is strained. If your mother is still living, does she know Jesus? Sometimes our mothers won't let us help them, but we can always pray for them. Let us all remember our mothers and all those women who have no children, but have been influential in the lives of other people.

### Mothers Give Life

Mother's Day - a day of mixed emotions for many people. Everything from sheer joy and pleasure to agony and pain comes to mind when many remember mothers. All of us have an image of what a mother should be. Reality often does not match that image.

Scripture tells us to: *"Honor your father and mother, which is the first commandment with a promise." -- Ephesians 6:2 (CSB)* Luke gives us this phrase: *"Blessed is the mother who gave you birth and nursed you." -- Luke 11:27 (NIV)* How blessed life is when those scriptures ring true for us! How often do those same scriptures stir up resentments and anger within us because we see the failures in our mothers. Consider these mothers:

- Those giving up babies for adoption.

- Those unable to have babies, but adopt.

- Those whose children become criminals or terrorists.

- Those whose struggle to survive which takes all their energy.

- Those whose role models gave them bad examples.

- Those who suffered watching a child with a terminal disease.

- Those whose child was taken from them.

- Those unable to find even food for their children.

- Those who view children as possessions, not people.

This list could go on and on! This Mother's Day, I invite you to look beyond those times of disappointment and remember that she gave you life, for better or worse. Each of us can go beyond what may be standing in the way of how we honor our mothers. In that very act of giving us life, we can find reason enough to honor our mother. So many mothers around the world consider that they did the best they could for their children, yet others wish they had done more. Today is today, we can't change the past, but we can affect the future as we experience it by choosing to honor our mothers per God's instructions.

Praise God for all those many mothers whose children have mostly warm, caring, loving memories. They are the lucky ones, as are their children. As we celebrate, let us also remember those whose pain is intensified on this day. Help us to acknowledge their pain, but invite them to move beyond and allow the Holy Spirit of God to touch their hearts, heal their pain and allow them to find something to be grateful for concerning their mother, whether it is their biological mother or the mother who raised them. How will you remember your mother today?

### Faces of Moms

As I ponder the mothers that I know, I see many faces, many different situations. All of us have a mother and we can honor her, living or already gone. An aunt loves her family, her children, and her grandchildren. She grieves the death of her lifelong husband and father of her children, who passed the day before. Mother's Day is forever changed for her.

My mother, while living with Alzheimer's disease, wanted to pass on knowing her life with Jesus is better than the one she endured. Nothing, - gifts, cards, phone calls - can take away the truth of the disease for her.

Another family awaiting being a mother for the first time, knows the baby she carries may not live or, if it does, may suffer severe problems. Then again, all may be well. Some women want to be mothers, but for various reason are not for their own biological children. The list can go on. Fill in your own concerns.

Many mothers have adult children serving in the military in harm's way. Other moms have children in prison, in detox units, under psychiatric care, and other such problems.

Jesus tells us, ***"I give you a new command: Love one another. Just as I have loved you, you are also to love one another. By this everyone will know that you are my disciples, if you love one another." -- John 13:34-35 (CSB)***

Sometimes loving one another is hard because we confuse behavior we do not like with the life of a person. Jesus did not always like what His disciples did, but He loved them as persons. Blessings come in many ways, and we need to search out those blessings amidst the events of each day. Help us each to be a blessing to someone each day, to find some loving kindness to share with someone even is small ways. Today we think of mothers, but loving one another every day honors life according to Jesus' message to us in John.

### *Job Well Done*

I was reminded in a card about these scriptures. *"Love is patient, love is kind. Love does not envy, is not boastful, is not arrogant, is not rude, is not self-seeking, is not irritable, and does not keep a record of wrongs." -- 1 Corinthians 13:4-5 (CSB)* How many mothers learn patience as they teach their little ones the many things they need to know - from walking, talking, dressing, manners, and you can add your favorite in here! God is so patient with us as we learn to praise Him, trust Him, and walk with Him as a daily part of our lives.

*"As a mother comforts her son, so I will comfort you." -- Isaiah 66:13 (CSB)* I remember the times of physical hurt and emotional hurt when my children needed comforting. Simply to be held, or perhaps putting a bandage on the wound, or listening as they spilled out details of some event of the day. God loves us so very much too! His compassion comes to us in so many ways - through others, through music, through cards, through sights in nature or scenarios around us, and through whatever other way He sees fit to use.

*"Her mouth speaks wisdom, and loving instruction is on her tongue." -- Proverbs 31:26 (CSB)* We pray for the wisdom to share with our children and for the ability to speak clearly with directions and hope. Sometimes we accomplish our task through the grace of God. Often, we feel inadequate to always say the right thing to our children, but when we rely on God to show us the way, His grace provides for our needs.

*"What is inside the heart — the imperishable quality of a gentle and quiet spirit, which is of great worth in God's sight." -- 1 Peter 3:4 (CSB)* Remembering to keep quiet first, then listen carefully and clarify before giving directions and instructions enables our children to trust us. Respecting them as individuals who have thoughts and feelings worth expressing teaches them to have respect for others as well. Let us not jump to conclusions based solely on what we see (or think we see) or on what siblings come running to tell us. Let love and respect for our children allow us to encourage the truth from them, even if it means they did something wrong. Help us to treat our children as God treats us. Hebrews 12 talks about discipline for those we love, just as God disciplines us whom He loves. Discipline is merely training for future correct behavior, and it is best done with a gentle and quiet spirit.

*"Strength and honor are her clothing, and she can laugh at the time to come."*
*-- Proverbs 31:25 (CSB)* Mothers need strength to endure the many demands from the children. Faithfully going to God in prayer is one way of developing the strength to endure. Dignity is essential, especially out in public when those adorable children decide to behave in another manner. Our children's bad behavior can often evoke equally bad responses from us, which never makes the situation better. When we yell at God, He never yells back. Think about the mothers who confidently guide their out-of-control child out of the store or into a private spot to bring calm. Allow God to lead you with strength and dignity rather than let the emotions of the situation overtake you.

### Warriors Lost

Reading the Old Testament used to be a chore, wading through all the difficult names and places. Keeping the multitude of wars straight was mind-boggling and unpleasant. I dreaded going there to read. Then the Bible Study Fellowship that I belonged to many years ago first studied Genesis for a year and then we studied the major and minor prophets (which were all Old Testament)! Wow, God knew I needed those two years. God knew I needed to know about the faith that developed for His people because of the conflicts. I needed to know about the people called to do impossible (for man) tasks on battlefields. God knew I needed to remember His soldiers from thousands of years ago who helped to keep His name alive.

Memorial Day is a day to remember members of the armed forces killed in war. Wars have happened since the earliest times with humans. Conflicts are and have been between nations and tribes for many reasons. This means to me that we honor not only those soldiers who died in modern day wars, but also the soldiers over the centuries that died to preserve our God's name and place in our lives.

Joshua fought battles for the land promised to Moses by God. Joshua took Jericho. Joshua fought when God told him to go to war. Joshua followed God's orders: *"The Lord said to Joshua, 'Look, I have handed Jericho, its king, and its best soldiers over to you. March around the city with all the men of war, circling the city one time. Do this for six days. Have seven priests carry seven ram's-horn trumpets in front of the ark. But on the seventh day, march around the city seven times, while the priests blow the rams' horns. When there is a prolonged blast of the horn and you hear its sound, have all the troops give a mighty shout. Then the city wall will collapse, and the troops will advance, each man straight ahead.' "*
*-- Joshua 6:2-5 (CSB)*

On this special day of remembrance, we remember the lives lost and the families missing a loved one. Yes, I hate war because of its destructive nature. I also recognize it is inevitable in our world of differing opinions. Until mankind becomes perfect and of one accord, wars will be with us. So, let us care for those caught up in the destruction and find meaning in their lives and in their deaths. Let us look to God in our pain and try to find ways to prevent future wars and seek peace. Will it happen in our lifetime? Probably not, but seeking peace is always worthwhile.

When war happens, we uphold and care for those in the battles. God is present to grant us grace and peace no matter how awful the circumstances. We must take God with us. God is present, His presence is available for anyone to accept, but each must take hold of His gift. Memorial Day is a time of remembrance.

### We Remember

On Memorial Day, we remember. We feel the grief of loss, if not from firsthand experience, then through empathy for others. Some feel a sense of purpose while others a sense of why. War existed in the Old Testament. Do we like war? No. Do we want war? No. Will we go to war over issues? Yes. Perhaps war can be shown in many ways.

I think of mothers who are MADD. Yes, mad against the drunk drivers who killed a loved one while they enjoyed their passion of drinking. I think of John Welsh and his war against those who harm children. Amber Alerts are the results of a war that a mother pursued after her child was abducted. War exists in every police department across the country as they fight distribution of drugs and the criminals who seek to live a way of life that brings harm to others.

However, on Memorial Day we think of those killed in war such as WWII, Korea, Vietnam, Iraq, Afghanistan, Ukraine, etc. These wars are for freedom for people who lived under a tyrant and others who seek to continue that type of tyranny. Lives on both sides are lost. Disturbing? Absolutely. Necessary? That answer is debated vigorously in many arenas.

Today, we reflect on the lives of the individuals who gave their lives defending freedom. The words of Jesus come to mind. ***"Don't let your heart be troubled. Believe in God; believe also in me. In my Father's house are many rooms. If it were not so, would I have told you that I am going to prepare a place for you? If I go away and prepare a place for you, I will come again and take you to myself, so that where I am you may be also." -- John 14:1-3 (CSD)***

It is my prayer for all those serving our country that they find God in their journey and know that He is there for them no matter what. For their families, He is also there to walk the journey with them. None of us know the time or day when God will call us home, regardless of where we are or what we are doing. Each day requires us to be ready for that call home to the place that Jesus went to prepare for us.

### Abba, Father

One of my favorite scriptures about Fathers is when Jesus was praying in the Garden of Gethsemane on the night Judas betrayed him. *"And he said, 'Abba', Father! All things are possible for you. Take this cup away from me. Nevertheless, not what I will, but what you will.' " -- Mark 14:36 (CSB)*

Many years ago, I heard a wonderful sermon about "Abba, Father" and have never forgotten the feeling the pastor conveyed to us about the depth of love a son has for his father. The word Abba is used to tell us of the especially close relationship Jesus has with His Father. All of us crave that kind of relationship with our earthly fathers and some of us never find it.

Our son in Texas now has seven sons. When he comes home after work, they ran to greet him with arms wide open, completely trusting that he would catch them and offer them hugs and kisses in return. What a joy to watch. He works for that relationship to exist between them. He is involved in their lives; he listens to them and to their mother. He shows respect for all in his family. Yes, he is not perfect, but he teaches them forgiveness and respect and he prays with them.

Not all of us are so lucky as to have a father like that. I know I did not, but the good news is that we can find that close relationship with our heavenly Father! Knowing that God loved His son and that He loves us enables me to cherish the word Abba as a description for a relationship with God, the Father.

Jesus only called God, Abba, once in the New Testament and that was at a crucial time in His life. Let's be sure to thank our heavenly Father on this Father's Day as He is waiting for us to call on Him. A phone call or visit to our earthly Father is always appropriate too!

### *Jesus Is Life*

Celebrate life! Our country is another year old! The day across the country finds lots of folks enjoying parades, picnics, neighborhood gatherings with food, grills, games and, of course, fireworks. Lakes are full of boaters, campgrounds filled with families, highways with travelers, and even stores are having big sales. Lots of life, good and difficult, continues for many amid the celebrations. Illness still claims many, death lingers close for others, disaster strikes during joy, family struggles distract and consume life, addictions claim power over normalcy, loneliness closes the door to joy, hunger dulls ability to function, and other such issues interfere with celebration.

Jesus came to bring us life even during struggle. *" 'I am the bread of life,' Jesus told them. 'No one who comes to me will ever be hungry, and no one who believes in me will ever be thirsty again. But as I told you, you've seen me, and yet you do not believe. Everyone the Father gives me will come to me, and the one who comes to me I will never cast out. For I have come down from heaven, not to do my own will, but the will of him who sent me. This is the will of him who sent me: that I should lose none of those he has given me but should raise them up on the last day. For this is the will of my Father: that everyone who sees the Son and believes in him will have eternal life, and I will raise him up on the last day.' "* *-- John 6:35-40 (CSB)*

It is for us to choose life with Jesus, regardless of the circumstances that surround us. Yes, as bad events or obstacles surround us, we can still grieve the events, but celebrate the life that Jesus came to provide for us. As we celebrate the joy of our country's founding and continued existence, we also celebrate the life we have with Jesus, which is life forever, life eternal, and never to be taken from us.

Thank you, Jesus, for life, thank you for allowing us to celebrate events in our life on earth even during struggles or sorrow. Help us to keep our focus on You no matter what else might surround us. You are the joy in my life, and I thank you for all the blessings You bring.

## America

"*America the Beautiful*" * is a song we see as we travel across our country. It is easy to see the "*spacious skies*," the "*waves of grain*," and the "*purple mountains majesties*."

"*God shed(s) his grace on us*" not because we are perfect, but because we call on His name. We seek His guidance in how we live and hopefully how we govern ourselves. With the disasters that hit in the form of 9/11, forest fires, floods, tornados, hurricanes, or perhaps the school and business shootings, the good in people comes out. By helping, supporting, praying, risking a life to save others is a form of "*brotherhood from sea to shining sea*."

Heroes emerge in many ways. Our war veterans, "*who more than self their country loved*," enabled us to continue to live in freedom. Yet, younger generations are often so focused on their own times and lives that they fail to appreciate sacrifices made by previous generations. Some show "*mercy more than life*" by risking their own life to give life to another. The "*gold that God refines*" is the good in us. Help us to also see that good and how God is refining each of us to a state of nobleness and divine gain.

Do you have a dream for our country? Can you see "*beyond the years*" toward that "*alabaster city*" which is "*undimmed by human tears*"? Let us allow "*God* (to) *mend our every flaw*, (to) *confirm our soul in self-control*" and grant us "*liberty in law*." May your Independence Day celebrations take on special meaning this year.

* "America the Beautiful," by Katharine Lee Bates, 1895, Public Domain

## Fill Me

What a "stuffy" feeling in the aftermath of Thanksgiving! Couldn't be that I over ate for several days! Is there a reason for calling the turkey dressing "stuffing"? It seems the stuffing goes from the turkey to me! It is so easy to fill my stomach with food. I seem to have no trouble in planning for, the obtaining of, and the consumption of food for my body. It comes so naturally, sort of like breathing; you just do it. The Thanksgiving meal is always one for the record books. A great deal of pleasure for the moment comes at that meal and the leftovers that follow. The pleasure in my case was short lived as the indigestion set in several hours later!

With the meal for Thanksgiving goes the part of remembering the people and things for which we give thanks. Isn't that more important than the food, especially on Thanksgiving Day?

Now we find ourselves in the Advent season of the Christian calendar. Once again, we made plans for Christmas. Will our plans include overindulging once again? Will the emphasis be on the earthly part of giving and consumption of material goods with a little religious flavor added to the mix? Or is our plan to fill our life with the true joy of Jesus birth and how we can share that news with others?

My hope for this season is taken from: *"You reveal the path of life to me; in your presence is abundant joy; at your right hand are eternal pleasures." -- Psalms 16:11 (CSB)*

If we all were filled to overflowing with the joy of Jesus, what would be different during this season? Would our plans change? How and what would we find ourselves doing? I bet there is no indigestion from being stuffed with God's word.

Lord, help me to learn more about living a holy life, fill me with your joy, and let me experience your pleasure forever.

### Thankfulness

Thankfulness for... Give thanks... Thank you... Yes, this is the time of year that we give thanks. We prepare great food, eat too much and, if we really think about it, we might even talk about some of the things for which we are thankful.

I spent some time looking up scriptures about thanks, thankfulness, etc. Five pages later, I have an extensive listing! A recurring theme as I read, was to "give thanks always" or to "be thankful." *"So then, just as you received Christ Jesus as Lord, continue to live your lives in him, rooted and built up in him, strengthened in the faith as you were taught, and overflowing with thankfulness." -- Colossians 2:6-7 (NIV)*

*"Let the peace of Christ rule in your hearts, since as members of one body you were called to peace. And be thankful." -- Colossians 3:15 (NIV)*

*"I urge, then, first of all, that petitions, prayers, intercession and thanksgiving be made for all people—" -- Timothy 2:1 (NIV)* Is our life always in a state of peace that causes us to feel thankful or even consider thankfulness? I doubt it. How do we maintain an attitude of thankfulness during turmoil or sorrow, disappointment, or fear?

Jesus set us an example knowing He was to die: ***"Then he took a cup, and after giving thanks, he gave it to them and said, 'Drink from it, all of you.'" -- Matthew 26:27 (CSB)*** Thankfulness is an attitude that we can choose to have. Often, we hear people who are suffering terribly say that they know others who are worse off than they are. They choose to be thankful for what they do have.

Life with Christ is the ultimate joy. No matter what happens to my physical body, my relationship with Christ is the most important connection to maintain. For that relationship I give thanks no matter what else is going on in my life. I choose to focus on thankfulness rather than suffering. I choose to give thanks when life gets difficult. Yes, the tears may flow, the heart may be burdened, the spirit in me may be afraid, but with Christ I can do all things. Those down times are when we most need to focus on thankfulness. Let's practice that spirit of thankfulness daily so that when the going gets tough, we automatically continue to focus on thankfulness that Christ is our companion carrying us through the deep waters. How will we express our thankfulness this Thanksgiving Day and every day?

## My Blessings

***"Therefore, since we are receiving a kingdom that cannot be shaken, let us be thankful." -- Hebrews 12:28 (CSB)*** Oh, these words are so appropriate for our week of Thanksgiving. I like to ponder the many blessings that I have and give praise to our Lord.

*For the blessing of life*, I give thanks to my Mom and Dad. Hey, Dad in heaven, thank you for having me! Mom, though your brain disease has deleted much of your life from you, I praise God that you do still know me for now. (She now is also in heaven.) Thank you for carrying me and nurturing me in my younger years. Though none of us are perfect, you did for me what you thought was best. I love you and pray for you to find peace in Jesus and a reunion with Charlie after all these years apart.

*For the blessing of marriage*, I give thanks for Rudy and his love for me, even though at times perhaps I didn't deserve it! How I praise God for Rudy's family who were so instrumental in the development of my Christian life. What an honor it was to love them, to learn from them, and to serve them in their final years on earth. Thank you, Rudy, for your love and for God leading me to you.

*For the blessing of three adult children and their spouses*, all of whom are joined in marriage to mates well suited to each of them. I praise you, Lord, for the answers to a mother's prayer for her children in finding the perfect mate for each.

*For the blessing of grandchildren*, what more could I want! My prayer now Lord is for them to grow into caring, faithful, and loving adults who know you and allow you to be their guide and companion. I picture each of them, and smile at the joy they bring to me as I follow their lives and adventures.

*For the blessing of health, home, safety, friends, and purpose in my life*, I thank You, Lord.

*For the blessings of gifts and talents* in my life that enable me to function, thank You. Thank You for the blessings that others have been to me!!!! So many people whose paths have crossed mine have enabled me to know more of You in ways I might have missed. I thank You for the many pastors and bible study leaders whose lives have influenced me. What a blessing many of them have been to me. To the authors of so many books that have blessed my life, I thank you.

During Thanksgiving, I know that the greatest blessing in my life is You, Lord. Your love for me, even though I don't deserve it, and regardless of all the above, helps me always from day to day. The blessings above all came from You and You put them in place for me. I thank You and praise You, not only for the past, but for each day yet to come.

## Small Blessings

I love Thanksgiving!! As I approach it this year, I reflect on many years of preparations, blessings, difficulties to overcome, and the joy of friends and family gathering. I even love cooking, though I'm not as wild about the cleanup. However, when done with a group of friends or family, it can also be a fun time too.

What can we count as blessings or things to be thankful for this year? Family and friends are always high on the list, and of course, thankful for a loving Savior who binds us together in ways we as humans could never bind together on our own. Could we dig a little deeper and find some of the events in our lives that cause us to pause and reflect on it as a blessing or something to be thankful for being in our life?

*"For the ground that drinks the rain that often falls on it and that produces vegetation useful to those for whom it is cultivated receives a blessing from God. But if it produces thorns and thistles, it is worthless and about to be cursed, and at the end will be burned." -- Hebrews 6:7-8 (CSB)*

How do we use the gifts and talents given to us by God to produce something useful to others? I remember a time sitting with my father-in-law in a hospital in a town 65 miles from his home; I was all alone trying to be helpful to him. God provided an angel in the person of Pop's minister, who happened to be in town at that exact moment, came to sit with me, listen to my fears, guide me, and pray with me. He was a blessing!

Another friend called one day when I was having a very bad day, asked me how I was doing, and I said terrible. After I explained the situation to her, her first comment to me was, "Have you prayed about it?" She was my angel that day that caused me to come back to the blessings of what prayer can do in our lives.

I have many stories like these that are blessings in my life. I praise God for each of the people who reached out to me in the name of our Savior to help keep me focused in those moments I drift away. I also count it a blessing when God taps me on the shoulder to see a need around me that I can attend to in His honor.

Perhaps as we come to the Thanksgiving table this year, regardless of tensions that might exist in our lives, we can also count the little blessings that come our way. May we gather around a table and give our praise to God for all our blessings, not just the big obvious ones, but the smaller and significant blessings that carry us through both the joys and difficulties of life.

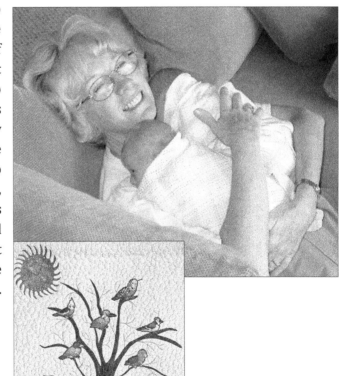

Asher Morris, my grandson, designed the birds with computer pixel art printed on vinyl for me. I designed the wall hanging for his birds.

313

# Christmas Thoughts

### Stressful Season

As I feel the pressure of the next two weeks getting all the preparations ready for Christmas, I have a choice concerning my response. I can be stressed out and unpleasant with those around me, or I can take one day at a time and remember that the celebration allows us to praise God for sending us His Son.

I approached the giving tree to choose an ornament that describes a child to receive a present. As I read a few of them, tears filled my eyes as I was suddenly overwhelmed by the simplicity of their requests - a 14-year-old boy wants a book, a 15-year-old boy wants shirts and underwear, a family of five needs toiletries, another family of six also needs toiletries. These families stress out for different reasons than the stresses I face, yet God knows all our needs. Hopefully, as I think of these families, I can put my own desires to complete my self-imposed plans into the perspective of nice, but not necessary.

Christ would far rather have me cheerful and able to serve others. The message of hope on this second Sunday of Advent reminds me that Christ will continue to be my guide, my friend, my counselor, my wise advisor, my strength, my refuge in times of trouble, and my source of forgiveness. Helping others to experience that sense of hope, for me, is a part of the Christmas spirit. I know from past experiences that God enables me to choose from day to day what it is He wants me to accomplish. However, I must allow Him to do that, and I must ask for His guidance.

Even during trials of the season, family disagreements, irate shoppers and drivers, excited children or lack of children, Psalms reminds us to: ***"Rest in God alone, my soul, for my hope comes from him. He alone is my rock and my salvation, my stronghold; I will not be shaken. My salvation and glory depend on God, my strong rock. My refuge is in God. Trust in him at all times, you people; pour out your hearts before him. God is our refuge." -- Psalms 62:5-8 (CSB)*** Where is your hope? What parts of the season cause you stress? What is God saying to you this week? My goal for this week is to make an appointment each morning to talk with God first, before I begin my hectic day. To help me get out of bed, I visualize an image of Jesus' hand reaching down to me. By giving my day this jumpstart, I know I take my friend with me to help make decisions and to guide me. Thank You, God, for giving us this season of celebration for the birth Your Son, Jesus.

## Birth and Death

The subject of birth is very current in our household for two reasons: first, it is Christmas, and we celebrate a most holy and important birth of Jesus, and second, because our son and his wife learned that they are expecting twins. The day after we learned about the twins, in my prayer time the Psalms that was next for me to read was Psalms 23. For many years, I have viewed that Psalms as one to be read at funerals and in times of great sorrow, but as usually happens when I read, a new thought occurred to me.

The first three verses provided me the comfort knowing that God is with us during this pregnancy. He knows our wants and needs and provides for them. *"He renews my life; he leads me along the right paths for his name's sake. Even when I go through the darkest valley, I fear no danger, for you are with me; your rod and your staff — they comfort me." -- Psalms 23:3-4 (CSB)* This made me stop and think about how fragile life is, not just for an unborn child, but also for any of us. Each of us is but a breath away from life or death. We read of accidents, sudden health events like heart attacks, and strokes that instantly take life completely away or change it forever.

How fitting this prayer is for saying even during a time of pregnancy to walk us through the many things that can happen to life during development. We take that walk, expecting continued new lives for ourselves and for the twins, knowing that You are walking with us just as You did with Mary and Joseph on their way to Bethlehem. Verse 3 talks about leading us and renewing us which is life affirming. Thank You, Lord, that I am never too old to have new thoughts about Your words and thank You for giving them to me.

### *Preparations For...*

This is the season for preparations once again! The Parable of the Ten Virgins (Matthew 25:1-13) reminds me of the need to be prepared for the second coming of Christ. Remember that five foolish maidens just took their lamps, but that the other five wise maidens took their lamps AND some extra oil to wait for the coming of the bridegroom. Since they did not know when the bridegroom was coming (and he ran later than some expected), the foolish maidens ran out of oil for their lamps and, while out to get some more, missed the coming of the bridegroom. *"Therefore be alert, because you don't know either the day or the hour." -- Matthew 25:13 (CSB)*

Having the perspective of the New Testament, we know to watch for the birth of Jesus on the designated day of December 25. With that knowledge we know how to prepare for a specific designated day! What about the second coming? Is Advent just about the birth of Jesus? What about using this time of preparation for having Jesus come again? What about using this time for preparing our hearts and lives for whenever He is coming into our lives? Is it time for us to consider renewal of our lives in preparation for His coming? Do our preparations include merely gifts for others, prayers of specific needs, study of God's word, helping others, lots of shopping, endless decorating, or too much of all the above?

This year finds many of us in different circumstances than ever before. Maybe the difference exists merely in our observation of life and what is important. How can we be ready for our coming Lord? What might we do that is aimed toward changing some of our worldly and spiritual preparations? My prayer for all of us is to allow God to lead us in our preparations, for Him to open our eyes and ears for seeing and hearing the ways for us to prepare, not just now, but throughout the year.

### *Highways to God*

Highways are usually convenience routes to take between two points of interest. We have Interstate highways, toll ways, US Highways, state highways, and county roads that all offer various types of travel. Many highways have some obstacles to endure when traveling on them. In planning a trip, we usually seek a highway that offers us the least number of obstacles for the type of trip we are taking. However, no matter how much planning we do, we nearly always encounter something unexpected. It might be construction, missing or poorly placed signs, weather/traffic, abused surfaces, or heavy/slow traffic.

God has prepared a way for us to His kingdom, a highway free from obstacles, free from head-on traffic and poor signage, with lots of individual attention and perfect warmth! Look at what Isaiah tell us in the following verses:

*"There will be a highway for the remnant of his people who will survive from Assyria, as there was for Israel when they came up from the land of Egypt." -- Isaiah 11:16 (CSB)*

*"A road will be there and a way; it will be called the Holy Way. The unclean will not travel on it, but it will be for the one who walks the path. Fools will not wander on it." -- Isaiah 35:8 (CSB)*

*"Prepare the way of the Lord in the wilderness; make a straight highway for our God in the desert." -- Isaiah 40:3 (CSB)*

During this season of Advent, I pray we all find the highway that God sent to us in the form of His Son, born in Bethlehem. Let's travel the Jesus highway to His Kingdom!

### Gifts for Jesus

*"Entering the house, they saw the child with Mary his mother, and falling to their knees, they worshipped him. Then they opened their treasures and presented him with gifts: gold, frankincense, and myrrh." -- Matthew 2:11 (CSB)* Christmas morning is near, very near. Gifts are about to be exchanged in abundance. The love in the gifts varies between required and most precious. As the events of my week came together, my focus is on another kind of gift we need to have under our trees on Christmas morning.

This gift needs to be just for Jesus. Perhaps it is a gift of gratitude or joy, or is it one of sorrow, longing, disappointment, hurt, anger, or guilt. You could perhaps add an emotion to the list. Why would we give such a gift? Sharing joys with Jesus is a celebration of happiness in our life. Sharing our sorrows with Jesus is a celebration of a decision to experience the fullness of life He has for us. Jesus was born, lived, and died so that we might experience a full complete life with God. His birth is a part of what He endured for us.

As we share gifts with our friends and family, we need to also think of giving Jesus a very special gift from our hearts. Once the gift is identified, perhaps even writing it down, placing it in a small box or envelop with a gift card to Jesus, and putting it under the tree. He wants these gifts. These are the special gifts for Him. It costs us nothing, but can free us from quite a load! What gift will you bring?

## *Preparations*

A church we attended presented their choir program with scriptures, messages, bell choirs, hymns, and of course children, youth and adults costumed for the shepherds, wise men, and the Holy Family. As I watched and listened, I remembered many years from my work as Christian Education Director helping to prepare for days like this. The days of finding or writing the right script, recruiting the people for the roles, organizing the costumes, props, lighting, sound, promoting the event, rehearsing, solving the problems that arose, keeping the spirit of the event paramount, praying for direction and the multitude of assistance needed, countering any objections or negativity and on and on flooded my memory. Those thoughts and memories all faded as I witnessed once again the coming together of that wonderful story of the birth of our Lord.

God prepared for a long time for the coming of our Lord. *"For a child will be born for us, a son will be given to us" -- Isaiah 9:6 (CSB)*

*"Then a shoot will grow from the stump of Jesse, and a branch from his roots will bear fruit." -- Isaiah 11:1 (CSB)* Luke 1 is a series of events that fulfilled scriptures throughout the Old Testament. Zechariah's wife, Elizabeth having John the Baptist, Mary hearing from the angel, Joseph also hearing from the angel are each dramatic stories in their own right. The preparations stood out to me. The totality of what God did to prepare the way for this event is amazing. God gave us the best gift with much thought given to the gift.

How do we approach the gifts we give? Do we strive to make them our best? Do we merely get something because we must? Are we trying to impress others or please others? What is our attitude about our preparations - chores or opportunities to serve? God gave us the very best, can we give back to Him our best as we reach out to others in Jesus name?

## *The Right Path*

During this season of each year, many of us find ourselves in conflict. Many things to do! People demand our presence. Everyone wants something, either our time or our money. The activities at our churches, our schools, our jobs, and time with our friends and family seem impossible to bring together in some kind of order.

Now add to this mix, events that perhaps you never envisioned having to add to the "normal" hectic schedule. Events such as the death of a loved one, getting laid off from your job, sudden disease, going off to war or other military service in a foreign land, (add the one in your life). How can I focus on the birth of our Lord Jesus! *"Listen, my son, and be wise; keep your mind on the right course." -- Proverbs 23:19 (CSB)*

The birth of our Lord represents the hope of tomorrow, the peace of today, the joy of living in the presence of our Lord, and the love of God. Jesus came to bring us a path to follow in our lives. His path allows us to deal with the present, knowing that He is with us always.

As I bring to Him all the confusion of joy and concern, a peace comes to me that only He can give. The path to take becomes smoother, clearer and the conflicts less entangled. I thank You, Lord, for reminding me once again to keep my heart on Your path as I journey toward the manger to celebrate Your birth.

### Our Eyes on Jesus

From Thanksgiving to Christmas, for some the season brings on memories of loss or memories of unhappy experiences during holidays. For others, we self-impose all the things we think must be done.

Jesus offers rest to a crowd of people through these words found in: *"Come to me, all of you who are weary and burdened, and I will give you rest. Take my yoke upon you and learn from me, because I am lowly and humble in heart, and you will find rest for your souls. For my yoke is easy and my burden is light." -- Matthew 11:28-30 (CSB)* Our preparations should be simple. How do we reflect on the coming birth of this Jesus who takes our heavy loads and gives us rest? Keeping our sights on the journey to Bethlehem, the ordinariness of the stable, the wonder of His birth, rather than the glitz and glamour of advertisements and store displays, helps to keep us focused on why we celebrate.

When I think of the journey that Joseph and Mary made to Bethlehem versus the way many of us travel to day, what seems a simple journey on a donkey had to be terribly difficult for a woman ready to give birth. We complain about a 2-hour ride in a soft cushy car or airplane. Even crowded airplanes are more comfortable than the back of a donkey. While standing in line to make purchases, think about how Mary made herself comfortable in a stable as her labor pains began.

When you feel the sorrow of loss or the anger of relationships that cause conflicts during the holidays, remember that this baby's birth is God's way of caring for those times in our life. Jesus birth, life and death were God's way of showing us the depth of His love for us, no matter what circumstances exist in our life. Those burdens of grief and sorrow, Jesus carries for you. He wants to give you rest. Allow His love and care to wrap around you and carry you through this season. Rejoice in His birth for all that He brings you.

Lord, help us to keep our lives simple and focused on Jesus this season. Allow us to celebrate Jesus birth by allowing Jesus to carry whatever circumstances exist in our lives.

### Children See

And on the night before Christmas, the tradition in our son's home was to gather around in the room with the piano and sing. With eight adults and nine children, the room was full. I got to hold my youngest grandson, who was one year old. When the music and singing started, his face and body communicated nothing but sheer wonder! With wide eyes and peaked attention, he listened and watched. Normally this little bundle was never still (except when asleep), but for this moment, his attention was captured by our gathering and activity.

Children's anticipation leading up to Christmas has a lesson for adults to learn from: ***"Then little children were brought to Jesus for him to place his hands on them and pray, but the disciples rebuked them. Jesus said, 'Leave the little children alone, and don't try to keep them from coming to me, because the kingdom of heaven belongs to such as these.' " -- Matthew 19:13-14 (CSB)***

Children are like little sponges, ready to soak up everything in their environment. They trust without reservations, they believe because they want to, and they are amazed by the simplest events. We adults bring too much baggage with us when we encounter Jesus. We question, we doubt, we want proof, we argue, and we try to do everything ourselves. Through our example, we often train our children to be like us! Perhaps we need to emulate our children on occasion.

How nice to view the world and others with eyes that always see things as new and fresh. I will long remember the sight of my grandson as a new happening came his way, and he absorbed the moment as we sang welcoming the baby Jesus to our midst.

Let us remember to be people who are like little children coming to Jesus. Let us encourage our children to know Jesus as their friend and savior. Let us also model for the children how Jesus is our personal friend and savior. If Jesus is just a name to you and you want Him as your Savior, all you need to do is ask Him, as a child would do. Simply, but sincerely, ask Jesus to come into your life.

### *Joyfully Pray*

We pray for safety as we hit the road in our car to travel to our daughter's home for Christmas. This time of the year, lots of us are on the roads either for long trips or short ones around town. Visits to family homes out of town. Going shopping. Attending parties. Traveling to and from work. Taking kids to activities. With many in a rush and others having one drink too many, but not willing to admit it, accidents happen.

During all the bustle of the season, this passage reminded me once again what we all need to do. ***"Now may the God of hope fill you with all joy and peace as you believe so that you may overflow with hope by the power of the Holy Spirit." -- Romans 15:13 (CSB)***

When you are standing in a long line waiting to check out at the store, always be joyful and patient. Use that time to pray for the cashier and the person checking out. Pray for the impatient person in front or behind you. Pray for those receiving the gifts being purchased. Pray for the workers at the stores handling all the concerns and questions of folks. Pray for anything else that enters your mind. Pray for the delivery people handling all the online purchases in time to be wrapped for Christmas. Pray for the travel personnel that deal with airlines, trains, buses getting people to and from during good and bad weather, delays, and cancellations. Pray for the children who are so anxious about gifts! Pray for the parents who struggle to get anything for their kids or to find the right gift that they want. Remember to share your blessings with others, however that looks - time, money, cards, joy, prayers, praises, gifts, share even with strangers!

Be open to whatever happens and be joyful in the Lord. Praise Him for each day. He is with you no matter what else happens. Jesus is the reason for this season, so keep Him first and foremost in all that you do.

## Birth Celebrations

The obvious celebration is the birth of our Lord Jesus. I often wonder if perhaps that celebration isn't one that needs to be all year long. Let us do it without the glitter and glamour of decorations, presents, and all the commercial activity which seems to accompany the season. The birth of Jesus allows us the privilege of knowing Him. That birth is something worthy of year-round celebration at least in our hearts and in our prayers as we thank God for sending us His son.

This time of the year finds other celebrations that take place as well. Celebrations, perhaps not necessarily related to Christmas such as birthdays, anniversaries, graduations, and weddings, continue to take place. Or what of celebrations when relationships are mended, jobs are found, or good news arrives? Health concerns bearing good news and results that cause us to celebrate. And during all these, God waits for us to keep Him in the center of the event.

*"I will praise you forever for what you have done. In the presence of your faithful people, I will put my hope in your name, for it is good." -- Psalms 52:9 (CSB)*

In Denver, we celebrated our daughter's second bachelor's degree (this one in Nursing). As we journeyed from the pinning ceremony to the graduation ceremony, we walked to lunch in downtown Denver near the Convention Center. It was cold!!!! All of us were in a great mood enjoying the day when suddenly my shoe caught a crack in the walkway, throwing me down face first! I became my daughter's first patient as a nurse out of school! With a growing black eye and very blue lips on the right side of my face, she did a great damage assessment. Rather than go home, I elected to stay for the ceremony! Why let a big blue lip and swollen cheek ruin our day! God is good and provided all we needed during a potential disaster. For the evening party, we thought of many stories to tell to explain my obvious injuries, but underneath all our laughter was much thanksgiving and praise for the good outcome of an unplanned event. Celebrations come in many ways for many different reasons. We continue our celebration of our Savior's birth.

## Happy Birthday

A time for sharing, caring, reflecting, and loving. When we consider the meagerness of the setting surrounding His birth, I must admit the surroundings of the elaborate church service we attended did not reflect that same meager setting. However, we now know Jesus as our King, our Lord, our Savior, and we now want to provide the best for celebrating His birth.

*"While they were there, the time came for her to give birth. Then she gave birth to her firstborn son, and she wrapped him tightly in cloth and laid him in a manger, because there was no guest room available for them." -- Luke 2:6-7 (CSB)*

As I read this scripture and thought about the Choir and the brass ensemble from the service we attended, I could only imagine the angels singing the praises of the birth of our Lord to the shepherds in the fields. Isn't that what we enjoy when we attend the Christmas Eve services? The celebrations are valuable in helping us to send our praise to God for the glory of the gift He gave to us through His son, Jesus.

That said, I also believe that God honors the humblest of settings when the heart is right for praising God for Jesus. Some people find themselves in places where humble praise is all they have and that is enough. Soldiers in the fields offer prayers in dire spots. Those in hospitals may not even know it is Christmas. The elderly with dementia in nursing homes simply exist on a day like the one before. Many celebrate Christmas with no mention at all of Christ, with their focus simply on gifts to be exchanged! Some people attend the greatest and grandest of celebrations with hearts that are not right with God, but go for other reasons. Perhaps through the celebration they can find a way for discovering a better relationship with God?

For me, I am so grateful for any services that allow us to collectively sing praises to God for the birth of Jesus and for all of His life that follows His birth!

### *Precious Gifts*

The gifts are all open now, some exchanged, some still sitting around, and some we wonder why we even received! Some of our gifts were exactly what we needed whether we asked for them or not. Are some gifts too precious to use? Perhaps some of us received a gift like this.

*"He looked up and saw the rich dropping their offerings into the temple treasury. He also saw a poor widow dropping in two tiny coins. 'Truly I tell you,' he said, 'this poor widow has put in more than all of them. For all these people have put in gifts out of their surplus, but she out of her poverty has put in all she had to live on.' " -- Luke 21:1-4 (CSB)*

Do we spend time wondering about some of the gifts we receive? Or is the message to us one of giving rather than receiving? Perhaps we need to give more thought to the types of gifts we give. Do we give from our wealth, or from our reserve which means a sacrifice? Do we give what we want others to have? Or do we take into consideration what we know suits the receiver's needs, passion, or wants? Do we give in anticipation of the recipient's future? Do we always give things? What about our time and love? How available are we in giving the most precious gifts of ourselves to our children, our spouses, or other loved ones?

Gifts need to be precious, not show pieces or junk. Let us think, as this year unfolds, about the precious gifts we received over the years and consider what precious gifts we want to give during the year. Jesus is the most precious gift God could ever give us. Does someone need a bible with specific emphasis for age level or study purposes? Help us to accept this gift in our hearts and live our lives acknowledging this gift. Allow us to use our gift by keeping Jesus alive in our daily lives and always praising His name.

### Gift Giving

This time of year, we concentrate on Jesus' birthday and our gift giving. *"In everything I did, I showed you that by this kind of hard work we must help the weak, remembering the words the Lord Jesus himself said: 'It is more blessed to give than to receive.' " -- Acts 20:35 (NIV)* Gifts go to family, friends, guests, co-workers, and yes, even strangers. Almost every organization takes on some group or family in need to help with gifts.

Yesterday, we took our list to the store and found items on our 6-year-old girl's list. What fun we had thinking of her (even though we know nothing about her but her first name and her list)! She had an item on that list that Rudy was helpful in obtaining and, since we have no young granddaughters, (*we do now have a granddaughter*) it was fun buying for her – dolls, girls' clothing, even a remote-control car! Even the shoe boxes of toiletries and other necessary items were fun putting together, knowing that they would meet the needs of someone.

*"Kore son of Imnah the Levite, the keeper of the East Gate, was over the freewill offerings to God to distribute the contribution to the Lord and the consecrated things." -- 2 Chronicles 31:14 (CSB)* It reminded me that these gifts are really gifts to God. He loves us so much that He gave us the gift of His Son as a baby. We didn't deserve this gift, but God gave us His Son anyway.

So many preparations go into gift giving! That is part of the joy. Preparing for any event is usually work, but do you choose to focus on the work or the joy? Imagine that you are preparing the gifts for the Lord and see how your attitude can change. Give as though each gift is for God. After all, Christmas is about the birth of Jesus and the gifts are representative of the gifts given Jesus by the Wise Men, and the greatest is God's gift of His Son to us.

Let us keep our focus on God's gift to us as we go about preparing gifts for others. Remember, the gifts don't have to be expensive, but they do need to be from the heart. Allow us to receive gifts with the same spirit.

### *Angels Watch*

One thought raged in my head! Get well. No time for this sick stuff. Glad I had most of my shopping done! I am so tired of lying on this couch, chilled and racking with coughs. The throat was so sore, the voice was gone, why, why, why! I was feverish enough that I didn't even want to sew, sit up or read a book. All I could think about was this 7-year-old little girl who needed items from the Angel Tree that I was responsible for getting. I wanted to do it, but the body said no. I agonized over that little girl, not wanting to disappoint her. Hoping each day, I would be better the next day to go get her things. Finally, the deadline arrived when the items were needed, and I was still not able to go to the store. Rudy got the bike she wanted, but had no idea about pants and a shirt. Fortunately, we gave the cash to the lady in charge of the Angel Tree for the RV Park, and she got the other things for me. Finally, the fever is gone, and the cough remains along with the congestion, but that too will disappear.

I am much more rested than I was. I read a book during the times I could hold it up. Rudy waited on me, took me to the doctor, did the shopping, got me ice cream and aspirin, and kept fluid coming my way, and fed himself, all for five days. He is still running errands for me as I continue to get better. Now I still ask, why at Christmas? Perhaps I needed to have quiet time to think and pray for others. I could not talk, no voice. I could not email, no strength. My mind was in gear, albeit at a slower pace. What blessings I saw during those days. First, I have a home (even one on wheels) that provides me with very nice shelter. I have a husband who loves me for better or worse. I have family across the country that cares for me. I have friends who kept asking about me (we wouldn't let them visit nor did they want to visit).

Most important of all, my greatest blessing is that Jesus cares for me and you. He doesn't care if I'm sick, he can't catch anything I have! He doesn't need me to talk, He listens to me anyway. His internet connection doesn't require a computer. He knew my needs and sent Rudy and others to take care of my needs. ***"But the angel said to them, 'Don't be afraid, for look, I proclaim to you good news of great joy that will be for all the people: Today in the city of David a Savior was born for you, who is the Messiah, the Lord.' " -- Luke 2:10-11 (CSB)*** Luke told the story of many angels watching over the birth of Jesus, and they continue to watch over us each day of our journey.

### *Our Gifts to Give*

Usually for gifts we think of material things to give. Perhaps we need to also consider gifts that take our time and effort to give. When money is tight, we can still give precious gifts of our time. When money is abundant, then perhaps a gift of time is also special! Suggestions for Christmas gifts:

- Spend time doing something the kids or grandkids want to do.

- Send a note of encouragement to someone you know who is in need.

- Prepare a meal for a family who suffers from an illness or the loss of a loved one.

- Sit and listen to someone who needs to talk over a problem.

- Search for acts of kindness to share with others each day this month.

- Pray *with* someone, even a stranger that God brings into your life.

- Pray for someone, even a stranger that might come to your mind.

- Open a door for someone whose arms are full of packages.

- Smile at the clerk who has been standing waiting on impatient customers all day, and then thank them for their work.

- Include gift coupons for tasks you can perform in the days to come.

- Tell those you love of that love with notes hidden in lunches, or briefcases, or wherever!

- Children can make special drawings, or items to give.

- Children can do any of the above as well as adults!

***"Just as you want others to do for you, do the same for them. If you love those who love you, what credit is that to you? Even sinners love those who love them. If you do what is good to those who are good to you, what credit is that to you?***

*Even sinners do that. And if you lend to those from whom you expect to receive, what credit is that to you? Even sinners lend to sinners to be repaid in full. But love your enemies, do what is good, and lend, expecting nothing in return. Then your reward will be great, and you will be children of the Most High. For he is gracious to the ungrateful and evil. Be merciful, just as your Father also is merciful." -- Luke 6:31-36 (CSB)*

Gifts are not just the material items we seek in the stores or online. What would Jesus want from us for Christmas? Perhaps it is time to reframe our wish lists for this year.

## *Waiting For A Baby*

We are waiting for the baby Jesus. Yes, at Christmas we wait for the baby Jesus and Christmas morning. In our family, we waited for another baby, our daughter's baby and it was the week for birth! Oh, the joy that resides in hearts as we anticipate the baby's arrival. How we longed to hold this child and gaze upon his/her face.

I can certainly imagine to some degree the joy and the concern of Mary as she told Elizabeth of her new child. As she and Joseph traveled toward Bethlehem, the journey was a rough one. Riding on the back of a donkey had to be uncomfortable! Yet she looked forward with anticipation to the birth of Jesus, to behold His face, to touch His soft skin, and to cradle His body in her arms.

Our daughter had a nice hospital to go to for the birth of her child. Mary had a stable with a manger and straw. Yet both mothers loved their child immensely. Mary knew that her Son had a purpose for His life, even though she did not understand that purpose. Some mothers believe that their children have a purpose in this life; some simply accept them as a biological result of life. A few mothers don't even want their children.

An angel gave this message to Joseph in his dream: " *'She will give birth to a son, and you are to name him Jesus, because he will save his people from their sins.' Now all this took place to fulfill what was spoken by the Lord through the prophet: See, the virgin will become pregnant and give birth to a son, and they will name him Immanuel, which is translated 'God is with us.' " -- Matthew 1:21-23 (CSB)*

Joseph and Mary followed the guidance they received. Each of us has a purpose for being. Finding that purpose and fulfilling what God plans for us is the life journey we live. I always saw my children as a gift to me from God, given for me to teach them about God and His place in their lives. They always belonged to God not me. I anticipated their arrival with joy!

I anticipated the arrival of another grandchild with joy! It is double joy as we await the celebration of the birth of Christ and the birth of our baby.

I share this joy with you, inviting you to remember the joy of the births of your own children or grandchildren and know that the joy of the birth of our Lord Jesus surpasses even that joy! How grateful to God I am for reminding me of the greatness of new life, especially the new life of Jesus. (*Yes, our grandson arrived in time to be home for Christmas.*)

## Advent Growth

Now that the Advent season is here, I am remembering many of the Advent seasons in the years past. The years as a child waiting for Christmas were all about anticipation and hope. Though I knew it was the birthday of Jesus, the main thing I remember is the exchanging of gifts. We did attend a midnight worship service and then went to worship again on Christmas morning.

During my college years, Christmas was only about gifts, time off from classes, and oh yes, it was Jesus birthday. The one thing that continued, though more from habit, was attending the midnight worship service. Then, during my last semester in college, I met Rudy and, at Christmas, we became engaged. During Advent of that season, I met Rudy's family and God began a work in me through them that was to be nurtured over the coming years. As those years passed, my faith grew as did my understanding of the Christmas season. Hope, light, and joy became the focus for me during Advent. The reason for the gifts took on a new meaning.

As our kids grew, activities that focused on the meaning of Jesus birthday became important to help teach them that Christmas is more than just presents. How effective those activities were is between the kids and their relationship with our Lord. We sure had fun. Helping others became something important to do since we were so blessed.

There are so many stories of what others do to celebrate and teach about the birth of our Lord. Some visit nursing homes, write special notes to friends and family, bake items to share, or buy gifts for families that cannot afford to get gifts for their children. Others sign up to help prepare and deliver meals to shut ins, homeless, and others in need of a meal. Some families adopt whole families and each of their children helps select gifts for the other family. Churches have special Advent programs and children's nativity presentations. We do many of these.

Do you smile at folks while waiting in lines to purchase gifts? Do you wish those in stores who must work a Merry Christmas, even if the store does not display the word Christmas? What honor do we bring to our Lord with our decorations? Are our outdoor decorations just snowmen, Santa Claus, and sleighs? What stories do we read to our kids about Christmas? How do we help them to know that Christmas is a celebration of Jesus' birthday? Some families have a cake and candles and sing happy birthday to Jesus, and then read the Bible stories of His birth.

*"Arise, shine, for your light has come, and the glory of the Lord shines over you. For look, darkness will cover the earth, and total darkness the peoples; but the Lord will shine over you, and his glory will appear over you." -- Isaiah 60:1-2 (CSB)*

### Fit for Heaven

"*Away in the Manger*" is a very traditional hymn this time of year. How many times have I sung it in my life? So many I can't count. As we sang the third verse, these words struck me, "*bless all the dear children in thy tender care, and take us to heaven to live with thee there.*" *

Jesus came as a man to do just that! My first thought is of actual children and then of adults who were once children and are still children of God. Yes, Jesus came to take us to heaven.

Are we fit for heaven? Is there anything we can do that makes us fit for heaven? Do we read our bible, pray, and have conversation with Jesus? Hum, are these the necessary things that get us to heaven? Technically, NO. Only Jesus fits us for heaven. He takes us warts and all when we ask Him to do so. So why do we even need to worship, pray, and study scripture? Because those activities enable us to live a life centered on Jesus. Being centered on Christ enables us to deal with life's difficulties with hope. Tragedies exist all around us. Yet we celebrate birth, life, and hope at Christmas time.

Mary, the mother of Jesus, certainly encountered what many at that time considered a tragedy of being pregnant before marriage. Her faith enabled her to say: *"My soul magnifies the Lord, and my spirit rejoices in God my Savior, because he has looked with favor on the humble condition of his servant. Surely, from now on*

**all generations will call me blessed, because the Mighty One has done great things for me, and his name is holy." -- Luke 1:46-49 (CSB)**

This example for us tells us to not get bogged down in details of daily life and the difficulties that surround us but to keep our eyes on Jesus. Mary considered her situation to be joyful since God chose her to be His servant. She used her situation to give glory to God. How can we see our difficulties as opportunities to give glory to God? The Bible is full of these stories that help us see how to praise God during our difficulties. Let us all worship, pray, study, and rejoice that Jesus fits us for heaven.

\* *"Away in a Manger,"* William J. Kirkpatrick, 1895 Public Domain

### Telling the News

Have you ever noticed how easily we like to spread words about wonderful events that happen in our lives? The birth of a baby or grandbaby lights us up! We can hardly wait to tell everyone we see, share photos of the new baby, and tell how proud we are of this new one. Yes, I'm guilty on this one. Of course, we know that this kind of news is acceptable in our society, and it feels good to tell others of this news.

What about news of how Christ works in our life? Are we as eager to tell this news? Why? Hmm....

Luke 2:8-20 talks about how the shepherds learned of the baby lying in a manger in Bethlehem. Imagine being in a field watching over sheep at night. Place yourself in this spot if you will. Angels suddenly appear telling them about the baby in the manger and how to find the baby. Then a company of angels began praising God.

Now imagine yourself and your team deciding that you needed to go see what this was all about. You find the baby, you confirm the story, and now what? Will people think you are crazy if you start telling them about these events? Do you care about what others think versus telling the true story of what happened? Decisions...

The shepherds in the bible: **"After seeing them, they reported the message they were told about this child, and all who heard it were amazed at what the shepherds said to them. But Mary was treasuring up all these things in her heart and meditating on them. The shepherds returned, glorifying and praising God for all the things they had seen and heard, which were just as they had been told." -- Luke 2:17-20 (CSB)** What would we have done? Would we just tell our Christian friends about what happened? Would we tell anyone who would listen what happened?

How has the birth of Jesus affected your life? What has Jesus done for you that you want to share with others? God gives us these events to bring joy into our lives. Many references in scripture, of acts done to change lives, results in the person telling everyone they see about what God has done for them. They were so changed they simply could not keep quiet. Perhaps we feel that the things that God changes in our lives are not important enough to share with others? Or are we afraid that others might think of us as religious fanatics? Are we willing to share the good news of Jesus birth and how His birth has blessed our lives?

### *Faithful Followers*

We are again preparing for the coming of our Lord. I couldn't help but think about the faith of so many people who walked with God before the coming of Jesus. They only knew of the prophesy of Jesus. Yet they believed Messiah was coming.

Those thoughts lead me to Hebrews 11, the Faith Chapter. *"Now faith is the reality of what is hoped for, the proof of what is not seen." -- Hebrews 11:1 (CSB)* Abraham was called to venture into a strange land, and he went knowing God was leading him. Sarah was told she would have a son at age 90 and she laughed! Yes, wouldn't we also laugh! The older I get, the more I can appreciate how ridiculous that thought was to her. God was serious and not happy with her lack of faith. Yet, she grew to know the truth about what God had planned for her, a baby boy.

Moses was born, placed in a basket, found, and raised by Pharaoh's daughter, and grew up to be a great leader for God. Though he was reluctant to accept the assignment, he had faith that God would provide.

David survived 17 years of being chased by King Saul and wrote many Psalms to express his emotions during those years. Those emotions included the depth of his faith and provide a lot of support for us today.

Finally, Paul summed up for us the meaning of all the examples given throughout Chapter 11 of the great people of faith, *"All these were approved through their faith, but they did not receive what was promised, since God had provided something better for us, so that they would not be made perfect without us." -- Hebrews 11:39-40 (CSB)*

Now we live after the birth of Christ and can see what was promised. Does our knowledge of His birth, life, and death enable us to live out our faith? Depends. Do we choose to live by faith? Or do we want to see everything first? We will always have decisions to make, journeys to take, and risks to ponder throughout our life. We can try to foresee the possibilities, but we can't know for sure. As we look forward to Christmas Day, let us see how our faith can help us to live faithfully day to day.

### Keep the Baby

The hustle and bustle of Christmas is upon us! Are all the gifts in place yet, almost? Is the Christmas letter written, cards sent out? Have I baked everything that I planned to do? Is the baby in the manger? What? Is the baby in the manger? Oh...

All mothers and fathers know how important it is to watch out for the baby. Babies are defenseless and therefore must always be watched over. Christmas is about the birth of Jesus, and He came as a baby. So, I ask again, is the baby in the manger? Technically, not until Christmas day. Mary was about to give birth, and she was watching over Him constantly in the days before His birth. That literal birth was over 2000 years ago. Today we celebrate that birth knowing Jesus was in a manger. Do we celebrate the holiday or is the baby in the manger?

*"Then Jesus cried out, 'Whoever believes in me does not believe in me only, but in the one who sent me. The one who looks at me is seeing the one who sent me' "* *-- John 12:44-45 (NIV)*

We have knowledge that enables us to keep the baby in the manger rather than get caught up in the activities and "must dos" that overwhelm us during this season. Let us fix our eyes upon Jesus, who was sent to us by God, as we celebrate His birth each year. Have a very Merry Christmas - with the baby in the manger throughout our celebrations!

### A Year in Review

Christmas is a day when I tend to reflect on my blessings for the year, important events, persons who made a difference in my life, and places that hold significant memories. Why Christmas day? For me the answer lies in the love that God showed for us by sending us His son, Jesus in the form of a baby. He sent Him knowing how we as humans would treat Him and yet knowing that we needed Him as our teacher, example, comforter, and savior. The question for me to contemplate is where during the year has His message been evident to me? Since we had such an unusual year, we put together a calendar for our family members. As a part of the calendar, each month has a scripture text that tries to reflect the pictures and feelings of that month.

- Jan. *"Let the little children come to me..." -- Matthew 19:14 (NIV)* in honor of our grandchildren.

- Feb. *"...let birds fly above the earth across the vault of the sky." -- Genesis 1:20 (NIV)* for all the new birds we saw in South Texas.

- Mar. *"...by this kind of hard work we must help the weak..." -- Acts 20:35 (NIV)* for our NOMAD work.

- Apr. *"By faith we understand that the universe was formed at God's command" -- Hebrews 11:3 (NIV)* for our tour of NASA.

- May *"You are my refuge in the day of disaster" -- Jeremiah 17:17 (NIV)* our visit to Oklahoma City with tornado damage and the Murrah Fed. Building bombing site.

- June *"I will sing praise to my God as long as I live" -- Psalms 104:33 (NIV)* for the magnificent views in Colorado and Wyoming.

- July *"I will pour out my spirit on all people" -- Joel 2:28 (NIV)* for our visits with many new people.

- Aug. "G*o in peace. Your journey has the Lord's approval" -- Judges 18:6 (NIV)* for our travels within Washington state with our kids.

- Sept. *"I hope to see you while passing through... I have enjoyed your company for a while." -- Romans 15:24 (NIV)* for the most states covered in one month and visit with a special couple.

- Oct. *"Your ears will hear a voice behind you, saying 'This is the way; walk in it' " -- Isaiah 30:21 (NIV)* for the trips in New Mexico confirming our decision to go that direction.

- Nov. *"Keep on loving one another as brothers and sisters. Do not forget to show hospitality to strangers, for by so doing some people have shown hospitality to angels without knowing it." -- Hebrews 13:1-2 (NIV)* as our grandsons reminded us of the importance of brotherly love.

- Dec. ***"The true light that gives light to everyone was coming into the world" -- John 1:9 (NIV)*** as I viewed the lights on our son's home that light the way for the Christ child.

Yes, it is a journey of memories much simplified for this writing. I invite you to look over your year, not to be discouraged, but to look for those positive memories of people, places, and events that just might have been God's touch of comfort, love, joy, grace, forgiveness, or simply His presence with you. Proceed with loving action as God's directs you.

# Alphabetical Index by Titles

Printed in the USA
CPSIA information can be obtained
at www.ICGtesting.com
LVHW070308251123
764285LV00001B/1

9 781957 077451